The Murder of Christ

Love, work and knowledge are the well-springs of our life. They should also govern it.

Wilhelm Reich

The Murder of Christ

The Emotional Plague of Mankind

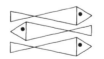

Farrar, Straus and Giroux
New York

Wilhelm Reich—Biographical Material
History of the Discovery of Life Energy
Written June-August, 1951 (Orgonon, Maine, U.S.A.)

Printed in the United States of America

TO THE CHILDREN OF THE FUTURE

CONTENTS

INTRODUCTION

The social crisis we are living through is basically due to the inability of people in general to govern their own lives. From this inability cruel dictatorships have grown over the past thirty years, with no rational social ends at all.

Serious men and women everywhere are deeply concerned with the misfortune which is threatening to extinguish our lives, our happiness, and cause disaster to our children. These men and women want blunt truth. They want blunt truth about people's true ways of being, acting and emotional reacting. To tell the people everywhere the full truth about themselves, means paying respect to their social responsibilities. The problems presented in THE MURDER OF CHRIST are acute problems of present-day society. However, the solutions to these problems, given in THE MURDER OF CHRIST are immature, emotionally blurred, insufficient or lacking completeness. Therefore, THE MURDER OF CHRIST is being published only as historical source material from the Archives of the Orgone Institute.

The Oranur Experiment, beginning 1947, has unexpectedly provided some basic solutions to emotional and social problems of man, solutions which have been entirely inaccessible heretofore. An extensive publication of the emotional implications of the Oranur Experiment is in preparation. THE MURDER OF CHRIST may well serve as an introduction of biographical background material to Oranur.

" God " is Nature, and Christ is the realization of Natural Law. God (Nature) has created the genital organs in all living beings. He has done so for them to function according to natural, godly law. Therefore, to ascribe a natural, godly love life to the messenger of God on earth is no sacrilege, no blasphemy. It is, on the contrary, the rooting of God in man's cleanest depth. This depth is there from the very beginning of life. Propagation is only added to genitality in puberty. Godly genital love is there long before the function of propagation; therefore, the genital embrace was not created by Nature and God only for the purpose of propagation.

Orgonon, November 3rd, 1952

And he came and found them sleeping, and he said to Peter, " Simon, are you asleep? Could you not watch one hour? Watch and pray that you may not enter into temptation; the spirit indeed is willing, but the flesh is weak." And again he went away and prayed, saying the same words. And again he came and found them sleeping, for their eyes were very heavy; and they did not know what to answer him. And he came the third time, and said to them, " Are you still sleeping and taking your rest? It is enough; the hour has come; the Son of man is betrayed into the hands of sinners. Rise, let us be going; see, my betrayer is at hand."

(*Mark* 14: 37-42)

*Then the soldiers of the governor took Jesus into the praetorium, and they gath-
ered the whole battalion before him. And they stripped him and put a scarlet
robe upon him, and plaiting a crown of thorns they put it on his head, and put a
reed in his right hand. And kneeling before him they mocked him, saying,
"Hail, King of the Jews!" And they spat upon him, and took the reed and
struck him on the head. And when they had mocked him, they stripped him of
the robe, and put his own clothes on him, and led him away to crucify him.*

(*Matthew* 27: 27-31)

Wilhelm Reich (1952)

Chapter I

THE TRAP

" Man is born free; and everywhere he is in chains. One thinks himself the master of others, and still remains a greater slave than they. How did this change come about? I do not know."

Jean Jacques Rousseau asked this question in the very beginning of his " Social Contract " some two hundred years ago. Unless the answer is found to this basic question, there is little use in setting up new social contracts. *There has for many ages been something at work within human society that rendered impotent any and every single attempt to get at the solution of the great riddle,* well known to all great leaders of humanity during the past several thousands of years: *Man is born free, yet he goes through life as slave.*

No answer has been found till now. There must be something at work in human society that obstructs the asking of the correct question to reach the right answer. All human philosophy is riddled with the nightmare of searching in vain.

Something, well hidden, is at work, that does not permit posing the right question. There is, accordingly, something in operation that continuously and successfully *diverts attention* from the carefully camouflaged access to where attention should be focused. The tool used by the well-camouflaged something to divert attention from the cardinal riddle itself, is human EVASIVENESS with regard to living Life. The hidden something is THE EMOTIONAL PLAGUE OF MAN.

On the correct formulation of the riddle will depend the proper focusing of attention, and on this in turn will depend the eventual finding of the correct answer as to how it is possible that man is born free everywhere and yet finds himself in slavery everywhere.

Certainly, social contracts, if honestly designed to maintain life in human society, are crucial tasks. But no kind of social contract will ever solve the problem of human agony. The social contract, at best, is no more than a makeshift to maintain life. It has heretofore not been able to remove the agony of life.

These are the constituents of the great riddle:

Man is born equal, but he does not grow equal.

Man has created great teachings, yet each simple teaching has served his oppression.

Man is the " Son of God," created in His image; yet man is " sinful," a prey of the " Devil." How can the Devil and Sin be, if God alone is the creator of all being?

Humanity has failed to answer the question as to how there can be EVIL if a perfect GOD has created and governs the world and man.

Humanity has failed in establishing a moral life in accordance with its creator.

Humanity has been ravaged by war and murder of all sorts ever since the inception of written history. No attempt to remove this plague has ever succeeded.

Humanity has developed many kinds of religions. Every single kind of religion turned into another way of suppression and misery.

Humanity has devised many systems of thought to cope with Nature. Yet nature, functional and not mechanical, as it really is, has slipped through its fingers.

Humanity has run after every bit of hope and knowledge. Yet, after three thousand years of search and worry and heartbreak and murder for heresy and persecution of seeming error, it has arrived at little more than a few comforts for a small sector of humanity, at automobiles and airplanes and refrigerators and radios.

After thousands of years of concentration upon the riddle of the nature of man, humanity finds itself exactly where it started: with the confession of utter ignorance. The mother is still helpless in the face of a nightmare which harrasses her child. And the physician is still helpless in the face of such a small thing as a running nose.

It is commonly agreed that science reveals no permanent truth. Newton's mechanical universe does not fit the real universe which is not mechanical but functional. Copernicus' world picture of " perfect " circles is wrong. Kepler's elliptical paths of the planets are nonexistent. Mathematics did not turn out to be what it so confidently promised to be. Space is not empty; and nobody has ever seen atoms or the airgerms of amebas. It is *not* true that chemistry can approach the problem of living matter, and the hormones did not keep their promises either. The repressed unconscious, supposedly the last word in psychology, turns out to be an artifact of a brief period of civilization of a mechano-mystical type. Mind and body, functioning in one and the same organism, are still separated in man's thinking. Perfectly exact physics is not so very exact, just as holy men are not so very holy. Finding more stars or comets or galaxies won't do it. Neither will more mathematical formulas accomplish it. Philosophizing about the meaning of Life is useless as long as one does not know *what Life is*. And, since "*God*" *is Life*, which is certain, immediate knowledge common to all men, there is little use in searching or serving God if one does not know what one serves.

Everything seems to point to one single fact: *There is something basically and crucially wrong in the whole setup of man's procedure of learning to know himself*. The mechano-rationalistic view has completely broken down.

Locke and Hume and Kant and Hegel and Marx and Spencer and Spengler and Freud and all the others were truly great thinkers, but somehow it left the world empty after all and the mass of mankind remained untouched by all the philosophical digging. Modesty in proclaiming truth won't do it, either. It is often no more than a subterfuge for hiding one's evasion of the crucial point. Aristotle, who governed thinking for many centuries, turned out to be wrong, and little can be done with Plato's or Socrates' wisdom. Epicurus did not succeed and neither did a single saint.

The temptation to join the Catholic point of view is great after the deleterious experience of the latest great effort of humanity, made in Russia, to come to grips with its fate. The devastating effect of such attempts has revealed itself too drastically. Wherever we turn we find man running around in circles as if trapped and searching the exit in vain and in desperation.

It IS possible to get out of a trap. However, in order to break out of a prison, one first must confess to *being in a prison*. *The trap is man's emotional structure, his character structure.* There is little use in devising systems of thought about the nature of the trap if the only thing to do in order to get out of the trap is to know the trap and to find the exit. Everything else is utterly useless: Singing hymns about the suffering in the trap, as the enslaved Negro does; or making poems about the beauty of freedom *outside* of the trap, dreamed of *within* the trap; or promising a life outside the trap after death, as Catholicism promises its congregations; or confessing a *semper ignorabimus* as do the resigned philosophers; or building a philosophic system around the despair of life within the trap, as did Schopenhauer; or dreaming up a superman who would be so much different from the man in the trap, as Nietzsche did, until, trapped in a lunatic asylum, he wrote, finally, the full truth about himself — too late. . . .

The first thing to do is to find the exit out of the trap.

The nature of the trap has no interest whatsoever beyond this one crucial point: WHERE IS THE EXIT OUT OF THE TRAP?

One can decorate a trap to make life more comfortable in it. This is done by the Michelangelos and the Shakespeares and the Goethes. One can invent makeshift contraptions to secure longer life in the trap. This is done by the great scientists and physicians, the Meyers and the Pasteurs and the Flemings. One can devise great art in healing broken bones when one falls into the trap. The crucial point still is and remains: to find the exit out of the trap. WHERE IS THE EXIT INTO THE ENDLESS OPEN SPACE? The exit remains hidden. It is the greatest riddle of all. The most ridiculous as well as tragic thing is this:

THE EXIT IS CLEARLY VISIBLE TO ALL TRAPPED IN THE HOLE. YET NOBODY SEEMS TO SEE IT. EVERYBODY KNOWS WHERE THE EXIT IS. YET NOBODY SEEMS TO MÁKE A MOVE TOWARD IT. MORE: WHOEVER MOVES TOWARD THE EXIT, OR WHOEVER POINTS TOWARD IT IS DECLARED CRAZY OR A CRIMINAL OR A SINNER TO BURN IN HELL.

It turns out that the trouble is not with the trap or even with finding the exit. The trouble is WITHIN THE TRAPPED ONES.

All this is, seen from outside the trap, incomprehensible to a simple mind. It is even somehow insane. *Why don't they see and move toward the clearly visible exit?* As soon as they get close to the exit they start screaming and run away from it. As soon as anyone among them tries to get out, they kill him. Only a very few slip out of the trap in the dark night when everybody is asleep.

This is the situation in which Jesus Christ finds himself. And this is the behaviour of the victims in the trap when they will kill him.

The functioning of living Life is all around us, within us, in our senses, before our noses, clearly visible in every single animal or tree or flower. We feel it in our bodies and in our blood. Yet it remained for the trapped ones the greatest, most inaccessible riddle of all.

However, Life was not the riddle. The riddle is how it could have remained unsolved for such a long period of time. The great problem of biogenesis and bio-energetics is easily accessible by direct observation. The great problem of Life and the origin of Life is a *psychiatric* one; it is a problem of the character structure of Man who succeeded so long in evading its solution. The cancer scourge is not the big problem it seems to be. The problem is the character structure of the cancer pathologists who in so masterly a way have obfuscated it.

It is the BASIC EVASION OF THE ESSENTIAL which is the problem of man. This evasion and evasiveness is a part of the deep structure of man. The running away from the exit out of the trap is the result of this structure of man. Man fears and hates the exit from the trap. He guards cruelly against any attempt at finding the exit. This is the great riddle.

All this certainly sounds crazy to the living beings in the trap. It would mean certain death for the speaker of such crazy things if he were within the trap together with them; if he were a member of a scientific academy which spends much time and money on studying the details of the walls of the trap. Or, if he were a member of a church congregation which prays, in resignation or hope, to get out of the trap. Or if he were the provider for a family whose only concern is not to starve in the trap. Or if he were an employee of an industrial concern which does its best to make life in the trap as comfortable as possible. It would mean death in one form or another: by ostracism, or by being jailed for the violation of some law, or, under appropriate conditions, the electric chair. Criminals are people who find the exit from the trap and rush toward it, with violence toward the fellow man in the trap. Lunatics who rot away in institutions and are made to twitch, like witches in the middle ages, by way of electric shock, are also trapped men who saw the exit but could not overcome the common horror of approaching it.

Outside the trap, right close by, is living Life, all around one, in everything the eye can see and the ear can hear and the nose can smell. To the victims within the trap it is eternal agony, a temptation as for Tantalus. You see it, you feel it, you smell it, you eternally long for it, yet you can never, never get through the exit out of the trap. To get out of the trap simply has become an impossibility. It can only be had in dreams and in poems and in great music and paintings, but it is no longer in your motility. The keys to the exit are cemented into your own character armor and into the mechanical rigidity of your body and soul.

This is the great tragedy. And Christ happened to know it.

If you live in a dark cellar too long, you will hate the sunshine. You may even have lost the power of the eye to tolerate light. From this comes hate toward sunlight.

The living beings in the trap, in order to adjust their offspring to the life in the trap, develop elaborate techniques to keep life going on a tight, low level. There is not space enough in the trap for great swings of thought or action. Every move is restricted on all sides. This has, in the long run of time, had the effect of crippling the very organs of living Life. The sense of a full life itself has gone from the creatures in the trap.

Still, a deep longing for happiness in life and a memory of a happy Life long past, before the entrapment, has remained. But longing and memory cannot be lived in real life. Therefore, *hatred of Life* has grown from this tightness.

Let us subsume all manifestations of this hatred against the Living under the heading " MURDER OF CHRIST." Jesus Christ had fallen prey to the *Hatred of the Living* on the part of his contemporaries. His tragic fate offers itself as a lesson in what our future generations will encounter when they will reestablish the laws of Life. Their fundamental task will be coping with human malignancy ("Sin"). As we search along this trail, trying to get a glimpse of future possibilities, good and bad, Christ's story acquires a tragic significance.

The secret of why Jesus Christ had to die still stands unsolved. We shall experience this tragedy of two thousand years ago, which had such tremendous effects upon the destiny of mankind, as a logical *necessity* within the domain of armored man. The true issue of the murder of Christ has remained untouched over a period of two thousand years, in spite of the countless books, studies, examinations and investigations of this murder. The riddle of the murder of Christ has remained hidden within a domain entirely removed from the vision and thought of many diligent men and women; and this very fact is a part of the secret. The murder of Christ represents a riddle which harrassed human existence at least over the whole period of written history. It is THE problem of the *armored* human character structure, and not of Christ alone. Christ became a victim of this human character structure because he had developed the qualities and manners of conduct which act upon the armored character structure like red color upon the emotional system of a wild bull. Thus, we may say that *Christ presents the principle of Life* per se. The form was determined by the epoch of Jewish culture under Roman rule. It is of little importance whether the murder of Christ occurred in 3000 B.C. or 2000 A.D. Christ would certainly have been murdered at any time and in any culture if the conditions of the clash between the *life principle* (OR) and the *emotional plague* (EP) had been socially given in a manner similar to what they were in the old Palestine of Christ's time.

It is a basic characteristic of *the murder of the Living by the human armored animal,* that it is camouflaged in many ways and forms. The superstructure of human social existence, such as economics, warfare, irrational political movements and social organizations which serve the suppression of Life, are drowning out the basic tragedy that besets the human animal, in a flood of what we may call rationalizations, cover-ups, evasions of the true issue; in addition to all this, it can rely on a perfectly logical and coherent rationality which is valid only *within* the framework of law versus crime, state versus people, morals versus sex, civilization versus nature, police versus criminal and so forth all along and down the line of human misery. There is no chance whatsoever to ever penetrate through this mire unless one has put oneself outside the holocaust and has made oneself inaccessible to the big noise. We are hurrying to assure the reader that we do not consider this noise and empty busyness as merely irrational, as nothing but aimless and senseless activity. It is a crucial characteristic of the tragedy that this nonsense is valid, *meaningful* and *necessary*, though only within its own realm and under certain given conditions of human conduct. But here the plague irrationality rests on sound rock bottom. Even the silence which engulfed the orgasm function, the life function, the murder of Christ and similar crucial issues of human existence for millennia makes good sense to the prudent student of human behaviour.

The human race would meet with the worst, most devastating disaster if it obtained full knowledge of the Life function, of the orgasm function or of the secret of the murder of Christ with one stroke as a whole. There is very good reason and a sound rationality in the fact that the human race has refused to acknowledge the depth and the true dynamics of its chronic misery. Such a sudden breaking-in of knowledge would incapacitate and destroy everything that still somehow keeps human society going in spite of wars, famine, emotional mass killing, infant misery, etc.

It would amount to insanity to initiate such major projects as " *Children of the Future* " or " *World Citizenship* " without comprehending how it was possible that all this misery went on for millennia unabated, unrecognized, unchallenged; that not a single one of the many brilliant attempts at clarification and relief was successful; that with every step toward the fulfillment of the great dream, the misery only deepened and got worse; that not a single religious creed succeeded in realizing its objectives in spite of the best of intentions; that every single great deed turned into a menace to humanity, as for instance, socialism and brotherhood which became statism and oppression of man of the worst sort. In short, to consider such serious projects without first looking around and learning what murdered humanity for ages, would be criminal. It would only add more misery to the existent one. At present, thorough investigation of the murder of Christ is far more important than the most beautiful children we may be able to raise. Every hope of ever breaking through the mire of educational misery would be lost forever, irretrievably, if this new and so hopeful attempt at a new type of raising infants would bog down and turn into its very opposite, as have all former hopeful tasks ever set up by human souls. And let there be no mistake about it: *The reshaping of the human character structure through a radical change in the total aspect and practice of raising children, deals with Life itself.* The deepest emotions the human animal can ever reach far outdistance any other function of existence in scope, depth and fatefulness. Also, the ensuing misery would be correspondingly deeper and greater if this crucial attempt would fail and degenerate. There is nothing more devastating than Life which was irritated and thwarted by frustrated hope. Let us never forget this.

We cannot possibly try to work out this problem in a perfect, academic, detailed fashion. We can do no more than scan the territory to see where treasures are hidden for possible future use, where wild animals are roaming the countryside, where hidden traps are set to kill the invader, and how it all works. We do not wish to get bogged down in our own impatience, in our own daily routine, or even in interests which have nothing whatsoever to do with the problem of education. At a meeting of orgonomic educators several years ago, the fact was mentioned that education is a problem for the next few centuries. It appeared most likely that the first few generations of Children of the Future will not be able to withstand the manifold impacts of the emotional plague. They would certainly have to yield here and there; we do not know exactly in what way. But there *is* hope that slowly a general awareness of Life would develop in these newtype children and would spread over the whole human community. The educator who makes a profitable business out of education would not be interested in education if he believed this were so. Let us beware of this type of educator.

The educator of the future will do systematically (not mechanically) what every good, true educator does today: He will *feel* the qualities of living Life in the child, he will *recognize* its specific qualities and *promote* their development to the fullest. As long as the social trend remains what it is to such an overpowering extent today, i.e., directed *against* these inborn qualities of living emotional expression, the true educator will have a double task: He will have to know the natural emotional expressions as they vary with each child, and he will have to learn how to handle the close and the remote social environment as it steps up against these alive qualities. Only in some distant future, when such conscious upbringing of children will have straightened out the severe contradiction of culture and nature, when man's bio-energetic and social living will no longer oppose each other, but will support, supplement, and enhance each other — only then will this task lose its dangerousness. We must be prepared that this process will be slow, painful, and that it will require much sacrifice. Many victims will be lost to the emotional plague.

Our next task is to outline the basic, typical characteristics of the clash between the inborn, highly variable emotional expressions of the infant and those qualities in the mechanized, armored human structure which will generally and specifically hate and fight these qualities.

Regardless of the innumerable variations in human conduct, character analysis has so far succeeded in outlining basic patterns and lawful sequences in human reactions. It has done so extensively with regard to the neuroses and psychoses. We shall not attempt to do the same with regard to the typical dynamics of the *emotional plague*. Specific descriptions of the individual plague reactions will have to be done amply in order to equip the educator and physician with the necessary detailed knowledge.

In the Christian world and the cultures directly or indirectly influenced by Christianity, a contradiction between "sinful man" and his "God" is sharply pronounced. Man was born in the "likeness of God!" He is encouraged to become "godlike." Yet, he is "sinful." How is it possible that "sin" came into this world if it was created by "God?" In his actual behaviour, man comprises both the godlike and the sinful. The "godlike" was there first, then "sin" broke into his existence. The conflict between the ideal of God and the reality of sin derives from a catastrophe which turned the godly into the devilish. This is true for his past social history as well as for the development of every single child ever since a mechano-mystical civilization has begun to drown out the "godlike" qualities in man. Man derives from paradise and he keeps longing for paradise. Man has somehow emerged from the universe and he yearns to return to it. These are factual realities if we learn to read the language of his emotional expressions. Man is basically good, but he is also a brute. The change from good to "brutish" actually happens in every single child. God is, therefore, INSIDE man, and not to be sought for outside alone. The Kingdom of Heaven is the Kingdom of the inner grace and goodness, and not the mystical "beyond" with angels and devils into which the brute in the human animal has turned its lost paradise.

The cruel persecutor and murderer of Christ, Saul of Tarsus, had clearly, but in vain, distinguished between the "BODY," which was god-given and good, and the "FLESH," which was devil-ridden and bad, to be burned at the stake one thousand years later when he turned Paul, the church builder, himself. In the distinction between the "*body*" and the "*flesh*" in early Christianity, our present orgonomic distinction between the "*primary*," naturally inborn drives ("God"), and the "secondary," perverted, evil drives ("Devil," "Sin") was anticipated. Thus mankind was always somehow aware of its crucial biological plight, of its natural endowment as well as of its biological degeneration. In the Christian ideology, the sharp antithesis of "GOD" (spiritualized body) and "DEVIL" (body degenerated to flesh), this tragedy is plainly known and expressed. In real man, the "god-given" genital embrace has turned into the pornographic 4-lettering male-female intercourse.

ORIGINAL SIN — A MYSTERY

Life is plastic; it adjusts to every condition of its existence with or without protests, with or without deformation, with or without revolt. This plasticity of living Life, one of its greatest assets, will be one of its slave chains when the Emotional Plague will learn to misuse the plasticity of Life to its own ends. One and the same Life is different at the bottom of the deep sea, and different on a high mountain ridge. It is different in the dark cave and different again within the blood vessel. It was different in the Garden of Eden, and different in the trap that caught humanity. Life knows nothing of traps in the Garden of Eden; it just lives paradise, innocently, gayly, without an inkling of a different kind of life. It would refuse to listen to an account of life in the trap; and, if it listened, it would comprehend it with its "brain" only, not with its heart. Life in paradise is fully adapted to the conditions in paradise.

Within the trap, Life lives the life of souls caught in a trap. It adjusts quickly and completely to the Life in a trap. This adjustment goes so far that nothing will remain beyond a faint memory of Life in paradise, once Life has been caught in a trap. Restlessness, hurry, nervousness, a dim longing, a dream long past — yet, still around somehow — will be taken for granted. No trace of an inkling that these are signs of a dim memory of Life in paradise long past will disturb the peace of soul of the captives. The adjustment is complete. It reaches proportions beyond the limits of reason.

The Life in the trap will soon become completely self-absorbed as Life in a prison is supposed to be. Certain character types will develop which will belong to Life in the trap, and would not make sense where Life walks the world freely. These characters, molded by bearing Life in prison, will greatly vary among themselves. They will disagree and fight each other. They will, each in his own manner, proclaim the absolute truth. Only ONE characteristic will they all have in common: *They will join together and kill in unison whoever will dare to ask the basic question:* " HOW IN THE NAME OF A MERCIFUL GOD DID WE EVER MANAGE TO GET INTO THE UGLY PREDICAMENT OF THIS NIGHTMARE OF A TRAP??? "

WHY DID MAN LOSE PARADISE? and

WHAT DID HE ACTUALLY LOSE WHEN HE FELL VICTIM TO SIN?

Man in the trap has, over the millenia, created a great book: the BIBLE. This book is the story of his fights and anguishes and glories and hopes and longings and sufferings and sinnings in the entrapment. It has been thought and written in many languages by many different people. Some of its basic features can be found in places far apart, in the written and unwritten memory of man. That things had, once upon a time long past, been quite different, that somehow man once had fallen to the devil, to sin and ugliness, is common to all accounts of the distant past.

The bibles of the world are the accounts of man's fight against man's sin.

There is so much the Bible tells about the life in the trap, and *so little about how men got into the trap.* It is obvious that the exit out of the trap is exactly the same as the entrance into the trap, through which they were driven from paradise. Now, why does nobody say anything about it except in a very few paragraphs which are as one to a million to the rest of the Bible, and in a veiled language which is meant to conceal the meaning of the words?

The downfall of Adam and Eve is obviously, beyond any doubt due to something they did against the Laws of God in a *genital* way:

" And they were both naked, the man and his wife, and were not ashamed."
(Genesis 2: 25)

From this it follows that in paradise man and woman were not aware or ashamed of nakedness, and this was *God's* will, and the way of Life. Now, what happened? The Bible says (*Genesis 3: 1-24*):

Now the serpent was more subtil than any beast of the field which the Lord God hath made. And he said unto the woman, Yea, hath God said, Ye shall not eat of every tree of the garden?

And the woman said unto the serpent, We may eat of the fruit of the trees of the garden;

But of the fruit of the tree which is in the midst of the garden, God hath said, Ye shall not eat of it, neither shall ye touch it, lest ye die.

And the serpent said unto the woman, Ye shall not surely die:

For God doth know that in the day ye eat thereof, then your eyes shall be opened, and ye shall be as gods, knowing good and evil.

And when the woman saw that the tree was good for food, and that it was pleasant to the eyes, and a tree to be desired to make one wise, she took of the fruit thereof, and did eat, and gave also unto her husband with her; and he did eat.

And the eyes of them both were opened, and they knew that they were naked; and they sewed fig leaves together, and made themselves aprons.

And they heard the voice of the Lord God walking in the garden in the cool of the day: and Adam and his wife hid themselves from the presence of the Lord God amongst the trees of the garden.

And the Lord God called unto Adam, and said unto him, Where art thou?

And he said, I heard thy voice in the garden, and I was afraid, because I was naked; and I hid myself.

And he said, Who told thee that thou wast naked? Hast thou eaten of the tree, whereof I commanded thee that thou shouldest not eat?

And the man said, The woman whom thou gavest to be with me, she gave me of the tree, and I did eat.

And the Lord God said unto the woman, What is that that thou hast done? And the woman said, The serpent beguiled me, and I did eat.

And the Lord God said unto the serpent, Because thou hast done this, thou art cursed above all cattle, and above every beast of the field; upon thy belly shalt thou go, and dust shalt thou eat all the days of thy life:

And I will put enmity between thee and the woman, and between thy seed and her seed; it shall bruise thy head, and thou shalt bruise his heel.

Unto the woman he said, I will greatly multiply thy sorrow and thy conception; in sorrow thou shalt bring forth children; and thy desire shall be to thy husband, and he shall rule over thee.

And unto Adam he said, Because thou hast hearkened unto the voice of thy wife, and hast eaten of the tree, of which I commanded thee, saying, Thou shalt not eat of it: cursed is the ground for thy sake; in sorrow shalt thou eat of it all the days of thy life;

Thorns also and thistles shall it bring forth to thee; and thou shalt eat the herb of the field;

In the sweat of thy face shalt thou eat bread, till thou return unto the ground; for out of it wast thou taken: for dust thou art, and unto dust shalt thou return.

And Adam called his wife's name Eve; because she was the mother of all living.

Unto Adam also and to his wife did the Lord God make coats of skins, and clothed them.

And the Lord God said, Behold, the man is become as one of us, to know good and evil: and now, lest he put forth his hand, and take also of the tree of life, and eat, and live for ever:

Therefore the Lord God sent him forth from the garden of Eden, to till the ground from whence he was taken.

So he drove out the man; and he placed at the east of the garden of Eden Cherubims, and a flaming sword which turned every way, to keep the way of the tree of life.

There was a serpent in paradise " more subtil than any beast of the field which the Lord God had made." To the Christian commentator, the serpent, in his Edenic form, is not to be thought of as a writhing reptile. The serpent originally was "the most beautiful and subtle of creatures." Traces of that beauty remain despite the (later) curse. Every movement of the serpent is graceful, and many species are beautifully colored. In the serpent, Satan first appeared as an angel of light. The serpent, thus, is a symbol of Life itself and the male phallus.

Then, somehow, out of nowhere as it were, disaster strikes. Nobody knows or has ever known or ever will find out how and why it happened: The most beautiful serpent, the "Angel of Light," the "most subtle of creatures," "less than man," is cursed and becomes "God's illustration in nature of the effect of sin ": it changes from "the most beautiful and subtle of creatures to a loathsome reptile."

And, as if a special counsel had met to veil the most dramatic, the most devilish, the most disastrous happening in the history of the human race, and to remove it forever and ever from any grasp by intellect or heart, this catastrophe becomes mysterious and untouchable; it becomes a part of the great mystery of the entrapment of man; it doubtless contains the solution to the riddle as to why man in the trap refuses to simply walk out of the trap using the exit through which he had come into the trap. The Biblical interpreter himself says at this point: "The deepest mystery of the atonement is intimated here," i.e., in the change of the serpent from the "most beautiful and subtle of creatures to a loathsome reptile."

Why all this? Let's hear.

There was a peculiar tree in the Garden of Eden, and God had said to man in paradise: "Ye shall not eat of every tree of the garden."

And the woman said unto the serpent, We may eat of the fruit of the trees of the garden;

But of the fruit of the tree which is in the midst of the garden, God hath said, Ye shall not eat of it, neither shall ye touch it, lest ye die.

(*Genesis* 3: 2,3)

Did anyone ever in the course of six thousand years explain that tree? No one ever did so. Why? The mystery of this tree is a part of the mystery of man's entrapment. A solution of the mystery of the tree could possibly answer the predicament why man is in the trap. The solution of the mystery of the forbidden tree would certainly point to the entrance to the trap, which, used the other way around, would become an exit *out* of the trap. Accordingly, no one ever thought of solving the riddle of the forbidden tree, and everybody in the trap was busy for millenia to scholasticize, talmudize and exorcise the predicament of being within the trap, using millions of books and myriads of words, with one single goal in mind: *To prevent the solution of the riddle of the forbidden tree.*

The serpent, still beautiful and subtle, knew better. "And the serpent said unto the woman, Ye shall not surely die: For God doth know that in the day ye eat thereof, then your eyes shall be opened, and ye shall be as gods, knowing good and evil."

Now, since the beautiful serpent thus brought about man's downfall, what in the name of sanity does all this mean:

If man in paradise, living happily the ways of God, eats from a certain tree, then he will be like God, his eyes will be opened, and he will "know good and evil." *How does such a devilish tree manage to get into God's garden in the first place?*

And if you eat from such a tree which bears the fruit of *knowledge* and you become like God himself, why then do you *lose* paradise? The Bible, to my knowledge, doesn't tell. And it is to be doubted that anyone ever asked such a question. The legend doesn't seem to make sense: If the tree is a tree of knowledge, to know the difference between good and evil, what's bad, then, in eating of its fruits? If you eat of its fruits, then you certainly can follow God's ways *better*, and not worse. Again, it doesn't make sense.

Or is it forbidden to know God and to be like God, which means to *live* God's ways, even in paradise?

Or is all this the cooked-up fantasy of man in the trap, regarding a faint memory of a past life outside the trap? It doesn't make sense. Man is haunted all through the ages by the request to know God, to follow God's Ways, to live God's love and life; and when he starts seriously to do so by eating from the tree of knowledge, he is punished, expelled from paradise, and condemned to eternal misery. It simply does not make sense, and we fear that no representative of God on earth has ever asked this question, or even dared to think in its direction.

> *And when the woman saw that the tree was good for food, and that it was pleasant to the eyes, and a tree to be desired to make one wise, she took of the fruit thereof, and did eat, and gave also unto her husband with her; and he did eat.*
>
> *And the eyes of them both were opened, and they knew that they were naked; and they sewed fig leaves together, and made themselves aprons.*
>
> (*Genesis* 3: 6,7)

When man thus was first trapped, confusion beclouded his mind. He did not understand why he got into the trap. He felt he must have done something wrong, but he knew not *what* wrong he had done. He had not felt ashamed being naked, and then, suddenly, he felt ashamed of his genital organs. He had eaten from the tree of forbidden "knowledge," which, in Biblical language means, he "*knew*" Eve, he *embraced her genitally.* For this now he has been expelled from the Garden of Eden. God's own most beautiful serpent had seduced them; the symbol of wavy, living Life and of the male sexual organ had seduced them.

From here to the life in the trap there is a wide, deep gap in comprehension. In its adjustment to the life in the trap, Life developed new forms and means of existence; forms and means which were unnecessary in the Garden of Eden, but were crucial for life in the trap.

A silent and suffering and dreaming and toiling mass of humanity, cut off from God's Life, provided the broad foundation on which grew priests, and the prophets against the priests; the kings, and the rebels against the kings; the great healers of man's misery within the trap, and with them the great quacks and the medical "authorities," the traumaturgists and the occultists. With the emperors there came about the freedom peddlers, and with the great organizers of man in the trap were born the political prostitutes, the Barabbases and the sneaking vermin of bandwagon riders; Sin and Crime against the law, and the judges of Sin and Crime and their executioners; the suppression of liberties unlivable in a trap, and the Unions for Civil Liberties within the trap. Also, from the mire grew great political bodies called "parties," designed either to keep up what they called the "status quo" within the trap, the so-called "conservatives" (since they tried to preserve the law and order which had been established to keep life in the trap going), and, opposing them, the so-called "progressives" who fought and suffered and died at the gallows for advocating more freedom within the trap. Here and there such progressives conquered power over the conservatives and began to establish "Freedom in the Trap" or "BREAD AND FREEDOM in the Trap." But, since there was no one who could "give" the broad herd of men bread and freedom, since they had to *work for it*, the progressives soon became conservatives themselves, for they had to maintain law and order just as their eternal enemies, the conservatives, had done before. Later, a new party arose which thought that the *masses* of suffering humanity in the trap should rule Life in the trap, and not the priests or kings or dukes. They tried hard to get the mass of people on their legs and into action; but apart from a few murders and the destruction of the homes of some rich men in the trap, little happened. The broad mass of humanity just repeated what it had heard and seen from above for millenia, and nothing changed; only the misery became greater when a very clever party was formed which promised to humanity a "*PEOPLE'S FREEDOM IN THE TRAP*" and brought about hell here and there by using all the old and outworn slogans formerly used by the kings and the dukes and the tyrants. The *people's* freedom parties had, to begin with, until their designs were found out, great success. Their slogan of a "PEOPLE'S" freedom in the trap, as distinguished from other freedoms in the trap, and the use of the old methods of the old kings, worked, since the leaders of this party had come, as little freedom peddlers, from among the herd of entrapped men themselves, and when they obtained power over a little area they were stunned to find how easy it is to push buttons and to see police, armies, diplomats, judges, academic scientists and representatives of foreign powers act according to brief, sharp pulls and pushes on neat buttons. The little freedom peddlers liked that game of push-button-power so much, that they forgot all about "PEOPLE'S FREEDOM IN THE TRAP" and just enjoyed themselves pushing buttons whenever they could in the palaces of the old rulers whom they had murdered. They just went power drunk with joy of pushing buttons on the tables of power machines. But they did not last long and were soon replaced by good, old, decent power-button-pushers, the good, old conservatives who had retained some decency and bearing in their souls as a fading memory from the days of paradise.

They all fought and quarreled with each other, pushed each other here and there, killed their adversaries with or without the law; briefly, they gave a true picture of man's Sin and the fulfillment of the curse in the Garden of Eden. The mass of entrapped humanity did not really partake in this holocaust of plague-ridden Life in the Trap. From among two billion human souls, no more than a few thousand partook in the turmoil. The rest just suffered, dreamed and waited . . . . for WHAT? The redeemer, or for something unheard of to happen to free them; for delivery of their souls from the trap called the body; for reunification with the great world soul or for hell. But dreaming, toiling and waiting were the main occupations of the broad herd of humanity far removed from the political turmoil. There was also great dying in the great wars within the trap, with enemies changing from year to year like people cashing money at a banking counter. It did not matter much, though it hurt. The mass of suffering humanity was waiting for delivery from this sinful life, anyhow, and the few noisemakers did not really amount to much, seen in the perspective of Life or " God " in the Universe.

And God's Life was born in billions of infants everywhere in the trap, but it was killed right away by the people in the trap who either did not recognize God's Life in their infants, or were frightened to death at the sight of living, moving, decent, simple Life. And so it came about that man perpetuated his entrapment. These infants, if left to themselves as God had created them, would certainly have found the exit from the trap. But this was not allowed to happen. It was particularly forbidden during the reign of " THE PEOPLE'S " freedom in the trap. All loyalty had to be for the *trap*, and not for the babies, under punishment of death by the " Great Leader and Friend of All the Entrapped Ones."

CHAPTER II

THE KINGDOM OF HEAVEN ON EARTH

The myth of Jesus Christ presents the qualities of " God," in other words, of the inborn, naturally given Life Energy, in a nearly perfect manner. What it does *not* know nor recognize is that Evil, *the Devil, is a perverted God, grown out of the* SUPPRESSION *of the Godlike.* This lack of knowledge is one of the cornerstones of the human tragedy.

In the Orgonomic Infant Research Center, we have seen those natural " godlike " characteristics in small children, characteristics which have heretofore remained the idealized, unreachable objective of every kind of religion and ethics. Similarly, every single religion which developed in the great Asiatic societies had pictured the animal Man as actually bad, sinful, malignant; and every religious philosopher throughout human history had only one single objective: to penetrate the fog, to find the answer to the origin of Evil and a remedy against the Evil in man. All philosophical striving and thinking has always been basically directed toward the riddle of the Evil and its elimination.

How can Evil come from God's creation? Here, in each newborn infant, God was there, to sense, to see, to smell, to love, to protect, to develop. And in each single newborn infant, to this day, God was squelched, restricted, suppressed, punished, looked upon with horror. This is only one of many realms of the chronic Murder of Christ. *Sin (Evil) is being created by man himself.* This remained hidden.

The Kingdom of God is *within* you. It was born with you. But you fail God, so all religion says; you do not recognize him, you betray him, you are false to him, and you are sinful as long as you do not return to God. So long, too, you remain tempted by the Devil and you must pray to God in order to escape temptation. How is it possible that man failed to see God right in front of him?

The qualities of the freely functioning orgonotic living system and the observation of children freely growing within their natural rights, bear out this mystified religious inkling of a basic truth. Let us remind ourselves that we are not interested here in an exegesis of religious belief or in approval of religious life. What we are keenly interested in is how much of the biological truth has been known to Man in the course of time, and how much of it he dared to realize in the face of his own fear and hatred of life. Christ represents this knowledge of man. Therefore, he must *die*. *The Children of the Future will grow out of the past.* The speed and efficiency of the change will greatly depend on how much of a happier future has been anticipated in the dreams of mankind and how much has been thwarted in the course of the conflict between Devil and morals. There is no hope whatsoever for education unless such basic orientation is accomplished. Discovering man requires awareness of the secret of armored man: *the hatred of the Living.*

Jesus knew that children have "IT." He loved children and he was childlike himself; knowing and yet naive; trusting and yet cautious; streaming with love and kindness, and yet able to hit hard; gentle and yet strong, just as the child of the future is. This is no idealization. We are fully aware of the fact that the least bit of idealization of these children would amount to looking at reality through a mirror where it cannot be grasped.

The Godlike, thus, is not merely revengeful and severe, nor is it merely good and meek, always turning the other cheek to the enemy. It knows *all* expressions of life. Orgonotic emotions are good and meek where goodness and meekness are due. They are hard and hit hard where Life is betrayed or offended. Life is capable of severe wrath, as demonstrated in the expulsion of the money changers from the temple of God. *It does not condemn the body,* it even understands the prostitute and the woman who was unfaithful to her husband. But it does not prosecute and condemn the prostitute or the faithless wife. When it speaks of "adultery," it does not mean the same thing as do the sex-starved, malignant, hardened, immobilized human animals in some big crowded city.

God is Life. Their symbol in the Christian faith, Jesus Christ, is a strongly radiating creature. He attracts people who flock around him in crowds and love him. This love actually is hunger for love; it turns easily into malignancy when not gratified.

Radiating creatures full of life are born leaders of people. They are leaders automatically, without effort, without proclaiming themselves as leaders of people, as the leaders of the emotional plague do.

Children who gleam with happiness are also born leaders of other children. The latter flock around them, love them, admire them, seek their praise and counsel. This relationship of leading child to led children grows spontaneously out of their games and talks. The child of the future is gentle, loving, giving freely and gladly. Its movements are harmonious, and its voice is melodious. Its eyes sparkle with a gentle glow and look into the world with a quiet, deep gaze. It is soft in its touch of hands. It can stroke so that the stroked one begins to radiate his own life energy. This is the badly misinterpreted "healing power" of Jesus Christ. Most people, including the armored small children, are cold or clammy, they have a narrow energy field, they do not radiate, they do not give strength to others. They need strength themselves and they drink it from wherever they can get it. They fill themselves up with the strength and the radiating loveliness of Christ, like men dying from thirst seep up water from a well.

Christ gives freely. He can give freely since his power to absorb life energy from the universe is boundless. Christ does not feel that he is doing much by giving his strength to others. He does it gladly. More, he needs this giving himself; he is full with strength to overflow. He does not lose anything when he gives to others richly. On the contrary, he becomes stronger and richer by giving to others. Not merely because of the pleasure of giving; he thrives on giving, for his energy metabolizes faster; the more he gives off in strength and love, the more new strength he gains from the universe, the greater and closer is his own contact with nature around him, the sharper his awareness of God, Nature, the air, the birds, the flowers, the animals, to all of whom he is close, knowing them with his orgonotic First Sense; secure in his reactions, harmonious in his self-regulation, independent of obsolete "thou shalt's" and "thou shalt not's." He is unaware that other "shalt's" and "shalt not's" will break in later in a most tragic fashion and murder Christ in every single child.

The "healing power" of Christ, later on so badly distorted by armored man into mercenary cheapness, is a *well-understood and easily observable* quality in all men and women who are endowed with natural leadership. Their strong orgone energy fields are capable of exciting the sluggish, "dead" energy systems of the "wretched" and the miserable. This induced excitation of the weak living system is experienced as relief from tenseness and anxiety, due to the expansion of the nervous system, and it even provides a quiet, kindly, lovely glow of true love in an otherwise hateful organism. The excited bio-energy in the weak is capable of expanding the blood vessels, of inducing better blood supply to the tissues, of improving the healing of wounds, of counteracting the stale, degenerative effects of stagnant life energy.

Christ himself does not think much of his qualities as a healer. No great physician struts around as a healer. No healthy child ever thinks of its redeeming powers. It is alive functioning that is at work. It is an integral part of the life expression of Christ in the child, in the true physician, in God himself. Christ even admonishes his mystical followers and stunned admirers not to tell anyone of his powers of healing. This will be misinterpreted by some future historians of Christianity as "hiding before the enemy," as "awareness of the possible accusation of sorcery." No, this has nothing whatsoever to do with enemies or sorcery. Though Christ later falls prey to the plague on these grounds, too. Christ really and truly does not pay much attention to his healing powers. They are ingrained in him and they are so much himself that they no more deserve special attention and are no more conducive of pride than walking or loving or eating or thinking or giving. It is an integral part of him. It is one of the basic characteristics of the GENITAL CHARACTER.

Christ tells his fellow men: The Kingdom of Heaven is right there within you. It is also outside of you, in all eternity. If you are aware of it and live according to its laws and meaning, you feel God and you *know* him. THIS is your redemption, *this* is your saviour.

They, however, do not understand Christ. What is he talking about? Where are the "signs"? Why does he not tell them whether he is the Messiah or not? *Is* he the Messiah? He should prove it by performing miracles. He does not tell. He is a mystery himself. He must be revealed; his secret must be disclosed.

Christ is no mystery at all. He does not tell because he has nothing whatsoever to tell them that might satisfy their mystical longings. Christ IS. He simply lives his life. But he is, to begin with, not aware that he is so very much different from all the rest of them.

To Christ, who is nature himself, Nature and God are one. Children know it, he tells his friends. And he believes they are all Children in God. To him, God *is* Growth and Growth *is* God.

They still do not know what he is talking about. God to them is a bearded, wrathful, punishing father. Therefore, Christ seems to speak in veiled parables. To them, God *makes* growth. To them, they are not children in God, but the subjects of a wrathful God. To them, Nature was created by God in seven days out of nothing. How then can God himself be Nature?

Christ knows of the inborn morality and natural sociality of life. He preaches the innate goodness of the poor and the wretched. The poor are like children. Faith is power. Faith can move mountains. Faith gives strength. Faith is the feeling of God or Life within oneself. It is self-assurance, strength, power of movement.

They do not know what he is talking about. They are miserably shut off from nature within themselves. They must be held by threats to obey the laws of morality and sociality. They have lost the Kingdom of God and forever are longing for paradise. Their conception of paradise is a land where one does not work to raise bees in order to obtain honey.

Honey flows by in big honey rivers, and you do not have to move a finger. Milk, too, of course, has not to be worked for. It, too, flows by in rivers. If it is true that God takes care of every sparrow in the universe, then, in paradise, he would take care of them just as well. No work, no effort, no worries, just milk and honey flowing in rivers. And manna too would rain right down to earth from heaven. They would have to do no more than bend down, pick it up and put it into their mouths. But somehow, manna does not rain down, and milk and honey have to be worked for, hard. This is so because God did not send his Messiah yet to redeem them. Moses had promised the land where milk and honey will flow in great streams. It turned out to be a dream which turned into a nightmare of Roman rule with soldiers, taxation, subjugation and persecution. Still, the Messiah is coming. Christ is so very much different from them. He speaks a language and lives a life they cannot understand. This confirms their convictions that he *is* the Messiah who is going to redeem them. People fear or admire what they cannot grasp. People feel better when they are near him. Children like him and flock around him as if he were God Himself. They had not yet developed the habit of having little children in white dresses bring flowers to the statesmen. This came about some two thousand years later.

Christ does not quite realize what is happening to him. He does not reveal himself because he has nothing to reveal. He just lives ahead of them. And since he feels and sees how miserable they are, how different, he tries to help them. He tries to convey upon them his own feeling of simplicity, directness and closeness to nature. *He loves women;* he surrounds himself with women as he does with men, and he lives his body " in the body " as God has created it. He does not live the flesh, but the body. He feels and lives God so very differently from the scribes and the Talmudists. These have lost God within themselves and are now frantically searching God, squeezing God out in their litanies, as it were, praying to Him-they-never-knew to reveal Himself. In vain; they cannot make it. So they hate everything that reminds them of God as he really is. They must *preach* to have faith, because they have no faith. They must *preach* obedience to God's ways and laws because men have lost the being godlike themselves. God, to them, is a strange, wrathful, hard God. He had scourged them once and had expelled them from paradise. He has put his angel to guard the entrance against reentry, with a flaming sword. They became victims of the devils.

The Devil is sickness and lust in the flesh and greed and murder and betrayal of the fellow man, and cheating and lying and money grabbing. They have lost God and know him no longer. Over centuries, many prophets have told them to return to God, but none dared to know God as he lives and works in man. The flesh had completely obliterated the body. Even the newborn ones were Godlike no more, but were rendered pale and sick and miserable in contracted, cold, stale wombs.

God, of course, was still within them; but he was buried and distorted so badly that no one could recognize him any longer. Feeling God within oneself was inseparably linked up with severe anxiety. From this came their belief that you must not know God. Somehow, they came to believe that you must not know God in spite of the fact that the Law commands people to know him and to live in His ways. How can you live in something you do not and are not ever to know? Nobody tells them. Nobody *can* tell them. Everything connected with God is transferred into a distant future, into a great, awesome hope, into a mirage toward which they stretch out their arms in despair. And still, God is right within themselves, unreachable, protected from their ugly grip by fright and agony. A fearsome angel is guarding the angels against themselves.

Christ knows that man is miserable; still, he cannot really know how they are since he is so very much different and does not know it. He believes that they are the same as he. Is he not their brother? Did he not grow up among them? Did he not play with them as a little boy, live their joys and sorrows? He did, so how could he know that he was so very much different? Knowing this would set him apart, render him lonesome, force him into solitude, prevent his little joys and sorrows from uniting him with all the children of God.

Still, he was so very much different from all the rest that only the glaring lack in them of what he possessed abundantly made it possible to know that he was different.

Christ did not pose as a saint. He just lived in a way dreamed of by his fellow man as being the truly saintlike way of living. Does a flower live " as if " it were a flower, or a deer " as if " it were a deer? Does a flower or a deer proclaim itself as flower and as deer? They are what they are. They live it. They function it. They exist through a continuous reality of being what they are without further thought or wonder. If anybody would tell a flower or a deer: " Listen, you are so wonderful, you are a flower, a deer," they would look at the speaker with utter amazement. What do you mean? I do not understand. *Of course* I am a flower, a deer. What else should I be?

And the mystical admirers would not understand what the deer and the flower tried to tell them. They would keep wondering at the miracle. They would keep wanting *to be like* the flower and the deer. In the end they will pick the flower and kill the deer. This is inevitable from the whole setup of things as they are arranged.

They love Jesus because he is what *they* are *not* and cannot ever be. They try to drink his strength and simplicity and spontaneous beauty into themselves. But they do not succeed. They cannot be like Christ nor take him in. They can feel better and stronger and wiser and different from what they were and are only by looking at him, by hearing him talk to them, by listening to the strange simple truth he tells them, which hits the nail on the head every single time, never missing the point. Christ does not miss the point because he has perfect contact with what is going on around him. He can see what they never see because he is not shut to seeing. He looks into a landscape and he sees the unitedness of it all. He does not see single trees and single mountains and single lakes as they do. He sees the trees and the lakes and the mountains as what they really are, integral parts of a total, unitary flow of cosmic events. He sees and hears and touches with his whole being, pouring his life force into everything he touches, and drinking from trees and flowers and mountains the same force a hundred times stronger back into himself. He does not retain and hold on to this strength. He gives it out abundantly, never giving a thought to whether or not he would get poorer by giving. He will not get poorer but richer by giving. Life returns in richly flowing metabolisms what it gets. There is no one-way road in giving or taking. It is give *and* take, back and forth.

Again, they do not know what he is talking about. To them, giving away things means getting poorer. Taking is the same as getting strength, filling up an emptiness, getting over a yawning gap within oneself. They can only take, they cannot give. The giver, to them, is either a fool or one to be sucked dry, taken advantage of. Thus, they shut up many a giver, drive into solitude many a loving soul. And the world is again a trifle poorer.

Christ, who loves people, lives alone. They who hate themselves and everybody else, live lonely and forsaken in big crowds. They are deadly afraid of each other. They pat each other on the backs and grin with friendly grimaces; they must deceive each other lest they cut each others' throats. And each single one among them knows that each single other one is cheating. They hold conferences now as they did two thousand years ago to get "final peace," well knowing that they cheat each other with evasions and formalities. Nobody tells what he really thinks. Christ tells what he thinks. He is not formal, he does not cheat, and he does not force himself not to cheat. He simply does not cheat. He can be silent, but he does not lie with intent and malice. They, on the other hand, cannot tell the truth simply because truth cannot be told; the organ with which to tell the truth has dried up within them when they lost the streaming of Life and living straight.

Thus it comes about that they worship truth and live the lie. Truth is inseparably linked up with the streams of Life within the organism and its perception. Life is not truthful because it should or is held to be truthful. It tells the truth by its every movement. The expression of the body cannot lie. You can read the truth if you know how to read the expressive language of movement from everybody's face and gait. The body tells the truth even if it has to tell that it lies habitually and that it has put up a veneer of truthlike behaviour to cover up the lie. Therefore, Life "reads the signs" just as Man has dreamed of Jesus Christ having been able to read the signs. However, in certain huge contexts where the very existence of the whole race is involved, it may easily happen that the truth is not expressed and remains hidden.

The ape in man is rarely expressed. So is his origin from segmentally wormlike functioning living beings. Though the history of an event is always somehow present this very minute, one has to know anatomy and physiology to learn certain truths which reach far beyond man's domain and scope. Christ's cosmic meaning, attributed to him by man in a mystical fashion, lay in his true expression of the Living, in his complete coordination of body and emotions, and in his immediateness of contact with things. Thus it lay beyond the scope of man who, through his armor, is confined to the strictly "human" domain. It is this confinement by the armor to strictly human affairs which is responsible for man's failure to reach the universe, to understand life around him and in his newborn infants, and to develop his society according to such knowledge which reaches far beyond his own biology. Thus confined, he is bound to develop dreams and utopias forever removed from any possible realization.

Now, man must experience everything from *within* this confinement, and he will be unable to judge his existence other than in terms of a miserable reality versus a mystical otherworldliness. He will be unable to change the first or to realize the true nature of the second. Life, functioning beyond his confinement, will automatically be conceived of as incomprehensible and unreachable.

We know from characteranalytic explorations of man's depth structure that it is his basic genital disturbance, his orgastic impotence, which keeps him confined. It is, therefore, quite consistent that he will persecute and punish nothing more severely, that he will hate nothing more abundantly and decidedly than the graceful appearances of orgastic potency, i.e., Life or Christ, i.e., his own cosmic origin and present potentiality. The first he misinterprets with an inexorable consistency as loveless 4-lettering, the second is forever removed into dreams unfulfillable.

From this hopeless entanglement ensues the Murder of Christ. The way to the final murder is long; the forms in which this murder operates are million; however, up till this twentieth century, the murder has never yet failed to occur in the end. That it has remained so secret and inaccessible is one of its basic characteristics.

The bio-energetic core of life and its cosmic meaning is the orgasm function, i.e., the involuntary convulsion of the total living organism during the embrace of male and female at the discharge of the bio-energy into each other. If there were no other way to identify the Life function with the orgasm function, it would be the identity of their fates during the written history of mankind. Removal beyond comprehension, persecution and punishment of their manifestations, mystical transformation of the awareness of their importance, and horror at meeting them at close range are the most typical as well as least acceptable characteristics of armored man.

A synoptical survey of the behaviour of Life and armored Life during the genital embrace will far better than anything else be able to convey the meaning of the hatred and consecutive murder of Christ. Christ depicted the Kingdom of Heaven in this parable, the deep biological meaning of which should be clear to anyone who deals with the human bio-energetic depths:

Then the kingdom of heaven shall be compared to ten maidens who took their lamps and went to meet the bridegroom. Five of them were foolish, and five were wise. For when the foolish took their lamps, they took no oil with them; but the wise took flasks of oil with their lamps. As the bridegroom was delayed, they all slumbered and slept. But at midnight there was a cry, "Behold, the bridegroom! Come out to meet him." Then all those maidens rose and trimmed their lamps. And the foolish said to the wise, "Give us some of your oil, for our lamps are going out." But the wise replied, "Perhaps there will not be enough for us and for you; go rather to the dealers and buy for yourselves." And while they went to buy, the bridegroom came, and those who were ready went in with him to the marriage feast; and the door was shut. Afterward the other maidens came also, saying, "Lord, Lord, open to us." But he replied, "Truly, I say to you, I do not know you." Watch therefore, for you know neither the day nor the hour.

(*Matthew* 25: 1-13)

CHAPTER III

THE GENITAL EMBRACE

The longing for the fusion with another organism in the genital embrace is just as strong in the armored organism as it is in the unarmored one. It will most of the time be even stronger, since the full satisfaction is blocked. Where Life simply loves, armored life "fucks." Where Life functions freely in its love relations as it does in everything else and lets its functions grow slowly from first beginnings to peaks of joyful accomplishment, no matter whether it is the growth of a plant from a tiny seedling to the blossoming and fruit-bearing stage, or the growth of a liberating thought system; so Life also lets its love relationships grow slowly from a first comprehensive glance to the fullest yielding during the quivering embrace. Life does not rush toward the embrace. It is in no hurry, except when long periods of full abstinence have made instant discharge of life energy imperative. Armored man, on the other hand, confined in his organismic prison, rushes at the fuck. His awful language already betrays the emotional feel of "taking her" against her will by force or seduction. To be with a human being of the other sex alone in a room for any length of time without "trying" whether "he can have her," or her fearing that he might attack her, appears unthinkable. From this derives the disgrace to any human dignity in the form of the chaperon. In these days it is on its way out, since natural genitality began to occupy the public mind.

Life can even be in bed together with a mate without thinking of the embrace if there is no spontaneous development toward it. Life does not begin with the fulfillment; it grows into fulfillment. It does it from love, for love, as it behaves in any other realm of functioning. Life does not write books in order to have written a book "too"; it does not perform its work in order to be written up right away in the newspapers; it does not write "for people" but about processes and facts. Life builds a bridge safely in order to cross a stream and not in order to get a reward at the next annual convention of the Society of Engineers.

So also, Life does not, in meeting a mate, begin with the idea of the embrace. Life meets because it just meets. It can separate again; it can walk together a stretch and then separate; or it may go all the way toward the full merger. Life has no preconceived idea of what will happen in the future. Life lets things run their natural course. The future here develops out of the continuous stream of the present, as the present in turn emerges from the past. There are certainly thoughts, dreams, hopes about the future; but the future does not govern the present as it does in the domain of armored life. Life, if it grows freely, is interested in functioning itself, and slowly develops certain skills to function well. The biologist or physician thus grows out of skills developing naturally from handling certain functions. Armored life dreams of being a famous physician, a surgeon with a big name who is admired by the population and strives for big write-ups about his big clinic in the big newspaper in a big land, and finally gets into big money. This is the armored man's idea of "success." One can vary this example *ad libitum* to suit the big fuehrer of the nation or the big leader of the people or the great father of the great Russians in greater Russia in the greater part of the globe. It is and remains always the same music, the same way of anticipating what should grow organically, of beginning with the end. Old cancer pathology began with the intention of solving the riddle of the origin of the cancer cell, and bogged down in airgerms. The riddle was solved exactly where it was least sought for: in the observation of silly grassblades soaking in silly simple water. Life does not start writing a book with the title and preface. The preface and the title are the last things to be written, since they are to encompass the whole, and one cannot survey the whole before it is finished. One does not start a home with the inner furnishing but with the rock foundations. But the layout of the foundations must be preceded by the general idea of what the inside will finally look like.

All sentimental marriage dreams start with the defloration in the wedding night, and land in the gutter of marriage misery. It is again armored man who keeps people from knowing that marriage has to grow slowly from the seedling toward the fruit. And it takes years to grow a fruit-bearing tree. Marital *love* has nothing to do with the marriage *license*. The growing of marital love is simple. It can easily be done. The growing itself, the constant experience of a new step, the discovery of a new kind of look, the revelation of another feature in the partner's make-up, no matter whether pleasant or unpleasant, in itself is great delight. It keeps you moving. It keeps you changing in your own natural direction of development. It keeps your appearance better looking than any advertised soap could ever do, and it keeps your face capable of flushing at the right moment. It takes many months, sometimes years, to learn to know your love partner in the body. The finding of the body of the beloved one itself is gratification of the first order. So is the victorious overcoming of the first difficulties in the adjustment of two alive organisms. He may not be gentle enough during high excitation, and she may be afraid of full sweetness in surrendering to the involuntary. He may at first be too "quick" and she too "slow," or the other way around. The search for the common experience of supreme delight in the complete merger of the two streaming energy systems we came to call male and female — this search itself and the mutual wordless finding one's way into the beloved's sensations and truly cosmic quivering, is pure delight, clean like water in a mountain brook, and delicious like the smell of a beautiful flower in the early spring morning. This heart-warming, continuous experience of love and contact and mutual surrender and body delight is the decent bondage which goes with every naturally growing marriage. The genital embrace emerges as the fulfillment of this constant delight, as a high point on a long mountain hike which takes you again and again back into the valleys, into the dark nights and into stormy weather. You know you are moving onward to new heights far above deep dark mountain valleys. And each time you reach another peak it is different from all former experience, since life is never quite the same even in two consecutive seconds of one and the same operation. You do not have the ambition to be "on top," to look down into the valleys or to tell others how many mountain peaks you have conquered in a fortnight. Your basic mood is silence. You simply keep moving along and you rejoice in every new height after the steady ascent. The preparation of the climb is just as delightful as the climbing itself. Resting after reaching the peak is just as beautiful as the first thrilling excitement when you first reach out for the landscape with your eyes and the rest of your body. You do not keep asking yourself painfully all through the preparations and the climbing whether you will ever reach the peak. And you do not invent a special pocket motor to get you safely over the last few feet. You do not choke the scream of delight in your throat when you reach the peak, and you do not start getting cramps when you feel the oncoming of delight. You just live fully each single step of it all. You know deep down that there is really not much to reaching the peak if you take care of every step toward it. You are sure of yourself, since you have reached many peaks before and you know the basic taste of it. You do not permit anybody to carry you up toward the top, and you do not think at all of what your malicious neighbor would think or say if he knew about what you are doing. You left them all far behind you, either doing the same or longing to do the same.

The full natural embrace is like such mountain climbing; it does not differ basically from any other life activity, be it of great or little importance. Full living means full surrender to any kind of functioning. No matter whether working, or talking to friends, or rearing a child, or listening to a talk, or painting or anything else.

The genital embrace grows out naturally from a slowly developing total body urge to merge with another body. One can easily see this basic characteristic in birds, toads, butterflies, snails, in mating deer and other freely living animals. The final delight of total energy discharge in the orgasm is the spontaneous result of a long continued build-up of smaller delights. These little delights have the faculty of providing happiness, yet creating desire for more. Not always do the smaller delights lead toward the final supreme delight. Two butterflies, male and female, may play with each other for hours and then separate again without embrace. They may go further and superimpose without penetration. But once they merge with their body energy systems, they go through with it to the end. They do not frustrate each other unless interrupted by a butterfly collector or a hungry bird. The total organismic excitation precedes the special genital excitation. The orgastic potency grows out of this total body delight and not from the genital. The genital organs are merely the means of physical penetration *after* the mutual merger of the orgone energy fields has occurred a long while before the last fulfillment. The contacts are gentle. There is no grabbing, grasping, clutching, pressing, pushing, squeezing, pinching in them. They go as far as is given in the special approach and no farther. A man may love a woman dearly for months, desire her deep down to the fullest, meet her every single day, and yet he may not go beyond a warm hand clasp or a kiss on the lips. When the embrace becomes necessary for both of them, it will happen, inevitably, and they both will know the moment without telling each other in words when they are ready. But then nature will develop its most beautiful powers of unification of two living beings.

Just as these organisms have permitted their love to grow organically and slowly, as far as it wanted to reach; just as they knew at the right moment to make the right move. their bodies will know exactly how to meet in the embrace. They will search each other's sensations and they will feel delight in finding them. They will find each other's curves of the body and the degree of mutual giving in each moment, the inevitably sure way. They may feel that their bodies were ready this first time to go so far and no farther. Unless the genital merger grows naturally out of what preceded this phase, they will not merge and will separate again, for good or for a few days only. They will " structuralize " their mutual experience, get accustomed to each other in preparation for greater fulfillments. No trace of possessing the partner, or of having to prove one's potency will darken the delight. Nothing is there to "prove" or to "achieve" or to "get."

The sweet melting together, is there or it is not there. It may come for moments and it may leave again. It cannot be forced or be kept by force. Unless it stays on and grows, no embrace will develop into genital merger. If genital merger develops ultimately, without the corresponding growth of the feelings of sweetness and melting, they will regret it later; it will blacken their delight and may ruin it forever. Thus the safeguarding of the full supreme delight is the best safeguard of the self-regulatory behaviour in the orgonotic superimposition of male and female.

The orgasm itself occurs when it has to occur, not when he or she "wants" it. You cannot "want" an orgasm and "get" it as you get a bottle of beer at the counter.

The orgasm in its true biological sense is a result of steadily growing waves of excitation and not something readymade to get by hard labor. It is a unitary convulsion of one single energy unit which long before the merger was two units, and which after the merger will divide again into two individual existences. Bio-energetically, the orgasm amounts to a true loss of one's individuality into an entirely different state of being: it is not the getting of an orgasm on her part from him and on his part from her, as the sick mind of man in the first as in the twentieth century was wont to believe. The proof of this is the fact that such "getting" the orgasm vanishes completely upon medical treatment, whereas the true bio-energetic merger does not vanish but rather increases in its vigor. These matters are crucial.

The orgasm is an event which *happens* in two living organisms, and not something "to be achieved." It is like the sudden protrusion of proto-plasm in a moving ameba. An orgasm cannot be "had" with everyone. Fucking is possible with everyone since all it requires is enough friction of the genital organ to produce discharge of seminal fluid or a feeling of strong itching. An orgasm is more than and basically different from a strong itching. One cannot "obtain" an orgasm by scratching or biting. The scratching and biting male and female is struggling to obtain bio-energetic contact by all means. Orgastic contact *happens* to the organism. One does not have to "make" it. It is there only with certain other organisms and is absent in most other instances. Thus it is the foundation of true sexual morality.

The fucking organism has to "rush" at it in order to "accomplish" it. It ends in "rubbing it off" or "making love." The loving organism lets himself submerge in the flow of feelings and drifts on the current as master of every move like an expert canoe rider is in perfect control of his boat on a wild mountain river. The expert rider of a full-blooded horse lets himself be carried away and still is fully master of the horse. The hardened organism labors for it, comparable to a runner whose legs are impeded by a bag around the feet. He can only hobble along with great effort. In the end he is exhausted and there was only misery in the run. The fucking organism keeps a cool head all through the " act " (the word " act " alone is significant of what is going on). He can " do it," " perform it," " make it," " accomplish it," " go through with it " anywhere and everywhere, like a frustrated, raving bull or stallion who was away from any female for years on end. And there are special, skillfully developed techniques to get at the female and to seduce her. The life value of such activity is worth as much as the pushing along of a disabled automobile on the road by way of a hauling truck — the two front wheels high up in the air.

The inner make-up of the love function determines every single feature in every single other activity of the individual. The fucker will always get it, push for it, rub it in or off, have special techniques for reaching his objective in an efficient manner; the suffering type will remain a victim to what the pusher does to him or her. The genital character, on the other hand, will always let things function and happen; he will submerge actively in whatever he is undertaking, from loving a woman or man to building up an organization or a job.

The pusher and the sufferer each will flock around the genital character to learn how to be like him. From this first impulse of the armorridden organism to emulate the freely functioning Christ, the tragedy ensues with steel-like logic. There is no escape from the final tragedy for both, Christ as well as pusher and sufferer, at any time, in any land, in any social stratum, as long as these two ways of life confront each other. In the No-Man's-Land between these two camps, the Children of the Future will needs grow up. To find an answer as to how to protect them from the emotional plague resulting from this tragedy is paramount to any future rational education. There is no problem of early or late upbringing that does not more or less depend on its structure and outcome from the conditions leading up to the Murder of Christ.

To the orgonomic characterologist of the twentieth century, Christ had all the characteristics of a genital character. He could not possibly have loved children, people, nature, have felt life and have acted with such great grace, had he suffered from genital frustration. The well-known signs of genital frustration — dirty thoughts, lasciviousness, cruelty, direct or moralistic, fake mildness — are absurd in the picture of Christ, as it came down to us, to such an extent that our attention centers spontaneously upon the riddle as to why no one has ever understood it. This is entirely in line with the fact that no biologist has ever mentioned the wavy, orgonotic pulsation in living things, and that no mental hygienist has ever mentioned the ravages of genital frustration in puberty.

Christ could not possibly have been clean like brook water and sharp-sensed like a deer, had he been filled with the filth of perverted sex due to frustration of the natural embrace. There can be no doubt: *Christ knew love in the body and women as he knew so many other things natural.* Christ's benignity, his gleaming contactfulness, understanding of human frailty, of adulteresses, sinners, harlots, and the lowly in spirit, could not possibly fit with any other biological picture of Christ. We know that women loved Christ — decent, beautiful, full-blooded women. This, too, is crucial to an understanding of the final murder of Christ. To think otherwise, appears to be out of the way of things completely. Independent writers such as Renan, have clearly expressed this thought, and every clear-minded knower of Christ's way knows the secret.

The greater is the riddle that from his life emerged a religion which, contrary to its originator, has banned the core of natural functioning from its domain, and has persecuted nothing more than love of the body. This, too, will find its rational answer.

CHAPTER IV

SEDUCTION INTO LEADERSHIP

Christ has, in accordance with his organismic harmony, the power of FAITH; he relies on his senses. He has contact with what is going on around him; he feels his body fully and has no frustrated, malignant flesh to carry along in a hidden manner. He does not " try " to do things; he DOES them. He has the full power of the God-given Life force. He understands the birds and he knows how to distinguish a grain of rye from a grain of wheat.

Christ knows the Kingdom of God which is the Kingdom of Life and Love on earth. It is here, right there in each flower, sparrow, tree and olive branch. His fellow men are not aware of God. They do not feel Life. They exchange money, they fornicate in a bad way, not knowing what love is. They pay heavy taxes and obey stupid, strutting, gulping, hideous emperors. They are squeezed, emotionally dependent people, pliable in any crook's hands, or they feel Life as a chauvinistic ambition to become emperors themselves. Christ sees, knows, suffers all this. He comes from among the poor who are like children, still close to God, still not completely warped and twisted, still knowing love. The poor are like children and they know and feel like children. They live apart from the big noise, take no part in it, though it can exist only because they do not or cannot care.

There are the Barabbases and Maccabees, necessary evils. You could not do without them. They are the ones who with their swords fight the emperors from foreign soil. Who else should fight and die on the battlefield? Christ does not fight the emperors. He gives Caesar what is Caesar's and God what is God's. Christ does not want to fight Caesar. He knows he cannot possibly conquer Caesar. But he also knows that Caesar will be long forgotten when what he himself feels in his body and what vibrates in his senses in harmony with the universe, will rule the world to the good of all men on earth. The Kingdom of God on earth, which is this feeling and vibrating of living Life in Christ as in all men on earth, is sure to come. It had been there, once upon a time. It cannot fail to come again. This is, in fact, so self-evident that it must be right around the corner. It is rather like a bad dream that the Kingdom of Heaven on Earth has not come already. There must be a reason for this since what it is is so evident, how it feels, how easy and lovely is this kind of being.

Christ, therefore, does not in the beginning consider himself as something special. He just is as he is. Why is not everybody else that way? You have it in yourself; just dip deeply enough into yourself and you will find it. Why did you lose it? How was.that possible? God has not forsaken his children. Man must have abandoned God. But why? How? When and where did it happen? We do not know to this day. But Jesus knows exactly *what* they have lost, yet *they* do not know what they still possess deep down within themselves. He does not know, but he will learn the bitter way, that they do not feel God because they are keeping on killing him every single second of every single minute in every single hour of every single day of the year through the thousands of years. This is too absurd a fact to be taken as a truly existent fact. Why should man kill Life in himself? What an utter monstrosity to think that such a thing were possible.

Yet this monstrosity is exactly what constitutes the realm of the adversary of God-Life, of the heathen and the devilish sin. Man got caught somehow long ago and he continues to tie the knot of this bondage, all the while he moans about his plight and dreams of the coming of the Messiah.

When they lost the feeling of God within themselves, they began to flock around men who radiated Life but did not possess the full force of Christ. They flocked around the *abortive* Christs, around the politicians of all ages, to get strength from them. The abortive Christs were swept to the top, and they began to enjoy people flocking around them. They liked the admiration they got and they felt a glow of warmth at the praising and the singing of chants, the dances in their honor and the call to leadership of impoverished man. In this manner the first chiefs, kings, dukes, fuehrers, generals, sergeants, Stalins, Hitlers, and Mussolinis were created and were carried to power by the people themselves out of perfectly rational reasons: *They needed outer strength to replace what they had lost in inner strength and faith and security.* Having lost the inner spontaneity of alive functioning they needed and got outer crutches of functioning, to this very day. But why did it have to last for so many thousands of years? Why did they not find right away the cause of their misery? Why was it even so very much forbidden to get at the scourge? You must not know God and you must not know Life. This became the most holy and the most powerful law that enslaved humanity. Incredible, ridiculous, but true. . . .

The little leaders have lost the sense of Life to a great enough extent to fall for this demand of the people. They are not down to earth enough, like Christ, and they do not, like Christ, sense the rotten quality of the present order, enough to abstain from such leadership. They assume leadership which is *necessary, crucial* for immediate existence. The high taxes have to be fought, the old religious customs must be upheld and protected, arrangements must be made with the pagan emperor to continue holy services in the temples even if these services are only corpselike shadows of a formerly sparkling, alive religion. And this religion is quite crucial to their very existence. Without it they would lose balance, orientation, hope, the support of their wretched souls. The Devil, thus reigning under restriction by moral laws, would otherwise reign without restraint.

Christ feels all this more than he knows it. He, too, is chosen to be a leader, a saviour, a fighter for their happiness. The tragedy is that what Christ wants and lives is so entirely different from what they want and live that there is no chance for the two ways of life ever to meet.

When Christ speaks of the Kingdom of Heaven on Earth he means the inner freedom of the animal man which is part of the lawful freedom of the whole creation. When Christ tells them that he is the Son of Man, or, which means the same, the Son of God, he means something very real, true, existent, crucial: He is the offspring of Life, of the cosmic force which he knows so well and feels so clearly within himself. They, however, do not understand him. They urge him to reveal himself and to demonstrate his divine power. They ask for signs of his divinity. This is the root of the future mystification of Christ.

To their plague-ridden senses, the Son of God should be different from what Jesus looks like. True, the Son of God would be like Jesus: sweet, gentle, understanding, always giving, always ready to help, feeling for the poor, loving children and being loved by children. He would walk gracefully as Christ does, and he would have his deep, serious look in his eyes. He would never tell a dirty joke, not because of any principle but simply because it would not occur to him to talk badly. His head would be, just like Jesus', radiant with a soft, invisible glow which would later appear on Ikons as a bright, yellow, hideous quarter-moon around his head, quite in agreement with the mystical, cheap way plague-ridden men experience the orgone energy field of the body. Only very great artists would in future centuries sense the quivering, gentle, fine quality of this orgonotic radiance and would try, with little success, to reproduce it in their paintings.

The expression of Christ has the quality of a meadow on an early sunlit spring morning. You can't see it, but you feel it all through you if you are not plague-ridden. You love it, it makes you glow softly and you do not laugh it off as does the dried out, emotionless, cunning brain of a red fascist, as petit bourgeois sentimentality. Can you imagine Molotov or

Malenkov on a meadow on an early sunlit spring morning watching deer graze? This is impossible. Christ is like a glowing, radiant flower; he knows it, he loves it, and he tries at first naively to convey this feeling to his fellow men in whom it is obviously lacking. He knows they are miserable because they lack it; that they have killed it, but he is not aware of the fact that they hate it as much as they yearn for it, more than anything else in Life. Neither does he know that they kill it in every single newborn infant right after birth, with mutilation of the genital, acid drops in the eyes and a spanking on the buttocks as a fond first greeting in this world. It will take millennia of misery, a huge heap of saints burned at the stake as well as mountains of corpses on all kinds of battlefields to give them an inkling of it. It is Christ's ill fate that he does not know it. He believes his fellow man is only ignorant, or dull from hunger or hard labor. He believes the fellow man will take to his knowledge like a thirsty man to a water well. In the end they will, they *must* kill him.

His fellow man does rush to his Life Force like a thirsty man to the water well. They drink it all in in big gulps, with eyes popping and faces flushed. They feel revived, radiating with a soft glow, they even get flashes of brilliant thoughts; they can ask good questions so the Master can give more of his abundance. And they drink it all and keep drinking. And the Master keeps pouring into them and keeps pouring, since they flock around him again and again and again to drink the crystal-clear words from his lips and the radiating strength from his body, and his consolations and advice and great wisdom. His fame as a rich giver is carried far over the lands. And more and more thirsty men and women fill up their dried-out vessels with the very sap of Life, the radiating grace of his simplicity and fullness of living.

They accompany him on his early morning walks into the fields and hear him say beautiful things about God's creation. He seems to understand the song of the birds, and the animals are not afraid of him. He has no trace of the movement of a killer within himself. His voice is melodious and fully expressive. It comes right out of the belly, not, as in them, out of a tight mouth or a hardened chest. He can laugh and scream with joy. He knows no restraint in his expression of love; in giving himself to his fellow men, he does not lose a grain of natural dignity. When he walks on the-ground his feet set fully into the soil as if to take root with each step, separating again to take root again. He does not walk like a prophet, or a wise man, or a professor of higher mathematics. He simply walks. When you see him walk, you ask yourself: What is he? Who is he? He is so very much different from all the rest. Every single one of his followers expresses something in his walk, something that really has nothing to do with walking. The one walks in modesty. The other walks in deep thought. The third walks as if he were running away from horror. The fourth walks like a king. The fifth like an obedient follower of the Master. The sixth walks like a deer. The seventh walks like a fox. The Master simply walks, not even like a deer. He just walks.

His walk alone is a challenge to any kind of scholasticism, be it Sophism, Solipsism, Talmudism or Existentialism. His whole behaviour is so much at variance with all kinds of isms that no one accustomed to " place " people, could tell where he belongs. This is most disturbing to common people, since everybody belongs somewhere, *has* to belong somewhere lest he become suspected of subversive activities. He has to be a member of a guild, or of the Sanhedrin, or of the class of priests, or of the legion for the rescue of the fatherland, or of the league of the heroes of the motherland. Christ is well known as a lecturer and teacher. But even here he does not seem to belong. In the very first place, he asks questions too bluntly. This is unpleasant. He gives very simple answers to most complicated questions, questions thousands of wise men have kept pondering about for millennia with no answer achieved. Thus he is the born leader of men. And people feel that he is. They keep asking him the one question: Who are you? What are you? Have you been sent by God? To save us? Are you the Messiah? If you are, tell us. We shall worship you. We shall follow you. We shall carry you to power and might over our enemies. Reveal yourself. Give us a sign, do a miracle to show who you are.

The Master keeps silent about his wherefrom's and whereto's. He keeps walking with them in the fields, visiting with them various places. He keeps giving simple answers to complicated questions, to give them strength to pour out great wisdom without touching a learned book.

He *must* be sent from heaven, they think. Not only is he different, he is also mysteriously silent about his true nature and his mission. He must have some mission. He has come to rescue his people, the poor, the nation from enslavement. Thus they are building up *their* distorted image of the Son of God, who is the Son of an unwarped Cosmic Life Force. He keeps silent because he has nothing to answer to their questions about any essence, mission, vision, signs, powers. He feels, of course, that he is different, otherwise they would not behave as they do. But he does not understand why they want him to give them signs from the heavens and to reveal the mystery of his being, which to him is no mystery at all. He feels like a son of the heavens, but he does not feel himself to have been sent by God. At least, he does not say anything about it. He does not feel as though on a mission. This idea is slowly being poured into him from outside, by his admirers and followers and pupils. In the beginning he does not dream of any mission. He just does carpentry or microscopy or healing people's wounds or tending fields. It is they, the ones hungry for salvation, the love-starved ones, who inject into him the seeds of the myth which is to kill him in the end, and many, many men and women and children after him. He only works differently, lives differently, talks and walks differently. That is all. AND HE LOVES PEOPLE. He knows their ills. And he learns to see their ills clearer every single consecutive day. He does not have an inkling of any idea of curing them. But slowly he learns that he IS helping them. That he possesses a power to comfort and to console people. This grows slowly into an obligation. If people suffer, you must help, do your best, give of your abundance to them, live modestly with the barest necessities of living. What you feel as a divine grace within yourself is so easy to feel and to live, it gives you so much and enriches everything you touch to such an extent that NOT to convey it to your sisters and brothers would be unbearable. In this manner meet divine grace and human longing for consolation. The one keeps giving, the others keep taking, drinking, sucking, filling up.

The basic thought of the bearer of the divine, natural grace, i.e., unthwarted Life, is simple: Every single soul has the God-given grace within him or herself. Let them drink from my abundance in their state of starvation, and they will become strong, will start giving from their own strength to others; and these others, rescued from their emotional starvation, will in turn give others again. Here our Master commits his first fatal mistake. He believes, quite consistently, as viewed from his own Life, that once filled up, the taker will turn into a giver himself. The master giver does not know that the chronic starvation has rendered the takers incapable of giving. They have become one-way dead-end roads. They are truly leeches. And this is exactly what is going to kill the master giver.

The good black earth produces grain. It receives the seeds and lets them grow into new grain, pouring nourishment, salt and water and life energy into every single fiber every single second of every single day. The soil enriches itself by retaining some of the straw, once the seed has matured and is carried away by the wind or taken away by man or animal. The soil, thus enriched, gives new life to new grain. And new grain gives new life to other Life.

An animal takes up the seed in the God-given union of male and female and reproduces the offspring, in its own image and yet different. It pours its Life strength into the offspring until it can do by itself. The offspring, grown up, will live and act likewise.

The whole universe is ruled by this cycle of give and take, absorb and reflect, grow and die, concentrate cosmic power and dissipate it again into the great cosmic ocean.

If a well has dried up in a hot summer drought, it can only pick up water when it rains again. Once filled up to overflowing, it will start giving off water to the soil around it and to distant brooks which in turn will give the sap of Life back to life.

In this manner Life reproduces, maintains itself and grows endlessly. Not so, armored man. He became a one-way-dead-end-road when he killed God in himself, when he lost paradise. It is often exactly the representative of God on earth who will block the entrance to the realm where the answer to the riddle of why man had lost his paradise, is to be found. This *verbot* is a part of the plague that ravaged humanity so long so mercilessly. You simply must not know God or Life as your body sweetness. This would inevitably lead you to find out why you lost God. Therefore, you must not ever know God. And all this nonsense is preached in thousands of places and by proficient masters in evasion, in thousands of universities all over the globe. You must, let's repeat, search God and Life, worship God and Life, obey God and Life, sacrifice to God and Life, build temples and palaces to God and Life, write poems and music about God and Life; but you must not ever, under punishment of death, *know* God as Love. There is not a single exception to this rule during the past several thousands of years. More: *Not a single man or woman has ever loudly asked any questions about this nonsense.*

Knowing God as Love would confirm God's existence, would make Him accessible, would make man capable of living actually what he is so utterly incapable of living now: It would fulfill each and every single demand of every single religion, constitution, law, morals, ethics, values, ideals, dreams. But NO! You must not ever know God or Life as bodily love.

This is all as it is because there is but one single approach to knowing God, and living Life accordingly: THE GENITAL EMBRACE; an approach banned and out of bounds. DO NOT EVER TOUCH IT! Every child went through this agony. *Do not touch it* — the genital, namely.

So it came about that man forever keeps longing for God and Life, drinking God and Life wherever it offers itself, sucking dry God and Life, killing God and Life inside and outside himself. But never, never can man give out God or Life. He does not know how God and Life feel when active. He only can experience them passively, take them in, fill himself up with them, enjoy them, use them to various ends; to feel better, to cure himself, to get rich with them, to obtain power, to influence people, to cheat. But never, never can frozen man give out God or Life. This is inextricably bound up with GIVING LOVE, GENITAL LOVE IN THE EMBRACE. Which is forbidden, cursed and killed already in the infant. *So Man can only take in, he cannot give out Love.* The Life Force he gets into himself becomes a means to quite a different end than loving giving. In entering his body it becomes "flesh," since the body became stiff and immobile. Godlike love turns into lust, the embrace into a hideous, grinning fuck, an expression of hating, getting, grasping, holding, possessing, ripping off or ramming in, jerking-it-off and rubbing-it-through, give-her-the-works and the marital-obligations racket, with lawyers, reporters, public defamation, tearing children's love apart, revenge, alimony and acrimony.

From this everything else follows with a merciless, cruel logic up to the final crucifixion of Christ.

CHAPTER V

THE MYSTIFICATION OF CHRIST

Read the prayer on the mountain slowly, thoughtfully. Substitute "*Cosmic Life Force*" for "*Father*" who is "*God.*" Think of "Evil" as man's tragic degeneration of the natural instincts. Keep steadily in your mind the entanglement of the *primary, natural* with the *secondary, perverted, cruel* drives. Keep clear the fact that "human nature" so-called, contains the "devilish" evil, i.e., cruelty born from frustration of the primary need for love and gratification of love in the mating embrace. Focus this "evil" as the dragon guarding the access to the Godlike love in man. And now read the prayer on the mountain:

Our Father who art in heaven,	*Our Love-Life who art from heaven,*
Hallowed be thy name.	*Hallowed be thy name.*
Thy kingdom come,	*Thy kingdom come,*
Thy will be done,	*Thy will be done,*
On earth as it is in heaven.	*On earth as it is in heaven.*
Give us this day our daily bread;	*Give us this day our daily bread;*
And forgive us our debts,	*And forgive us our guilt,*
As we also have forgiven our debtors;	*As we also have forgiven our debtors*
And lead us not into temptation,	*And lead us not into distortion of love*
But deliver us from evil.	*But deliver us from our perversions.*
(*Matthew* 6: 10-13)	

God-Father is the basic cosmic energy from which all being stems, and which streams through your body as through anything else in existence. But also: God-Father is the unreachable reality of BODILY LOVE, mystified and idolized into Heaven.

Mystification consists of worshipping in the mirror the image of an unreachable, tantalizing, unlivable, untouchable and therefore unbearable reality within oneself.

Humanity does *not*

1. Distinguish between and separate primary and secondary human nature.

2. Comprehend the devilish Evil ("Emotional Plague" – "Sin") as the prime result of the frustrated GOOD – GOD – LIFE – LOVE (*including* THE GENITAL EMBRACE).

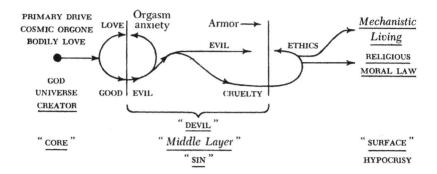

3. Know, accordingly, how evil *could* come about when the creator is good.

4. Have the power to disentangle itself from the Devil and the mechano-mystical dichotomy.

5. Arrive at laws protecting (*not* the moral laws *but*) the primary, godly, bodily love against the emotional plague, which is called " sin."

6. Reach God, the Good, brotherly Love by opening the gates out of the trap where the biological foundation of man finds itself entrapped.

7. Stop protecting the Evil emotional plague.

8. Make the core accessible to put the middle layer plague (— " sin ") out of function, thus:

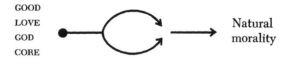

GOOD
LOVE
GOD
CORE

Natural
morality

The love from the core, once made unreachable, constitutes the essence of the mystification of God.

The murder of Christ, who represents the Godly love in the body, ensues henceforth through the ages with an inexorable logic.

From now onward, Life can only be conceived of as godlike and unreachable, as beyond and unknowable. From now onward, through the ages, every single experience of man concerning his living Life will be seen as if in a mirror, like Fata Morgana. From now onward he will spend all his strength, his wits, his skills, his creativity in keeping the reality of life away, and in transforming every single reality (except lifeless, mechanical machinery) into a mystical image in order *not* to have to grasp it. He will feel Life, but from far away, as it were, as through a wall or a fog. He will know that a godlike something exists, whether he calls it God or Eternity or The Higher Destination of Mankind or Ether or The Absolute or the World Spirit; but he will tightly shut all entrances to knowing it, handling it, developing it. This removal of the true, real, living Christ did not happen only once, at the beginning of the Christian era. It went on long before Christ's name appeared in man's history; and it went on long after Christ was murdered. Christ was only the most prominent exponent of the chronic tragedy. More: Christ became the symbol of suffering and redemption from Man's sin through the fact that nobody before and nobody since has shown the qualities of living Life so clearly, and was murdered in such a hideous, shameful manner. *In the legend of Christ, man has tried, in vain, to comprehend and to solve the riddle of his own miserable existence.* He did it without success since, again, as always before and after the Murder of Christ, he could not get at what he wanted most: *to get at himself.* He established Christ as the symbol of his own mystery and suffering and, at the same time, shut tight and sealed for good by the MYSTIFICATION OF CHRIST, the access to understanding Christ. By seeing Christ as if in the mirror only, in his true image but unreachable, man has made himself inaccessible to himself. It is comprehensible now that many thousands of books were written about Christ without a single hint at the fact that it was *man himself who had killed Christ* because Jesus represented Life.

But somehow the same man who had murdered Christ and later made Christ his most beloved God must have sensed his tragic, logical mistake all through the ages. Not only did he show this in the magnificent churches, in the great art, in the most beautiful music, in the most elaborate thought systems developed to honor and worship Christ. We cannot escape the impression that the great noise about Christ was to drown out the committed murder, to obliterate every trace of the last bit of an inkling of such murder and to secure its continuation all through the immediate post-crucifixion period and the later middle ages up to the burning of crosses, the murder of softspoken and softbodied Negroes in the South of the USA, and the killing of six million helpless Jews and Frenchmen and others in Hitler's Germany.

From the actual Murder of Christ and what had led up to it till the murder of Negroes in Cicero, USA, of pacifists in the USSR and Jews in Hitler Germany is a very long stretch of time, packed full with events of first rank order. However, no detailed elaboration of these single events will ever reveal a trace of the true nature of the Murder of Christ, since it is the very essence of the plague to conceal the murder and its motives. The victims of the murder vary. The reasons given *post hoc* for the murder vary. The methods of murder vary from land to land and from time to time. It does not matter whether Danton gets the guillotine or Lincoln the bullet into his head; whether Gandhi gets the bullet into his chest or Wilson or Lenin, suffering agonies in seeing their life dreams perish, are struck down by a cerebral hemorrhage; it is always the same basic red thread that marks the hidden way in which Dreyfus is put away for five years for a crime he did not commit, or an innocent man in America spends twenty years in jail, sent there by a criminal judge, saying " thank you " in a truly Christian, forgiving fashion, while the judge and the criminal district attorney go free, or whether millions of plain people who KNOW do not dare speak up because there is some malignant gossiper and slanderer around in town. It all really starts with the first mystification of Jesus Christ by his own pupils.

Christ's disciples do not really understand what he is talking about. They are only faintly aware of the great promise he holds out for them. They sense it, they drink it up in full sips, but cannot digest it. It is like pouring water into a barrel without a bottom. Empty men are soaking up water like sand, drying out right away again, wanting more. This, of course, means a constant agony of frustration. Here is Christ, the redeemer, right in front of them, feeding them, comforting them, thrilling 'them, telling them of the age of the reign of God on Earth, and more: showing them the signs of the reign of God right now and here, and yet. . . It all remains unreachable, inaccessible, frustrating; they can only take in the image of it, but not its substance itself. They can only gulp down the pure fluid, but it does not stay with them. It passes quickly through them, like a quiver through the nerves, but it does not stay on, and, worse, it does not DO anything. They listen to his words with tense ears. But these words do no more than thrill them. They try to reproduce these words; it does not really work. Or, if it works, it sounds hollow, without meaning, like the mechanical echo from a distant mountain. When the WORD stops flowing from his lips, the echo stops echoing from

the mountain. THEY ARE COMPLETELY EMPTY. THERE IS NOTHING WHATSO-
EVER IN THEM TO PICK UP THESE WORDS AND TO RECREATE THEM.
They find themselves to be deserts, complete wastelands. This realization is not clear; it is well concealed as are most of their experiences of
their selves. But an awareness of this awful situation is there, undeniable
and painful.

They try hard, as best as they can, to learn from Christ and to reproduce him. But soon they find that they simply do not and cannot understand him. Therefore he seems to speak in mysterious parables. Christ
is not mysterious at all. He just tells them good, poignant stories. But
since they are shut like a tight shell, they feel him as mysterious, somehow
dark, far away, not quite present, strange, so very much different, as
through a fog or a haze. The fog and the haze are truly *theirs* and not his.
But to realize this would inevitably mean to realize their living death.
Therefore the fog seems around him, and not around themselves.

The better Christ hits them with his sharp, acute remarks, the further
removed they feel him. And here sets in what you can watch in every single town meeting in every land where town meetings are still held: The
simpler the speaker, the clearer his words, and the emptier the speech or
expression of the participant in the discussion from the floor, the greater
becomes the distance between the platform and the floor, and the closer
comes the audience to mystical, helpless admiration of the speaker on the
rostrum.

A wide gap opens up, never to close again: *The wide gap between
the factual impotence of the crowd and its mystical identification with the
speaker on the rostrum.* Into this gap the Hitlers and the Stalins and the
Mussolinis and the Barabbases and the evildoers of all ages and lands pour
their influence upon people. They do not know, of course, how they are
doing it. Here it is, exactly here, where the misery of the twentieth century was bred out to the brim of endurance. Yet, no one ever mentions it.

The mystification of Christ, which begins with his removal into an
ever greater distance, does not mean that they do not truly love him or
admire him genuinely, or are not ready to die for him. At this point, it
only means that they feel they can never, never be like Christ, while Christ
always feels certain that they CAN be like himself. It is not Christ who
removes himself, it is they who slowly, unnoticeably remove him from
themselves. This is the first step toward the pedestal where he will finally
be put for good, untouchable, impossible to equal. He is, as they usually
say, "A thousand years ahead of his time," i.e., made ineffective. They
try to be as he is. They suffer agonies because they try so hard and do not
succeed. And the harder they try the worse becomes the feeling deep

down of their own worthlessness. With this, slowly *hate* develops, never quite obvious, never quite outdrowning the love for Christ, never reaching their own full awareness; but the hate is there to stay through the ages. Christ challenges their very existence; emotional, social, economic, sexual, cosmic. And they are utterly incapable of any change or challenge to their established ways. They are rigidly armored, rendered emotionally sterile, immobilized, devoid of development.

Really, they are without any contact and cannot establish contact with his teachings. They only feel the prickling warmth of his words. His teaching is to them a means of getting warmed up in their cold desert. It does not mean anything in itself. These words and deeds of Christ serve them only as another splendid means of escaping the realization of their true selves, the nothingness, the emptiness. No glorification at a later date, backward into the distant past of mankind, of the " simple fishermen " and the " simple-minded peasant " or tax-collector will or can obfuscate the fact of the emptiness of these simple people and what it means to every single one of them to meet a living being like Christ.

Not to face this crucial issue of the emotional emptiness of people and of their rut, means giving up hope of ever changing the lot of man-kind. It is tragic to realize what the people do to their potential leaders, and that the leaders later retaliate by doing the same thing to the people: Mystification, idealization, patting on the back, glorification of suffering, false admiration of simplemindedness. In this manner the leader seduces the people into remaining what they are, instead of getting them moving; just as the people seduce their leaders into the distance where they become harmless as true changers and shapers of basic improvements which always are, and are bound to be unpleasant and painful. From this mutual back-slapping, smearing sugar around the mouth, between people and leader, stems all the hideousness of politics, its inner emptiness and futile gestures, and the final wars which are Murder of Christ again — on a mass scale.

Since the led ones are thoroughly and deeply incapacitated in help-ing themselves, the leader must be made the more powerful to help them. Since he usually is an average mortal himself, he has to be elevated to high, even if fake, power and splendor. This fake power and splendor, house-sized pictures, uniforms, medals and the like, are the necessary comple-ments of the helplessness and emptiness of the people. Both together heave each other to the great heights of fake state power and fake national strength. Think of the " thousand years' " reign of Hitler's ten years in power, or even the eighty years of the German Reich as compared with a single biological event. The mystery is not the power of the men in the Kremlin but the gaping nothingness and emptiness of its foundation.

The difference between a Jesus Christ and a Hitler or Stalin in this tragic relationship to people, is this: The dictator abuses and misuses the helplessness of people to the fullest. He does not hesitate to say so frankly, and people still hail him, even for this. He tells them they are not worth a thing except as victims of glory to die for the Fatherland, and he gets them. Not because he tells them to die, but because he is the right person; magnetic enough to enable them to fill themselves up with his strength and show of vigor. They drink from him and he pours the stuff into them as much as they please. It never really fills them up since it seeps out right away again; but it tickles and thrills them to shout, to march, to hail, to yell, to identify with the greatness of the nation. No sociologist in this century has as yet dared to look into the deep abyss of the structure of people's behaviour. This is so because the plague has shut and concealed the exit from this trap.

Stalin does the same thing, more subtly, in a more refined way. He keeps hidden, and pulls the strings in a most cunning way from behind a screen. He lets only his pictures speak. He behaves modestly, wears no medals, but it is exactly this modesty which is the fake show in the big parade in Moscow square. He has a different background from Hitler's, and it is this background of the great revolution of 1917 that determines his behaviour. Deep down he really admires the greater, quicker efficiency of a Hitler, as evidenced in his pact with Hitler in 1939. He must transform show-off into silent cunning. And he does so skillfully. But in this he does the same as Hitler: He creates an image for the helpless people to identify with, to drink fake strength from the leader, which seeps out again right away.

And as long as they keep giving the people the opportunity to drink from them the mystery of leadership, they are safe. They will not be murdered. But many Christs are murdered, as a matter of course, as it were.

It is different with Christ. He does not fall for the mystification right away. He does not accept leadership right away, and when he finally falls prey as a leader, he does so in such a manner that murder in the end is inevitable. *He accepts leadership without sacrificing his true nature, and therefore he must die.* This marks his true, cosmic greatness.

Two thousand years will pass before human thought will reach the crux of the Murder of Christ, so safely put away and hidden in millions of written pages filled with words of admiration, exasperation, adulation, interpretation, commiseration, expectation of salvation and excitation. Two thousand years will pass before in a lonely nightly hour in some far

away corner of the wide world, a lonesome man will understand the nightmare; and will tell

THE SUCKER

I am rich like the black fat Earth.
I nourish the things that suck.
The sucker knows not what he gets.
Yet:
The good old Earth had not rebelled
when they ravaged the land,
eroded the soil,
cut every tree in the forest.
The land was covered with sand
when the soil was gone.
They never gave back to the land;
Does the litter return what it sucked?
They took my knowledge
To heal the soul of the sick,
And the tool I built
to capture the very essence of God.
And they took my name
and wrapped it around their necks,
For protection against the icy cold
which chilled their aching flesh.
They did not take the grace
of love and care.
They had no eyes to see,
Nor hands to touch;
No sense to live the grace.
They merely ravaged the land.
And Mother Earth did not rebel,
Nor did she shake off the lot.
She only covered herself with grief
where the crowd had dwelled.
The good rich soil,
once fat and yielding,
Had gone,
Because they never returned the grace.
They had no souls:
They gave to get ——
They learned to earn ——

They worshipped to gain ——
They never, never reached out into space
with arms or heart or brain.
The motion of yearn
was gone from their chests
except to GET.
Their lips could not kiss,
Their smile was frozen to grin.
This is what they called their " sin,"
To be freed from which
They had nailed their redeemer
to the cross of the witch.

The universal importance of the Murder of Christ is this:

Fifty years of technology, out of two hundred and fifty years of experimental natural science, has promoted man from the horse-drawn buggy to the rocket air ship. Eight thousand years filled with the grave problems of human nature had not brought man an iota closer to understanding himself.

It is obvious that man failed in understanding himself because he *did not dare to understand himself;* he had shut all entrances to knowing himself. There must be a reason for this. We saw some of the things man hides from himself. But HOW DOES HE MANAGE TO HIDE THEM SO LONG AND SO EFFECTIVELY?

There is no use whatever in proclaiming the crucial importance of understanding human nature, of establishing great societies for the study of human nature and of meeting at mass congresses to such ends, unless we first realize THAT MAN DOES ALL KINDS OF THINGS TO *avoid* THE UNDERSTANDING OF HUMAN NATURE.

Among the things man does to escape from knowing himself are the make-believe conferences on human nature. And his social future depends entirely on whether or not he will keep running away and continue murdering Christ unabated everywhere.

Through the continuous Murder of Christ, man keeps sawing off the bio-energetic branch he is sitting on, and thus does he keep himself away from the very sources of all he has. All this has been very well known since early social sex-economy which, in the process of refuting certain psychoanalytic theories in the late 1920's, brought the character structure of the people to the foreground as the decisive sociological factor in history. However, this knowledge is no longer a novelty, nor would it stop the Murdering of Christ, since there are some sociologists who took over the knowledge about the character structure and emptied it again completely of its essence, *the bio-genitality of man.* For this, now, they are hailed as the great sociologists of the time.

We know now that the dynamo of man's whole existence is driven by bio(*genital*)-energy. We also have learned that the total body convulsion has been extinguished in man through the armoring of every single child newly born into his society, and that, in this manner, man has shut off the only powerful valve of social self-regulation and his only emotional access to his own nature. We have learned many other minor things, too, such as the representation of the early parental environment of the infant and child by the ideas of gods and goddesses, who continue to stand for father and mother.

However, all this will remain academic stuff unless we get to the root of the horror which obviously keeps man from knowing himself and governing his own Self as he has learned so perfectly well to govern his mechanical environment. Before anything can be done about *Ending* the Murder of Christ, the manner in which man keeps this murdering hidden must be detected. Otherwise, the Murder of Christ will continue unabated in spite of all the knowledge collected in the books and at the congresses about human nature. It would be like knowing the very last details about motors but knowing nothing about how to make them run. And in order to know how it was possible that man kept Murdering Christ so long, it will be of decisive importance to know the ways the Cosmic Life Energy works and what it does to man if it works freely, unimpeded by a character armor.

It is crucial to learn why man has put an angel with a flaming sword to guard the entrance to paradise. To get into paradise you must not only know what paradise is like, you must also *be able to get into its inner sanctuary.* And somehow, to see the inner sanctuary is forbidden; nobody except the highest priest of God must ever enter the holiest of the tripartite holy temple. Moses must not look into God's face; God is mystified in the Catholic creed. God is removed from the concrete touch of man's body and mind, and guarded with flaming, threatening swords. The true guardian is, of course, man himself; HE IS GUARDING HIS VERY LIFE AGAINST DISASTER. DISASTER WOULD ENGULF HUMANITY IF MAN AS HE IS TODAY, WOULD FIND AND KNOW GOD. He would make of God what he made of love of knowledge, of his newborn babies, of socialism and exchange of goods all through the ages: *a mess,* a Little Man's abominable mess.

This sounds rather peculiar and nonsensical. Why should knowing and touching God with bodies and minds spell social disaster? If God is the Life Energy which is the creator of all the Living and, outside and before the Living, the creator of the whole universe, why then should touching and knowing it, which would be the surest way to live God's life, be disastrous and so severely forbidden?

Before we can learn more about this, we must pursue some of the results of man's ways of murdering Christ.

The murderers of Christ will remain victorious against Christ's true teachings and intentions. They will murder his meaning by mystification, beginning with his disappearance from the tomb where his body was laid after the crucifixion. Only two women, Mary Magdalene and Mary the mother of James, saw where he was laid. The following morning when they returned to the tomb to embalm the body, it had disappeared.

The Christian religion could have arisen from the manner alone in which a spiritual leader like Christ was crucified: from his radiance and his simple wise sayings; from his fighting the scribes and the Pharisees; from his reinterpretation of the Old Testament as it is transmitted to us in the gospels; from his great love for people and children, and the help he rendered to the sick. Nothing miraculous need necessarily have been connected with the healing of sick minds by a man who possessed great powers of radiance. Every good psychiatrist in the twentieth century performs such "miracles" of alleviation of emotional distress and, in some cases, even of bodily pain. Thus there were, ready for use, ample emotionally high-pitched experiences for the development of a religion.

Let us now for a moment imagine what such religious belief would have been like had the mystical transformation of Christ after his death *not* taken place.

Its basic elements would still have been the major tenets of present-day Christian belief: To love the neighbor and to forgive, i.e., to *understand* the motives of the enemy. To do good as in most other religions. To worship God, who is Life, and to be faithful to the creator of all being. To revive the alive elements of the old Jewish religion which had been ossified by corrupted priests. To lead a moral life and not to succumb to evil temptations. To help the sick and to give to the poor.

The moral tenets would have been the very same ones we find today in so many reformed and modernized Christian churches. Christ could still have been conceived as a Son of God, like Mohammed or Buddha. However, the great momentum of the Christian church does not rest in these elements of religious belief which are common to most religions and vary only slightly. *The great force in Christian belief, as felt especially in Catholicism, derives from the mystification of Christ.*

This mystification, no matter what forms it takes, shows clearly one common center from which all details emerge and derive their specifically Christian timbre:

IT IS THE DISEMBODIMENT OF JESUS CHRIST AND HIS COMPLETE SPIRITU-ALIZATION.

The bodily ugliness of the last agony screamingly contradicted Christ's high-spirited faith. Esteem of the body collapsed. The spirit rose the higher to God's heaven. The Christian refused to realize that a *man* had been cruelly maimed. The mangled body itself was spiritually transformed.

The heirs of Christ are aware of the existence of the cosmic love of the body, but, having imprisoned it, they exhort a yearning humanity to reach their God who is behind bars. Live your God in your body, but do not ever touch him — thus they speak to mankind.

With the complete disembodiment and spiritualization of Christ, the pure bodily love he had lived was lost, never to return again. If the Catholic church would include Christ's *pure bodily love* again, as *distinct from the perverted "sin of the flesh,"* it would solve with one stroke most of the contradictions of its cosmic aspects. Many impossible devices to maintain the exclusion of the pure bodily love, such as the "virgin birth," "the condemnation of bodily love," etc., would become unnecessary. The deep gap between the cosmic aspects of Christianity and the exclusion of the very gateway to man's cosmic origin is a screaming discord and an insoluble, dangerous contradiction. Is it too much to ask from the heirs of Christ that they open the gateway to heaven again? Otherwise, "sin" will continue to be. The heavens will continue to be closed. A great error will continue to harass hundreds of millions of human souls. And the plague will continue through the ages to ravage the lives of man.

This is obvious to anyone who has ever seen at close range the transformation of bodily desire into spiritual ideas of purity, in the mentally sick and in the insane, as well as in normal minds under stress of acute frustration: *The mystical transfiguration of Christ emerges from the great need to outscream and outdrown the tremendous biophysical implications of his earthly being and his teachings.* The very fact that in the most orthodox of all churches, in the Catholic creed, the sin of the desire of the flesh is the hub of all moral theology and Christian spirituality, tells us why and how Christ's teaching HAD to become mystified.

To have established a Christian religion *in accordance* with Christ's true biological nature would have led in a straight manner to where bio-energetic orgonomic knowledge is tending to lead today in 1952.

This is a sweeping statement of such tremendous proportions that it will require some very simple reasoning to prove its correctness.

Christ had, as has been amply stated, led the life of a simple man of great emotional power, amongst simple people and amidst a natural peasant environment. Every social worker, every physician or educator who is or has been dealing practically with so-called " plain people " in their every-day lives, knows that their genital misery constitutes the center of their interests and worries. It not only far outdistances the economic worries, it is also infinitely more widespread than material want in the Western world, and it is the *immediate* cause and source of the economic misery in the great Asiatic communities.

No amount of effort to alleviate the great economic misery of the Asi-atic masses will or can ever succeed unless their emotional and genital misery is alleviated first (See: THE SEXUAL REVOLUTION). It is this misery which renders those millions helpless to do anything or even to think about their economic misery. It is agony to these millions to emerge from an age-old slavery, chained by the mystification of their bodily love. This spells new disaster, and there are the freedom peddlers ready to exploit it. But, in the face of a drowning civilization, no statesman dares mention it. Not to see this is in itself a major case presenting the basic features of the Murder of Christ all over again. And the father or mother or teacher or adolescent would be rare, indeed, who would tell you right away that this is *not* so.

The colossal economic misery of the great Asiatic masses cannot ever be touched without a clear-cut, thorough and most resolute attack on their genital misery (overpopulation through lack of birth control, cruel moral-ism, etc.) from which stems their great social misery. The patriarchal structure of their societies only forms the framework within which this misery is continuously being created and can flourish. And nowhere is the Murder of Christ as tangible as in these great Asiatic societies. Accordingly, no other part of the world is as prone to fall prey to Red Fascism, which is the mechanistic Murder of Christ *per se*, cloaked in an obsolete, rationalistic thought system that knows nothing of the cosmic nature of the emotions in man.

CHAPTER VI

THE GREAT GAP

MAN'S SITTING

Christ will be murdered in the end, 30 A.D. Not because he is good or bad, or a traitor to his people or a challenge to the Sanhedric Talmudists, not because his words are mistaken by a jealous emperor's governor to mean that he is the "King of the Jews"; not because he was a rebel against Roman rule, nor because he had come to die on the cross for the Sin of Man. Neither is he a mere myth, a mere invention of the Christian hierarchy, maintained to secure its "rule over people's souls." Christ is not the result of economic developments in a certain period of society; he could have lived at any time, in any place, under any circumstances and social conditions. He still would have died the same way. He would have had to die everywhere and in all ages. This, again, is the emotional meaning of Christ.

The Christ myth derives its strength from cruel, well-hidden realities in the existence *of armored Man*. In Christ man has searched for the key to his own nature and his own fate for two thousand years. In Christ man has found the access to a possible solution of the tragedy of mankind. Christ had been murdered long before Christ was born. And Christ continued to be murdered every single hour of every single year since. Unless Christ's fate is understood fully and practically, the murder will continue with no letup. Christ's fate represents the secret of the tragedy of the human animal.

Christ had to die all along the stretch of time and continues to die because he is *Life*. And there is, at present as in the past, a deep, unbridgeable GAP between the *dream* of Life and the *ability* to live LIFE in man. Christ had to die because man loves Life too much for his own structure. He simply cannot take Life as it is being created by God, ruled by the laws of the Cosmic Life Energy.

An ugly woman, seeing herself all the time in the mirror as beautiful, as she dreams of being and as she could have been had the conditions of her growth been different, is bound to smash the image in the mirror. Nobody, not a single living soul could stand to live an ugly life, continuously having in front of one's eyes the inner potentialities developed to the fullest outside of oneself, walking alive on two graceful legs.

You can keep hoping for salvation as long as salvation is a matter of a lifeless interpretation of the Talmud, or a mere idea in a church song or in a prayer. Then you even enjoy the hoping itself, the thrilling expectation of a future day far away where everything will be as you dream it to be one day. Hope gives you strength, it makes you glow with a pleasant inner warmth; it is like a stiff drink taken during a strenuous trip on a steep mountain trail.

With the hope directed toward a distant future, with no obligation whatsoever to move a finger to realize the hope in single steps every hour of your life, to *turn hope into actual Life*, you can remain sitting just where you have been sitting twenty or thirty or five thousand years ago.

SITTING on the spot is the most logical consequence of man's immobilization. Everybody prepares himself in early life to remain sitting, comfortably if possible. The girl goes fast through a period of acute dreaming of the blond hero on a white horse who will save her from slavery or will awaken her from a thousand years' sleep and will marry her, to remain happy ever, ever after. Every movie shows you this moving up to a secure place to remain sitting. It never shows you what happens *after* boy gets girl. Never. This would stir up a strong *emotion* and with it *motion*.

You remain sitting as an office man, or as a country doctor, or as a tax collector, or as a Chinese laundry man even if you came from China to America, or as a Jewish *restaurateur* selling " gefilte fish " in New York as you did in Minsk. Sitting makes for skill and craftsmanship, which in turn makes for greater security. All this is not bad at all; it is highly necessary. Without such sitting, man could not possibly exist or maintain his family under the present actual conditions. Without remaining sitting in life, man could not be an expert bridge engineer nor an expert designer. He could not, without getting used to sitting on one spot, tolerate a life-long service as coal miner or grave digger or cement mixer or steel construction worker. The absolute necessity and rationality of sitting on one spot in life shows up clearly in the job of a window-washer in New York, just as it does in the life of a coolie in China pulling his ricksha.

It is, therefore, quite consistent that all social development heretofore was the result of an outer commotion, be it war or revolution, ripping the people from their spots of sitting. Not a single development from an inner motion on the part of people has yet happened. All social movement was political in its nature, i.e., artificial, imposed from outside, not homegrown. To move outward, man would first have to *stir inside* without outer excitation. The impulse to move on, to change things, to end the endless sitting, would have to be ingrained in his structure from the very beginning and skillfully developed as a basic characteristic of his being, as was the case, of necessity, with the American pioneers or the old nomadic peoples.

No deer or bear or elephant or whale or bird or snail could do the sitting man does. They would dry up and die right away. You can see in the zoo what sitting does to wild animals.

The immobilization through the physical and emotional armoring, makes man not only capable of sitting; it makes him *desirous* of sitting. Movement is painful under the condition of rigidity of soul and body. You can live in a neighborhood for ten years and see the same people doing the same thing at the same hour of the day every single day all through the years. Sitting keeps the energy metabolism down, does not permit of high-pitched excitation. It makes it easy to be "easy-going," always friendly with people, to take things as they come along in the daily routine, not to get excited over small or big things. Sitting is to armored, civilized man a "godsend." Sitting on the spot becomes one of the most precious possessions and habits of mankind.

From the sitting of armored man comes the sitting of nations and cultures. China sat for thousands of years, complacently, brooding like an ocean, in one spot, with only ripples on the surface and occasional storms causing fifty- or a hundred-foot high waves. But what are such waves compared with four miles' depth? Nothing at all. Nothing can disturb a brooding ocean, and nothing can disturb or really put out of composure millennia of armored man's culture. True, cultures come and go, civilizations are born and perish again. But this does not, in the light of the basic tragedy of mankind which culminates in the chronic Murder of Christ, mean very much. True, a civilization perishes if its sons and daughters become fed up with continuous sitting. They cause a big or a little revolution, or they make war upon other nations, but in the end it does not really amount to much. It does not mean a thing because after making a very big noise in overthrowing a thousand years of some culture, within a decade or two the new nation or culture looks and acts exactly like the one it went out to destroy. Think of how little has changed basically between the first and the third world wars.

It all depends on the point from which you view such events. It is true, a bird is shaped like a whale, that is, basically. If you view the bird in relation to the tree where it has its nest, everything it does is in proportion with the size of the leaves and the worm it carries to its young ones. It loses its detailed greatness the moment you watch it from the standpoint of a whale.

The philosophical discussions on science and morals you hear at some university panel meeting are most intricate and truly great in the elaborate exactness of wording and thinking. But compared with the issue of man's existence which it is resolved to EVADE, it really does not mean much. The difference between the IS and the SHOULD *is* important. It pertains to crushing, mass-killing issues. But the secret of Christ's story, which holds the key to man's cosmic existence, is incomparably bigger. In its light, the IS and the SHOULD are no problems at all. The IS and the SHOULD depends on the solution of the cosmic issue.

These discussions do not differ much from Plato's dialogues or Socrates' discussions with his pupils. Of course, they are different, too, since so much has changed during these last two thousand five hundred years. Still, they are basically the same, and you discover with amazement that since the inception of written human history, everything has remained sitting on one and the same spot.

Of course there *is* a great difference between an automobile in the USA in 1950 and a camel in Palestine in 30 A.D. Of course, the people lived differently and thought differently and had different problems and clothes and dwellings. But still, it is not entirely foreign as the moon's surface would be. And even the moon's surface would look somewhat like the Dolomites in Italy.

Christ's problem is much more comprehensive. *It concerns the conflict of motion against frozen structures.* Motion alone is infinite. Structure is finite and tight. Basically, the way people act and the fates they meet are the same. History somehow has remained sitting because man, who writes his own history, has remained sitting. The Murder of Christ could happen and does happen today as it happened then. The economic and social conflicts are even exact duplicates today of what they were then: Emperors and foreign governors and an enslaved nation, and tax burdens and national hatred and religious zeal and collaboration of the subjugated people's leaders with the conquerors, and tactics and diplomacy and all the rest of the show. In order to comprehend Christ's story, you must start thinking in cosmic dimensions.

Christ somehow does not fit into all this. He did not fit then; he would not have fitted six thousand years ago, and he would not fit today. Can you imagine Christ walking around alive, speaking as he spoke, living and eating with sinners and harlots as he did, in the Cathedral of St. Stephan or of St. Peter? This is impossible. Yet these cathedrals were built to worship him. Why, then, could he not walk into such cathedrals? Not, as is said, because man has degenerated or forgotten Christ, or because the priests have been corrupted. We have good reason to believe that the people and the priests and their emotions and hopes and fears have not changed much since they worshipped Christ in the body, to this day when they worship his spirit. This too, all of it, has remained *sitting*.

No, it is not a later degeneration of the church which made men forget Christ, but it is today as it was then, thousands of years ago, THE GREAT GAP between the great hope and the true, real Self; between the phantasy of the Self and the reality of the Self; between mobile, productive energy and frozen energy.

When Christ began his mission when he was thirty years old, he still did not disturb anything or anybody. He only walked gracefully among them and they liked to look into the mirror to see their hope. The murder began to develop when the hope began to stir up motion. Christ was too mobile. Not too mobile in the sense of living Life. On the contrary, here we have at times the distinct impression from what the gospels tell us, that he was a little bit too demanding, a little bit too much set on principles. He had to be, of course, and we shall soon see why living Life in man develops — why it has to develop — strict principles and a strained seriousness if it is to prevail against the sitting human nature.

But Christ, in all his naiveté, meant business. He took himself just as seriously as a deer takes itself seriously. " I am Life, *of course!* What else should I be? ", so we hear him say.

Christ did not like to remain sitting in the home with his brothers and sisters and his mother, though he loved them dearly. He liked to wander about the beautiful countryside, to greet the sun when it rose over the horizon in glaring pink. He liked to see people in different places, though he never left Palestine. There is no indication whatsoever that Christ felt himself to be a saviour of mankind in the beginning of his wanderings. However, there is ample evidence from the history of his life as well as from what we know about human functioning, to the effect that at first he was different and felt different from the rest in that he could not sit still. He did not intend to spend the rest of his life at the carpentry bench. He loved people. He felt kindly toward them. His family was too narrow a domain for his lively agility, and, we may assume, also for his lively views. We know that his mother reproached him for not staying within the family bonds. He was not on too good terms with his brothers and sisters.. And later, after he had already been seduced into Messianic leadership, he requested his followers to leave their brothers and sisters and mothers and fathers, and to follow him and his mission. He knew that compulsory family life kills every movement beyond its confines.

This, too, is comprehensible against the background of the contradiction between Life moving onward and Life remaining sitting. If Life is truly Life, it moves onward into the unknown, but it dislikes moving on alone. It needs not pupils, not followers, not yes-sayers, not admirers, not worshippers. What it needs badly, what it cannot live without, is companionship, comradeship, friendship, closeness and intimacy, the warming understanding of another soul, the possibility to talk it out and to confide one's depth. There is nothing supernatural or extraordinary in this. It is an expression of true living, of natural sociality. No one wants or can live quite alone without risking lunacy.

Now, this deep urge for companionship is bound to turn sour, that is, to become a request, otherwise incompatible with living Life, if the friends and companions remain bound to their families, their wives, their children, their professions. These bondages act like dragchains on them. They rip them backward whenever a great expanding leap is required. Every great leader of men had to cope with this trouble. Every great leader of people requests the followers to abandon everything and to follow only him. This was true and still is, for the Catholic church as well as for the Red Fascist creed. It is true for every ship captain and his crew. It holds for every military leader or similar task group which has things to do, which has to keep moving and to remain mobile.

The difference between Christ's requests and that of the rest just mentioned, is that the latter are already fully established, rigidly organized associations of men which require abandonment of the sitting in any and every form; whereas Christ originally does not intend to create a church or a political movement. He just wants friends to wander around with, and he finds them petty, cumbersome, holding him back, impeding his joy of living. This would not matter or amount to much if he were not captured soon by his friends as the future Messiah. It is they, the friends, who slowly become admirers and followers. It is the led ones who determine the rules they get from their leaders, and never the other way around *originally*. There is nothing in this social world of ours, and nothing can be, that is not primarily and basically determined by the character and the behaviour of the people. There is no exception to this rule, no matter wherever we turn.

To begin with, it is, therefore, Christ's friends, turning into admirers, who induce him to request that they leave their families and jobs, and not Christ himself. This is not so because Christ is exceptional in this respect but because living Life would have to act the same way in any age and under any social or cultural circumstances if it wanted to move onward into the unknown without staying quite alone.

In this manner, life everywhere turns into leadership, rule, requirement, order, restriction, sacrifice, wherever it begins to move against the sitting of the crowd, the "culture," the "civilization," the set opinion in science, the established routine in technology or education or medicine. If all people were mobile, there would be no reason for all this. They would love to move around, themselves. And they themselves, not single leaders or groups, would carry the burden of progress.

The vast majority of living men in any age or phase of history did not move out beyond their village district. Some do not move because they are poor. Most men do not move because motion is painful to them. They have just enough Life energy to make the motions that feed them and their sons and daughters. Only some merchants and gypsy-like people travel. It was not before the middle of the twentieth century that traveling became a commercialized mass product and that people began to go "abroad." However, the great majority still sit out their steaming summers in New York, Chicago and other such places. It is wrong to speak of *people* travelling, if only a minority travels, because it is the greater majority that is responsible for all that happens. And even if a majority would travel, travelling alone would not change their basic structure.

Those who travel today are not travelling because travelling is wholesome and good, but because "one travels" nowadays, and the neighbor would look upon them as peculiar if they had not seen what the Joneses had seen. Also, one travels because "one buys so cheaply with the dollar in Europe." Thus one sits again.

Christ does not travel to Europe because the dollar buys more in Europe than in the USA. He travels because he wants to see European people. He visits museums, like other people. But he does not go to the museum because "one has to have been" in a museum or one "has to have seen" this or that picture. He goes simply to see the picture. And this one does not really do, just as one does not really embrace a man or a woman for the sake of the happiness in embracing but in order to beget children. All this is foreign to Christ. And therefore he will and must in the end be murdered.

The immobility, the sitting go with the traveller wherever he or she moves. Therefore they admire and worship the real mover. On his travels Christ keeps to himself, though he meets people. He travels alone, with only a very few companions. Even when with his companions, he is mostly a bit separated from them, either a hundred or two hundred feet ahead of them or going alone somewhere into the woods to meditate. The followers rarely meditate. They mostly talk about their master, wondering what he is doing now or how he could possibly have done this or that. Thus they follow their own mirror image, the thing they so very much would like to but really cannot be.

They dream of him as their leader who will with all his might and god-given furor one day certainly drive the Romans out of the holy city. He is only waiting still and preparing. But the day of revenge will certainly come. Isn't he a leader? *Their* leader? They are ready to follow him through fire, and they already glow at the thought of going through fire with him. In the end, they will abandon him.

They try to persuade him to perform miracles, to demonstrate his divine power. This divine power to them is thunder and lightning and crushing noise from a thousand fanfares or cannons, and a bursting sky, and a ripped curtain in the temple. The dead will rise from their graves, the -greatest miracle of all will happen: The souls will return to their bodies, and they will walk around again just as they did a thousand years ago. This is the least he can do for them.

In their future religion, the true Christ will have disappeared entirely, and only the thunder and the lightning in the sky, and the earthquake will be retained together with the return of the dead.

Christ knows nothing of all this. He never spoke of or promised any thunder or lightning in the sky or earthquakes or ripped curtains. He lives and travels around on an entirely different plain. He does not think or even dream of any revolt. The Kingdom he feels in himself is not of this world, and he will tell them so shortly before the last agony. But nobody understands what he is talking about. They take him literally. A Kingdom is a Kingdom, isn't it? And a kingdom goes with a King and marches and trumpets and siege and conquest of cities. A leader has power and exerts power upon others.

This it is that 'they expect from Jesus Christ. He is only still hiding. He only did not reveal himself yet. And they urge him to reveal himself, to give them a sign, again and again.

Christ begs them not to talk to others about his graceful influence on people and sick ones. He never speaks of miracles. In the end, a hundred years after his murder, the miracles will dominate the scene, not his rebuttal of the miracle-making.

Christ is *against* armed revolt. He refuses to lead any such revolt. He preaches the revolution of the soul, the turning outside of the deepest inside. Christ knows that unless the deepest inside is turned outside and made effective, soon doomsday will come upon his very generation. Christ feels more than he knows that man must find again and love his CORE if he is to survive and to establish the Kingdom of Heaven.

Christ slowly begins to realize the gap between his way and the others' ways. He begins painfully to realize that he must die sooner or later, and he begins to prepare his friends for this event. He knows he has to die because there is no place in this world for the Son of God to put his body to rest, but every sparrow has its nest.

If he would take the sword, as requested by his followers, he would not be killed, or he would be killed honorably, in action, and not dishonorably at the cross between two thieves. Christ knows he must die because there is no place for him in men's hearts or minds. They simply do not know what he is talking about. He does not speak in mysterious parables. He speaks clear words about crystal clear things. But they have no ear for these words. More, they will misinterpret these words and therefore he will have to die.

He quotes Isaiah who said:

> " This people honors me with their lips,
> but their heart is far from me;
> in vain do they worship me,
> teaching as doctrines the precepts of men."
> (*Matthew* 14: 8,9)

He knows disaster will strike soon; it will *have* to strike. And nobody, not a single soul will help to save him, because, again as Isaiah said,

> " You shall indeed hear but never *understand*,
> and you shall indeed see but never *perceive*.
> For this people's heart has grown dull,
> and their ears are heavy of hearing,
> and their eyes they have closed,
> lest they should perceive with their eyes,
> and hear with their ears,
> and understand with their heart,
> and turn for me to heal them."
> (*Matthew* 13: 14,15)

This is the ARMOR: No, they do not hear nor see nor feel with their hearts what they see and hear and perceive. Never, never will they understand, and the words of all prophets of all times have been wasted upon them. The martyrs have died in vain, the saints were burnt for nothing, and the Murder of Christ continues unabated.

Everything that human hearts have known and human thoughts have ever thought and human suffering has ever revealed about the tragic secret of man has been wasted. The books were stacked away or were rendered impotent by empty admiration. Men only want to be filled up where they feel empty. *Nothing can fill them up.* God was buried in them irretrievably. He will only be found again in their newborn sons and daughters if their hands can be kept from injuring their offspring. And Christ has to die because he came too close to their secret, because he refused to accept *their* misinterpretation of the Kingdom of Heaven, because he stuck to his guns.

And this is the way they finally delivered him to his enemies:

He withstood the temptations of the evil and the devil. He withstood the temptation of power. Heartbreak went with the search for a way out of the trouble, out of the dilemma: how to be a leader of people and not to fall prey to the ways of people's leaders. He knew well that power would not do it, *could* not do it.

Power, ultimately, is the result of the helplessness of the people. Power over men is either grabbed by leaders by force or leaders are pushed into power over people by the people themselves. A Caligula or Hitler or Djugashvilli grabs the power with clear contempt for people, out of the acknowledgment of what people are and do. This type of power is taken because people let it happen, do not object to it, or even admire it.

The other type of power, *the seduction of leaders into powerful positions, is an active accomplishment of empty, helpless men. Men change new liberating truths into new power of man over men.* This sounds incredible. It is self-evident once one rids oneself of the commiseration and idolization of people and man in general. This very commiseration and idealization is a major tool of the protection of the mass plague. As long as you pity people, pat them on the back, refuse to see them as they are, you will fail to find this hidden trail to the understanding of a huge mountain of age-old miseries. Christ's story reveals this secret only through the failure of Christ to fall prey to seduction into power.

The way people mislead and seduce their great leaders into evil power devils is this:

At first people pay tribute to the ideas of what is called "progress," hail the developers of such ideas, but they themselves remain sitting. If they have not killed the new idea right away, they still might slander or otherwise torture to death the pioneer. The gap between the ability to *hope* and the ability to *do* will in any case force people to feel the new idea as a burden, as a constant reminder of their immobility and deadness. This feeling of lagging and hobbling behind needs must develop into hatred of the new, the moving, the stirring. In this respect the hate for everything alive is *rational* on the part of ruined man. The new, moving idea moves people right out of their emotional security and safety. *Here conservatism becomes rational.* This security, even if it deadens man, is essential to his existence. He would perish without it. The big noise of the lout of freedom, the freedom peddler, should not distract from this realization. The freedom lout, who out of pure ignorance and lack of responsibility clamors for freedom because he would like to do as he pleases *the bad way,* would, after having killed the conservative defender of the status quo, thoroughly fail in securing any social functioning at all, and will certainly, in order to save his head, become more cruel, more rampant in the suppression of living Life than any conservative man ever would dream of. This history has demonstrated, at a terrific cost to human lives, in the Russian imperialists of the twentieth century who came from the ranks of the people.

People are and must be conservative under the given conditions of their ways of living. There is no use in marching out of your village into the unknown if you have no blanket to protect yourself against the cold and no bread to eat. You had better remain sitting where you are with the little vegetable garden in the backyard. Therefore, people do and must hate the disturber of their emotional security. This, of course, means advocating the rights of the devil, but there is little use in fighting the devil unless you know why there are devils in this world in the first place.

The disturber of the secure sitting habits of man may fall prey to the hailing of his greatness and remain sitting himself. There are many such fates. In this case, nothing has really moved onward. There was only a little commotion, a stir in the deadened genitals of some men and women, but nothing much happened to endanger the community. Watch " sitting " orientals and you know and *see* what is meant here.

The disturber of the emotional security may not yield to the pressure of the sitting of man. In this case, he will be hunted, *must* be hunted like a wild animal. Or he dies and does not impede any longer the drag toward staleness. Here again, nothing much will change in the communal situation, except some dust will be stirred up on the road or in an innocent row in some tavern.

The real danger to man's existence arises if the innovator or prophet does neither remain sitting himself nor die away silently. The real danger stems from the *success* of the prophet. Here are the steps to general social disaster:

1. *The mass of inert men pick up the great hope entailed in the new message through a few little great men.*

2. *These little great men are not as inert as the big herd of men. They are alert, keen, out for success and power; not for power over people as yet.*

3. *The prophets who had condemned the sinful existence and saw new lands, hold out the promises unaware that they are creating the very foundation of a new evil power which they themselves would be the first to condemn.* Unless they have reached the degree of self-denial and true

vision which puts into the glaring daylight the gap between hoping and doing in men, social disaster is bound to strike.

4. *Little great men will seize the new idea.* They will become drunk with the potentialities of the new vision. They will have neither the skill nor the patience to realize the danger and to acquire the necessary knowledge to handle the new vision. The great vision will inevitably make them drunk with dreams of power: *Powerdrunk.* These little great men will not want power right away. Powerdrunkenness is the unintended but certain result of the mixture of a great vision and little know-how. In this manner, new, worse evil is being created out of a splendid vision of redemption. It is this turning of vision into powerdrunkenness which has increased in scope over the ages as the prophets became more numerous and more people from the big herd entered the social scene. The *sitting of man,* the *vision of the prophet* and the *turning of vision into power-drunkenness* in the little apostles of the great prophets constitute the trio that is the reproductive system of man's misery.

This turn from vision to power over man is inevitable; it will endure as 'long as the gap remains between the great dream and the factual impotence of man. Both, John and Caiaphas, Christ and the Inquisitor, arise from this gap in man's nature.

It is the dynamic vicious circle which turned every single *socialist* leader during the first half of the twentieth century into a bureaucrat of statist power over men. The sequence of these events is inevitable as long as the gap is not closed. The powerdrunkenness is nobody's fault but it is everybody's responsibility. *There is no greater danger to people's futures than commiseration and pity.* Pity will not remove the gap in men between the dreaming and the doing. It will only perpetuate it. *In this sense of the perpetuation of man's misery, socialists are enemies of men.* The conservative does not pretend to improve man's lot. He tells you frankly that he is for the status quo. The socialist appears as the " progressive leader " toward "freedom." He is in reality a builder of slavery, not out of evil intent, but simply out of the seduction into leadership; he suffers from the mystically hoping but factually impotent masses of men.

Socialist sentiments are bound to lead into statism. They *have* led into statism everywhere, to the extent that socialism as an idea was taken seriously. Where socialism was no more than a humanitarian ideal, it did not force the leaders into statism, as in the Scandinavian countries in the twentieth century. But it wrought havoc in England and it brought disaster to Russia, exactly to the extent of the seriousness of the socialist ideal.

Nobody would blame the socialist leader for not seeing the gap or for mistaking people's hopes for freedom for a capability for factually building freedom. They are, however, to be blamed for impeding, misusing, killing everyone who pointed toward the gap and proposed measures, good or bad ones, to close it. This concerns especially the Russian imperialists. To them, the pathological sitting of people meant conscious "sabotage" of state interests. The abysmal cruelty of Russian imperialism toward man cannot be understood unless one sees the shock the leaders suffered when they encountered human inertia while building "heaven on earth." Not the hopes of mankind distinguish Roman Catholic from Russian imperialist creed; not the degeneration of a great teaching into a petty cheating. What distinguishes them from each other is their different attitudes toward man's frailty. However, during the Middle Ages, Catholicism was of the same quality and caliber as the fascism of the twentieth century.

All this is, of course, most tragic. That it should be more wholesome for man NOT to take ideals seriously rather than to do so, is only one more of the many paradoxes created by the great contradiction in human structure between man's longing and his inertness.

Christ does not yield to the herd and their seduction of the leader into power. He does not, in his lifetime, create a large movement; he does not even abandon Judaism. And he himself does not turn his prophecy into powerdrunkenness. This remains for Paulus of Tarsus to do. In modern times, Stalin is to Marx what Paul is to Christ. Lenin is to be counted out. He fell victim to his own sorrow over the degeneration of the Russian dream which he witnessed in its inception. Accordingly, he fell prey to a cerebral stroke, just as did Franklin D. Roosevelt in 1945, when he realized what the Moscow Modju had done with his friendly gestures. *The true Paul of Red Fascism is Stalin, the cunning Modju from Georgia, Russia, down to details of language, doctrinarism, cruelty, conversion from Saul into Paul.* Stalin had only an easier job of getting powerdrunk than Paul. There were not as many millions of men involved in the disaster at Paul's time. But the cruelty that developed in both cases is well matched.

Christ does not develop any organizational chapters in various lands. He does not intend to convert the Gentiles into Christians; he is only including the Gentiles among the children of God, and he is far removed from the idea of making converts against their will. He does not bring Christianity to the people. He waits till people come to him. Then he simply tells them that the Kingdom of Heaven ON EARTH is possible and is close by. He believes, as the liberals and the socialists two thousand years later will, that man is good and only suppressed and prevented by *outer* force alone from living his goodness. He believes, as many will after him, that the Kingdom will come if you only keep praying long enough and seriously enough and truthfully enough. He is as so many others before and after him, the victim of the mistaken belief that the many can be suppressed by the few emperors and Talmudic scribes, against their will. He has no inkling of the fact that *suppression of life works within the people themselves.* Centuries full of cruelties and death and despair and error and hideous crimes will pass before an awareness of the emotional sickness of man will begin to dawn upon a few. And even then, the few knowers will cling to the error and refuse to see the truth fully, face to face. They will believe that the mentally ill are bad by heredity, just as their predecessors believed that they were possessed by the devil and had to be burned at the stake.

The big evasion of Christ, who is Life, will keep murdering by the billion into the ages. They will convert foreign nations to Christianity by force, without an inkling of what Christ meant when he spoke of the Kingdom of Heaven within you. In the name of Christianity, in order to evade Christ, blood will flow in rivers, corpses will be dangling from the trees, screams will rebound from thick stone walls within prisons, and the insane, who are in touch with Christ, will be chained for life, all in the name of Christ.

And the nightmare will continue under a different name, this time under the disguise of the Anti-Christ who pretends to exterminate the Christian faith for its cruelty and ignorance, while it itself will surpass in method as well as number anything that any inquisitor may ever have dreamed of doing. It took eight years to get Giordano Bruno to the stake; it takes only a few hours to put hundreds of innocent men and women to the wall today.

Hate will reign in the world and words of love and peace will at the same time drivel from frozen mouths. Christ knows nothing of the structural hate from frustration within man. It will take hundreds of years and hundreds of saints and wise men to *conceal* the one single fact that one could put an end to the nightmare by stopping the Murder of Christ within the womb of billions of love-starved women who bear children.

The disaster is *too big, too stupid, too obnoxious* in its monstrosity for even Christ to be aware of its dimensions. He loves people too much. He believes in them too much. With such deep and sincere love in one's heart, it is not possible to conceive of man as an evil hater. Man does not show his hatred openly. He hides it and lives it clandestinely in a masterly manner. This hatred is too well disguised as hatred of the eternal enemy, of the emperor, of the outer evildoer, so that no trusting, loving soul would or could ever dream of suspecting it right *within* righteous man. Yet, this is true: The sticky love of the mother toward her child is true hatred; the rigid faithfulness of the wife is true hatred; she is full of longing for other men. The dependent caretaking of men for their families is true hatred. The admiration of the crowd for their beloved fuehrers is true hatred, potential murder. Let the redeemer turn his back on his flock, let the shepherd for a single day only abandon his sheep, and the sheep will turn into howling wolves and tear the shepherd to pieces.

All this is too unbelievable to be conceived and handled. Yet it is true. It is true to such an extent that we suspect, with good reason, that it is at the bottom of the big evasion of any and every truth, the big as well as the small one. To get at the truth, this big lie has first to be uncovered. And uncovering this big lie means disaster to every soul involved.

The big hatred is well concealed and well enough controlled on the surface not to cause harm at close range. The child which was strangled emotionally by its mother in early infancy will not show the results until it has grown into a man who faces the task of loving a woman or into a woman who faces bringing up her child.

The distortion of gracefulness in a little girl by a frigid, ugly-faced mother will not show up until this girl has grown into a mother herself and has made her man and child unhappy for life. The last thought on the deathbed in many such a mother's mind will be the worry as to whether her daughter has preserved her virginity.

This is only a small glimpse onto the backstage of human misery. The big hatred will only be visible to the man or woman who fights for the survival in decency of their own love and life. It will only be accessible to the skilled surgeon of human emotions who knows how to open up a human soul without killing the body with a flood of hatred. The hatred's form and appearance will be manifold and varied in a thousand ways, but it will always be well hidden. In fact, all rules of good conduct and polite sociality feed on the necessity to conceal this big hatred. Certain strata of society through the ages will develop a special etiquette to cheat everybody into forgetting the existence of this structural hatred. The diplomats of the later post-Christian era will go to a peace conference fully aware that they are facing bitter hatred, ready to cheat, knowing that cheating is the only way to cope with the big hatred. Nobody will trust anybody, and everybody will know exactly what is going on in everybody else. And nobody will mention it. In the great conventions of the great mental hygiene councils, every single man and woman will know the misery of puberty from his or her own experience and from the mass misery they encounter in their offices and medical centers. Every single educator will know exactly why juvenile delinquency exists and what it means deep down: SEX STARVATION AT THE HEIGHT OF GENITAL DEVELOPMENT. But nobody will mention it. The big hatred is in between the juvenile misery and its potential healers. And everybody pretends not to know about this hatred in the great cheating politeness and socialitis, because everybody is afraid of everybody else. And accordingly, everybody keeps patting everybody else on the back, like petting wild animals into mildness and harmlessness. All this will be the inevitable consequence of the chronic Murder of Christ.

The Murder of Christ is inevitable, not because they hate, but because they *love* him too much in a way *he cannot possibly satisfy.*

Christ refuses to acknowledge his great differentness. His love for his fellow man forbids him to know that he is so very much different. That he has got what they have not, and that he can do easily things they try in vain to accomplish. This is so because he feels and lives Life as it runs its course, while they first kill life within themselves and then try to bring it back by force. Life, however, cannot ever be forced. You cannot force a tree to grow, the greatest fact of hope against all evil dictators.

Christ thus remains close to his fellow men. He continues to be the great giver. They, the fellow men and women, continue to take from him, and they become so used to getting that it grows to be a second nature to be around him, as it were.

His continued presence and closeness will be the very reason to kill him. If he were remote, distant by way of haughtiness or false dignity, he would be safe. But he is close and humble and simply there, easily accessible to each one of them, day and night at any hour, another man among the crowd. Secretly they ask themselves: Why does he, the Master, let us, who know and do so little about his message, be always around him? He is splendid, but a little bit of a burden. To be solemn all the time, and to live the life of God all the time is high-minded but troubled living. Oh, true, the Master jokes with us, he teases us, we are wandering over the hills and the fields, and we see many people and children come to us, and people are curious about us, but we are not what we appear to be. We are not holy, not perfect enough; We are not pupils fully worthy of him. Did you ever hear him make a juicy, dirty joke? Never. Yet he associates with courtesans and tax collectors. He is so friendly to everyone; a bit of stand-offish dignity would help. The most standoffish man will certainly be his successor and represent him after his death.

We know nothing about his love life. He never speaks about it, and you never can find out with whom he goes. Women love him, he is very attractive and manly. Did you ever see him kiss or make love to a woman? Never! He *must* come from heaven. He *cannot* be an ordinary mortal. Mortals joke, and drink, and get drunk at times, and tell each other little, dirty stories about their little love affairs; they 4-letter right and left, and they have their little secrets which everybody knows and talks about. Sometimes they go into some faraway land and live it out, to be solidly virtuous again afterwards. They live for their wives and children only. Oh, we know, many hate that kind of life, but they stick to it and they tend their gardens and harvest their crop, and during the rainy season they do nothing very important, just talk, or dream or sleep a little nap. They distrust and despise each other but they are always friendly with each other. Sometimes they stone a woman who dared love a man out of wedlock, but on the whole they live quiet, orderly lives.

Why does not the Master have a woman? He left his family and asked others to leave their families and to follow him. He always lives and talks us away from this life of ours. It is burdensome to switch over to his world from the usual, the well accustomed. We love the thrill it gives us, but when will he reveal himself, lead us, make a sign, crush our enemies? He is always silent about this. He should start doing something. Something big. Make the world aware of his greatness. Then, to be his disciple would be so much easier and closer to our way of life. We cannot go on forever walking around in the fields, comforting the poor and bringing a little happiness to the sick here and there. We are looked upon as a queer, strange lot. We need something big, noisy, something with fanfares and marches and banners and shouting, and let us tell the Romans that we are their enemies.

The continued love and giving and filling of their empty egos did not help in the least. They want *their* way of life. And Christ does not realize this. They succeed in conveying upon him the feeling that he must do something big, noisy, impressive to be acknowledged as the Son of God. He, who withstood the temptations of sin and power, permits himself to be talked into a " March upon Jerusalem." And since Christ is so very different from a Mussolini who will march on Rome two thousand years later, since such marching is out of tune with Christ's true nature, he will die miserably on the cross.

For all his love for man, Christ does not fully realize man. He feels himself as being a leader who never should abandon his flock of men. He has an inkling of impending disaster. He feels his life is incompatible with the common run of things. He knows nothing about the plague in man and for two thousand years nobody will know about the rampant plague in man. And so he yields. His enemies only waited for such an occasion to kill him. He was safe as long as he lived the life of Life. He was doomed the moment he began to mix his life with their lives.

He humbly mounts an ass and rides ahead of a few followers toward the big city with the big temple manned by powerful priests and toward the fortress of the emperor's governor. He knows that he is going to die. "Behold we are going up to Jerusalem; and the Son of Man will be delivered to the chief priests and scribes, and they will condemn him to death, and deliver him to the Gentiles to be mocked and scourged and crucified, and he will be raised on the third day." (*Matthew* 20:18,19) He knows it, yet he goes. He tells them that he will be captured and killed, but they do not know what he is talking about. It is only another one of those thrills to them, one of those mysterious sayings that keep them filled with prickling delight for another day or two, until the next thrill is due them. Nobody warns him not to go. Nobody holds him back. He is abandoned already, though nobody is aware of it. He has not a single friend to count on. Friends would have understood, would not have wanted this. Friends would have known that his ways are not of this world of Talmudism and conquest, and that Life does not storm a huge city riding on an ass. Friends would have told him that this was ridiculous and would appear so to everyone; that crowds would gather to watch his procession out of a morbid curiosity only, like watching a circus. A few will shout "Hosannah in the Highest," but this will not alter much.

Two thousand years later, politicians will arrange hunger marches of the poor in big cities on cold winter days to show off the future proletarian rulers of society. A few will sing freedom songs, another few will shout "Down with the bourgeoisie," and a thin line of indifferent spectators will gather at the sidewalks to look at the procession of destitution and poverty and misery. The few Hunger Marchers will try desperately to imitate the march of a big military column. They will even have some guards in shabby uniform-like apparel marching ahead of them, and a few drums will beat the rhythm of the miserable march. Well-armed police will march in file on both sides of the column in order to protect the miserable ones from the wrathful hatred of the many. The pity for the wretches will one day get hold of the whole nation. . . . . . and the end of it all will finally be this:

and this will still continue

And just as Christ knew well that he was going to his death, so these "liberators" of mankind in rags will know (they will say so in plain words) that they will be going to get nowhere and that they will only establish another, more cruel, more godforsaken rule of power. They will march the marches of misery in full awareness of the futility of the undertaking. They will march because there will be nothing else they will be able to do in compliance with the rules that governs human conduct at the time.

They will be *against* revolt two thousand years later as Christ had been two thousand years before them. They will know well that "it" was "within them," to be liberated from their oppressed lives and not to be obtained by marches. But their leaders will know no better way. It will be the *usual* way. The outwardness instead of the inwardness.

CHAPTER VII

THE MARCH ON JERUSALEM

The march on Jerusalem is to drown out the constant reminder that Christ's way of life keeps pounding away at their hearts. Two thousand years later the streaming of love and life in the body will be finally known and understood. People will flock around the knower of streaming life, they will try to get orgastic potency from him, to have it poured from barrels into them, to suck it from his presence, to obtain it through what is called "therapy." But no one will really know what he is talking about since no one has ever felt it, or *if* he felt the stir of life, he felt it with horror. Therefore, they will want to get it but not let it live or develop from their total life. They will work hard in bed for it, to "*get*" it; they will study books in order to find it; they will search for it in many embraces of hatred and disgust; they will kill themselves for not being able to obtain it, but they will kill true love the moment it appears in their senses or they will choke it when they will see it in newborn babies. Mothers will scream in horror at the sight of their newborn infants, "It moves! It moves, really, oh, horror!"

All this is somewhere, somehow known to the marchers at Jerusalem as it will be two thousand years later in big European cities, to every single one of them, because there is nothing the lack of which makes them as miserable as this lack; there is nothing else they call their God and Life and Christ. But they keep murdering it, fearing it, talking or marching it away, shooting it, hanging it. It is a constant reminder of their true misery, and therefore it must die. The American Medical Association has not recognized it yet, and the Sanhedrin is still searching the words of the prophets to find the meaning of life in 1950. But they will kill, will *have to* kill life which at this very moment is riding on an ass toward Jerusalem, seduced into compliance with the accepted way of life, the murderous way of life. Man has taken over God's ways and from now onward he will keep God's ways imprisoned and safely removed from any grasp of mind or body, worshipped away into mechanical litanies, transformed into dead crosses and skyrocketing cathedrals.

The ridiculous ride on the ass has to be effaced forever.

They seduce Christ into the march on Jerusalem not because they see him as he really is, not because they understand what his very being signifies. They seduce him because of THEIR OWN IDEA OF WHAT A PROPHET OUGHT TO BE AND DO. Doesn't it say in the books of the prophets what has to be fulfilled?

> *" Tell the daughter of Zion,*
> *Behold, your king is coming to you,*
> *Humble, and mounted on an ass,*
> *and on a colt, the foal of an ass."*
> (*Matthew* 21: 5)

It is not Christ's way. It is *their* way. And then they tell the world that it *was* His way, which isn't true. Even their dreams are too heavy a burden for them to carry. Somebody else must have dreamed their dream for them to feel comfortably free of responsibility. Christ never dreamed of conquering Jerusalem. It has never been in his vein. He has rebuked the ways of the Barabbases and the emperors many times, in vain. But there is no way out for him.

Two thousand years later the cosmic life force will be finally discovered and made usable for mankind. It will overturn millennia of human thinking. It will fill gaps which were left gaping in old human knowledge full of errors. It will reveal God's meaning which was made inaccessible by chemistry and bigotry alike. It will fill the cosmic space which was declared empty. It will establish the lawful harmony of the universe. It will open up man's souls to their own sources of faith and comfort. It will heal with great power and in simple ways. It will establish new ways of thinking, neither mystical nor mechanical, but alive ones, according to man's place in the general scheme of things. This will be the way of the Life Energy.

But they will not permit this to happen. They will drag the discoverer to a hopeless bacteriology department and want to obtain confirmation of his findings. They will rush to the physicists who were busy all their lives with killing every trace of the existence of such a cosmic force, and ask them to " control " the discovery of Life. They will want write-ups in the very newspapers where the killers of life hold the public scene in ignorance of Life.

The " liberators of the working class " will tell the public that the discoverer is not a member of the very psychiatric association which they are slandering in the motherland of the proletarians. They will ask why the name of the discoverer of Life is not in " Who's Who " and why the producer of ice boxes has never heard of him. They will ask him to give a big lecture in the Academy of Medicine where one otherwise only hears about " Dolson," the chemical promoted on the radio as a cure for everything.

They will, in short, only want the *image* of the change and will want to retain what they hate. They will bury their big hope before it will be born, just as they kill life in the newborn before they are born, in order to obtain quiet, orderly babies, easy to manage.

They will want redemption without the trouble of change and without the bother of knowing themselves. Every word will become an empty slogan, every move of a living body a sum of mechanical moves. They will talk nothing but corpses of words and think corpses of thoughts. Zero will equal zero in the accounting books as in the universe of empty space, and it will tell nothing whatsoever about factual human problems.

Since love goes only into them and nothing out of them, they must finally hate the giver and the redeemer. To lose one's source of replenishing strength means losing one's life. To fall back on one's own emptiness and desert-like existence has become intolerable after contact with the Master. From this many ideas, widespread and detrimental to man, have developed and persisted through the ages.

There is the cherished idea that the common man should have the right of free movement, of choice of a place to work, the right to choose his or her profession, to come and to go as he pleases. This very same common man will not grant the same right to the working people when he becomes a dictator; he will refuse this right to his leader. The leader, no matter whether a state agency, a commercial boss or a military leader, must under no circumstances leave his flock or abandon it to it's own devices. He has to stick it out, to be their public servant, and the captain must never abandon the sinking ship. Everybody else, first of all the hero of the street, can, of course, abandon anything.

From this very same sucker-need arises the MARTYR ideology. The need for martyrs has grown big over the centuries. The discoverer *has to* suffer for the good he brings to the people. "This has always been that way," which means, of course, it should always remain that way: Do not " THE PEOPLE " need somebody to admire, something to worship, somebody to emulate? The suffering of the martyr must be all visible and hearable. If it is silent suffering many may know, but nobody will give a damn about it. In order to become a hero, a child has to fall into a narrow well pipe and be stuck there for days to be rescued by great crews of engineers. The whole nation stands by. But when thousands of children suffer the silent agonies of their maturing, frustrated desires, nobody gives a hoot; it is even forbidden to mention it in the schools and universities where future parents and teachers are being hatched out by the thousands.

The great man has to suffer. Nobody will ever blame the emotional skunk who makes great doers suffer. The great giver must suffer and never abandon his plight lest he fall prey to public condemnation. The public needs its hero to fill empty souls with the glow of admiration. Can you imagine the American General after having won the second world war, refuse to accept the agony of settling European quibbling in the preparation for a third war? This is impossible. He must not rest, he must not retire, he must serve the public. If he doesn't, disgrace and defamation are his certain fate. Another ideal deriving from all this is " Love thy Enemy." This is a very practical and useful thing — *to the enemy*. Christ does not love his enemies. He curses the scribes and the Pharisees in no uncertain terms. He scourges the money changers and throws over their tables spilling their money all over the place.

" . . . . *woe to you, scribes and Pharisees, hypocrites! because you shut the kingdom of heaven against men; for you neither enter yourselves, nor allow those who would enter to go in. Woe to you, scribes and Pharisees, hypocrites! for you traverse sea and land to make a single proselyte, and when he becomes a proselyte, you make him twice as much a child of hell as yourselves.*"

" *Woe to you, blind guides, who say, ' If any one swears by the temple, it is nothing; but if any one swears by the gold of the temple, he is bound by his oath.' You blind fools! For which is greater, the gold or the temple that has made the gold sacred? And you say, ' If any one swears by the altar, it is nothing; but if any one swears by the gift that is on the altar, he is bound by his oath.' You blind men! For which is greater, the gift or the altar that makes the gift sacred? So he who swears by the altar, swears by it and by everything on it; and he who swears by the temple, swears by it and by him who dwells in it; and he who swears by heaven, swears by the throne of God and by him who sits upon it.*

" *Woe to you, scribes and Pharisees, hypocrites! for you tithe mint and dill and cummin, and have neglected the weightier matters of the law, justice and mercy and faith; these you ought to have done, without neglecting the others. You blind guides, straining out a gnat and swallowing a camel!*

" *Woe to you, scribes and Pharisees, hypocrites! for you cleanse the outside of the cup and of the plate, but inside they are full of extortion and rapacity. You blind Pharisee! first cleanse the inside of the cup and of the plate, that the outside also may be clean.*

" *Woe to you, scribes and Pharisees, hypocrites! for you are like whitewashed tombs, which outwardly appear beautiful, but within they are full of dead men's bones and all uncleanness. So you also outwardly appear righteous to men, but within you are full of hypocrisy and iniquity.*

" *Woe to you, scribes and Pharisees, hypocrites! for you build the tombs of the prophets and adorn the monuments of the righteous, saying, ' If we had lived in the days of our fathers, we would not have taken part with them in shedding the blood of the prophets.' Thus you witness against yourselves, that you are sons of those who murdered the prophets. Fill up, then, the measure of your fathers. You serpents, you brood of vipers, how are you to escape being sentenced to hell? Therefore I send you prophets and wise men and scribes, some of whom you will kill and crucify, and some you will scourge in your synagogues and persecute from*

*town to town, that upon you may come all the righteous blood shed on earth,
from the blood of innocent Abel to the blood of Zechariah the son of Barachiah,
whom you murdered between the sanctuary and the altar. Truly, I say to you,
all this will come upon this generation.*

*" O Jerusalem, Jerusalem, killing the prophets and stoning those who are sent
to you! How often would I have gathered your children together as a hen gathers her brood under her wings, and you would not! Behold, your house is forsaken and desolate. For I tell you, you will not see me again, until you say,
' Blessed be he who comes in the name of the Lord.' "*

(*Matthew* 23: 13-39)

Christ's well-put "forgive thine enemy" meaning "understand
thine enemy," was distorted just as anything is being distorted
and defaced that gets into the hands of empty souls. The plague
will never forgive its enemies; the safer and better to be able to kick the
fellow who is down on his knees once more, the kicked one must love his
enemy. A pestilent district attorney will imprison an innocent man knowing well what he is doing; he will put away a father or a husband for twenty
years into a fortress with bars at the windows. Someone discovers the mistake after twenty years and it happens sometimes that the innocent victim
is released. Upon release he has to say publicly — this is expected from him
lest he expose himself to further lawful persecution — that he bears no
grudge against anyone. The pestilent character will go unchallenged to
commit another crime against another victim who again will have to love
his enemies and bear no grudge.

In this manner, a great idea born in a great soul was turned into a killer.
From this request that the leader must not abandon his flock of helpless
men will stem, after the leader will have been nailed to the cross, the other
still more monstrous idea that he *had* to die to take all of the sins of mankind upon his shoulders. It is clear why, and this is exactly why nobody
ever mentions it, never dares to touch this little gem of truth: *They can go
on sinning* and *the crucified one will be always merciful and take over all
their sinning in all his great grace.*

What a nightmare of a moral setting! *Crucify an innocent man to be
freed of sin yourself.*

Christ feels all this when he enters Jerusalem. But he is tied down
through his love for people. He is their captive, they do with him what they
please; a leader should die for them. It is not Christ's way. It has nothing
whatsoever to do with Christ or his mission or his way of life. It is THEIR
way. And it will kill him.

Even if he knew the full story of the plague, how it works and how it
captures its victims, he could not do a thing about it. He would soon find
out that the plague knew how to protect itself against any attack; that it

has shut tight every single entrance to its own domain of evil-doing from the inside. THE PLAGUE IS BEING PROTECTED BY ITS VERY VICTIMS. For thousands of years nobody knows anything about the plague which roams the region of every living soul, killing, slandering, gossiping, murdering openly and clandestinely, causing wars, defaming, mutilating children, distorting great religious beliefs, fucking, farting, stealing, cheating, grabbing the fruits of the work of others, lying, knifing in the back, soiling everything that is clean and translucent, messing up every clear thought, taking over and destroying every single attempt at bettering man's lot, looting, scourging the land, making slaves out of free people, shutting them up so they can not talk or complain, making laws to protect its own existence and misdeeds, strutting, uniforming, medalling, diplomatizing, decorating, visible to every single eye, and yet seen by no one.

Empty souls do not ever drink great thoughts to change the world for the better. They only drink great thoughts to fill their empty souls. Nothing will ever be done about the misery. They honor, if they do not kill, their great sages and prophets not for the betterment of their lot but for the HOPE which warms their cold and barren souls. They will never point their fingers toward the plague which ravages the land and their own lives right in front of them. They accuse the tyrant but not the people who make tyrants powerful. They accuse the lawmaker but not the people whose eternal sitting on the spot makes bad laws possible. They will condemn the usurer but will not move a finger to stop it. Why bother? They will hail Christ for his attack upon the moneychangers but they themselves passed by the stands of the moneychangers for ages and did not say a word.

The crowd spread their garments on the road, and others cut branches from the trees and spread them on the road where Christ travelled toward Jerusalem. And the crowds shouted, "Hosannah to the Son of David! Blessed be he who comes in the name of the Lord! Hosanna in the highest!" When Christ will walk the road up to Golgatha, there will be not a single soul to sing Hosanna in the Highest. WHY? WHY in heaven's name is this so, and why in the Devil's name has no one ever mentioned or pointed out this discrepancy? Because people will easily shout Hosanna to the Highest and turn their backs just as easily when the victim of the Hosanna-yelling will be down on his knees. This does not make sense, and only the defender of the plague will find it quite natural. It should be, emotionally no less than reasonably, the other way around:

When a leader is on his way toward possible victory, he should be met with silence. One should wait and see what he is and how he acts in tough situations. When this same leader has shown that he is reliable and well set, and later gets into trouble, ought not " THE PEOPLE " come to his rescue, shout HOSANNA IN THE HIGHEST *then,* free him, support him? NO! WHY? They will always be absent when the leader, hailed when it was safe enough, gets into trouble. And this is the *plague within the people.* It is to their own disadvantage to be that way. It harms their own lives, not only the leader.

In this manner the plague is protected from attack of any kind. And since the plague dwells and acts within the people, it follows logically that people must not be criticized. Did you ever hear anyone criticize people? No. Oh, yes, you can ridicule them in plays and movies; you can say generally that people are evil, just as you can fume against sin in a general way. But start being concrete, tell people how they *really* are in great detail, and see what happens. People must not be criticized in this age of worship of " The People." The people themselves don't like it, and the politicians are powerful enough to punish the critics of people.

Yet, there is nothing more important, nothing more crucial to people's lives than to know how badly arranged they are. They and nobody else are responsible for what happens to them.

Christ refused to acknowledge his differentness and to tell people what they truly are, and therefore he had to die. He did not choose any other way out of the seduced leader's plight. These ways are:

To despise people, to have had no hope about them in the first place and to exercise truly Machiavellian power over them, as did Genghis Khan, Hitler, Nero, Stalin.

To adopt people's ways and people's favors, after a start in an independent direction.

To abstain from any attempt at improvements and just function as a people's administrator.

Instead, Christ adhered to his basic tenets without attacking the people's ways, and so he died because of his pity. He died and had to die because he refused to acknowledge the terrifying fact that not only Judas, whom he picked out at the last supper, but every single one of his followers wanted him to be killed; a fact that clearly turned up in the complete abandonment he suffered later. The multitudes which had shouted, " Hosanna in the Highest," only a few days before, just watched him carry the cross to Calvary, without moving a finger to rescue him. They had not given him what they had granted Barabbas, i.e., active support.

History has not shown so far another way of escaping the back-drag of people's sitting. But also, nobody has yet attempted to tell the people of the earth the full truth about themselves and at the same time to refuse to accept the role of being their leader; in other words, of falling prey to their compulsive mystification, which always is the Murder of Christ. The results of such a procedure will doubtless show up clearly and will tell their own story in due time.

The mass of human animals does not kill the leaders or drag them back onto the spot they sit upon out of conscious malice or in order to kill deliberately. People generally, except a few, are not sadistic. They are morosely immobile or stale, but not sadistic. But they have exerted the decisive influence upon human development through prohibition of any attack upon their own way of emotional existence. It was man who created his religions to begin with.

The sitting on the spot, the drinking of strength, the sucking of hope, the silent knowing of their own depth is not made-up in any way. It is *structural*. It is automatic. It is altogether a result of simultaneously still being an animal and yet being immobilized through armoring. People do; in general, they do not philosophize about doing. They do the minimum necessary for their existence. People are in general and everywhere the source of all conservatism. The conservative leader can better rely on people than the one who has visions about a possibly better future. The czar, the emperor, is closer to people's real ways than is the prophet; closer to their sitting. The prophets only reflect their silent hopes and dreams. It is clear why the prophet and not the czar is the one to be killed.

To realize all this and to abandon the adulation and embellishment of people is a first requirement for any valid approach to social matters. It is so very characteristic of social writers that they see either only the realities of people's way or only their dreams. They rarely see both together. To the social writer in general, people are either only the ideal, the good, the decent, which is outwardly suppressed: Socialism. Or, people are a passive mass of pliable material to be shaped at will: Fascism. Liberalism knows little about people's realities, but it keeps the great dream alive.

People are the determining factor of any happening in social processes. There is nothing whatsoever that can or will ever happen without basic rooting in people's ways. It does not matter here whether people determine the course of things social by dullness and sitting, i.e., by passive suffering, or by active behaviour like upheavals. Everything social emerges from the big herd of people and returns to them. People are like the mass of an ocean upon the surface of which the dukes and the prostituted politicians and the czars and the rich and the social crackpots and the freedom peddlers cause a few ripples. These ripples may be fifty feet high waves which easily overturn small schooners, but in relation to the ocean it is nothing at all. The waves emerge from the ocean and return to it. They cannot exist or come about without the ocean. The depth of the ocean does not enter into the making of a ripple at all. Still, without the ocean there are no ocean surface ripples, and the depth of the ocean is active even in the littlest ripple.

The ocean of human living had not begun to stir before some one hundred years ago. The stillness of the ocean of human living was mistaken by the ripples for non-existence of an ocean at all. The ripples were like flies crawling along an elephant's back. The fly is not aware of the elephant, particularly when the elephant is asleep. The social upheavals of the first half of the twentieth century are only the first stirrings of an elephant baby's skin. There is a thick skin which makes the flies on the surface imperceptible. They simply do not matter. A single shiver in a single small spot can cause havoc among a heap of flies on the back of an elephant baby. And the baby will grow to be a huge, wild elephant. This elephant will live in huge elephant herds. And the huge elephant herds will roam about the countryside, for food and for fun, for water and figs, or just for the sake of mere roaming about. And there is little anyone will be able to do about it. No one can ever predict what the elephants are going to decide about their destinies. Maybe they do not want any destiny; they may just want to roam around the countryside, without any respect for the tiny, tinder huts of peculiar human philosophers. The elephants will graze and sip water through their trunks and scream and mate and feed their young and kill tigers and smash up and uproot huge mast-sized trees and trample to pulp many a philosopher's hut. And there still will be nothing any philosopher or social scientist will be able to do about it. It is high time to recognize this fact: The ocean of human life has begun to stir, this is certain; and nobody can do anything about it, or direct it, or prevent it from happening. Nor can anybody reasonably complain that the ocean began to stir. It is not the communists who make the stir. It is the stir that makes the communists and the fascists and the other funny vermin. The fascists were swept away by the same stir, and the communists who believe they are the true world-shapers will find themselves one day trampled to a flat mud pie under the foot of one single elephant. There is far more, infinitely more to an elephant or an ocean, than any hack writer in a small office in Moscow or Chicago dares even to dream about. They are perfectly ridiculous and impress one as the movers of the ocean or the elephant herds only if one has the wrong perspective which mistakes the ripple on the surface as the result of a move of a fly. There is no greater difference between the little flies in brass in the Kremlin, or in any other similar place, and the mass of a thousand million people, than there is between a boat riding upon the waves of an ocean and the ocean itself. There are forces in and around this ocean in the face of which the boat or the fly are rendered completely negligible. This the sly business lawyer at the head of the Un-American Activities Committee does not understand. He promotes the power of the vermin by proclaiming it to be the very ocean itself. It isn't; and the chairman of the committee was not the right person to erase the mistake about vermin in the first place.

The Catholic church grew out of and rested upon a sleeping elephant and an immobile ocean. The priests thought they ruled the sleeping ocean and the resting elephant, unaware that the ocean and the elephant did not even sense their sitting on their backs. The Catholic religion had an inkling, due to its origin from Christ, of the depth of the ocean and the power of the elephant herd. It all ended in mechanized litany, in the Little Man's work once more. Litany murders Christ in every single prayer.

The Communist movement grew out of a ripple on the surface of a tiny part of the ocean. It was carried onward by a sweeping stir caused by a dream which faded away again. And the Little Men who rode the boat at that time, still think they caused the stir and, worse, they still cause the philosophers to think that it is they who make the stirring with " truly bolshevik courage, determination and conspiracy." And this foolish notion is broadcast by many an American radio commentator all over the globe, just as the greatly impressed American newspaper man seems awed by the long-past emperor of Austria. It is all dead ducks, you great descendants of the tough pioneers in New England's forests and in the Western vastnesses. Stop broadcasting about the foolish little men in the Kremlin, but don't stop telling the people exactly what these Little Men are doing. And stop broadcasting about the Austrian emperor's pretender to the Austrian throne. Watch the huge American elephant and the tremendous ocean of American potentialities, or you will be swept away with no trace left of you; a thing that would not matter very much regardless of who you are or whatever your name.

Christ did not believe that he was causing the stir in the ocean. He said he was the Son of Man, which he truly was. He felt what is in the big ocean and in the elephant herd and in his own blood and in his senses, and he said so freely. It was the flies who did not understand and made him go to Jerusalem to fight the emperor. Christ knew exactly what would happen because he felt that it was not his business to fight the emperor. Let the emperor have whatever he wants. Do not despise the tax collector. It does not really matter whether the emperors reign or the collectors collect

taxes. The emperors and the taxes will be gone down the drain long before the Kingdom which Christ knew would come and stir itself into ruling
the fates of the human species. And this will be when men will feel and
know God, when the ripple on the surface of the ocean will become aware
that it is a tiny bit of the great ocean, coming from it and returning to it, a
beautiful passing event, but no more than an event vibrating with vigor
and direction and motion as long as it lasts. The meaning of the existence
of a wave ripple on the surface of an ocean is exactly what it does: *Being a
wave*, rolling onward, spraying a beautiful gust of water all around itself
and vanishing again. But the *principle* of the ripple remains as long as
the ocean lasts. So, let us realize the principle of our existence.

Christ knows exactly that he is a stirring ripple coming from the big
ocean and scheduled to return to the big ocean. He knows it in fact in
such perfect lucidity that here alone is reason enough to kill him. The
flies on the back of the elephant don't like it. It disturbs their philosophy
of life. Had Christ not made the fatal mistake of yielding for a moment
to the ways of the flies on the backs of the huge elephants, he may have
lived out his natural lifetime.

Christ is truly the Son of Man and he is to be understood as the Son
of God. He is *both* because Man is the Son of God, and God is the Cosmic
Energy Ocean of which Man is a tiny passing part, a ripple, coming from
and going back into God, returning to the Great Father. Christ saw the
deep meaning of being an ocean wave, i.e., being a Son of God. You are
all children in God and of God, he told them; and they killed him because
they believed that *they* ruled the earth, that *they* could bribe God with
bloody sacrifice of animals or with preputia cut off from newborn boys'
penises, or with empty handwashing while retaining dirty souls, or with
morbid attempts to find the meaning of God in the dot on top of an " i "
as they still do today. They still force two- and three-year-old children to
seek God in the dot of an " i " in their schools, using the rod for cruel punishment. This is a rotten lot, indeed. Their doings have nothing whatsoever to do with religion but only with sadistic compulsion neurosis,
grown from deadened pelvises. The little men have done to religion what
they have done to everything else: Turn it their own way. But there will
once be a prophet who will realize this and not give a damn whether they
believe him or not, whether they reach the Kingdom of God or not,
whether they will be killed by the billion over the ages or not. This
prophet will care only about seeing and sticking to the Kingdom of God
within them. He will only stick to the *principle* of the ripple as a returning event and not to the single ripples or even a group of single ripples.
And the ripple will be no more to him than a tiny stir of a whole ocean,

and it will be the ocean that matters in the ripple, not the ridiculous, pass-away ripple itself.

This prophet knows these ripples would as big waves swallow and drown him in silence if he were too much concerned about them. He discovered the ocean in them and doesn't even care if they know it or not. This may save him from their fly fury.

They will ask him as they asked Christ in Jerusalem:

" By what authority are you doing these things, and who gave you this authority? "

He will not ask them a counter question impossible to answer. He will not say to them, " Neither will I tell you by what authority I do these things."

He will tell them off plainly. He will tell them it is none of their business, that he has acquired his authority to do what he does himself, that they are a nuisance, that he does not care whether they believe him or not, recognize him or not, take up his teachings in their schools and temples or not; whether they " recognize " him as a prophet or not, give him the Medal of Honor or not; that he is not out to convince anybody, that he does not care about anything except one thing: *To keep in touch with the ocean within and without men.*

And since every tiny fly has the ocean within itself, it will respect him and . . . maybe . . . . . will let him live out his natural lifetime.

He will know exactly as Christ knows, from experience, from living Life, from deep within, that the tax collectors and the harlots go into the Kingdom of God and not the Pharisees. Christ does not despise the harlots. He knows they carry to men an inkling of the big ocean of love, even if distorted and dirty. But the Murderers of Christ will burn the harlots as witches at the stake. Much worse will happen.

If you know the ocean, be it asleep or stirring or fully awake, you know God and you know what all the Christs in the history of man have talked about. If you do not know the ocean, you are just simply lost no matter who you are. You may know about the ocean as if in a mirror only if you are afraid to drown in its depths, but you can never stop being a part of the ocean, emerging from its depths and returning to its stillness. And in coming from and returning to the ocean, you take its depth with you; not a little bit of depth as against the great ocean depth. Not a milligram of depth as against a thousand tons of depth. Depth is depth, no matter whether in a gram or a ton. It is a *quality,* and not a quantity. It is fully at work in a glowworm, as it is in an elephant. The tiny nerve in a butterfly does exactly the same thing, basically, as does the large nerve in a whale.

And you KNOW God. You refuse to believe that there is such a thing as NOT knowing or even not daring to know God. It was sick, forsaken, dried-up men who created the tale of God's forbidding people to look at him, to know him, to feel him, to live him. It is they who caused miserable men to try to find the hard way – on mere hearsay, on mere belief and trust – what they had abandoned so easily. It is, again, the people who caused Moses to issue the strict laws against worshipping the golden calf, against eating pig's flesh, and to wash the hands before meals. All this was necessary because, having lost God in yourself, and having lost your FIRST sense of Life, you began to worship gold.

And this the scribes and the Pharisees will never forgive Christ; this it is that will force the scribes and the Pharisees to kill him:

That he told his people where and what the ocean is, while they kept searching the ocean in the books and had built little pools which they stirred with rudders to create a make-believe ocean.

Christ dares to show them the ocean depth. And therefore he must. die. The Pharisees are no better or worse than are our geneticists and bacteriologists and pathologists and Marxologists in matters of life. They will unite, no matter how great their disagreement, to kill Christ, the common foe who has challenged their ghastly evasions. They will kill him because he told the people where life is to be found: in their own souls, in their guts, in their newborn babies, in the sweetness felt in their loins during the sexual embrace, in their burning, glowing forehead when they think, in their limbs stretched out toward the life-giving sun. They will kill him for all this, because he did not hide it away in Talmudic books.

But they will not kill him outright. Not without first covering up their murder with all the legal trimmings they can muster. And they will not lay hands on him directly, not personally. This would soil their dignity which they carry like gowns of silk in front of little people. They will do two things:

They will first trap Christ with the help of one of his closest followers. And, second, they will induce the emperor's governor, their worst foe and suppressor, to crucify Christ in the " perfectly legal " way.

This is the way it has been and has remained to this very day and will go on being for quite some time. They will not cease to kill this way until they have been rendered powerless to kill the soul in every human fruit already in the womb before it saw the light of day.

They will kill Jesus Christ for a crime *they* themselves imputed, *they* themselves invented, *they* themselves committed a thousand times; a crime Christ never dreamed of, never was close to, never possibly could have concocted.

If they are habitual spies themselves, they will kill Christ for espionage. If they are looters of people's efforts and goods, they will kill Christ for sabotage of public property. If they are robbers of banks, they will kill Christ for bank robbery. If they are cancer quacks, they will kill Christ for cancer-quackery. If they are dirty pigs in sexual things, they will accuse Christ of immorality, moral turpitude. And if, in order to gain riches they are promoting killer drugs by the million, they will accuse Christ of promoting cures. If they are dreaming of ruling the land like kings, they will accuse Christ of proclaiming himself King of the Jews.

They are the keepers of the rot of the world and they will continue to attend to their ugly jobs. They drivel words about truth, but they are not out for truth. They are out to *murder* truth wherever they meet it. They talk about the ideal of the spirit, and they will kill the spirit wherever it lights up in a boy's or a girl's eyes. They will organize congresses of mental hygiene, and they will not mention or permit anyone to mention the very essence of sanity of the mind — the sensation of God's sweetness in the bodies of the young.

They are the curse of the world of Man, but their power they derive from the very men they destroy.

Man knows the truth but he was frightened into deadly silence. Where will the crowds be who once shouted " Hosannah to the Highest " when Christ will carry his cross toward Golgatha? They will be absent. But later the Church will have huge pictures painted showing Christ walking up to Golgatha with the multitudes standing admiringly by. Why don't they do anything to save their saviour? Did they shout Hosannah in the Highest? *The saviour should save himself.* Now, Son of Man, perform your miracle. , And they will spit into his face, and will scourge his back, and tear down his honor, and they will let him suffer agonies to destroy his love for people and people's love for him. For they are hideous, beasts as no beast in the wild forest has ever been, cruel devils of hatred which has smoldered in their stale flesh, only waiting for the proper occasion to kill what it never, never was capable of feeling inside. And all this will come true, with inexorable logic and unavoidable consequentiality. Not only in 30 A.D., but all through the ages.

Chapter VIII

JUDAS ISCARIOT

It will happen in front of the very noses and ears and eyes of the great judges and wise men of all nations, but they will not mention it except in special cases when it belongs to the past and serves their ends only. The people will keep silent, knowing well what the dirty game is, and they will protect the evil betrayer of Christ, not the grace of love.

You can find Judas Iscariot in every land, in every association of men gathering around a rich giver, in any age in the history of mankind. It is the follower, the ardent pupil, the one ready to die for his master ahead of all the rest. It is the Little Man with the tight lips and the pale face, the burning eyes and with steel in his heart. It is the child beaten down into the mud, his soul flattened, grown up to be traitor by structure. It will be the hater and taker, the empty bag full of fury in expectation of heaven. The one who will not grasp with his body a single move or word or sound or look or graceful stroke of his master. It will be the empty bag waiting to be filled with joy he himself can never, never create in others. It will be the sharp-tongued, snake-like admirer of greatness he can never, never live up to. He is not out for thirty shillings of traitor's money. He is out to get the grace of God out of his sight. He must end the torture of daily meetings with the great soul. He is the one who will suffer agonies in having to turn green-yellow envy into a hideous love every single second of his being together with Christ, the Son of Life. He will be the one who has lost his soul and life and joy and childhood and his love for women and children. He will be the one who rides the band-wagon to get rich quick on the back of the giver, to get fame for nothing, knowledge without effort, love without sweetness, and first of all his daily filling up of his empty, dreary soul. He will cling to the rich giver like a leech. And he will feel desperate if he is kept from sucking the giver's riches for a single hour only. He will feel like a dirty rat, but he will not have the courage to kill himself. Therefore, he must kill the constant reminder of his own misery. He must destroy even the picture, the last memory of the torturing, life-giving strength right in front of him. He can no longer bear to look into an honest face, like a clean brook, a straight expression of quiet, patient love and understanding.

He would never dream of killing a torturer of innocent children. Through the nights he nourishes his nightmares of a lost Life. He knows well his soul will never, never return from the dead. It is dead already and there is nothing to return to. There is no Kingdom of Heaven for him, and why should he wait so long, anyhow? Get going, Master. Get famous and be King of the Jews right away, to comfort my dried-up carcass, to fill me with pride, even if for a brief hour only. Let me feel my hardened heart beat faster with joy at the sight of your triumphs. Why do you always talk of things I cannot grasp or live or feel or ever hope to reach? Why don't you perform the things I *can* understand; the display of power, the howling of the herd of men, the uprising of all the suppressed of this earth toward a sudden victory of Heaven on Earth? Why should I have to search my soul, to repent, to change my ways, to take the pain of heartbreaking thoughts, to go through transformation of my Self?

It all can be had so much more easily, so much more to my liking, with trumpets and fanfares. If you are the Son of God, why don't you destroy the enemies of my national honor? Why don't you fill my heart with sweet quiver at the sight of a thousand soldiers of the great emperor falling to pieces with one stroke of your fist armed with a flaming sword? Paradise is forever closed to me, and, roaming through this life without purpose, aim or love, sword and fire and death have been my only delights. My God is a God of revenge and thundering wrath. If you are the Son of God, why don't you act like the Son of *My* God? *Your* God is strange and out of my reach. Love is not of this world and never will be. You must force Man toward love, if love must be. I cannot bear your love. I cannot any longer bear the pure rays of heavenly light. I must kill you, I must, I must, because I love you, and need you and cannot live without you any longer. And live I must, so die *you* must.

I must not ever go to his enemies, but I will. In heaven's name, I must not betray my Master, but I surely will. I cannot forego the thrill of supreme hatred, the tickle of remorse, the emotion of feeling like a stinking skunk. So betray I must. Christ must and will *prove* that he is the Son of God. He will rescue himself. He will at the last moment perform the great miracle to give me the faith I so badly lack.

I shall not really do him any harm. *I shall force him finally to reveal himself as God's true Son.* He is my beloved master, isn't he? I trust his strength, his godlike power. I shall not do him any harm. I do not want to do him any harm. But test I must his ways. He is too modest; he is not what I want him, must have him to be. He hides his power. He must prove it, show it, so I can be redeemed, freed from my eternal misery.

Chapter IX

PAUL OF TARSUS

BODY VERSUS FLESH

Christ knows all this with a calm glow of bitterness. Christ tries to push away this knowing, but it keeps returning and nudging him. They are no good. They do not understand a thing. They hate me for disturbing their lives. They will certainly run away when disaster strikes. I must die. There is no other way. My world is not of this world. This world would have to change or at least be ready to change soon in a crucial manner to accept me. It cannot be done by the sword. It must be done by love. But the love of God has gone from their hearts in times long past. Therefore they do not understand. Children still understand; then they lose it fast.

I must die, since I cannot win *now*. They will crucify me. I must tell them, prepare them for the event. They must not suffer too much. But they do not really understand. I shall meet them and talk to them at my last supper with them.

Christ does not, in his great outpouring love, find the way to *live* for his world's sake. To add a few years to finish his mission of living Life. The single accidental soul is still too important to him. He does not reach the conclusion of the unimportance of the single life, of the importance of the principle of Life itself, which will preserve billions of single lives. He should abandon his flock. He should retire, go away, hide until the storm is over. His sacrifice won't help a bit. All will remain as it had been through the ages. His great grace and love will be wasted. They will never understand. They will only *take* again, mistake his death to have happened to save *their* souls and to free them from their sins. They are and remain selfish to the core, without grace or love to the last. He has to die, to die to save them from their sins. He must die " for them." Otherwise his mission is not fulfilled.

How great must be the love for man to deliver Christ to this sacrifice for worthless, thankless men? Is it worth it? This deep immorality — is it worth a single life like Christ's?

It will not save a single child from the cruelties of distorted life. It will increase the suffering of innocent souls. His love which embraces *all* love, of the body *and* the soul, will be transformed into the Killer of God's love, and only a hard face with a fake smile will remain. The cosmic meaning of man which he sensed and tried in vain to teach to his fellow man, will become a mirror image, and wherever this true meaning will turn up again it will be killed cruelly, mercilessly, by his very representatives. He has forgiven the adulteress because he knew the sexual misery of man. His church will kill the adulteress as did the old Jews. There will be no mercy. He has lived with sinners and with harlots and with publicans, and he knew that persecuted life lives its bits of joy in hidden, dark, filthy caverns. His representatives will not know this and will have no mercy with publicans and sinners and harlots. They will turn the very love of God into a grave sin, and they will not distinguish the love of God from the love of the Devil. Two thousand years will pass before man's minds will dare approach the love of God again. And what will they do then? Repent? Change their ways? Find and admit their error? Discover Christ again? Return to his great love? Impossible. They will remain sitting in Paul's cathedrals as they and their kind have been sitting through the ages.

They will forbid the feel of the sweet love of God even in the very holy marriage they themselves are blessing at the altars. Husbands will never in their life see the bodies of their spouses. Darkness will engulf their senses. God's love will be driven out from their churches completely several hundreds of years after Calvary, and the devil will reign. New churches will be formed, in the search for God's love; the Protestants will restore some direction toward God's sweet love, but again God's love will submerge in Puritanism. They will know the truth somewhat more clearly, but they will never say so. Some will regain mercy with the love of God, will forgive the Young for loving with their bodies, but they will never restore the Love of God to its proper rights.

They will hide away the evidence of Christ's love for women, as God himself has created it, into deep, dark catacombs with heavy locks at the doors and the keys thrown into the river. No human soul will ever know the full truth about Christ's love of the body.

Christ's ways lend themselves as the seeds of a future religion. It is, essentially, a religion of love. Love encompasses *every* kind of love: The love of your parents, the love between man and woman, the love of your neighbor and of your enemy, and the child, and deer and God and the whole world. One cannot cut apart love and say: You may let your love stream in this, but you must not let love stream in that. As a little boy you may love your mother fully, but as a young man you must not love your girl fully, with all your glowing senses. Senses are bad, sinful; kill them.

And sensual *don't* will reign in the lives of men.

One cannot tell love to be there at one time and not to be there at another time. One cannot possibly tell a bridegroom to love his future wife up till ten o'clock in the evening, and after ten, when the marriage ceremony has taken place to love her in a different way. This is not the way of God's love, which cannot be neatly subdivided into parts nor restricted in time one way or another.

If you are a man and you love a woman, you may start loving her the full way, wanting to melt into her as God has established it. How can you stop the flow of love? Christ, according to his apostles, is against adultery; but did he say that to desire another man's wife even in thought is a grave sin? How much did the narrators of Christ's story put into his mouth that was not his meaning?

One can with certainty put characteristics together which do belong together, and separate those that do not belong. It is entirely possible that a man of spirit and love makes women happy but dislikes adultery, especially the type practiced in average life by the average man or woman. However, it is unthinkable that a man with a glowing body and a sane mind, who always had made women — young, desirable women around him — happy, should preach asceticism or restrict love to a type of marriage which at his time does not exist in the form in which it later appears in the age which carries his name. Where does the sharp, merciless battle against the " Sin of the Flesh " originate? What does the cruelty mean — the cruelty with which *this* sin especially is being punished through the ages? Why the tale of the virgin birth of Christ, never mentioned or even hinted at by Christ himself or even by his apostles in the four gospels?

The condemnation of the flesh in the Catholic form comes late in the history of the Christian church. It first appears in Paul, who creates the empire of Christianity by carrying it out of the narrow domain of existence as a Jewish sect. And the strict asceticism for the priests does not appear until nearly four centuries after the death of Christ. Christ never mentions asceticism, and we cannot, from what we hear in the four narratives about Christ, imagine him demanding abstention from the genital embrace, either for himself or for his followers. *There is no indication to the effect that he lived in abstinence with the women he knew, and there is no indication in his whole being to such effect.* It would not fit the picture of a man, young, strong, attractive, desirable, and surrounded by young, healthy women, associating with sinners, publicans and courtesans, knowing as he well did the ways of life among the poor, a carpenter by profession, to be an ascetic. He could not possibly be an ascetic as he is presented to us, with full loving. And it would not fit the picture if he were conceived as a God in a Paulinian world which had taken so much over from Greek religion. Gods are not and never were, in the Greek world, depicted as abstinent creatures. And Paul's later raving scorn is directed toward the " flesh," that is, the *dirty* way of sex and *not* against the natural, i.e., the " body." But this distinction will disappear entirely in the church of the Popes.

Why, then, the condemnation of the sexual desire as the dynamic core of the whole Catholic world to this day and with such severity?

We must, in accordance with what is known to man about the ways of love in the animal as well as in his own world, assume that the Christians, in building up their empire all through the world, beginning with Paul, hit upon the pornographic structure of people at large. This structure, which does not know love except in its dirty, distorted, unclean manner, seized upon the religion of love to justify its own rampant dirtiness. This very same thing repeated itself when the function of the orgastic convulsion of the living protoplasm was finally discovered in the twentieth century. Natural love and the natural right to live it were taken over by the perverted spirit and thwarted desires of armored man, and put to its evil services. There is no way to delineate the Godlike from the Devilish once the Godlike starts flowing. This is so since the Devilish is only the perverted Godlike. Therefore, the Devilish will at first be hard to distinguish from the Godly, and it will often slip through disguised as the true love. In the end, these two ways of being are incompatible, exclusive of each other. But in the beginning, at the onset of the flow of love, the distinction will be unsharp.

THERE IS NOTHING MORE EASY THAN TO CREATE A RELIGION OF FREE-FOR-ALL 4-LETTERING OUT OF A TEACHING OF LOVE WHICH INCLUDES THE NATURAL GENITAL EMBRACE.

And no greater disaster could strike mankind than such a development of a brothel religion from a message of love including the genital embrace. Every founder of such a movement would of compelling necessity have to do *one* thing first of all and above all other things. He would have to curb the pornographic flood of a free-for-all fucking epidemic by all means. This would have to be done in any land, at any time of history and with any kind of historical background, since the genital action of animals, including man, is a bio-energetic function and the valve of the life energy itself. Any kind of excitation of the living organism will needs increase the inner pressure and lower the natural resistance of the valve mechanism. In times of crises such as wars, famines, floods and other great disasters, and in great ideological revolutions such as the birth of a new religion, the inner pressure of Life must increase a million fold.

Under natural conditions and with a biological structure capable of harmony and gratification, which is a temporary lowering of the urge and calming within one's self, there would be little danger to individual or community. Here and there somebody would overdo, but little harm would come of it.

The situation is entirely different with organisms incapable of gratification. The excitation of the biosystem and the increase of inner pressure would not give way to discharge and gratification, and thus to calmness, but would inevitably lead to an increasingly stronger inner pressure with no way out of it. The valves to let the stream flow off are shut and the dams would burst everywhere. There is little doubt that such a free-for-all-fucking period as we sometimes witness during wars, would swamp away every vestige of human existence WITHOUT PROVIDING ANY HAPPINESS OR GRATIFICATION.

When the Christian faith began to grow out of its local, restricted area of influence; when it began to spread over ever widening territories, when it especially began to act upon formerly pagan countries, the old religious cults of natural fruitfulness and of the phallus poured into the new vessels, threatening to demolish the very foundation of the religion of LOVE OF CHRIST. These old pagan cultures were at their decline, whereas the new Christian faith was in its beginning, flourishing stage. Without the sharp turn against the development of a fucking religion in the multitudes who joined the Church, the Christian faith could not have come through with its basic gospel of Love of Man for Man; it would have been swamped away by the fucker chaos, the loveless, hateful, dirty, piggish, cruel, reckless rubbing of cold penises against the walls of dry vaginas with subsequent disgust, remorse, hate, contempt and murder of the fellow man and woman.

It is immaterial here whether or not the builders of the Christian Empire were aware of the nature of the danger. One can, however, be certain that they must have sensed the danger, apart from all personal aversion to fully functioning natural love. They must have seen or felt, during the declining phase of Roman rule, the sweeping tide of dirt and loveless embraces ruin human lives. And they were forced to clamp down on it. Paul's procedures to this effect are quite unmistakable. In the twentieth century, soon after the Russian Revolution had opened the gates of love, new and more cruel restrictions set in, for the very same reasons.

Paul, of course, had no clear idea of the contradictory nature of what he calls the " body " and the " flesh." " Do you not know that your bodies are members of Christ? " This is fully true in the sense of Christ's being the love of God and the body being a member to this love. " Every other sin which a man commits is outside the body but the immoral man sins against his own body." The modern orgonomic physician must fully agree with this commandment if the body is understood as the executor of full natural love. A man or a woman of full genital love capacity will feel miserable after an ugly, empty, disgusting act of rubbing a cold penis against dry vagina walls. He or she will feel it as a disgrace, as a smutting of their clean limbs. Did Paul mean *this*, which is true and right? We have reason to doubt it.

Christ never seemed to have been concerned with the fulfillment of natural full bodily love in the human animal. We can assume from what we know about man, that Christ understood and lived the clean, natural way of a full gratifying love; that he abhorred the dirty fuck out of nowhere into nothingness.

In Paul, such awareness seems equally unlikely. Neither was he concerned with the natural sex-economy of the population. He knew nothing about the emergence of mental ills from the frustration of natural love, and he was probably far removed from any awareness of the physical consequences of a religion of pure love; " pure " here taken as not dirty, not pornographic, not slimy, not cold and empty, and not cruel and reckless. The purity of the heart and the purity of love at the same time still do not exclude the genitals of mankind, at least they do not do so in clear words.

Such a ban on the genitals of Man, even in the sacred marriage, appears much later, in the beginning of the development of the social power of the church, which means a church encompassing millions of multitudes. Here the Catholic's rigid ban on the genitals begins to make sense, though it only leads into a dead-end-street without any hope of a solution to this crucial problem of man's existence.

IT IS THE ARMORED MAN'S PORNOGRAPHIC CHARACTER STRUCTURE WHICH CAUSES THE BREAK-IN OF THE CATHOLIC IDEOLOGY OF BODILY SIN AND OF THE BAN OF THE DESIRES OF THE FLESH.

The universal, all-encompassing love of Christ must be curbed, restricted; the genitals must be excluded, and even the sweet streaming in the loins must be condemned lest the first stir in man's loins lead to the free-fuck-for-all way of life.

It is probably the greatest lesson taught to humanity ever since the inception of written history. *Natural love pouring into dead genitals turns into hatred and stale murder of social living.* With this, the great misery begins, and man becomes ensnared in the complications of a life full of taboos.

Every founder of a religion had to face this very same problem, being ill-equipped to cope with it. This emerges clearly from the teaching of

Gautama Buddha and the faith of Mohammed. The great mistake is not the curbing of man's evil urges for free-for-all-fucking with dead genitals. The great mistake is the burying of the very natural powers in man's body which alone are capable of putting out of function the perverted sex in mankind. The alternative to the pornographic genitality of the Catholic priests of the Middle Ages was not the Puritanism of Luther's origin, but the cleanliness of the original Christian love-life.

The clear distinction between the *primary*, natural, socially fruitful genital desires and needs, and the *secondary*, barren, filthy, cruel, unsatisfactory, perverted drives of man will not be made before twenty centuries will pass; and then there will be great agony in the way of the clearing of the rubble from ruins of thousands of years standing. The first great and deep-going psychology in man's history will take over the great confusion of primary and secondary drives and will implant the great evasion in the minds of thousands of physicians, educators, nurses and parents. Nobody will dare touch the grave problem of the orgasm function which is so badly mingled with the sexual filth of the ages.

The sexologists in the beginning of the twentieth century will deal with the perverted sex of man as if it were naturally given. There will be little inkling of the origin of the perverted nature of sex from the suppression of the streaming love in the child and in the adolescent. There will at first be no organ to understand what sweet streaming love is. They will deal with the homo-sexuals as a third kind of sex. They will exhaust their interest in phalluses and condoms and Indian love techniques. They will give advice to the ignorant and the impotent as to how to be " successful " (mark the word " successful ") in " performing " (mark the word " performing ") the sexual act. They will teach love " techniques " (mark the word " techniques "), how to play with each other's genitals, how to excite each other, what to do and what not to do, what positions to take in the sexual embrace. They will, rightly, try hard to reduce the great guilt feeling that drowns out all genital activity, from the self-satisfaction of the maturing adolescent to the first embrace after the marriage ceremony. But they will not touch or permit anyone to touch the streaming of love in the body of the children, of the maturing young ones and in the natural full embrace. The Catholic church will issue warnings and pontifical declarations against all these attempts to remedy the greatest tragedy that has befallen a whole living species, Man. The Christian church will try hard to hold its own territory which rests on the condemnation of the flesh, which truly, in the deep sense, means chronic Murder of Christ.

Politicians will seize the opportunity which offers itself here, and will promise the " freedom of love " for " the masses." They will know little of what love is, how it works, what happened to it in past historical times; they will even ban any inquiry into the laws of the body from their rostrums when the great power of this problem will threaten to outdrown the noise of their economic propaganda. In the great Russian revolution, they will first issue laws to free mankind sexually, but the free-fuck-for-all epidemic will soon appear, and, to maintain some order, they will begin to suppress ALL love, forbid the teaching and learning of love, and finally they will reinstate laws of marriage worse than the ones given by the czars.

All this will be ugly, but necessary and unavoidable. It will repeat itself until man will permit his loins to feel the streaming of life again; not until then will dead, dry female organs stop receiving pushing, rubbing, piercing cold male organs, the source of all frustration and the dread of all true love which they came to call the Love of Christ.

All this explains satisfactorily the sharp ban on all genital acts which mean happiness and gratification even in the sacred and Church-blessed marriage. It is impossible to feel the beginning of the stir of life and not to feel the urge to merge with another body. And one cannot ever hope to let nature run its course without danger to human living if the stir turns into fright, and the fright into a rush-fuck " to get rid of tension." There is no hate greater than the hate emerging from this frustrated and thwarted love of Christ. And there is no temptation to murder greater than that emerging from this sense of living Life forever unreachable, forever receding from the outstretched hand. And all this was implicitly entailed in the preparation of the Murder of Christ 30 A. D.

CHAPTER X

PROTECTING THE MURDERERS OF CHRIST

The most fantastic, perverted, incredible fact is this: *The murder of Christ through the ages is protected by the people themselves who suffer from it most.* The murder of Christ is protected by:

SILENCE on the part of the multitudes; the people know the truth. . . Why don't they speak up?;

OPEN DEFENSE OF THE MURDERER if and when it happens that a finger is being pointed at him, defense especially by so-called " Liberals ";

SLANDERING AND PERSECUTION OF CHRIST on the part of pestilent little Fuehrers risen from amongst the people;

THE WHOLE SYSTEM OF PROCEDURE IN COURTS AND THE SHAPING OF PUBLIC OPINION: SILENCE THROUGH THE AGES ABOUT THE WAYS AND MEANS OF THE EMOTIONAL PLAGUE in the books of learning of all nations.

NOBODY HAS EVER DARED TO ATTACK THE EMOTIONAL PLAGUE AS AN IN-TEGRAL PRINCIPLE OF BASIC HUMAN ORGANIZATION. THERE DO NOT EXIST ANY LAWS DIRECTLY PROTECTING LOVE AND TRUTH.

Incredibly perverse as the protection of the murder of Christ by the victims of the plague themselves is, the *rebuttal of the prophet is perfectly correct,* following a cruel logic:

If the prophet does not compromise with the prevelant public opinion, if he refuses to fulfill the people's demand to become their oppressor, if he sticks to his ways and beliefs and, naturally, is not able to ever satisfy the expectation on the part of the multitude of miracle performances, he must of necessity die. The cruelly valid reason is this: If the prophet's demands were to be realized right away, the general state of affairs would be far worse in man and society alike, than the immobility and the rot which he defies. The impossibility of the realization of his dream is given in the impossibility of the human character structure to live, to carry on, to secure, even to understand or to be aware of the prophet's world without shattering anxiety.

In this tragic entanglement of man is rooted everything that protects the status quo; everything that is directed against man's dream of paradise, which, from the standpoint of the prophet, *is* rational and fulfillable. In this tragic Gordian knot, everything is secured in an insoluble entanglement that makes the irrational rational, that establishes and maintains the rule of the Devil which is the perverted love of Christ, which is the Emotional Plague of the ages. The sergeant carrier of the Emotional Plague is usually a productive but abortive great doer or lover.

The whole situation is incredible and fantastic to such an extent that the sages of the ages have failed to see it. The "logic of the illogic" begins with the fact that everything is perfectly rational and correct *within* the realm of the Devil's reign. Everything is as it should be, and accordingly is secured by law and institution. People protect it and *must* protect it, since otherwise, as persons and as carriers of certain functions in this present setup, they would perish.

Only such a leader of men, as he who on account of this very insight abandoned the ambition and resisted the temptation to become a leader of men at all, can be the true guide. Standing far outside WITHOUT THE URGE TO BETTER THE LOT OF THESE PRESENT GENERATIONS, such a leader will be able to prepare the way out of the entanglement and the rut. The true leader of man will think and act far beyond his own age, beyond the age of written history, beyond the age of past society as a whole. He must, if he wishes to see man within his setting in the domain of what he calls GOD, write man off, as he was and is, completely, without remorse, without hesitation.

It is, again, phantastically enough, the Christian love for man in the cosmic sense, the very principle of Christ, to love one's neighbor as oneself, which has been perverted like anything and everything else into a powerful weapon to kill Christ through the ages. This godly principle is being used to protect the killer of Christ. And this is as it must be, again *within* the framework of man as he is and must be. The cosmic, tragic fate of Christ is that his death is necessary and absolutely logical as a consequence of man's character structure which cannot ever be changed by any means once it has been formed. Once a tree has been forced to grow a crooked trunk, no power in the world can straighten it out. And since in the realm of man the crooked stem is being transmitted to the future generations by the mere force of adaptation to the conditions of crooked trunks, the murder of Christ will remain necessary as long as the tree trunks continue to grow crooked. The crooked tree trunk will hate and will have to murder the straight tree trunk until the tree trunks will start growing straight all around and will no longer cause terror in crooked tree trunks. It is exactly here where the task of our " *Children of the Future* " sets in.

The ways of the chronic murder of Christ are many and varied. Let us survey the territory:

The final, shameful crucifixion of Christ is not accessible to comprehension unless the hidden, devious, well-set methods of the Emotional

Plague are thoroughly understood. The very fact that the secret of the murder of Christ has remained unsolved until human knowledge succeeded in penetrating beyond the domain of man's armored existence into the *core* of his Life principle, is a major accomplishment and expression of the devilish rationality of the Plague. Protective guards of the secret were:

The principle of Christian Love for the enemy, i.e., the killer of Christ.

The evasion of *truth* as a principle.

The repression of man's childhood experiences over the ages.

The armor of man's Life system, which did not permit him ever to search for the solution of the Christ tragedy within himself.

The transformation into the mystical of everything that is real in Christ's existence and teachings, i.e., the inaccessibility of the image in the mirror.

Finally, on top of it all, and well rooted in its inner logic, the sum total of all human ideas about morals and ethics and law and the state and the beyond and the cosmic destiny, things all of which are part and parcel of man's great evasion of his rooting and origin in the genital organs, the symbols of fertility and creativity in the old pagan religions.

At least a thousandth part of the futile effort made through the ages to understand Christ's tragedy, could deservedly be used to find out whether the monotheistic religious systems, beginning with the Jewish, were not strenuous efforts to cope with a fucking, farting, gossiping, maligning, sitting, dull, malignant, murderous, envious, underhanded, empty, unthinking, stubborn character structure as it had been created in the subjects of the great patriarchal empires of Asia and the Mediterranean Sea. In order to save the Jews from persecution in Egypt, Moses had to organize and to civilize them. Was it not this that forced him to give them the ten commandments and the rules for cleanliness and orderliness? And this in turn could not be accomplished without full suppression of the malignant *secondary* character structure. It had to be replaced by an ethics which in its cruelty and rigidity of demands only took over from the perverted drives, the cruel qualities it had to keep in check with all the severity and brutality it could muster. The rule of circumcision as one of the most sacred beliefs of the Jews, points clearly to the genitals as the source of the evil.

From this, finally, Christ recoiled, as had many prophets before him. But it appears that no one before him had had the character structure which not only in thought penetrated to the core of man's origin, but in addition LIVED the very LIFE OF GOD as it is here understood, as a *Life of Nature including uncut genitals* and LOVE of LOVE ITSELF.

One cannot possibly imagine the Jews in Christ's time being capable of switching over *en masse*, and in a short time, to Christ's teachings. They could, of course, admire him, wish him success; they may have believed in the usefulness and rationality of his revolutionary criticism of the Judaism of those days, but never would they have been capable of LIVING Christ's life. Their society and daily routine would have been shattered at the first attempt to do so.

Seen in this light, the severe, murderous animosity which the teachings of orgonomy had met first in the twentieth century become perfectly understandable. Can you imagine men in the twentieth century of Hitler and Stalin and Mussolini, living according to the great insights of an unconscious mind and of the importance of natural orgastic genitality? This is quite impossible. The character structures of man in the twentieth century seemed ready to listen to it, but *not* to *live* it. Psychoanalysis accordingly degenerated into a cultural philosophy of a very bad kind within three decades after its birth, and Sex-economy had to fight for its life more than three decades to prevail against the murdering and slandering and gossiping and tearing down of honor and police persecution. It did not succeed in getting a firm foothold till the general sexual misery became too obvious to everyone to ignore; till American military medicine had to reject every fourth or fifth man from military service because of mental disorders; till adolescents fell prey to addiction *en masse* due to their burning genital frustrations in an incipient sexual revolution; till marital happiness marred the conscience of all concerned and the courts and newspapers were filled with reports of marital murder. This age was still far removed from grasping the close connection between " private " misery and the great wars, the mass killings in Germany, Russia and Korea. But *the sexual revolution* had come under way. Thus Sex-economy escaped the fate of the Murder of Christ so far. It also had powerful support by the discovery of the Life Energy in 1936, which turned public attention toward the BIOLOGICAL nature of man's trouble. The sharp distinction of Sex-economy between the PRIMARY, natural, and the SECONDARY, perverted drives found its formal expression in a change of terms which pertained to sexual matters, and this, too, helped to keep the atmosphere clean. The term " sexual intercourse " had come to mean filth to everybody; the term GENITAL EMBRACE distinguished the clean from the dirty act and it is here to stay. The word SEX, abused and smutted into a horrible nightmare, into a rubbing of cold penises within stale vaginas, was completely abandoned and the new findings of the glowing, streaming of Life in the organism during the embrace were subsumed under the term ORGONOTIC, which as yet had not been besmirched by the withering, cruel hands of the plague. There can be little doubt, however, that sooner or later the plague will try its hand again on this clean function, too. But this time we are better prepared to cope with the evil.

Slander, defamation, snooping of pornographically oriented state officials, of frustrated women and piggishly minded men are, of course, still around and quite busy. But they are less successful lately since it has been learned that one can use the TRUTH as a WEAPON against the plague; since it has become possible to break the deadlock and the ban on attacking the carrier of the plague. The Christian principle of " Love Thy Neighbor as Thyself " and " Forgive Your Enemies," which is inherent in all great deeds far beyond the domain of the Christian church, which is given by the closeness to the principles of life and depth and truth, is centered on the protection of Christ and God and love and genitality in the newborn infants. It is no longer as easy as it used to be to protect those who murder Christ in millions of innocent children and adolescents in agony with genital frustration.

The murderer of Christ has been recognized; the mask of joviality and uprightness has been torn, on principle, from his ugly face. His basic character structure, which is a murderous mixture of frustration, envy, intolerance of living Life, impulses to pierce, to kill Life, to besmirch whatever is clean and lovely, of stiffened faces and limbs, and a mind full of dirty dreams, has been carefully studied and is being revealed, to be known far and wide to everyone.

This is only a beginning. The murder may still occur and there are many hideouts inaccessible as yet to the weapons of reason and of interest in the future fates of unborn generations. Murder of Christ will certainly and abundantly still occur. But the spell has definitely been broken. The ENDING of the murder of Christ is at hand, not as the Kingdom of God, not as a dream, but as a crucial task for generations of educators and psychiatrists and physicians and administrators.

It is no longer a matter of proclaiming any truths but of searching out the hideouts of the plague. Will the plague succeed in turning this job again into a nightmare of human agony? Possibly, but not probably.

Let us learn more about it in one of the many ways the plague killed Christ again, many centuries after the Murder of Christ: this time in the form of a great natural philosophy which taught the totality, continuity and comprehensive aliveness of the universe. The originator of this natural philosophy, and thus an anticipator of some basic orgonomic thoughts, was Giordano Bruno.

Chapter XI

MOCENIGO

THE MURDER OF CHRIST IN GIORDANO BRUNO

There are empty souls which thirst for excitement of some kind to fill their desert minds. They will, accordingly, hatch evil. Not all of them, true, but a few will do it, and their victims will most likely be a Giordano Bruno. And Giordano Bruno is chosen as a victim because he rediscovered Christ in the Universe, i.e., the love of God in terms of astrophysics.

Bruno had, in the sixteenth century, by mere thought, anticipated the factual discovery of the cosmic orgone energy in the twentieth century. He had discovered and captured in a system of thought, the interrelations between the body and the mind, the single organism and its environment, the basic unity and multiplicity of the universe, an infinite universe embracing infinitely numerous worlds. Everything exists for itself, and yet it is an integral part of a whole. Therefore, the individual unit or soul exists for itself and, at the same time, is a part of the whole which is infinite, one and multiple at the same time. Bruno believed in a universal soul which animated the world; this soul to him was identical with God. Bruno was basically a functionalist. He knew about the simultaneous functional identity and antithesis, even if only in an abstract manner. He moved within the general stream that carried human thought to the concrete formulation of functional orgonometric equations four hundred years later. He described, according to his orgonotic sense, many qualities of the atmospheric orgone energy which the discoverer of the Life Energy in the twentieth century made visible, manageable and usable in a practical, bioenergetic way. To Bruno, the universe and all its parts had qualities identical with life. In his system there was no unbridgable contradiction between individualism and universalism, since the individual was an integral part of an all-encompassing whole, and not a mere number to a part in a sum of parts, as in mechanical mathematics. The " World Soul " was in everything, acting as an *individual* soul and, *at the same time*, as an integral part of the *universal* soul. These views are, in spite of astrophysical formulation, in accord with modern orgonomic functionalism.

Bruno had discovered the road that leads to knowing God, and therefore he had to die. And die he did, indeed, a death of nine long years, from

1591 till 1600, when on February 16th in the early morning he was led, with prayers, by the heirs of Jesus Christ, to the stake and given over to the flames, all in the name of love of the Creator.

Though the Catholic church, due to the great power it exerted over millions of human souls, had developed the cruel techniques of empire builders; though it developed them into a great art, among them the burning at the stake of dangerous searchers of the realities of Christ's world, it would be wrong to attribute these ways of the devil to the church only. The church is no more responsible for the creation and maintenance of the methods of the emotional plague than was Nero or Caligula or Genghis Khan or, in modern times, the Hitlers and the Stalins. The plague has developed its rampant malignancy wherever leaders had to face the grave task of holding sick, deadened, cruel multitudes together in unity and cooperation.

Bruno's teachings, in the right direction as they were, carried with them too much force, too much power to change the order which kept the still-slumbering mass of human animals together — a mass which within the next three centuries would develop its dreams into upheavals that were destined to shake the world of man to its very foundations. To permit the discovery of God and his Kingdom to become a practical reality, to let men grasp with their minds and hearts and their practical lives what the church had transformed into a mystery, removed far away into unreachable heavens, would have amounted to precipitation of an early general disaster. This is the tragedy of all knowledge which emerges at the wrong time into an unprepared world. Therefore, Bruno the Nolan, had to die.

It is rarely the inquisitors in high places, the attorney generals, the high pontiffs of established beliefs, who start the trouble. It is not the multitude of passive, suffering and dreaming mankind which takes the Bruno's before the tribunal of inquisitors, condemned in advance to die, and thereupon delivered to the stake to burn. Neither inquisitor nor sleeping mass of mankind are or feel responsible for the death of a knower. The sleeping men are entirely unaware of what is perpetrated in their behalf, and the inquisitor only follows the set rules of certain laws, mechanically, in a wooden manner, like a robot, without mercy or freedom to act otherwise.

The true killer who starts the ugly show, is usually an inconspicuous, " upright " citizen who has nothing to do with either the problem of the sleeping and dreaming herd of men or with the grave administrative responsibilities of the inquisitors and judges. The true killer is the bloodhound who stirs up the escaped prisoner, not because he hates the prisoner or because he is out to restore justice or because he knows anything at all what it is all about. *The true killer is an accidental nuisance*, a mishap that strikes the victim without rhyme or reason, like a stray bullet from the gun of a hunter who misses a deer and kills a casually by-passing game warden. The true killer does not intend to kill this specific person or any other individual. The victim becomes the prey of the pestilent killer for reasons which have nothing whatsoever to do with his true life or with his beliefs or his relationship to the killer. The victim only happened to cross the way of the killer at a certain moment; a moment which bears importance to the life of the *killer*, but not to the life of the victim. An executioner who is paid for his job of killing, does not hate his victim, he does not choose it or wish it evil. The executioner kills because he chose the profession of killing, no matter who happens to be under his ax or guillotine blade or in the electric chair. The killer, on the other hand, kills because he *must kill*. The victim happens to be a victim only because he happened to be around at a certain opportune moment.

The killer of Giordano Bruno happened to be a Venetian nobleman by the utterly unimportant name of *Giovanni Mocenigo*. This name has no rational meaning whatsoever. Nobody had heard of it before the killing, and nobody even cared to remember it after the killing. His name could have just as well been Cocenigo or Martenigo. It wouldn't matter at all. Mocenigo is a nonentity of some proportion. He knows nothing, does nothing, loves nothing, cares for nothing except for his complete nothingness. He sits around or walks around, not necessarily always in a palace, habitually breeding evil. He produces dreams of evil like a hen lays eggs, one every once in a while. He is too smart to just do evil like a simple, daring, foolhardy criminal, such as robbing a bank to get money the easy way, or attacking a girl on the street at night out of sex-starvation. The pestilent killer does not even produce a sound reason for his evil deed. Since there is no sound reason within himself to commit a crime, he must search in someone else for a reason to kill. His own barrenness of soul and emptiness of mind is no good reason to kill; why should he kill somebody else if he himself is empty like a desert? Therefore, the pestilent character will hatch out a most elaborate reason to kill somebody, no matter whom. The victim must only have one characteristic to provide the good reason to be murdered: He must in some way be at variance with the ways of the sleeping or sitting crowd, preferably a soul like Christ who knows the smell of eternity.

The pestilent killer will, in contradistinction to the reasonable killer who goes after money or rape, gain nothing from the murder. He murders his victim simply because he cannot stand the existence of such souls as Bruno's or Christ's or Ghandi's or Lincoln's. He may be anybody in any government or commercial office, in a bacteriological university institute or in a cancer society. He may be young or old, a man or a woman. What matters is only one thing: *He breeds evil out of frustrated, cruelly perverted genital desire, and hates the Love of God which he is resolved to kill in the name of God or Christ or national honor.*

Accordingly, Mocenigo, the empty do-nothing nobleman from Venice, writes two letters to Bruno, who at that time lived in Frankfurt, inviting the scholar to teach him the " art of memory and invention." That means: Mocenigo knows Bruno is very rich in a quite different manner than he himself, and he plans to suck dry his future victim. Bruno believes in the power of love which binds all together in all and is the urge to all good. Therefore, he is scheduled to be killed by Mocenigo. Believing firmly in the great love in the universe which binds all men together into one and creates the great good in man, just as Jesus Christ believed in the power of Love as the great force in the Kingdom of God, Bruno agrees to move into the home of his murderer.

Bruno is expected to impart his knowledge of the great art of thinking to his murderer, Mocenigo. He is not supposed to give this knowledge to anybody else. When Bruno expresses his desire to return to Frankfurt to get some works printed, Mocenigo objects and threatens Bruno with the holy office. Mocenigo, of course, as every similar killer, has his connections with the inquisition. He is going to use them to the detriment of the rich giver should the latter not be willing to convey upon the killer his great art of thinking and memory. Mocenigo is firmly set to get what he wants, even at the price of murder. Of course, Mocenigo does not care for knowledge. He would not know what to do with it, how to handle it, how to let it grow or how to apply it.

He is only capable of sitting and breeding evil out of dead genitals. He does not care in the least for knowledge for the sake of knowing or learning or finding or solving riddles. He just wants knowledge as you want a nice car or a juke box to play gay tunes, or a rowboat or a girl from a certain bar, or just a dish of fish to fill your belly. *It is the getting,* the getting it from somebody else who has worked and toiled hard for it, *that matters.* Mocenigo must be filled up with knowledge which he can neither produce nor digest himself when he gets it. He cannot stand anybody else having knowledge or the skill of obtaining wisdom. He cannot bear seeing somebody, even a thousand miles away, enjoying the belief in love and a universal soul which, possibly, sometime in an uncertain future, could or even factually would bind men together in peace. Whether you call them Mocenigo or Caiaphas or Judas or Saul of Tarsus or Stalin, it is and remains always the same old story. They just cannot stand it; it makes them green with envy; it fills them with unbearable desire for something they are utterly incapable of possessing, and therefore, they will deliver Christ to the cross and Bruno to the stake or scientific sociology to the dogs. The closer the future victim is to the Kingdom of God with his knowledge, the surer will he be chosen to be murdered by the pestilent character.

All this goes on with not a single soul, not even the murderer himself being aware of what is happening. When Bruno insists on departure, perhaps sensing the malignancy of his murderer, Mocenigo seizes him at night from his bed with the help of an " arm of the Law." From here onward the machinery of the organized emotional plague of all ages takes over like a robot grindstone, never to stop until the victim is squeezed to pulp. The envy and evil plotting of Mocenigo does not count and does not even appear among the arguments in the protocols. The true motive of the murder is not mentioned or even admitted to court at any time, neither in 1592 nor in 1952; neither in Italy nor in the USA nor in the USSR. The true motive of the cowardly killer is banned from inquiry all over this planet, except where simple routine murders are concerned, never in cases of the Murder of Christ. The Bar Associations of all lands do not tolerate even the discussion of the motivation of such killing. The judges who sentence and the executioners go free, no matter how innocent the victim. If, occasionally, after decades, the error can no longer be kept hidden, the victim, if alive, must say, " Thank you very much," or, if dead, somebody kneels in prayer at his grave. But nobody dares to attack the true killer.

From now onward, it is of no importance whatsoever what fills the protocols, whether it is forbidden to have the Earth circle around the sun or to believe in a Soul of the Universe or in Universal Love or whether one has lectured here or lectured there, whether one has been decent all his life and committed only the blunder of meeting accidentally a pestilent sniper shooting from ambush. Nothing matters, since the true motive is the murder of Christ who could actually accomplish the dreaded realization of the Kingdom of God on Earth. It does not matter whether Jesus actually proclaimed himself as the King of the Jews or not. It is merely a pretext, and everybody is aware of this; therefore, nobody mentions it or does anything about it. The established law is geared to eternal *seeking* of the Kingdom of God, but not to the *finding* of the Kingdom of Heaven, not to the ways of Christ who knows the ways of the Kingdom of God. Only formalities count. Every appearance of fairness and precaution *not* to commit a judicial murder will be carefully guarded in order to commit the murder in the " proper, legal " ways. No one should ever be accused of injustice. The record of honor must remain clean. Everybody knows what has been done, and nobody moves a finger.

Much later, when the victim will have been long dead, when his screams to heaven in the evocation of God will have been silenced forever, when the myth of " justice done " will have evaporated, historians will dig out the facts, when all is fairly safe; and it might happen that a Pope kneels at the grave of one of the victims to restore his posthumous honor. Thank you, Sir! we hear the victim whisper. And God once more turns away from his Godlike creation, Man, and continues to send his prophets to preach in vast, empty deserts. Mocenigo is forgotten. Nobody investigated him, nobody even thought him guilty, though a few may despise him. More, there will be many who will tell you that Christ has been justly crucified, for he has acted as a common rebel against established government, that he had unnecessarily provoked the scribes, that he would better have sat still and quiet and left the souls of men alone in peace to sit it out forever and ever after. And books will be written and read by the multitude, books that tell you how to escape the truth about the Murder of Christ, how to obtain peace of mind. Don't touch it, ever!

CHAPTER XII

TOWARD GOLGATHA

Christ must die on the cross at Golgatha. Not because he endangered the Roman Empire. Others have endangered the Roman Empire and lived. Christ would die, not because he aroused the caste of the priests by his harsh words of criticism. Others had criticized the Sanhedrin; others had cursed the hypocrisy of the mechanized, Talmudic Jew, and continued to live. Christ did not die in shame because he pretended to be King of the Jews. He never dreamed of being the Emperor of the Jews. He would have rejected such an idea if it had been offered to him by the Roman emperor himself.

Christ would not know how to be a " King of the Jews." Can you imagine Christ riding a fiery white stallion, galloping ahead of a column of mounted Maccabeans, with sword drawn, blinking in the early morning sun, and shouting, " Heigh Hop! Hop Heigh! Forward, Charge! "? This cannot be visualized. It is unthinkable, impossible; it would be perfectly ridiculous. No worse degradation of living Life in Christ can be imagined. You can imagine Caesar, Napoleon, Hitler, but not Christ in this situation. Christ simply does not fit here.

Accordingly, Christ will be scourged and crucified by the people as the " *King of the Jews.*"

Christ does not fit and looks ridiculous in any attire which means aristocratic honors and high standing in the world of armored man. You cannot imagine Christ rattling down a litany, nor can you imagine him ever receiving the Honorary Degree of Doctor of Law at X University. He was a stranger in Jerusalem, and he would have been a stranger in any city in any place in the world at any time during written human history. Christ has a natural dignity and a direct, charming acuity of speech which is not fitting. One just does not behave that way. People love it and flock around a man having such gifts; but they would never do it themselves. They would blush, feel uncomfortable, somewhat out of place in any gathering of men behaving like Christ — simple, and straight, sharp-witted but not smart alecky, radiating love and contact but not obtrusive or clinging.

Christ does not fit into this world except within the small flock of innocent, ignorant admirers and followers in the midst of the green hills and vineyards of Galilee. And even with his admirers he is out of place. He is incapable of fully enjoying the hailing as does a Mussolini, the abortive genius who fits people's dreams of a hero like a glove made to fit the hand. It is more likely that the admirers feel uncomfortable in his presence, not being quite free to make their usual sex jokes or to engage in small chit-chat and talki-talk.

Christ is entirely out of place anywhere among armored men, yet he is their very hope, the essence of their dreams about a better future life. His greatness in simple, straight thinking turns out to be a handicap in the twisted and complicated arguments with the scribes. One just does not think straight and simple. It amounts to being offensive. You tell the scribes that you can see life moving in a bit of heated coal, easily and without any difficulty. The scribe does not simply look into a microscope. He keeps arguing with you about how unseen molecules push the particles around. You keep telling the Pharisee that you can see, easily, without effort, that deadly rot bacteria develop in deadened organs out of the tissue itself. The scribe will never look into the microscope, but he will tell the multitude that you have not sterilized the tissue and that it was " only air-germs," though he himself has never seen or demonstrated the airgerms. Life is completely out of place in this world of Pharisees and Talmudic scribes and medical councils on pharmacy.

You tell the Talmudist that to cut the skin off of little boys' penises hurts; that it hurts badly and that the screaming of the baby is a sign of utter agony. The scribe will tell the multitude that the child really does not feel anything at all since soon after birth no sheaths of the nerve fibers have yet developed, or similar nonsense; and " the people " will ask you whether your idea about the pain connected with the cutting off of pre-putia without anesthesia has been recognized by the scribes.

In order to save babies from the agony of circumcision, you must fight, and you get involved in a tangle of all kinds of things. The fact that cutting off preputia hurts horribly cannot prevail. Christ is against many rituals of such a cruel nature, and therefore he must die.

There are simple things in this world, clearly visible to everyone, which require little thinking to understand, just a bit of common sense and judgment. The agony of genital frustration in adolescence is such a thing. Every single man and woman has gone through this agony. Every single man and woman has struggled with its pain and hopelessness. As long as you are alone in stating the fact that puberty is maturing of the genital function and readiness for the full embrace, you are all right. The moment you get into a physiological institute of any university of the early twentieth century and talk about this simple matter, you get hopelessly entangled.

First, you feel out of place in a university auditorium talking about the genital embrace in puberty. It just does not fit and it is looked upon with frowned eyebrows as unfitting, bad behaviour. The professors have never talked about it; they have never permitted anyone in their classes to take up this crucial subject. In order to hide the self-evident fact that you were built, by nature which is God, to mate in puberty, a hodgepodge of *ad hoc* theories were created, all kinds of arguments, the details of which cannot possibly ever be reconciled with each other, a tangle of ideas and assumptions that everybody has a right to be wrong and to have his own private opinion about excitation in puberty, which he acquired during his desperate battle to hide his own masturbation from the eyes of the father in order not to get beaten up. After a while, you just have to give up the debate. There is no hope of ever penetrating the tangle, and you decide that you must keep away and remain alone.

The scribes are the guards at the gates to the palaces of knowledge. They let no truth about essentials pass through the gate to the inside. They let truth pass to the outside only.

All this is true at any time. Everybody knows it. Many have written large volumes about it. And nothing happens. All knowers of the simple things were out of place, a great embarrassment to any type of scribe. The scribe is the personification in science of the sitting of people, of their immobility in mind and body.

In Galilee, Christ can somewhat be what he is. Nobody, except his closest relatives, questions his natural dignity, his place among the hills. One may feel that he is different or that he is exaggerating or unnecessarily "dreamy." But in Galilee he can still mix with people, talk, eat like an ordinary human being, and enjoy a few friends.

In Jerusalem he cannot be quite himself. He is torn from his home where he so naturally belongs. He is forced to become a bit like the rest if he wishes to be with the rest. One apostle, according to Renan, hints at Christ's having been lured into Jerusalem to be killed.

In Galilee among the hills where he is left alone to his own world, he can say simple things in a simple way, and they will remain valid for thousands of years. In Jerusalem everything he says sounds funny. He has to argue, he loses his harmonious totality of existence, he must split up his great oneness and start knowing point 23 in number 5638965 of the Talmud in order to prevail. Christ's way of life is valid over the ages. It is not valid and could and will not stand up in any court in this man-shaped world.

In order to understand the murder of Christ, one must see things in their perspective of common living, which, distorted as it is, has the power to distort even eternal truth into a social crime. This is true to such an extent that anyone in the place of Christ would do well to warn the world against his own teachings. Not only he, personally, does not fit. His teachings do not fit, either. Not only do his close friends and relatives and disciples not understand what he is talking about; the world of man at large does not, cannot, dare not understand.

And this is the true tragedy of TRUTH itself; that it cannot possibly be accepted without being watered down, distorted, flattened, deprived of its sharpness. Oh, yes, a little truth, a useful truth such as improvement of wine growing or radio receiving or military ballistics — all this is well and good, acceptable and respectable. Not Christ's basic truth. It cannot stand up in any court. It is, seen from the standpoint of armored, immobilized, well-set man, a crime, a dangerous stirring up of life. True, without such truth nothing whatsoever can ever change. No ill can be really exterminated. The misery must remain. But the truth itself *is* a crime, a crime against the very life of any nation geared to things as they are.

This is valid to a frightening extent; the fake dealings in social improvement on the part of evil politicians are necessary in spite of their horrible emptiness, even to such a degree that NOT to advocate the devil and be against God's reign is paramount to treason. And because the tragic dilemma as just outlined is so severe and insuperable, nothing moves or has moved in thousands of years since the inception of human mechanical civilization as far as man himself is concerned. The murder of Christ is true today as it was two thousand years ago.

Thousands of years of Chinese and Japanese immobility in social and personal matters makes good sense. Moving freely would have meant disaster and actually spelled disaster when the Chinese Red Devil took over from Sun Yat Sen.

The evil thing is not the sitting in the rut over millenia, not the ideas of the reformers, not even the misery of the multitudes, but, by comparison, the evil that is bound to emerge the moment the freedom vulture starts rearing its ugly, pernicious wings and dispatches his freedom peddlers to the farthest corners of the earth.

To hide one's senses before these truly tragic contradictions in the basic existence of mankind is to help the devil and to worsen the misery. There is, according to experiencing of and conscientious reasoning about the plague, no trace of a hope for mankind as long as the ostrich policy will be upheld in the face of the necessity to Murder Christ. It is because the total problem is so tragically rational that mankind has recoiled from tackling it; man always has evaded it and will continue to evade it for quite some time to come, as long as infants will be subjected to character armoring. ARMORED MAN IS BOUND TO MURDER CHRIST IN ORDER TO EXIST. This is a realization directed against the practical effectiveness of any insight of some rank. It can no longer be circumvented. It will bother and torment humanity for ages, and it will slay many innocent victims. One cannot expect that a ruined species will dissolve its greatest trouble easily and speedily once someone gets a bright idea and starts with the proper kind of political propaganda. This, again, is grasping realities in the mirror only.

The big noise created by philosophic students of man's nature is an expert device to keep this realization of the magnitude of the tragedy away from man's senses and intellect.

This is the practical dilemma:

If a truth is too monumental, it turns into a nuisance and is rendered useless. If a truth keeps itself little and innocuous in order to survive, it will be submerged in endless arguments and remain ineffective.

It is like facing a beloved child who is dying from an ailment that could be cured by a remedy which cannot be reached and applied in time. It is like the feeling of a mother in Korea in 1950 whose child was lost in the meleé of confusion, who knows that it must be somewhere, still alive, perhaps in the orchard of the old shattered house, hiding and crying bitterly; that you could reach it easily and save it within a few minutes' walking time, but that it is finished because there is a battle raging exactly inbetween the mother and her lost child.

It is like being hopelessly caught in a burning house and knowing with perfect lucidity that you could have saved yourself and your dear ones if you only had in time put up an escape stepladder at the window.

It is like all this, only multiplied by the billion. *If the chronic Murder of Christ could be stopped, which it cannot be, the reign of God would become a reality.*

Christ did not dream mystical dreams. His ideas were not unreal or impracticable in themselves. They are real and practical. They could solve a lot of problems, disperse a great heap of misery. Unfortunately, the use of Christ's truth by man would kill mankind. This is true because man is set up the wrong way for this truth that could save him. The character armor came into being from terror of exactly the same truth which alone can stop the armoring process that kills life in the womb already. And the Murder of Christ will continue to occur as long as the hidden pathway is not found that leads from the ill-fated structure of man towards the saving realization of the truth. Proclaiming the truth — this alone will never do it. The truth will be and will have to be killed.

In this sense and seen in this crucial perspective, even the scourging and ridiculing of Christ makes horrible sense. There is a truth and a rationale in everything irrational that happens, in every murder, rape, war, suicide; so also in the scourging of Christ.

Christ *must* be ridiculed, defamed, scourged, rendered helpless and despicable, handled worse than a common thief, because his lucid, unbeatable way of showing the hope must be fully, thoroughly and irreversibly exterminated. It cannot, must not any longer face a people who have lost the capacity to reach it and to live it; who would inevitably go to ruin if it were really touching this truth, if it would succeed in taking the glory of God out of the mirror and making it touchable right in front of its eyes with its own bare hands.

This now begins to make sense, though utter, perfect nonsense it truly is. It begins to make sense how it was possible that ethics and morals always have been and still are mere mirror images, something to look at but not to grasp or live practically. The look into the mirror and at the image of an unreachable God still has retained some power of restraint, of conscience so as not to go too far, to feel the last remainder of inner clean emotions within oneself when listening to church music played at an organ, to behave decently in the presence of an attractive woman when one is sexually starved; not to cheat the neighbor all the way but just a little stretch; not to shoot one's nagging wife completely dead right away when she had slept with another man but only to beat her up, with inner remorse afterwards; not to kill one's child for touching his genitals, in accordance with a cruel religious law, but only to smack its fingers; not to keep murdering thousands of Negroes in the South of America for being constantly reminded by them of soft limbs and sensual lips and the dreamed pleasure of the genital embrace as it once was in the bush, but to kill and hang only two or five Negroes during a year's time; and to have to quibble, at least morally, about solving the Negro problem in the great democracy of free Southern Americans; and finally to have to give in an inch out of a mile in this struggle for the dignity of man by permitting one in a hundred Negro students to enter a university, or a white soldier unit; and not to keep them out and talk badly about them altogether. Is the Negro himself not a bit responsible for what happens to him? How would *he* behave if the whites were in his place? He already hates the Jew no less than the Jew hates and despises the Negro. It is all rooted in the people themselves, and nobody dares to mention it.

All this is necessary, though an advocation of the devil it really is. But filthy water in a desert is better than none at all. OR IS IT?

It is. At least we can do little about it by despising it. The freedom peddler is required to come into being in order to provide some substitute for Christ. The freedom peddler comes in when man realizes the transposition of Christ into a mirror image and turns once more to searching the real, touchable, livable Christ. The freedom peddler is a very late product of man's struggle for release from his emotional trap; he does not really establish himself as a public figure till the Catholic peace and brotherhood peddler has succeeded in shutting every single exit from the trap toward the domain of Christ, the Kingdom of Love and eternal happiness. Enlightenment, renaissance, reformation and the first political revolutions will have to pass before the socialist freedom peddler will begin to occupy the public mind. He introduces for the first time the idea of filthy water in the desert being better than no water at all. It will take some three hundred years from the crucifixion of the prophet of total love to the transformation of his message into a political power that will kill love of the body wherever it will meet it. It will reign for more than a thousand years, until the Renaissance and Reformation will begin to grope again toward the forbidden truths; and another six hundred years will pass before the first ideas about "sexual freedom" and "equal rights of women" will begin to stir men's minds. It will take only fifteen years from the establishment of the first sexual freedom laws until their revocation by little freedom peddlers in power. And again, in the United States of America, a new thrust toward Christ's Kingdom will develop in psychiatry, while the churches of Christ will anxiously search for the means to stop the beginnings of a realization of Christ's Kingdom of Love on earth. Toward the end of the twentieth century after the Murder of Christ, his church will still condemn as sinful the streaming of love in the loins, and will proclaim now, as before, the virgin birth.

All this will happen with a cruel logic.

The freedom peddler will emerge in the story of the chronic Murder of Christ at the right moment and in the proper place. But first, Christ has to suffer mental agonies before he submits to scourging and crucifixion.

Christ feels that he has fallen victim to the ways of doing things as they usually are done, as they have been done thousands of years before and as they will continue to be done thousands of years after him. The people to whom he tried to give the vision of the Kingdom of Heaven take the word "kingdom" their own way and expect him to ride a white stallion in glittering armor. They simply cannot visualize a Kingdom without a king and a stallion, and his messenger without a sword. Centuries later, they will actually carry wars of the Cross to the Holy Land. No matter what Christ does to show them the true ways of God, they are structurally incapable of understanding him. And this must slowly begin to be felt by Christ. Christ did not care to be a prophet or the Messiah in the first place. He was seduced into it by the burning expectation of the admirers around him that he actually had a message to deliver from his God. In this he was perfectly honest, not a faker or an epileptic mystic, not a lunatic, nor a common political rebel who misused the confidence of the people. When he felt that he was able to comfort men, to pour a new hope into their sick hearts, to make them feel better, lighter, to cause their eyes to glow again, he was led to believe that he actually served some mission in the holy sense people used to think of it. He accepted the role of a religious leader, and he got himself into trouble. At first he was not aware of what began to happen to him. But when the demands for miracles and signs and demonstrations of power increased in number; when they began to ask him more and more frequently whether he was the Messiah who had been announced by the old prophets; when he at first did not know what to answer but slowly realized his power over people and thus overlooked people's power over him, he fell victim to a sickness within the people which had not ever been understood or even known until the very day when this writing will reach people. Unintentionally, unknowingly and naively, he took over the role they imposed on him and he began to develop the language of a prophet or Messiah and the ways of a religious leader. This is easy to see, now, as it was easy for him to do, then. In this manner, Christ became a victim of the people's craving for an idol from whom to drink hope and strength into their desert souls. Christ, out of love for man, could adapt to man's ways; man could not possibly adapt to Christ's ways. Not even a half-way compromise was possible. The people were stronger all along the line of development and have remained to this day the sole victors, in good as well as bad ways.

Christ would not have been human as he was, nor would he have loved people as he did, if he had not enjoyed the praise and admiration which was bestowed upon him. And this praise and admiration is the bait on the hook which is on the line held by empty, love-starved people to capture a decent, loving, glowing carpenter as a leader to fill their needs.

The inner turmoil in any true leader who emerges from this mess, soon impresses its marks upon his face, long before he meets with final disaster. If he is a true lover of man and a true friend and helper, he will needs realize the hidden trap which was set, the unrealities and impossibilities of the expectations, the pernicious sitting on one spot on the part of the multitudes; and if he is firmly rooted in his inner depths, he will be torn to pieces between his way of life and the armored people's way of life. The two ways are, as things in emotional matters stand, irreconcilable.

The prophet will keep the principle clean because his emotions are clean. The multitude will force him, because of the sitting, to give up his principles and to adjust to their ways, i.e., to transform the realities in the principle into a mirror image of a *fata morgana*.

Can you imagine Christ delivering a speech on the day of the Bastille, July the 14th, from the rostrum of a huge meeting hall? This is not possible.

Can you imagine Christ receiving a decoration, a medal of this or that kind, for the greatest contribution to the idea of peace on earth and brotherhood of mankind in Jerusalem in his time or in any land in our time? This is quite unthinkable.

Can you imagine Christ who lives and thinks in truly cosmic spaces and according to the laws of the cosmic Life Energy, approaching the Sanhedrin or the priests in the temple for approval of his teachings, for " recognition "? And this it always is that people want: Not to be separated from the big herd; not to lose the common way of life; their leaders to be esteemed by their enemies and honored by the powerful of the day who are out to destroy them. Christ is expected to deliver a speech on Bastille Day in a convention hall before thousands of delegates of the international peace party of the liberators of mankind and the peaceful people's democracies. He is expected to be decorated with the legion of high glory or the yellow star.

And therefore, Christ never meets the Christians, and his way leads farther and farther away from theirs if he definitely refuses to become a freedom peddler in the First Century in the Christian era.

What is true for the Christians is also true for the Buddhists and the Mohammedans and the Hitlerians and the Stalinists and the Freudians and all the other popular movements. And the people always remain the victors, the final determinant of things and events — to their own detriment as long as they keep sitting and force armoring in their newborn infants.

Some interpreters of Christ believe that the revival of Lazarus was " put over " on Christ by his friends who wanted to help him to fame, to victory over the apathy towards his teachings in Jerusalem (Renan). According to this interpretation, Lazarus, who was reported dead, emerged from a tomb with bandages on his head and body, to meet Christ. Christ was shaken into a tremor, to see his friend alive, and had really nothing whatsoever to do with the whole performance. The onlookers mistook this scene for an act of supreme traumathurgy.

In the minds of the admirers of Christ, the divine virtue is expressed in epileptic convulsions. This is true as far as it refers to the involuntary convulsive action in the life system in a great emotional upheaval, a function which is closely allied with the orgastic convulsion which is the supreme, coordinated discharge of surplus Life Energy. Epileptic attacks are truly *extragenital* orgastic convulsions, thus, in a deep sense, manifestations of the divine, i.e., Life.

Christ is torn between these sharply conflicting emotions:

He spoke the truth as he knew it and felt it, but he knew that nobody really understood.

He loved his people but he also felt trapped by them into an expression of life which was not his.

He knew he could never conquer his enemies and that he would not accomplish anything by using the sword.

Their ways were of this world and his ways were not of this world.

He knew that he would be betrayed and he even knew that it would be one of his closest friends who would betray him.

He continued to adhere to them in deep friendship though he knew perfectly well that they did not understand, that they dragged him off his way and that they were just sitting on the spot, dreaming of the ready-made heavens on earth.

Christ had, however, not reached the full realization of having fallen prey to the most serious sickness of the human race: THE NEED TO FILL IT-SELF WITH HOPE, FOR THE *FILLING'S* SAKE AND NOT FOR THE HOPE'S SAKE. Christ spread and poured out hope for the *hope's* sake. And therefore they could never meet. And filling up with hope for the filling's sake remained the guiding line of men to this very day. It does not matter *what* they hope for. The only thing that matters is the hoping itself, the thrill of hope, the glow of hope. And therefore there are many kinds of hopes in this world of man, but none that has ever been fulfilled. And: The more numerous and varied the hopes that thrill the nerves, the worse becomes the social chaos.

Christ knows he is trapped. There is no way out. He had gone too far, and worse still, he had gone too far on a road that leads away from his Kingdom of Love and God and Peace on Earth and Brotherhood of Man. He knows with perfect lucidity that he must die in vain. He is trapped in something he never intended to perform; he never dreamed of dying for the Sin of Mankind. This will be imputed to him by a humanity which wants to get rid of its big heap of sins and which needs a victim to take over the heavy burden.

If he were a God who came down to earth to die for the sins of mankind, he would not suffer the agonies of Bethany. He cries out, " O Jerusalem, Jerusalem, killing the prophets and stoning those who are sent to you! How often would I have gathered your children together as a hen gathers her brood under her wings, and you would not! " *(Matthew* 23: 37)

Christ, the eagle, has hatched the eggs of little, blind chicks, thinking that he would hatch some eagles to carry his message into the wide world. The shame of it is, the blind chicks had seduced him into hatching out their eggs, and he did not know what he was doing when he kept hatching eggs.

Christ knows he is finished, and finished for nothing, nothing at all. He knows he will and must die for something he had never thought, taught, lived, dreamed of, claimed or even hinted at. He knows it long before the actual false accusation. He knows it because he learned to see man's ways. He knows it because he suffers the trap he is in.

Christ's humanity is his Godlike quality. It is the quality of all creatures who remained creatures of Life and Love; who know the sweetness in their bodies during mating; who know how to let this sweetness stream into the bodies of their babies, their children, their lovers and their friends. Their love is in their bodies and not in a mirror. It can be grasped and lived and loved itself. It radiates from the eyes in a warm glow and in a sad look; it goes through you in gentleness, it knows you when it looks, and it strokes you lovingly with its gentle grace. And this very love for his fellow man has led him into the ghastly trap and to the cross.

Chapter XIII

THE DISCIPLES SLEEP

The tragedy of Christ is so moving because it is the universal tragedy; a tragedy that encompasses the tragedy of man *per se*. Man is armored. Everything passes to the inside only, little or nothing to the outside. Man sits because his movements are painfully restricted. When Life moves ahead, he will go a stretch with it, then he will remain sitting on the spot. And he will hate Life for it moves onward while he is left behind. From this the Murder of Christ develops irresistibly. Sitting man does not want to be left behind. He wants to be loved, protected, taken care of, secured, warmed. He wants to get all the comfort from Christ and he is willing to pay amply in admiration for it. If he loses some or all of these comforts, the emotional plague rears up in him. He will slander *one* thing: The giver. *He will never cut loose from the past giver of love and stand alone or turn somewhere else.* No hate can compare with the hatred deriving from this frustration.

Christ knows his cosmic meaning. "Heaven and earth will pass away, but my words will not pass away. . . . But of that day and hour no one knows, not even the angels in heaven, nor the Son, but only the Father. Take heed, watch; for you do not know when the time will come. . . . Watch, lest he come suddenly and find you asleep. And what I say to you I say to all: Watch." *Be alert,* do, change, keep changing, moving, giving, loving, building.

It is completely useless. Christ still hopes that they understand. They do *not*. They only suck in his glowing words. But they do not, they *can not understand*. "I will strike the shepherd, and the sheep will be scattered." Christ tells them that they will all fall away when the ghastly hour strikes. They do not understand. Every one among them thinks all the others will fall away only not he himself. Christ knows differently. He knows it because it is written in their faces, it is expressed in every single one of their motions and words. Therefore, feeling it, he *knows*. And still he loves them, because *he* understands. He would be better off to curse them, to stop seeing them, because one among them has already betrayed him to his enemies.

This is the way of Life: It suffers far worse for the doing of its murderer than for its own death. It suffers more from the principle of betrayal

and persecution than from its results. It is suffering since the murder and
the betrayal are, seen from Life's own vantage point, unnecessary, an ugly
rasping tone in a beautiful symphony, like the smashing of the head of an
infant, sucking at the mother's breast, by the gun butt of a raving, warring
soldier; it is like killing off the mothers and fathers of little children that
leaves them prostrate on the roads, with a bleak sorrow in their little frozen
hearts.

But disciples have no hearts. They only want to get inspiration and
warmth from the master. At Gethsemane, shortly before Christ is taken
away, he wants to pray, and he asks them to stay a little behind and to
pray, too. He takes only three of them farther along with him, and then
he leaves these behind, too, asking them to stay and pray. His agony is
heartbreaking; he is troubled and greatly distressed. He falls to the
ground and prays, a child of the great heavenly Kingdom like other children of the heavens who fall to the ground and pray in many lands and at
all times in all nations: Their fathers and mothers had been shot away by
the emotional plague waging wars and pestilence, and nobody does or can
do anything about it. All hearts had died out long ago and the will had
withered away in the many. Life has been drained away from their blood.
It is not their fault that they sit or sleep. Forgive them for they know not
what they are doing.

Christ begs them: "My soul is very sorrowful, even to death; remain
here and watch." He prays to his Father, humbly, to let this hour pass by
him, and, if possible, to remove the cup of the final agony from him. Yet,
if it cannot be done, he is ready to drink it all to the end, in utter submis-
sion to the will of God.

When Life returns to its children, after the great agony, it finds them
all asleep. Not a single admirer and getter of love is awake. They do not
care; they have no hearts, only emptied souls to be kept alive by continuous pouring in of Life's heavenly sap. It is all quite clear. It cannot be
otherwise. It must be and will remain as it is for a very long time of agony
to come. This is so because the soul was killed in every baby already in
the womb. Therefore it cannot do otherwise, try as honestly as it may.

The gospel repeats the account of the sleeping, fleeing, betraying
disciples several times.

*And Jesus said to him [Peter], " Truly, I say to you, this very night, before the
cock crows twice, you will deny me three times."*

(*Mark* 14: 30)

*And he came and found them sleeping, and he said to Peter, " Simon, are you
asleep? Could you not watch one hour? Watch and pray that you may not enter
into temptation; the spirit indeed is willing, but the flesh is weak." And again*

he went away and prayed, saying the same words. And again he came and found them sleeping, for their eyes were very heavy; and they did not know what to answer him. And he came the third time, and said to them, " Are you still sleeping and taking your rest? It is enough; the hour has come; the Son of man is betrayed into the hands of sinners. Rise, let us be going; see, my betrayer is at hand."

(*Mark* 14: 37-42)

And Jesus said to them [the captors], " Have you come out as against a robber, with swords and clubs to capture me? Day after day I was with you in the temple teaching, and you did not seize me. But let the scriptures be fulfilled." And they [the pupils] all forsook him, and fled.

(*Mark* 14: 48-50)

In its primitive manner, this account tries to impress upon us something crucial, something awfully important that concerns all of us everywhere and at any time:

It says:

Be on your guard, men who guard the ways of living Life. You will be betrayed into leading ruined men toward a freedom which they cannot ever bear.

You will be misled into giving them all and getting empty admiration out of them right away again in return. Therefore they never get enough and must be filled all the while. They do not return comfort to the giver, it seeps out of them, dispersing uselessly in the sand.

You will believe that they mean what they say. They do not. They only speak to please you in order to get more of the very sap of life from you.

They will follow you awhile, then they will, sooner or later, begin to smile about you in secret and say how wonderfully silly you are in your great enthusiasm, how unrealistically convinced that the great hope can be accomplished. It can *not*, to their minds. They know it and they are right. You are a dreamer to them, a phantast, something queer, strangely affected like a lunatic. They are right from where they are and what they are. But, *you are right from where you see the world.* The gap between you and them is deep and unbridgable.

They will remain sitting on one spot and will drag you down to sit with them, too. You will follow them for awhile because you love them and continue to give them the sap of life they cannot get from within themselves. You think, after a while of rest, they will move on very soon and follow you. They won't. They will remain sitting, and they will hate you for moving onward yourself, alone. They want your strength, not your worries nor your thrust into things obscure and dangerous and laden with future fateful events. And finally, after having filled their Selfs with everything they need, and continuing to sit on it, they will slowly begin to hate you for disturbing them in the enjoyment of their comforts.

And in the end it will happen that some among them will deliver you to your enemies, inevitably, with the perfect logic of evil, entangling you and smothering you.

If they will not kill you physically or deliver you to be killed by their very own enemies, they will besmirch your name, or kill your thought which you have born with pain and much sorrow, of which they know nothing, with their confusion of words and scholastic quibbling over nothing.

If they do not kill your thought, they will flatten it into a Talmudic mire. Do not blame them for it because they cannot help it; they cannot act differently. But do not fall prey to their ways either. Do not yield to their temptations held out to you with admiration. It does not mean a thing. They admire you to get your sap of Life.

Do not pity them. It will not help them in the least, and it will harm your cause and with it many, many unborn ones who will need it badly. It will only render them more helpless and far more dependent.

Use them the *good* way as helpers, and tell them that you are using them to serve a good cause. They will be grateful to you if they can serve a cause *with sacrifice*.

Stay alone, be your own. Your heart will be less oppressed. And leave them alone to themselves, to their own devices and ways of life. In the end they will be grateful. And a very few will find their way to where you are and will begin to understand.

Your loneliness will at first be unbearable because you love people, you love friendship, and you are a man like them — alike in spite of the great gap. But you must take your loneliness as an inevitable condition of your way of life. There is no other way than loneliness as long as man is empty and does not know what love in the BODY is.

Do not save people. You will be seduced by your admirers into saving people. LET PEOPLE SAVE THEMSELVES. This will be the only way to salvation: true, real, wholesome salvation. Life is strong enough to save itself. Just live your life ahead of them.

Do not write for people but *about* the essentials of Life. Do not speak to people in order to get acclaim, but do speak *about* people to clean the air from the pain of emptiness of emotion.

Let your words and thoughts stream out into the wide world and leave them to the world to do with as it pleases. Let them take it or leave it. The evil fruits of distortion will be *theirs*, just as the comfort your thought may carry will be theirs.

And, Christ of Love and Life, look down deep into your own soul and test your own emotional attire. Did you not also *fear* the mission imposed upon you? Did you not shrink from living lonely and forsaken even before the betrayal by Judas? Did you not join them and wander around the countryside with them because you did not dare to be quite alone? You needed them, too, in many ways: To talk to them, to hear your words rebound from your fellow's mind, to hear the echo of your words in their early ways, to see the light in the eyes of your friends glimmer with hope when you spread out your hopes and visions richly before them; to test the ground on which your seeds in the end will fall, to see how they carry the fruit and yield your riches manifold.

Your error was mistaking the glow in the eyes of your friends for a glimmer of penetrating realization of the nature of the Kingdom of Joy and Peace. You erred in accepting the role of redemption as saviour of man. True, they got your hope and fed on it for ages, but your supreme sacrifice was in vain. It did not help; it prolonged their sleep. It did not stir them into action that would move their souls. They have no souls. Their want is only consolation. What they need is regeneration. Not in heaven; *on earth*. Each infant brings your heavenly Life back to this world. Here is the reign of your eternity. Here the torture you suffered reveals its universal meaning beyond man and the angels and even beyond the Son of God himself: *To learn the language of heavenly Life, to end the Murder of Christ.* Only the heavenly Father who is the Life in your limbs, knows when your sacrifice makes sense.

CHAPTER XIV

GETHSEMANE

When the Emotional Plague strikes its victim, it strikes hard and fast. It strikes without mercy or regard for truth or facts or anything else except one thing: *to kill the victim*.

There are public prosecutors who act as true lawyers, establishing the truth by evidence from many sources. There are other prosecutors whose only goal of the prosecution is killing the victim, no matter whether right or wrong, just or unjust.

And this is the murder of Christ today as it was two thousand and four thousand years ago.

When the emotional plague strikes, its victim is exposed to everybody's eyes and judgment; all accusations against it are spread out in full daylight. The victim stands naked before its judges like a deer in the open clearing in a forest ready to be shot by the hunter well hidden in the bushes. The real accuser rarely appears on the scene, his identity is kept secret until very shortly before the final kill. There exists no law to punish the sniper from ambush.

To be standing in the middle of an open clearing in a dense forest, widely visible to everyone, and to be shot at from the bushes on all sides is the situation of the victim of the emotional plague, no matter what form it has.

When the emotional plague strikes, justice quietly recedes, weeping. There is nothing in the ancient books for justice to call upon to prevail. The sentence of death is perfected before the investigation of the crime. The true motive of the prosecution never meets the cleaning force of God's daylight. The reason for the killing remains in the bushes well hidden from anybody's eyes.

When you meet the accused but not the accuser, the charge but not the defense, the exact point of formal law but not the true reason for the accusation, you are dealing with a killing by the plague.

When the plague kills, it kills for wretched reasons. Therefore, to assure the murder, it will not permit weighing accusation against the true, full being of the victim. It will tear down the victim's honor, besmirch every bit of innocent intention or act; it will pronounce innocuous details in a tone and with a slant of intonation which is meant to kill the last vestige of love or esteem for the victim in the hearts of most devoted friends.

When you hear the deadly, poisonous intonation of the prosecutor, you know a Murder of Christ is going to happen again.

Who in this world has not at any time dreamed of removing a king, or of living a forbidden love, or of cursing God for injustice suffered; or who has never touched his genitals or thought of "adultery" or seen in his dreams the temples of the whole world tumble together with their emperors and kings and dukes and fuehrers and God-sent liberators? Nobody has *not* done all this except the image of a Babbitt, manufactured for the purpose of making thoughtless obedience and deadly conformity the idol of a wretched nation.

The victim of the plague has done all this, one way or another, early or late, with or without real intent to execute the dream. And this, together with the exclusion of justice from the court of justice, renders the victim mute and helpless.

When you see in the victim a gentle face and a sad, helpless look in his eyes, you may be sure that another Murder of Christ is about to be committed.

True justice operating according to the laws of life and truth does not tear down the victim's honor. It tries to understand how it came about that a Son of God (and all men are sons of God) got himself into the predicament of being brought to court in the first place.

True justice will find the particular setting of living Life in which any man or woman has violated an existent law.

True justice will even judge the very law it is about to apply. Does it fit the case? How old is the law? When and under what conditions was it made, and who was it who made this law? Are the conditions still valid that created such a law? Were there specific reasons at the time of the making of the law which are no longer alive nor valid today?

When you meet a court which does not judge the law itself which is to be applied in a living case of human fate, which does not ask for its history, its function, its maker, the reasons for its existence at the time of the new application, you are dealing with a potential or actual tool of the plague which is intent on committing another Murder of Christ.

When a law was given two hundred years ago at a time when nobody knew anything about the love of God in the child and in the adolescent, a law that made it a crime to love before reaching a certain age; and when two hundred years later such knowledge is widely available and well secured in the mind of man, and a judge refuses to apply this gap in his judgment, you are dealing with a law made to secure the Murder of Christ by the emotional plague. And the true criminal is not the victim but the law itself which refuses to change in accordance with the change of living Life.

When you meet with a law that was given six thousand years ago, you must be six thousand times more careful in applying it. How otherwise shall true justice ever be done? Such laws are the most powerful tools in the hands of evil men to be used against Christ which is Love and Truth and movement onward with the rest of the Kingdom of God. Here are rooted the reasons which keep man in bondage, which make the dictators because people are afraid to talk and to say what they so well know, deep down and well hidden, to be true and just.

If you hear somebody talk of progress and freedom and happiness and peace and the brotherhood of mankind, and he does not say which law is to stay and which is to go, he is a hypocrite and he means nothing whatsoever. He is only out for votes or riches or power or a seat in this or that chamber, or he is out to continue the Murder of Christ.

Christ does not hide from the law and the prosecutor, as the prosecutors hid their true motives for the killing, and the ancient law hid its actual meaning from Christ. He does not try to escape. Whereto shall he escape? Why should he escape? He would carry his way of Life everywhere with him and he would meet the same fate in any place on earth.

Therefore, he does not hide or flee. Neither does he conspire. He has nothing whatsoever to hide. When he tells his pupils not to talk about his healing power, he does not hide, he only tries to curb their fantastic thirst for miracles.

Christ knows the soldiers will come and get him. He awaits them and meets them. And Life knows so perfectly well how the plague works, that it says to the captors:

> *Have you come out as against a robber, with swords and clubs to capture me?*
> *Day after day I was with you in the temple teaching, and you did not seize me.*
> *But let the scriptures be fulfilled.*
>
> (*Mark* 14: 48,49)

Two thousand years later, the discoverer of the Life Energy will be held for police investigation of his activities, to find out whether he was a spy of this or that country. They could simply have asked him, since he had nothing whatsoever to hide and would have been glad to tell them what he was doing. So they themselves sneaked around like thieves to neighbors who knew little, to find out what he was doing. They avoided the clean air of his workshop. And nine years later they still did not know what he was doing, in spite of thousands of pages written and published by him. They did not know because they were not capable of understanding. They had no organs to know about Life. And therefore they sneaked around like thieves in the night to see what was cleanly and clearly to be seen in full daylight. They lay hidden in bushes with gun muzzles pointed, while he stood on the meadow to be seen by all.

And this again is how the plague works and thinks and acts.

Christ is Life. And Christ was manhandled just as Life was manhandled long before him and long after the crucifixion and is still manhandled today.

And all his admirers fled and forsook him while he was captured, just as they all had fallen asleep again and again before he was taken and while he went through the agony of the innocent one in supreme distress.

And even his God seemed to have abandoned him. But Life within had not abandoned him. His Life within kept acting as Life acts, up till the last breath. And this is so because God is Life within and without. God did not abandon him at all, except as an image of misled men, corresponding to no reality.

Life had known who would deliver it to its enemies. It had known it for a very long time. It saw the traitor step up to it and kiss it on the cheek as he still said, " Master! "

And this, again, is the plague.

Christ's story has moved and stirred humanity to tears and sorrow and great art because it is humanity's own tragic story. Men are Christs and victims of the plague, helpless before their own courts and fleeing disciples and sleeping admirers and Judases kissing the Master with a kiss of death, and Marys who give Christ a forbidden, godly love, and deadened bodies that seek in vain God's sweetness in their frozen limbs, but never cease to sense his presence within and without themselves. Men, basically, in spite of all armoring and sin and hate and perversion, are living beings who cannot help but feel the Force of Life within themselves and without themselves.

Christ is Life, dying innocently for many millenia at the hands of a Life that had lost and could not restore God's ways, and therefore kept guarding the ancient laws with glowing, murderous eyes, and swords ready to kill whoever has lived God's life.

Christ is the infant tied down or filled with nuisance drugs until it vomits, not knowing why all is so terribly painful, and slowly settling down into a living death, to grow into a future murderer of Christ.

Christ is the agony of a boy or girl of four lying in his bed in the darkness, desperate because God is stirring in its little body, terrified that mother or father might come and yell or hit because the hands are not above the covers.

Christ is the nightmare of a suppressed God in God-made genitals in infants and children in the first puberty, returning from suppression as terror of ghosts and robbers with knives, and bleak shadows at the windows, as multiarmed octopuses and devils with glowing forks, and a fire burning in hell to engulf the little, poor souls jammed in between God's stirring in their bodies and the parents, the representatives of God on earth, who punish for feeling God in the limbs. This is the source of all sin punished in Dante's inferno, a man-made, madman's nightmare.

And the Judases are the educators and the councils for mental hygiene and the doctors and the priests who guard the entrance to the knowledge of God with threatening words and flaming swords. Did you ever think of how many billions of small children on this earth went through the nightmare of Christ at Gethsemane and Golgatha over the millennia? Did you? *You did not.* You were "social" and "good to your neighbors" and "liked your enemies like yourselves" and you sent prayers up to heaven for salvation and redemption of your soul, and you knelt before altars of many kinds to obtain forgiveness of your sins. But never, never did you think of the billions of babies and children who bring the very sap of God's fresh life from your endless universe into this miserable world of yours; and you maimed and punished and frightened these children, and do to this very day, for knowing God and living the Life of Christ. And you guard well every single entrance to the houses of knowledge against intrusion of the truth about these countless Murders of Christ committed by you and your appointed ones in the name of God.

And you, defender of the honor of God in some darkened room in some village in some country, don't you think right now, hard, of how you could get at the writer of such "blasphemies" and tar him and put feathers on his skin and put fire to the tar and feathers and make him run screaming with agony through the streets, a warning to every good citizen? You are doing this this very minute. But the times are against you. Some well-guarded gates at the entrances to some of the palaces of knowledge have been broken down and we begin to get an inkling of what has been committed in the name of God for such a horribly long time on so great a number of innocent little Christs, sons of Life and God.

The knowledge of God as the love in your body, which you persecute, is breaking down your guards at the entrance to paradise, which you yourself have put up in your dreams, and your obstruction of living Life on this earth.

You kept brooding over the riddle of the Murder of Christ for centuries and it is *your* failure to find the answer which revealed you as the true and only murderer of Christ. You kept hiding this well and for a long time. But not much longer will hiding be possible.

Chapter XV

THE SCOURGING

The High Priests, led by Hanaan and Caiaphas, are only the final executors of a social situation which had bred evil for a long time within the foundations of society. It was not the high priests who had caused the rotted, " sinful " state of man, a state which clamored for prophets and redeemers. The high priests only administered the *status quo* which was created by the people themselves. The administrator always is the executor of the public will, no matter what is said or what appears to be to the contrary. And the public will can express itself as apathy toward continued injustice just as in active revolt against it or as direct support of evildoing. Nothing whatsoever in matters social can prevail against the multitude, passive or active, good or bad. To blame a single person or caste for social evil is to concede the perfect inertness of the masses of people.

It was not Caiaphas or Hanaan who rendered false witness. It was men from among the people. It was not Caiaphas or Hanaan who scourged Christ before the crucifixion. It was men from among the people. They only did not interfere and gave the way of the people free reign.

The very fact that the decisive role played by the people at large in the course of social events is never mentioned, clearly points to the source of the trouble: *Nobody dares to touch the burning pile of human misery at the very foundation of society.* To evade the responsibility of people at large for the social misery and their own predicament very much longer, amounts to obstruction of the very thing one professes to pursue. It was people who seduced Christ into Messiahship; it was people who expected miracles from him; it was people who brought him to Jerusalem, and it was people who forsook him when he was submerged in trouble. It was the simple, average man from the street who did all this, who added the false witness and the scourging to the rest, and is busy doing all this and similar things to this very day.

There is no escape from this realization, and evading it further will only prolong the misery. It would be the way of the politician who infests the people with the belief that they govern when they vote.

To get the full truth out about people's ways of living and acting is the first rate requirement of the time, at any time and in any society.

To repeat: The crucifixion of Christ was the ultimate result of the action of men in general, and not of any high priest or governor. It was the result of man's action, from the first proclamation of Christ's Messiahship to his last breath.

Neither was the crucifixion the specific result of the Jewish people or their priests. The crucifixion of Christ happened and happens in many lands and nations. It is a general human affair, and not specifically Jewish. Christ's death only brought together in concentrated form what otherwise either happened in single doses at various places or ages, or is submerged in the turmoil of history, never reaching the attention of a writer or a historian. The agonies of newborn infants and small children through the ages are graver, yet they have found no ear and no historian. And there, too, it is people at large who again are responsible for the great silence that engulfs the deep misery.

DO NOT EVER TOUCH IT!

Only when a butchery reaches the proportions of a public scandal, if it claims sufficient blood, will the public mind be aroused to cause writers to note the event.

The attempt on the part of the high priests to avoid a scandal by arresting Christ in his " hide-out " instead of in the temple where he went every day during his stay in Jerusalem, failed completely. Not because they had not been careful enough in the preparation of the judicial murder, but because of the bearing of Christ. It was only this bearing which caused the scandal and everything that followed it. Had Christ fled, or resisted arrest, or had he held great speeches on behalf of his belief or his God, had he cried or screamed with pain, there would have been no Christianity.

Christ's behaviour during the torture does not fully emerge from either the accounts in the four gospels nor any account of later date. It is, however, depicted in many great paintings of the Reformation, which dealt with the Passion on Calvary; it is depicted far more movingly in expression than in words; in the discrepancy between what the crowd does and what the victim represents rather than what cruelty he suffers.

It is the stunning discrepancy between the spirit of the torturers and the spirit of the victim that goes right through our guts to the core of our awareness of living Life.

The more astonishing it is that this crucial experience cannot be found in the accounts of the Passion. It is replaced by pity for Christ, by picturing the evil in the torturer, by immediate transposition of Christ into the distant realm of the heavenly which is to say that he really did not suffer much since he was the Son of God and only fulfilled his mission of supreme sacrifice.

A careful, sympathetic reliving of Christ's last hours reveals a secret of a basic nature at the very foundation of human existence. It reveals again that the story of Christ derives its great power from its universal validity rather than from the particular fate of the Son of Man. The pity and the metaphysical or mystical transposition of his suffering seem only to serve to obfuscate the true meaning of his agony. Not even Renan, who came closest to an understanding of Christ's true being, is aware of the general character of the Passion.

It is, briefly put, this:

God-given Life or "Nature," if you prefer to call it so, meets the plague or "sin" in man every single time a new life is being born and is to adapt to the ways of armored man. Each single life has to go through Gethsemane and Golgatha. Every single man and woman carries deep within himself or herself the deep scars from the early experience of Golgatha, a sensitive memory which is vibrating with sorrow and past agonies: It is the agony of the killing of Life within the organism, which every single man and woman went through, that unites them with Christ.

Let us now trace the distinct features of this identical experiencing of the plague in accordance with the happenings before and at Golgatha. The distinct experiential characteristics of Christ's Passion are:

The deep trust in and love for the people, father, mother, siblings.

The utter ignorance of malice, within oneself and within the friend.

The utter horror at the first experiencing of being spat at and defiled *for nothing*, being hurt *having done nothing wrong*.

The heartbreaking sorrow of having done good to the neighbors and being hated by them and persecuted for having done good to them.

The utter helplessness on the part of Life in the face of human bestiality.

The complete inability of the victim to fight back with the same weapons as those used by the plague, such as the lie, calumny, strategy, defamation, or cruelty.

The feeling of being trapped by one's own deep understanding of the ignorance on the part of the torturer: "Forgive them; for they know not what they do."

The feeling of being paralyzed by one's own fundamental love and sweetness of being.

This seems a rather incomplete account of how Life feels when it meets the scourging plague. The expression in the eyes of a dying deer looking for the last time at its killer may come closest to the emotional expression of the situation.

It is not rational, reasoned determination not to use the weapons of the plague in retaliation. It is the utter *incapability* of doing so which renders the victim of the plague helpless and puts it at the mercilessness of the torturer. It appears that the Russian torturers of the twentieth century relied on and used these deepest resources in the human soul to extort the fantastic confessions of its innocent victims. It cannot be drugging alone. It is a general characteristic of the plague to wrap its poison and its dagger in the cloak of Christ.

This utter helplessness in the face of the scourging plague is not due to any set plan of executing an idea, as, for instance, the fascist traitor and spy will follow a certain typical line of protest or proclamation of his mission. Where the true mission is really given, if we must speak of mission at all, it does not proclaim itself; it lives it ahead, in front of the fellow man, or it works it in visible, durable results. It never proclaims itself; does not make any propaganda for itself.

People know this when they use the terms " Christlike behaviour " in cases of persecuted truth; they very often sense the identity of the attitudes of life in danger, where no fighting back is possible.

The plague character will in situations of danger, conspire, call meetings, make resolutions, stir the people to action, organize this or that, go underground, set up spy organizations to replace him when he is in jail. He will occasionally make use of secret murder as in the case of Trotzky or Liebknecht or Luxemburg or Landauer or Lincoln or Gandhi. The defender of the principle of Life, up till now at least, has never used any of these techniques.

This has a very good reason. Such weapons not only disagree with the basic mood of Life; they would not accomplish anything and would only cause Life to lose its bearing. Using power, it would inevitably degenerate. But using the principle of Love against the principle of hate and murder would also not be in its vein, since it inevitably leads to voluntary martyrdom or to hypocrisy.

Christ does not play the role of a martyr. He becomes a martyr against his will and intent. He never practices an " absolute " Love for one's neighbor and enemy. His unequivocal behaviour in the temple at Jerusalem is witness to that. Christ is capable of great rage and scorn, as he is capable of great love.

This, once more, upsets many a false legend in Christian mythology, and reveals the true laws of Life: *Life could not possibly love where love is needed, if it were not able to hate intensely where hate is required.*

In true Life, love and hate alternate according to the situation. This has little in common with the eternal, even, false attitude of love on the face and in the bearing of the fake Christian who bursts inside with hatred. Here, a fake love covers a brutal, murderous hate. There is no more cruel human beast than the eternally and evenly good and loving one. Every fascist torturer, every murderer from reasons of pervert lust shows this fake kindliness in his face together with piercing, sharply gleaming little eyes.

No, Life *can* hate. It hates fervently, in the open, exposing itself to the enemy in disregard of its own security. It would never murder for the sake of murder alone or for riches or for revenge's sake. But it could kill in an open honest fight.

Life as it appears in the depth of the human soul is incapable of revengeful, dragged-out adherence to an injustice suffered in the past. When the hatred has been discharged there is sunshine again just as after a thunderstorm, and in perfect accordance with the Life within the organism and the Life energy in the atmosphere.

The plague hates silently, brooding and tortured by the continuous pressure of the hate it is hiding until the right situation and the proper victim offer themselves. Then it strikes mercilessly from behind a screen or a bush of a well-protected office in some department of social administration.

Christ meets his enemies entirely in the open. He hides nothing, but he knows when they are out to catch him in a well-set trap, and he is smart enough to be aware of it in spite of his basic trust. He is not always suspicious, but he has a fully developed sense of danger just like a deer.

Christ's enemy is well hidden and nobody knows what he is going to do. Then the situation changes. Christ becomes silent because he has nothing to oppose the plaguey crime, and the plague occupies and governs the scene of public attention. Its devices of murder are ready. The torture is to satisfy the public lust for blood. The truth has become homeless and weeps once more.

LONESOME

Lonesome and lonely I am ——
Yet rich and amidst all of them.
Silence engulfs my domain,
Yet in every one's words I am.
Oh, give me a friend
Who does not request
The endless safety of my name.

Who helps to finish my struggle
For the infant to come.
Who has not imprinted
The plague on his face,
And despair in his glance.
Who will play fair in this game
Of Vision through fog,
Of hope in despair
And courage in fear.
Within, yet without —
Piercing the mask of the fake,
To detect the hope in the lout.

CHAPTER XVI

"YOU SAY IT"

There is nothing whatsoever Christ can do but die a martyr's cruel death. He knows that whatever he will tell them, they won't understand. His language is not their language since they have been confused at Babylon.

Therefore, he is silent or, if an answer is required, he says: "YOU SAY SO."

When the plague asks Christ through the mouth of Judas, who in his heart had already betrayed his idol a hundred times — when it asks him at the last supper in that certain innocent, sneaky voice, "Is it I, Master?", he answers "YOU HAVE SAID SO."

It does not mean *yes* and it does not mean *no*. It keeps us wondering, if we wonder at all and do not put Christ away into a mystical box on the wall which is to comfort us. Christ will repeat these words several times before he dies.

Did Christ himself know why he said these words? Nobody can tell. They make sense only if one hears them telling the plague:

"I did not appoint myself the Son of God. *You* distorted the meaning of what I said and *you* will squeeze it to fit *your* meaning and *your* kind of spirit. *You* say that I am the Son of God.

"God is something else to you than it is to me. To me it is the sweet streaming of love, of all kinds of love, even that in sinners and harlots, in the body and its loins. To you it means the Son of a God in heaven, with a white beard, and a bolt of lightning in his fist to punish poor mankind for its sins. This is the way you will paint God and me sooner or later on canvas.

"In the gospels there will be confusion as to what *I* have said and what *you* have said. And the world will take the words' meaning as YOU say it, not as I. You strive to be as I am. But you will never be as I am unless you feel me in your body."

It is not what Life says or does that smells like rotted corpses. It is the same words, clean and wise and true coming from Life, that are poison in the mouth of the plague-ridden soul. An innocent speech can be intonated and accentuated in such a way that it would spell death to the speaker at any time in any land or nation. A truth can spell disaster for generations if spelled out wrongly in sick minds.

Life will once find words which will be useless in the mouth of the plague, new words for old things and doings, words never defiled by the mud in man's pestilent emotion.

Christ had said that the temple of God could be destroyed and be built up again in three days. In Christ's mouth these words have a deep meaning. It meant that a temple is nothing compared to Life's force in the universe. In the mouth of the plague these words only mean malicious destruction of the temple by a rebel who proclaims himself as the King of the Jews. Christ had nothing to say since he knew his words would not be understood or only misunderstood and misused. Therefore, he was silent.

When the chief priest implored him " by the living God " to tell them whether he was the Son of God, Christ answers, " YOU SAID SO." The high priest understood it in his own way, and not in the way of living Life, and began to tear his robes and to rave about blasphemy.

When two thousand years later, the quacks and fakers in the cancer racket will meet the discoverer of the origin of the cancer scourge, who saw the roots of the scourge as deeper and more difficult to uproot than they, they, who are the promoters of cancer cures, will tell the public that *he* had promised a cancer cure. Just as only an ass can say IJAH, so the plague can say only what it thinks words mean.

And Life is silent against this. It has nothing to say to this.

The high priest had asked Christ whether he was the Son of God. This was his frame of mind, never to be overstepped, dark and tight like a shell.

The traitor Judas had asked Christ whether it was he himself who betrayed Christ. This was *his* frame of mind.

In both cases, Christ had given the same answer: " YOU HAVE SAID IT."

Now, before the governor of Jerusalem, who had only one major worry — whether the Jews would revolt and proclaim a new independent King of the Jews —, Christ again, when asked, " Are you the King of the Jews?," answered, " YOU SAID IT."

You say so, not I, Son of Man. I only use the same words that you are using. But there is no bridge between your meaning and mine.

Within your frame of mind, Judas is a traitor who gave away his beloved master for thirty shillings. This is what *you* would do at any time. In *my* frame of mind, Judas is a traitor *to himself*, to his own beliefs and his soul. He loved me but he did not know what he loved. He admired me, but he admired in me the image he has built himself, the image of a mighty emperor of the poor who rides a fiery white stallion at the head of a column of riders in shining armor toward Jerusalem, the sword drawn and trumpets blasting away. And you wanted to test me, the Christ. *Therefore* you gave the Christ away, and not for thirty shillings. You are far better than the high priest, to whom you delivered your great friend, thinks you are. He calls your money " blood money." It was merely your mask.

Within *your* framework of thinking, I claim to be the " Son of God " sitting at his right side and throwing his lightning out of blackened skies down upon you. In *my* mind, I am the Son of God because we are all sons and children of God, who is Life, who has shaped us all and is in us as he is outside of us, since he is everywhere. I feel God in my body and in my loins. You see him only as an image in heaven. Therefore the words " Son of God " mean such very different things to you and to me.

And you, governor of a mighty Caesar over Jerusalem, conceive of me as a dangerous King of the Jews who will, quite in agreement with Judas' dream, ride out against your soldiers and start killing them off.

Your ideas of empires derive from the dreams of the Judases, in *my* sense not in yours, and the Judases are thriving on the dreams of the Caesars. This is as it should be, and Caesar should get what is coming to him.

I request what is coming to me. But I am outside your domain. Far outside, so far, indeed, that my words are mere distorted echoes in your ears.

Therefore I remain silent when I am caught in your domain, and you wonder why I am silent, as your captive, when asked not to remain silent; they accuse or they defend or they curse themselves, or they bring their own witnesses. My witnesses have all fled; they, too, did not understand.

I have nothing to say to you. You will not grasp my meaning now, as you did not ever grasp it before and will not grasp it in the future. I do not wish to add to the confusion by further talking to you. I have learned my lesson.

You do what you do to me and my words as you do to everything you touch. I know this, and therefore, I have tried to show you the true domicile of God, in the souls of the poor and the sinners and in the loins of men and women who know what the love of the body is, and in women whom you call bad and prostitutes with whom I have associated because they can give the love that you, dried-up Pharisee and scribe, have never had or given or sensed, of the existence of which you have never known.

You say it, not I. I have never said that little children's hands should be bound or smacked for touching the Love of God; and I have never said that there should be no delight when man and woman embrace in God's Love, even in holy matrimony; and I have never poured endless litanies from my mouth; and I have never spoken of angels in heaven or of burning women as witches at the stake because they felt me in their bodies.

All this and much more YOU HAVE SAID AND DONE, NOT I.

Let me be silent and withdraw into the great silence of the Infinite. Let me wait for another child of Life or Son of God who will again try to convey the meaning of my being to you, miserable souls, and who, maybe, will invent a device or find a way to soften your heart and your body to make you feel God in your blood again. Then, maybe, then and no sooner, will my Kingdom, in my meaning, not in yours, come upon this earth. Maybe. . . . Until then, let us pray to keep up the hope to this end:

" Blessed are the poor in spirit, for theirs is the kingdom of heaven.

" Blessed are those who mourn, for they shall be comforted.

" Blessed are the meek, for they shall inherit the earth.

" Blessed are those who hunger and thirst for righteousness, for they shall be satisfied.

" Blessed are the merciful, for they shall obtain mercy.

" Blessed are the pure in heart, for they shall see God.

" Blessed are the peacemakers, for they shall be called sons of God.

" Blessed are those who are persecuted for righteousness' sake, for theirs is the kingdom of heaven.

" Blessed are you when men revile you and persecute you and utter all kinds of evil against you falsely on my account. Rejoice and be glad, for your reward is great in heaven, for so men persecuted the prophets who were before you.

" You are the salt of the earth; but if salt has lost its taste, how can its saltness be restored? It is no longer good for anything except to be thrown out and trodden under foot by men.

" You are the light of the world. A city set on a hill cannot be hid. Nor do men light a lamp and put it under a bushel, but on a stand, and it gives light to all in the house. Let your light so shine before men, that they may see your good works and give glory to your Father who is in heaven."

(*Matthew* 5: 3-16)

CHAPTER XVII

THE SILENT GLOW

THE PEOPLE WANT BARABBAS

It is never rulers who rule people but always people who force rulers to rule people.

It is Pilate who orders the crucifixion of Christ, but it is the people who force him to do so. Pilate understands that the plague has delivered an innocent man to be crucified. He does not believe, from what he sees in front of him, that Christ has had any intention of conquering Caesar. This is what the plague says, and Pilate in accordance with the plague, against his own conviction.

It does not matter in the least whether the historical detail of the account is a true happening or not. It would be true had the human race in a large sector of the world managed to dream up such a tale. The story of Christ remains the true story of man himself even if not a single reported incident ever really happened. Even if Christ had never existed as a man, his tragedy would still be what it is: *The tragedy of Man under the reign of the well-protected Emotional Plague.* Every feature of it would be true even if it were only the dream of one single man, because it happens every single day of every year in daily life.

The agony of frustration of Life is no less real and tantalizing if it occurs in a dream than if it happens in real life.

Therefore all quibblings about whether Christ had lived or not, whether his story is an invention of the early papacy or not, whether he was a mere Jewish rebel or a true Son of God, as " YOU SAY IT," are again no more than another detail in the continued Murder of Christ. It is designed *not* to find the real Christ, *not* to find oneself, one's own evil-doing all through every single day in a lifetime. It is the way of the scribes all over again, no matter what they now say or do. At the very moment they will read this account of the Murder of Christ, they will inevitably again sit together and hatch out a new Murder of Christ, and the people who shouted " HOSANNA IN THE HIGHEST " yesterday will want Barabbas and not Christ freed tomorrow.

The people always want Barabbas, because they fear and refuse to comprehend Christ. They always let Barabbas rule over them. Barabbas knows how to ride a white stallion and how to draw a sword; he knows well how to march past an honor guard and how to smile when he is decorated, a hero of this or that battle. Did you ever see Barabbas decorate a mother for having protected the Love of Life in her child against the four-lettering bastard in the Society for PEACE in the people's democracies? You have not, and you never will see this.

People need, as they are structured, both Barabbas and Christ. Barabbas to ride white stallions at their earthly parades, and Christ to worship in heaven after the killing. This is so because the soul must be fed here and in the hereafter, too. Thus the mystical supplements the mechanistic.

But the eternally living Son of Love will not be permitted to govern their lives unless he adjusts to their ways in the flesh, to the ways of a prostitute whom they then call sinner, for the redemption of which Christ had to die.

Pilate has some hope that the people will see who is the true killer deserving of the cross. He hopes they will see Christ as what he really is: To himself, one who knows Life as it is, and to them, possibly, a dreamer who had committed some foolishness, but innocently so.

Armored people when seeing Christ in the body can only see red. He is what they had lost and were yearning for in agonies all through their lives, and what they must forget, never to see it again. Christ is their lost love and their long forgotten hope. Christ is the stir of sweetness which causes terror in their frozen flesh from which only hate and rage, and not even pity can emerge in the face of the silent, suffering Christ. Therefore, they chose Christ for crucifixion, and not Barabbas.

The tale of the high priests' turning the people against Christ is an invention of the freedom peddler. How could ten priests turn the minds of the multitudes against anything if what *can* be turned against Christ were not within the people.

Stop apologizing for the people and what they do. Before they can ever hope to face Christ squarely, they must first face *themselves* as they truly are and act. Only nuisance freedom peddlers idolize people.

The Love of Life has been forsaken. *Where are Christ's many friends and admirers at that moment?* Not a single friend, not a single admirer is around. Where are the multitudes who shouted " Hosannah in the Highest " to the Son of David, or " See and look; the Son of David is coming." All admirers and Hosanna-in-the-Highest-shouters have disappeared. Not a single " Hosanna " is to be heard when the people choose Barabbas.

What is friendship, what is admiration worth? You can have it for thirty shillings if you are not in the predicament Christ is in right now.

Christ realizes for the first time the gap that separates him from his countrymen and his age.

He takes it calmly. It does not even hurt. His friends have never been true friends. They were friends as long as they could get something from him: thrill, comfort, peace, delight and inspiration. Now, when the emotional plague is howling all around him, they are gone. Not a single one of the leeches is present. Christ does not hate or despise them. He just realizes the true situation, and he is solemnly silent. He looks into a deep, dark abyss where man's sick mind will place the tortured in Hell for centuries to come.

Christ is surrounded by an aura of outer silence and *inner peaceful glow*, as if shielded. Nothing really touches nor can touch him. He is beyond the silly spectacle all around him. Out of his silence creeps pity for the wretches. Are they worth being saved? Certainly not. Yet, he fully lives through what they do to him.

The peaceful, glowing silence in Christ at this moment can be felt by some who are witnessing the ugly turmoil. The wife of Pilate loves Christ; she had dreamed about him and is full of sorrow about his fate. Women always truly loved him. They loved him just as happy women feel for men they love. THEY KNOW. They know such men *in their bodies*. Pilate's wife tries to save him, in vain. She feels the silent, warm glow that is in Christ at this moment. And from such feeling of the silent glow of confidence far beyond men's wretched ugliness, will later arise the silent strength of the early peaceful Christians. It will continue to be felt until the very moment of the writing of these lines: Nothing in this world that is an ugly expression of man's plague can touch this silent, warm inner glow. It is the glow of Life itself.

It is this silent, warm glow which carries Christ through the hours of agony. The world will soon picture him with a glow around his head. He will be silent when pain will make his body twist. He will be silent when exhaustion will overtake him. He will be silent when people will curse and ridicule him, but this will hurt most — from a distance, as it were. At the very end he will question his God.

From the sensing of the silent, warm, inner glowing in the face of danger and ugly happenings and doings, the love for *spirituality* will arise, and a low opinion of the value of the body will prevail. The spirit truly can conquer the body if it is possible that Christ can remain silent and calm and composed and dignified suffering this holocaust of human pestilent dirt. It will continue to exist in the silence of the big cathedrals, in silent monasteries, and it will swing to exuberance and delight in such pure

Life expressions as the music of Bach or in the "Ave Maria," or in the "Song of Joy" in Beethoven's ninth symphony.

The capture by man of this silent, warm glowing within oneself in the middle of ghastly, dirty doings on the part of men who have lost their lives, will be his basic mood when hope or faith will possess his heart. It will be there when a mother looks at her newborn baby for the first time. It will be there when a loving man will calmly wait for the melting into his beloved woman's body. It will be there when Curie will watch the glow of radium for the first time, or when the discoverer of the Life Energy will for the first time see tiny bits of formerly dead rock move with slow undulation.

This silent glow does not scream "Hosanna in the Highest," nor "Heil mein Fuehrer," nor "Red Front," nor does it do any of the many silly, stupid things which the plague does. It is just calmly glowing in the silence of knowledge of the feeling of Life. Whether you call it faith or confidence or self-reliance or bearing or fortitude, it does not matter. From this natural strength of living Life all human ideas of virtue derive. They have nothing whatsoever to do with the later "ethics."

Can you imagine a deer shooting a bullet at its little one? Or torturing another deer? Well, set the mood conveyed by a deer on a meadow, grazing quietly and solemnly in the first gleam of the rising sun, against a picture of "the great father of all the peoples" carried along in big parades of people screaming "down" and "viva," and you feel the essence of the inner calm glow of Life as against the raving plague. By the way, in the beginnings of the great revolutions, when American frontiersmen or Russian workers fought for their very existence, and not for any fuehrers, the same silence pervaded their movements on the streets and in the hills.

This silence, then, was conveyed by Christ to men and women who witnessed the ugly demonstration of the plague. They must have felt pity instead of anger toward the perpetrators of the crime who shouted: "His blood be on us and on our children."

The blood of Christ had been on man and his children long before and long after his crucifixion.

We have no reason to doubt the rationality of the happenings related in the Old as well as the New Testament. These things are true because they represent crucial realities in man's behaviour. But these accounts are rendered useless by the later additions on the part of the scribes and Talmudists in both the Jewish and Christian worlds. The essence of the calm glow expressed in the silence does not prevail against the mystical glorification which is to obfuscate the way Life behaves at the moment of undeserved agony.

Then the soldiers of the governor took Jesus into the praetorium, and they gathered the whole battalion before him. And they stripped him and put a scarlet robe upon him, and plaiting a crown of thorns they put it on his head, and put a reed in his right hand. And kneeling before him they mocked him, saying, " Hail, King of the Jews! " And they spat upon him, and took the reed and struck him on the head. And when they had mocked him, they stripped him of the robe, and put his own clothes on him, and led him away to crucify him.
(*Matthew* 27: 27-31)

The Bible is still being read by the million because it relates what is going on all around us inside man all the time and everywhere. Mechanistic science and rationalistic reasoning have failed to detect these so very crucial things typically human. Therefore, the *science of Man* could not develop, since in the church the glow of bodily love is tabooed as " sin " and in science the feeling that leads to what is called faith is removed as " unscientific." Let's forget the " angels " now. Even our mechanists have already begun to hear the music of the sphere. To them it is only the dry clicking of the Geiger counter in response to cosmic energy, The Creator, God.

The silent, calm glow of living Life cannot ever be destroyed by any means. It is a basic manifestation of the very energy that makes the universe run its course. This glow is in the dark night's sky. It is the silent quiver in the sunlit sky that makes you forget bad jokes. It is the calm glow of the love organs of the glowworms. It hovers over the treetops at dawn and dusk, and it is in the eyes of a trusting child. You can see it in an airtight, evacuated glass tube charged from the air with life energy, and you can see it in the expression of gratitude in the face when you relieve sorrow in man ill with the emotional plague. It is the same glow which you see at night on the surface of the ocean or at the tops of high masts.

Nothing whatsoever can destroy this glowing, silent force. It penetrates everything and governs every move in every cell in the living organism. It is everywhere and fills all space, which was emptied by empty man. It causes the glowing of the stars as well as their twinkling. This glow in the feel of the skin is to the true physician a sign of the health of a human being, just as its absence is a sign to him of the presence of sickness. In fever, this glow grows fierce since it fights the deadly infection.

It is the glowing of the Life force which continues after the death of the body. It is the glow of the soul, but *it does not persist after death as a shaped form. It dissipates back into the infinite cosmic ocean, the " Kingdom of God," from where it came.*

This ocean of the primordial energy of the universe is the source of the single eruptions into single living lives; therefore, rightly, men from time immemorial have called it their " GOD " or " FATHER IN HEAVEN " or " CREATOR " or one of many other names. The knowledge of this universal *Life force* and its background of endless heavens full of it, is indestructible in man since he *feels* it. This is the basis of all his notions of heavenly virtue and basic emotional cleanliness and angel-like patience and endless love and endurance and fortitude and diligence and thriftiness and all the other virtues which were set up by all religions alike as eternal ideals for mankind, ever since man lost contact with the inner glow due to the desecration of bodily love. It has remained to this day the essence of all cosmic longing in mankind. It is even active, as murderous fury, in the pestilent killer of *Life*.

It is this glow which, in the feeling of mankind, unites Christ during his last agony with the great universe. Now, let us forget the angels once more. They are results of the ways the Little Man understands the existence of God's kingdom when he feels no glowing any longer within himself and still knows it is there, around, somewhere.

It is this glow which is foreign to the brutal usurper of earthly power over men. Men of power are hard men, men without love, nor desirous of the softness of great strength. The strength of Christ in his last hours is so very much different from the strength of a Nero. They are two entirely different, even contradictory kinds of strength. This will be important when men will have to start overcoming the chronic Murder of Christ.

Christ is helpless during the scourging and he transmits to posterity the basic sense of passive endurance and martyrdom. The glow of Life within Christ, however, which makes his endurance and suffering the basis of a great religion, will surpass the phase of passive endurance. It will bring down heaven upon earth, in the sense of Christ, by conquering the cunning, sneaking malignancy which makes the work of cruelty possible.

The Christian world knows nothing about the ACTIVITY of the glow of Life. Moreover, Christianity, which was to preserve the glow in its music and its solemn churches, shut the access to its domain by killing this glow early in the life of every single human child. Thus it undermined its own foundation. It is this impediment of the glow of *Life* which makes possible such horrid scenes as the coronation of Christ with a crown of thorns as the symbol of the " King of the Jews." It is perfectly clear that nothing ever will or can change in man's existence unless the spirit that governs the scene of crowning Christ with a crown of thorns will vanish from the hearts of men. It is the killing of the glow of Life in the newborn infants which is at the very basis of the crowning of Christ's head with a crown of thorns, and of the ridicule heaped upon him in such a ghastly manner. The Little Man is still doing all these things to this very day everywhere, whether it be in a Siberian camp or some Psychiatric State Hospital in the USA.

Chapter XVIII

CRUCIFIXION AND RESURRECTION

The leader, the governor, the king, the fuehrer — is an expression and tool of people's ways of life. *One* Ivan the Horrible cannot make into passive creatures two hundred million peasants, but the appropriate number of peasant mothers can. And these two hundred million silent, enduring peasants can make the reign of Ivan the Horrible last.

Pilate can do nothing against the people's will which wants Barabbas freed and Christ crucified. They choose Barabbas because he agrees with their way of being and thinking, and Christ does not. And they would turn Christ, if they chose him, fast into another Barabbas, if he would let them. Or they would kill him. They certainly would kill Barabbas, too, if he did not satisfy their hunger for the sight of Kings of Jerusalem riding white stallions with swords drawn against the eternal enemy, and they would soon choose another Barabbas, and not Christ. This man has done now for some six thousand years, as far as our knowledge goes, to this very day, and his dream of the Kingdom of Heaven was just as long put away into a mirror with an image safe enough never to be reached.

This dichotomy in men's being which has existed for such a long period of time is so obvious that there is some hope that it will sooner or later be mentioned at some international congress of mental hygiene or even in some European sociological or ethnological journal.

Unless the barabbasic inclinations and redeemer-longings of people at large will be grasped and managed by the people themselves very soon, there will be many more Barabbases and murdered Christs. This much is certain. There can, in fact, be no doubt about it, and nobody should try to fool himself out of it or to permit himself to be talked out of it by some freedom peddler. The situation has become extremely serious, and it is high time to get going and to stop pretending that one does not really know what one knows so clearly and sees so penetratingly all around oneself.

At Golgatha, the basic split in people's actions once more emerges with all its ghastly cruelty, though one might have had enough of it in Jerusalem and whatever had led up to it. When the people clamor for Christ's crucifixion (and we have no reason whatsoever to doubt the truth in the account of the gospels, *since the very same thing is and has been going on for ages all around us),* Pilate is stunned and asks, " What wrong has he done? " Pilate does not understand. It is exactly the fact that Christ has *not* done any wrong but *only good* to the people — *it is this very fact which will cause him to be manhandled worse than a common thief.*

In order to outscream one's feeling of rottenness in sending Christ to be nailed to the cross, one MUST, *one cannot do otherwise* than heap all the humiliation one can possibly muster, upon the victim of one's own devilish procedure. The screaming rottenness has to be outscreamed by defilement of the victim. This is exactly the way the plague works and has worked since it began to ravage mankind. Not to be aware of it is another characteristic of the procedures of the plague and its popular protectors.

Christ carries his cross silently up to Calvary. He breaks down in silence, and he remains silent when Simon helps to carry the cross. Silently he reaches Golgatha, the place of the execution. Silently he suffers the full dose of man's cruelty.

This cruelty is well calculated to add as much agony as possible to the already unbearable suffering of the victim: The cross is not ready-made for use when Christ arrives at the place of the execution. It is put together in his presence. Nails are driven into live hands which had so often caressed and smoothed the sick and suffering. Nails are driven into the live feet which had so many times walked over God's fields and meadows and through the brooks. A support for the body made of a piece of wood was placed between the legs.

Christ is fully aware of what is going on. His silence is his only weapon that sustains his courage to the last. He suffers burning thirst, and he asks for a drink. One soldier dips a sponge into his posca drink, fixes it to the end of a reed and puts it to the lips of Christ, who according to one account, sucked it.

Out of his far distant reaches, Christ lives through both the horror suffered by his body and the horror of seeing man act like this, able to act like this, not being aware of what they were doing; of man as a tool of a justice machinery, the gleam of pity gone from his heart or drowned in a feeling of performance of duty, or simply in a deadly insensitivity. These men have nothing whatsoever to do with Christ or with his beliefs or his Kingdom. They are just machines and no more, the essence of mechanized government that forgets man in whose behalf government should be. It IS. Man is the way such government is, otherwise it could not be at all. It is man who creates his government, and his government only maintains what man permits it to maintain.

They put a writing at the top of the cross, bearing in three languages, Hebrew, Greek and Latin, the words " THE KING OF THE JEWS." The dream of the people about what Christ *ought* to have been prevails. Christ's own world is *beyond* the cross. "FATHER, FORGIVE THEM: FOR THEY KNOW NOT WHAT THEY DO." They really do not know what they are doing, at Golgatha or at Belsen or at any Russian prisoners' camp; they *never* know. *This is their priceless hideout!* This innocence must be unmasked: IT IS TIME TO START KNOWING WHAT YOU ARE DOING, COMMON MAN IN THE STREET. Your innocence no longer suffices to excuse you from your guilt of such crimes. You will not hide much longer behind your innocence. You will start knowing what you are doing when you murder Christ.

No admirer or disciple is present at or near the cross. John claims to have been present. This appears doubtful to some inquirers of the gospels. However, the belief seems to prevail that Christ's devoted women were present: Mary Cleophas, Mary Magdalene, Joanna wife of Chuza, Salome, and others according to Renan's compilation, were there and remained there to the very end. Also, Christ's mother was present at the cross.

It is self-evident that the women who had loved Christ *in the body*, and not his admirers and disciples who had only sucked Life from his body, should be present at his last agony. Accordingly, the women will recede into the background when man will take over Christ's tragedy for the purpose of deification, and the absent disciples will be put in the foremost foreground. The fight among the disciples for occupation of the first rank in the order of their closeness to Christ had already begun in Christ's early wanderings, and will continue at a faster pace after his death. There will be certain leading apostles and other less prominent ones. There will be an Ivan the Horrible to make an earthly power out of Christ's Kingdom, and there will be a Francis D'Assissi who will desperately try to return to Christ's Kingdom. There will be among Christ's future representatives those who were chosen by the people to succeed him because they behaved in a very standoffish, highbrow manner. There will be those who will be chosen because they will excel in display of eye-stirring pageantry. There will be those who will be chosen because they will be excellent diplomats and masters of intrigue. There will be those chosen because of their great statesmanship, and those chosen because of their skill in inquisitive, cruel execution of Christ's commands. And there will be those who will be chosen who will be great warriors to carry the sign of the cross to distant pagan countries, though to convert by force to his belief Christ would not and could not ever have consented. Man, and not Christ, will in the end prevail.

But there will be no trace of the very essence of Christ's life, of the women who had loved Christ's body. A lonely, persecuted writer will, two thousand years later, understand this deepest secret and write a little book, "The Man Who Died," which will present Christ in a truer, more Christlike light. Accordingly, this book will not be as widely known as Paul's interpretation of the Kingdom of Heaven and the sin of the flesh.

Christ's women, who knew and loved his body, were present to the last and took him down from the cross later. It was a woman who sat by the tomb and found it empty, a finding from which the whole mythology of Christ's ascent to heaven arises.

Christ said the Kingdom of Heaven shall be compared to ten maidens who meet their lovers.

Then the kingdom of heaven shall be compared to ten maidens who took their lamps and went to meet the bridegroom. Five of them were foolish, and five were wise. So when the foolish took their lamps, they took no oil with them; but the wise took flasks of oil with their lamps. As the bridegroom was delayed, they all slumbered and slept. But at midnight there was a cry, "Behold, the bridegroom! Come to meet him." Then all those maidens rose and trimmed their lamps. And the foolish said to the wise, "Give us some of your oil, for our lamps are going out." But the wise replied, "Perhaps there will not be enough for us and for you; go rather to the dealers and buy for yourselves." And while they went to buy, the bridegroom came, and those who were ready went in with him to the marriage feast; and the door was shut. Afterward the other maidens came also, saying, "Lord, Lord, open to us." But he replied, "Truly, I say to you, I do not know you." Watch therefore, for you know neither the day nor the hour.

(*Matthew* 25: 1-13)

Christ knew well the difference between women who gave their sweetness in the embrace and women who had lost their sweetness and dried up in their love organs and therefore cried, "Lord, Lord, open to us!"

The silent presence of women who had loved Christ in the body at one time or another of his earthly life, each one of them in her special way of love and caress, point to the true reason for the defilement of Christ during his last hours.

There is only one single crime that is met and punished by pestilent men in such a vile, ugly, stupid, pernicious way: THE CRIME OF GOD'S TRUE BODILY LOVE. This is the sole comprehensible explanation for the outrage. It is in full agreement with what is known today about the emotional plague, its reasons for existence, its hidden motives of cruelty, its ardor in persecuting true, bodily love as God's creatures live it. Accordingly, except for close hints in books on Christ, such as Renan's or Lawrence's, there is no mention of it anywhere. How could it be mentioned in the books of the Christian church if it is not mentioned, concerning our adolescents, in any book of psychiatry, not even in psychoanalysis. *How could it?* It is too obvious to be mentioned anywhere.

DON'T TOUCH IT! It could reveal Christ's meaning and with it the meaning he acquired for humanity. It could reveal the meaning of many Christs who have died for living Life through the ages, at the cross, at the stake, in the lunatic asylums now as long ago, in the hospitals as those sick from rheumatic fever, infantile paralysis, leukemia, anemia in puberty, cancer of the womb, of the breasts, of the genitals, and from here, of all kinds of organs; as schizophrenia, phobia, nightmares of all kinds; as murder and rape and addiction to dulling drugs; as marital agony, as marital rape protected by an evil ancient law, as marriage divorce racketeering, as suicides in silent drops from high buildings to hard, head-smashing pavements; as agonies of a horribly silent kind and of many other kinds of suffering.

DO NOT EVER TOUCH IT! ! !

This agony cannot be talked about in academic words. The scribes do not let it be discussed. It has to be smashed through in flaming words no matter what the scribes say. THEY MUST FINALLY BE MADE TO LET OTHERS TOUCH IT.

They do not dare to touch it because they never dared to feel their bodies and to touch their genitals. The parents had punished it, the schools had excluded you for it, the church had declared it sinful, and the congresses of mental hygiene had banned it completely from public discussion.

It will not stop ringing in man's ears, as it never stopped emaciating his secret soul, as long as man is born by and will live with genitals.

Nothing whatsoever in this world, no power will ever be strong enough to eradicate this fact which is in exact agreement with the secret of the continued Murder of Christ.

Christ was killed in such a shabby way and he was defiled by a sick and sickening crowd because he dared to love with his body and did not sin in the flesh.

Christ was tortured because they had to destroy his truly godly, i.e., orgonotic way of life, strange and dangerous to them.

They mocked him and laughed at him and threw ugly words at him because they could not suffer to be reminded of godly life within themselves.

Even the two thieves at their crosses nearby mocked Christ. In this account, whether historically true or not, the Christian legend has grasped an awful truth: "A thief is preferable to a godlike lover of women." In the American South, they do not tar and feather Negroes for theft, but for "rape of white women."

Frozen white men cannot bear to have their women feel the warm bodies of strong black men. From this all race hatred of white men primarily derives.

The young, lively, beautiful, attractive Jesus Christ was killed because he was loved by women the way a scribe never could have been loved; he was killed because he was built and alive in a manner no Talmudic priest could ever suffer to continue to live. And the Talmudists in later temples of creed as well as knowledge did not suffer even the mention of this very core of the secret of the murder of Christ. Renan was excluded from the French Academy for coming closest to it. What will they do to the present true account of Christ's secret?

Renan writes from sources of the Talmud:

> The invincible obstacle to the ideas of Jesus came especially from orthodox Judaism, represented by the Pharisees. Jesus became more and more alienated from the ancient law. Now, the Pharisees were the true Jews; the nerve and sinew of Judaism. . . They were, in general, men of a narrow mind, caring much for externals; their devoutness was haughty, formal, and self-satisfied. Their manners were ridiculous and excited the smiles of even those who respected them. The epithets which the people gave them, and which savor of caricature, prove this. There was the "bandy-legged Pharisee" (Nikfi), who walked in the streets dragging his feet and knocking them against the stones; the "bloody-browed Pharisee" (Kizai), who went with his eyes shut in order not to see the women, and dashed his head so much against the walls that it was always bloody; the "pestle Pharisee" (Medinkia), who kept himself bent double like the handle of a pestle; the "Pharisee of strong shoulders" (Shikmi), who walked with his back bent as if he carried on his shoulders the whole burden of the Law; the "What-is-there-to-do?-I-do-it Pharisee," always on the search for a precept to fulfil; and, lastly, the "dyed Pharisee," whose externals of devotion were but a varnish of hypocrisy.[1] This strictness was in fact often only apparent, and concealed in reality great moral laxity. (Ernest Renan in THE LIFE OF JESUS, Modern Library Edition, 1927, pp. 299-300.)

---

[1] Talmud of Jerusalem, Berakoth, ix., sub fin.; Sota, v. 7; Talmud of Babylon, Sota, 22b. The two compilations of this curious passage present considerable differences. We have, in general, followed the Babylonian compilation, which seems most natural. Cf. Epiph., Adv. Harr., xvi. 1. The passages in Epiphanes, and several of those in the Talmud, may, besides, relate to an epoch posterior to Jesus, an epoch in which "Pharisee" had become synonymous with "devotee." — Ibid, p. 300.

The Talmudists seek God by killing him; they kill him the way they are searching for him, *by tests of torture.* God is treated like the prince who must go through all kinds of cruel tests of his endurance and strength to prove that he deserves being the king of his people. This is the way the people dream and think about their kings. If a three-year-old Jewish boy cannot endure sitting it out in school before the Talmud from six in the morning to ten at night seeking the meaning of God in the point of the " i," he is no good Jew, no son of Abraham who was the father of the people of God. And children must behave well, be good toward father and mother, obey them, no matter what they do to them or demand of them; children of God must not doubt their forefathers' words and must not challenge their beliefs lest they be punished by death. And they must not behave badly nor violate the good morals of their forefathers who consumed love as mating guaranteed to them by Law, forcing the wives to gratify them.

The hatred stemming from lawfully guaranteed love given by revolting bodies, violated by the absence of God's streaming in the limbs, knows no limitations in killing living Life, which needs love as it was given to all creatures alike. This hatred deriving from Godless mating, bare of sweetness, makes the Love of God lawless and ugly. It roams the streets at night in dirty rags, or sneaks from corner to corner like a thief. The outlawed love of God must keep its ears sharply pointed while it drinks from the well of its being; it must be on the alert all the while; the bloodhounds are roaming around the countryside to capture it in *flagrante delicto*. The bloodhounds are directed by the scent of warm, healthy blood, the smell of which sets evil men to murdering Christ. These men who send the bloodhounds on the track of their prey have lips like paper edges and little eyes gleaming with cruel darkness; their faces are tight like drums, the skin shrivelled into dried-up folds like ancient leather. The noses are pointed and the tongues speak only poisonous words. In their hands is a rope with a knot at the end of the sling, or a gun ready to shoot Life drinking its sap from the well of Love.

Christ had drunk the sap of Love from the well of Life according to its own law. A great courtesan had turned toward saintly living, and maidens were turned away from the godless ways of loving. They, too, learned to drink from the wells of a living God of Love, first fighters on the road toward the very origins of Man in God's infinities, the first to feel again in their bodies what paradise was like:

ONCE UPON A TIME

Mothers were sitting at water springs,
dancing, singing,
gently caressing their children,
guiding them into the currents of Life. . . .
Ocean waves gently rushed
at beaches of a peaceful world. . . .

Men and women drank the joy of Living
from the movements of their limbs
and their melodies into the eternities.
Children's laughter sounded
in exuberance of voices
filled with gayety and delight.
Joyful glances in young men's eyes,
regleamed in smiling faces
of maidens gay with love
and drunk with youth
in tender bodies.
Suddenly . . . . a howling . . . .
What a jowling!
Never heard and never felt before,
uninvited, perpetrated. . . .
It was the plague that penetrated:
Stiffened faces,
Falsehood's grinning,
Tired arms and deadened loins,
Weeping cheeks and dulled-out gazing,
Hardened backs, polite in bowing;
Bodies bare of love,
Wanting bare of will,
Longing bare of sensing,
Fighting bare of victories,
Martyrdom of marriage torture. . . .
Moaning, Groaning,
Children's screaming, agonies. . . .
Murder, misery and crooked thinking. . . .
Cowards' gallows and parades,
Marching, medals, rotting corpses;
What a scrambling idiocy,
hunting, tripping, nightmare fooling. . . .
Woe to Men
a million fold. . . .

Christ had drunk from the wells of Life. His world was, he told the
ruler, not of this world of rule and power. It was the world of God, long
past for Man, yet expected to return. It was the world of Love in the
limbs, and there is nothing that could replace it.

And Man always had known that Love in his limbs, the sweetness of melting delight, was truly his God, named by various names and worshipped in many lands in various temples in many tongues. But Man kept silent about the truth he knew, and still he keeps silent like Christ from Bethany to Golgatha. There is no ear nor sense nor feeling for God in this world full of the noise of quarrel and war and beating and gulping and wallowing and four-lettering and cheating and Talmudizing, which, altogether, is to outscream gentle stirrings of Love in the loins and the limbs.

And therefore, they manhandled Christ when he hung at the cross.

Imputing to Christ their own vicious thoughts he never dreamed of or meant in the way they said it, they soiled his honor and grace, the appearance of which they could never bear to see. They needled: " Ah, You who would destroy the temple and build it in three days, save yourself and come down from the cross," and: " He saved others; he cannot save himself."

Christ had never claimed that he could save others. It was his admirers who had invented this. He had never said that HE would destroy the temple. He only said the temples would be destroyed, as it truly happened some years later. It is as if a writer in this age of ours, for having predicted the Third World War in one generation, would be defiled by the false accusation of having proclaimed himself as the *cause* of the Third World War.

They had, incited by his disciples, in secret expected the very miracle to happen for which they later nailed him to the cross; in secret they had wished that Christ would really be what THEY claimed him to represent. They reeled in disappointment, for Christ did nothing of the kind. Accordingly, now, when he hung on the cross, they jibed at him: " Let the Christ, the King of the Jews, come down now from the cross, that we may see and believe."

Thus they had cooked up the miracle expectation they had nurtured all the while; they had persecuted and accused Christ for their own invention; they had put Christ to the cross for their own ghastly dreams of power and might and sorcery and traumathurgy and healing the impossible, and having delight poured down their throats into deadened guts and genitals with no effort on their part at all, and for their expectation of his bringing down heaven to earth for them for sheer amusement, and bringing a paradise where surely honey and milk would flow in rivers, and where there would be no need to think or to worry, to care for the sick and to love one's children with God's love and to build up one's life and to tend the gardens and bring in the fruit and to sweat it out. . . . . This is THE SIN.

Poor soul of Jesus Christ. . . . How trustingly and lovingly he had gone into the ghastly trap set by evil, empty, cruel, godforsaken men. These living corpses, carrying within themselves a last little gleam of a lovely memory of a lost paradise forfeited by themselves, had to have their way to the last drop of Christ's agony. They even saw darkness settle over the land from the sixth to the ninth hour of Christ's suffering. And they did not cease to mix their filth of defilement with their drinking of hope from Christ on the cross in front of their eyes; they did not for a second stop sucking Christ's rich soul to fill the empty bags of their dried-up carcasses, still clinging to the last vestige of a hope that they had nailed to the cross a *true* God and a *true* Messiah.

Christ, at last realizing fully, as the final few breaths were passing through his lungs, what had happened to him, what a nightmare of a dirty game had been played upon his whole life by a worthless, godless, forsaken generation of vipers and vermin, feels that even his own holy God must have gone back on him. He screams in agony:

"E'lo-i, E'lo-i, La'ma Sa-bach-tha'ni?" "My God, My God, why hast thou forsaken me?"

What a nightmare. . . . . .

And over thousands of years the offspring of these vipers, surrounding and passing by the cross, will study, investigate, digest, reproduce, Talmudize, exorcise, embellish and embalm the story of Christ, but the gist of his meaning will slip through their fingers and brains unnoticed lest they hang themselves from the trees of the closest forest.

THEY MURDER AND DEFILE CHRIST TO FIND OUT WHETHER, POSSIBLY, IN THE END, HE WILL STILL TURN OUT TO BE A TRUE, GOD-SENT MESSIAH WHO CAN SAVE HIMSELF.

When they hear his last words, they drivel: "Behold, he is calling Elijah," the prophet. He MUST, he cannot, dare not fail, being a holy, god-sent Son of Israel.

Christ can not, dare not do such a thing to them. They are very "sensitive," very "delicate" in their feelings about their own dreams. They cannot possibly be left hanging in the air, holding the bag. Christ *must*, in this very last minute of agony, do *something* for them, thrill them, give them another dose of hope in the existence of Messiahs and redeemers and holy men, eager to die for *their* sins, of martyrs bleeding to death to pour some meaning into *their* dried-up lives. Christ can not do this to them! He must not simply die like any other Son of Man they have murdered before for this or that law of theirs. He cannot, must not, dare not, the scoundrel!

They have no souls. They worship to get. The feeling of love has gone out of them, forever and ever. Therefore, Christ can not do that to them. And they tried to prolong his life to force their ugly dream to come true. One among them, out of pity or out of cruel desire to prolong the agony, filled a sponge full of vinegar, put it on a reed and gave it to Christ to drink. The others among them, more in line with their whole being, not caring about even the appearance of pity, tell him:

"WAIT, LET US SEE WHETHER ELIJAH WILL COME TO TAKE HIM DOWN. . . . . . ."

Thereupon Jesus Christ uttered a loud cry and gave up his soul.

The beasts continued to abuse Christ after his death. They dreamed up the tale that the curtain in the temple was torn in two, from top to bottom, when Christ gave up his soul. It is still possible that somebody, in agony about Christ's fate, actually tore up the curtain to show the Pharisees a last sign of protest over the crime.

"And when the centurion, who stood facing him, saw that he had thus breathed his last, he said, 'Truly this man was a son of God.'"

Why, you son of the Devil, did you not see this in time to run to your governor to rescue Christ? For this you and your kind will die on the battlefields in many lands through many ages with no hope whatsoever for an end of the slaughter, you will keep dying for your cowardice in the face of dying Life, defiled by your own kind.

For all the evil you do to living, kind Life, you will wander about this earth, patting your neighbors' backs for *fear* of them; you will gather your kind in "social parties" with loud, empty laughter and glasses of brandy in your hands to dull the pain of your souls; you will kneel in churches and beat your breasts in synagogues for ages without end or hope except the new hopes you will suck from the rich souls of new Christs; you will run after happiness like the hound on the race track runs, panting, with tongue dry and hanging from your jaws, after a make-believe rabbit which will always be exactly the same little, unsurpassable stretch ahead of you.

You will hunt and crucify other scapegoats for your sins that you will never, never get rid of unless you start seeing why and how you murder Christ all through the ages. There is no way for you other than this one.

You will start, finally, to stop murdering LIFE. The Murder of Christ will be ended, and dark night will fall upon your whole past existence.

Christ has conquered you in a way you never suspected to be possible. He died, not to free you from sins, but to show you up in the full, glaring light for what you really are. It does not matter that it took so long to recognize this true meaning of the Murder of Christ which you have tried so very hard to hide from Men's minds.

Christ's agony is your own, both the active and the passive way.

You are hanging at the cross, dying a death of agonies a million times, in vain, for nothing, cheated out of your possibilities and great dreams of a higher, cleaner destiny.

You will awaken to this reality, sooner or later, and you will scream Christ's last scream, this is quite sure. It will happen sooner or later. And you will stop murdering, torturing, Talmudizing, framing, lying, spying, politicking and pretending you do not know a thing about it all, you innocent son and daughter of the devil.

You carry Christ right there within you, *and you know it*. You may succeed in hiding and killing him again and again within yourself and within your children for quite some time to come. But finally you will start talking Christ's language and shiver in learning to live his way of Life.

Your belief in the *resurrection* of Christ is *true:* Living Life remained *unthwarted* and walked on this earth clean, without sin, without dirt of the soul, for thirty-three years until it ended on the cross. But, being Life, it did not really die. Life can not be killed, ever. It hung from the cross bleeding in agony from many wounds, but it is truly invincible. Having expired in one body, it will certainly return in another body. It will bleed again and again for ages at the hands of thwarted, hardened, armored life which can not feel sweetness in the limbs or bear the look in the eyes of a deer on a sunlit meadow, without shooting or knifing or choking to death the reminder of its lost paradise. Still, in the end, Life will resurrect and conquer the evil, sinful devil which is the Life force gone stale in the body.

Christ, who is Life in this true sense, is being born in every one of the fibers and cells of every child, in every generation, in every single nation on earth, irrevocably, irresistibly, due to the lust in your loins which one day will be the *Love of God* again. And wise men with flaming words will keep watch to drive the Hell of your miserable Little Men out of your paradise.

PRAYER

OH, LIFE ETERNAL . . .
WITH THE BEING OF THE STARS —
FOREGO THY MERCY WITH THY KILLER . . .
SPEND THY LOVE ON THE NEWLY BORN
OF MAN AND ANIMAL AND PLANT . . .
RETURN MAN HOME IN THY PEACEFUL GARDENS.
LET, LIFE, THY GRACE ONCE MORE
POUR OVER THE FORSAKEN SOULS . . .
FULFILL THY TOWERING POWER.

End

ON LAWS NEEDED FOR THE PROTECTION OF LIFE IN NEWBORNS AND OF TRUTH

A careful study of the realm of social pathology reveals the fact that there exists no law in the USA *which would directly protect factual truth against underhanded lie and attack* motivated by irrational interests. *Truth is at present at the mercy of chance. It depends entirely on whether a law officer is personally honest or dishonest, emotionally rational or irrational, subjectively inclined toward or against factual functions. It is most difficult to operate as a pioneer in new fields of human endeavor, if any emotionally sick individual anywhere on the social scene can — unhampered — destroy work or knowledge he dislikes, and if truth is in no position to defend itself against underhanded attack. It is obvious that the future of the* USA *and the world at large depends on the rational upbringing of the newborns in each generation which will enable them to make rational decisions as grown-ups. (See Wilhelm Reich: Children of the Future, OEB, October, 1951). There do not exist any laws as yet to protect newborns against harm inflicted upon them by emotionally sick mothers and other sick individuals. However, there are many old laws rendered obsolete long ago by progress in the understanding of the biology of man, which threaten progressive educators with extinction if they transgress* technically *these old laws. These facts, together with the operation on the social scene of emotionally sick individuals, block progress and the search for better ways in medicine and education. Although laws which are serving the welfare of people at large can never accomplish factual changes, life affirmative laws can protect those who strive practically for betterment of the fate of humanity. Therefore, two laws, one to protect* LIFE IN NEWBORNS, *and a second to protect* TRUTH *against underhanded attacks (beyond the scope of libel laws which are not suited for this purpose), should be studied and formulated by legislatures, institutions of learning and foundations whose work is primarily devoted to securing human welfare and happiness.*

To illustrate: Truthful and thorough investigation of natural love life in children and adolescents, one of the most crucial tasks in present day mental hygiene, is held up and rendered helpless by the single fact that any biopathic individual who himself has been emotionally warped in childhood or adolescence through frustration of his needs for love, is in a position to put in a complaint to an Attorney General's Office to the effect that those who investigate the subject of love life in childhood and adolescence, and make certain suggestions as to its solution, are committing a crime, the crime of "seduction of minors." If the attorney happens to agree emotionally with the complainant, the investigation of fact is completely at the mercy of chance. There exists, according to rich experience in actual situations, no provision on the statute books to prosecute the biopathic individual on the basis that his motivation is not truth-seeking, or helping children or adolescents, but only hate of such scientific procedures. The motivation of an accusation should always be taken into consideration, just as the motive for a murder is taken into consideration.

This example must suffice to illustrate the situation. The Archives of the Orgone Institute contain enough factual evidence to prove that the situation is bad indeed where pioneering efforts are burdened with the rather hopeless struggle with such irrationalism in addition to the factual difficulties entailed in the pioneering job.

[This is the text of a proposal made to the Congress of the USA in November, 1952 by THE WILHELM REICH FOUNDATION.]

APPENDIX

THE WEAPON OF TRUTH

The Lesson of THE MURDER OF CHRIST applied to the
Social Scene of the American Period (1940-1952)

CONTENTS

THE BIO-ENERGETIC MEANING OF TRUTH

Truth is full, immediate contact between the Living that perceives and Life that is perceived. The truthful experience is the fuller the better the contact. Truth is the more comprehensive the better coordinated are the functions of living perception. And the living perception is coordinated exactly to the extent of the coordination of the motion of the living protoplasm. *Thus truth is a natural function in the interplay between the Living and that which is lived.*

Truth, basically, is not, as many believe, an ethical ideal. It became an ethical ideal when it was lost with the loss of " paradise," i.e., the loss of the full functioning of the Living in Man. Then truth was suppressed and the ideal mirror image of truth seeking appeared. Neither is truth something to be striven for. You do not strive to make your heart beat or your legs move, and you do not, by the same token, " strive " for or seek truth. Truth is in you and works in you just as your heart or your eyes work, well or badly, according to the condition of your organism.

The Living, in its constant interplay with its environment, *lives* truth fully to the degree in which it is in contact with its own needs or, which means the same, with the influencing of the environment to satisfy the natural needs. The cave man, in order to survive, had to know the ways of the wild animals, i.e., he had to know the truth about their manner of living and acting. The modern flier, in order to arrive safely at his destination, must be in full contact with and fully reactive to every gust of wind, to the slightest change in the balance of his plane, to the clarity of his own senses and to the movements of his body. He flies truthfully. The slightest blurring of his sensory reaction to his inner and outer environment would kill him. Thus he lives truthfully when he manages the elements and survives. Yet, he does not " search " or " strive " for truth while flying.

Truth, therefore, is a natural function, just as is walking or running or hunting the bear by the Eskimo or finding the tracks of the enemy by the Indian. It is, within the framework of the totality of natural functioning, an integral part of the organism and it depends on the integrity as well as integration of all the senses. *The first,* ORGONOTIC *sense must be intact.* Truth, no matter in what realm of life or whatever its scope, is thus a tool of the Living, in line with all other tools that are given or shaped by the senses and the organismic motility. The use of the weapon of truth is, therefore, the use of the fullest possible contact with all situations of life, the sensing, the knowing, the contacting and the influencing of everything within and without. Therefore, truth is a function most akin to growth, since development is reaction of expansion and variation to various outer and inner stimuli. Only the truthful organism can grow experientially, and the organism that cannot grow is not truthful, i.e., not in accord with its own bio-energetic necessities. It remains sitting on the spot.

There are certain truths which are *a priori* given by one's senses and movements. That Life, Living, is constant MOTION, is such a self-evident truth itself. That Love is the merger of two organisms, is another such truth, self-evident from the sense of longing for merger, actual merging and loosing one's circumscribed individual identity during the embrace. That there exists something very alive and emotionally enlivening and vibrating and life-giving in the atmosphere around us, is another such self-evident truth, no matter whether it is called God or the Universal Spirit or the Great Father or the Kingdom of Heaven or Orgone Energy. This experience is common to all men and indelible. It is far older and more persistent than any other, less comprehensive perception of one's being. Watch a cocker-spaniel deliver and care for its puppies, and you know what is meant here, *what naturally given truth is*. Truth is not something to be learned or imparted to the organism. It is born as a crucial function within the organism and it develops as long as the organism maintains its unitary functioning, which means full orgonotic sensing.

With the loss of paradise, that is, with the loss of living Life, with the exclusion of crucial functions from man's senses, such as the genital embrace according to natural needs, the " TRUTH SEEKER " broke into this world of a ravaged humanity. What is called " Sin " by the Christian world, " Sabotage " by the Red Fascists, " Ignorance " by the scientist is the expression of the loss of the full orgonotic contact with one's life; accordingly, *substitute, false, inadequate contacts* had to develop to maintain life, as if on crutches. (About " *contactlessness* " see CHARACTER ANALYSIS, 3rd ed., 1948.) And this is the plague at its inception. With the sin the prophet came about, with sickness, the medicine man. And among them there was rarely, very rarely, a Christ who dared to touch upon reality fully, without restriction, still here and there being bound down by the apron-strings of his time, his culture or his people's customs.

It is so very significant for the understanding of the emotional plague that the searching for truth becomes the more artificial and futile the closer what it searches for is to the genital emotions of mankind. Because Christ had touched exactly upon man's loss of living Life within himself, which is, ultimately, the loss of his genital functioning replaced by the dry, empty, frustrating 4-lettering, pushing desperately toward the lost paradise, his truth was deep, of cosmic dimensions, and it won a great part of the world — and was distorted *worst* of all, the distortion centering upon the " Sin of the Flesh." With the seeking of the truth, instead of the living of the truth, the EVASION OF TRUTH became the inseparable companion of truth-seeking. Evasion of truth, not truth-seeking has prevailed so far.

This is easily understandable. Truth, as a manifestation of Life's fullest contact with itself and its environment, is inextricably bound up with Life's energy economy. Truth, accordingly, if lived fully, stirs up the deepest emotions, and with the deepest emotions it stirs to high activity the urge for the genital embrace. *Since, now, the core of the energy release of the Living has been excluded and ostracized by men for ages, truth needs must be evaded, too.* Every movement toward truth inevitably brought man closer to the lost function. It is, therefore, no wonder that every truth-seeker was accused of " immorality " at all times and in all cultures built on genital suppression, and that the reactionary mind always fought truth as the way of the devil toward " immorality."

The more genitality is excluded from man's senses and activities, the harder the fight against the truth, the more complete is the transformation of a *biological* truth into a *mystical* " truth." The Christian religion is a *mystified* religion of the Living, directed against the very reality of what it represents and adores as an ideal. All lost *actual* virtues of nature reappear as *ideal* virtues, to be striven after. With this the dichotomy between the devil, who is a perverted God, and the realm of ethics is ever being born.

The EVASION OF THE TRUTH, so characteristic of man who lost paradise, i.e., who lost the feeling of God in his body, has, accordingly, its well justified *raison d'etre*. Truth, under the conditions of the full suppression of the laws of Life, stirs exactly those emotions which would upset the orderly way of life which became crucial to *armored* man's existence. Truth, penetrating to the core of man's misery, would *impede* the joys he learned to obtain in his substitute life: the little, secret love affairs, the little two weeks vacation, the little joy in listening to the radio, the little squanderance. It would disturb severely his *necessary* adjustments to the hard way of life under given structural and work conditions. Let an American Indian or a northern Eskimo or even a Chinese peasant live in full use of the most advanced technical acquisitions of civilization, and they would be rendered helpless in their usual way of life. These are banal things. What is meant here, essentially, is that the crooked character structure of present-day man has its *rational* meaning and function which cannot be lightly discarded as the freedom peddlers of all nations would advocate doing. They are ignorant of what "adjustment" means. They could not manage a single nervous breakdown due to inability to function actually according to the dreams.

Even the dream of paradise, no matter in what form it appears, is rational and necessary. It fills the heart with a remainder of the old glow of Life within a dreary actuality, as a pin-up girl adds strength to the soldier's guts in the firing line. The pin-up girl acts as a continuous torture, true, but it also helps to maintain the dream of life.

All this tells us that, though crucial and the only weapon capable of disarming the plague as the truth is, it cannot possibly be commanded or injected or taught or forced upon anybody who has not grown it in his organism from the very beginning. TRUTH IS BEING EVADED BECAUSE IT IS UNBEARABLE AND DANGEROUS TO THE ORGANISM WHICH IS INCAPABLE OF USING IT.

Truth means full contact with oneself as well as with the environment. Truth means knowing one's own ways as distinct from the ways of others. To force upon the fellow man truth which he cannot live, means stirring up emotions impossible for him to carry; it means endangering his existence; it means kicking off balance a well-set, even if disastrous, way of life.

Truth is not what the Russian political prostitute thinks it ought to be: a tool of power, to be changed at will. One cannot change the truth, as one cannot change one's basic character structure.

This must be constantly born in mind as a protection against the prophets who, it is true, see the light but do not know how to enable their fellow men to take it in peace and full enjoyment. This, now, amounts to advocating the devil.

There is, however, an irrational rationale in the persecution of the truth, which cannot be overlooked if truthful living is eventually to prevail. Truth turns critically toward itself, as it were. If it has been persecuted through the ages, it reasons truthfully, there must be a good reason for it. There was a good reason in the rise of fascism of both the black and the red variety: *Fascism has awakened a sleeping world to the realities of the irrational, mystical character structure of the people of the world.* The rationale of the evil influence of fascism in the twentieth century upon the Asiatic masses is a serious reminder of what harm the mystical transformation of living Life has done to billions of human beings over the ages. Such rational functions within the ugly irrational are a part of living Life, and the truthful organism will acknowledge it. If we do not

exactly agree with the command to love one's enemy, we can readily agree
that "Love Your Enemy" had the meaning of "*Understand* the motives
of your Enemy." Not a single leading politician in Germany before Hitler's
ascent to the reign of terror had really studied Hitler's gospel. So they
kept babbling about his being a "bought servant of the bourgeoisie." *To
know the rational in the deeply irrational is the mark of truthful living,*
that is, of fully alive perception of the conditions of one's life. Only the
stupid self-righteousness within the empty bag of a freedom-peddler manages to believe itself fully perfect and the enemy fully bad. There is a
rational motive in the most evil happenings. The grave situation in which
adolescent youth finds itself today, the so-called juvenile delinquency,
which means in six out of ten cases simply the performing of the natural
embrace under the most devastating circumstances, inner as well as outer,
— this situation is truly a reminder, directed toward a sitting world, of the
laws of living Life within a maturing organism. And this voice will not
stop screaming until the world stops sitting and starts moving onward.

The evasion of the truth in matters of adolescents' plight is *rational*
on the part of the educational and medical bodies carrying grave responsibilities; they *would not know how* to start doing, *what* to do, *where* to
proceed in a single case of adolescent misery. They have, due to the
chronic evasion and the continuous misrepresentation of the issue, lost the
ability to learn and to know how to act. The old laws do not fit. They
never did. The police is not the proper agency to deal with juvenile misery,
except in cases of full crime against life and safety. The physicians
brought up in medical schools which either eschew the subject completely
("DO NOT EVER TOUCH IT") or adhere to old, wrong, outworn concepts
given by old, outworn, dried-out lifeless parents and educators, cannot
possibly take responsibility or do anything. The educators are in a similar
situation. Therefore, the plague maintains itself. Evasion of the issue
becomes rational in a very bad way. And proclaiming the full truth about
the plague without preparation for its successful extermination would be
equally criminal. What could millions of adolescents without parents who
understand their plight, without public support, without help of any kind,
and in addition, with a frustrated structure and with sick minds, do with
the full truth about their lives?

The knower of the misery of adolescence keeps off the way of the
freedom peddler. The peddler peddles "freedom of sex" for adolescents
as he used to peddle "bread and freedom," not having the slightest whiff
of an idea as to how bread and freedom are to be had; so he would, as he
actually *did* for a while until he was stopped, peddle "freedom of sex for

youth " in a most dangerous manner.   No solution of any major social problem is possible without the full support of the public and without full knowledge of what is entailed.   We must, by all means, nip in the bud the flourishing of a new brand of social nuisance, the *Truth Peddler.*   He will do more harm than any lie has ever done.

The solution of the problem of adolescence and with it of juvenile delinquency requires:

A complete turn in matters of extramarital living together of boys and girls, secured by law.

Full cooperation of the parents based on rational, medical understanding of adolescence.

An upbringing of children *from infancy onward* which would insure a character structure which could take the severe jolts of a rich life and would be capable of full adaptation to the laws of bio-energy.

Full support on the part of the social administration.

Housing of the population which would take into account the need for privacy for adolescents.

Sufficient numbers of educators and physicians, *healthy themselves,* who would stand by in emergencies.   This would require full public recognition of the evasion of truth on the part of psychoanalysts who today help to form public opinion on mental health.

A thorough revision of our ancient laws concerning rape and seduction of minors, to distinguish between *love in adolescence* and true criminal *seduction.*

Full endorsement of the subject of human biology (in the *orgonomic* sense) in the schools.

Adequate protection against the emotional plague which could and certainly would wreak havoc among the young ones who live happily.

And many other grave matters which would turn up in due time.

All this is unknown, and if known, it is inaccessible to the *freedom peddler.*   It will be equally inaccessible to the *truth peddler.*   Their only interest is to get youth into their organizations by way of political exploitation of the sexual misery of youth.   The freedom peddler will in the future, as he so often has done in the past, start youth movements and later betray the very core of the life of adolescents by becoming more reactionary than the old, good conservative, since he had promised more than he could possibly fulfill.   Beware of the freedom peddler in matters of love and Life.   He does not mean what he says.   He does not know anything about Life and the obstacles in its way.   He transforms all realities into formalities and all practical problems of living Life into ideas about a future paradise of humanity. Actually, in this very manner, he lands himself and, if brought to power by gullible masses of people, he lands the whole population too in utter misery.

The freedom peddler makes out of matters of truth a bait to lure people into a trap. Truth to him is an " ideal " and not a daily *way* of doing things. He believes that he defends the truth if he is righteous. The conservative, who, out of an instinctive knowledge of the great difficulties connected with the pursuit of truth, defends the *status quo* in social living, is by far more honest. He has, at least, a chance of remaining decent. The freedom peddler *must*, if he wishes to get along, sign his soul over to the devil.

Truth should be used cautiously against the *fear* of truth *which is justified* by actual conditions. Truth cannot be used as a tool without the infliction of pain, often severe pain; but neither can it be used like a medical drug. It is an integral part of the way of life of the future and *has to grow organically within the senses and primal movements in our children from the very beginning* in infancy. And this requires social and legal protection which no freedom or truth peddler is ready or able to give.

All truth as *a way of living* requires an opportunity to express itself freely. It then will grow by its own devices. All it needs is an equal chance with the lie and the gossip and the maligning and the killing of Life.

Is this too much to ask for?

Truth can be used as a weapon against the Murder of Christ only if it has grown straight like a tree and is branching out like an oak in the forest.

A body that lies by way of its very movement, a soul which lies in the way it expresses itself, not being able to help it, cannot have truth implanted or injected into its veins. Truth in such containers would turn into a far worse lie than the simple lie that had been developed for the protection of the remainder of one's Self. Such truth, injected and turned into a lie, would be a horrible killer. It would have to *prove* continuously that it is NOT a lie, that it is TRUTH *per se*, that *not* to believe that it is the very essence of truth is sacrilege versus the holy smoke of the church or the state or the patron or the matron or the ruler or the nation or the this or that. Listen to the proclamation of " true bolshevist truths " and you will know right away what truth injected into crooked bodies and turned into lies looks like and what it does.

Therefore, beware of the freedom peddler who peddles truths like shoestrings in the market place. He is worse than a horse thief. The horse thief does not promise heaven on earth; he just steals a horse. The horse thief is strung up by the neck with a rope from the tree, but the freedom peddler goes free.

The freedom peddler refuses to learn why there has been lying in the world for so long a time and in so many people.

Learn how to recognize the freedom peddler by his righteousness, by his stalwart uprightness, by his erect forefinger kept up high in the air like a teacher's rod; learn to know him by his cruelly glowing eyes and his rasping voice, by his rigid mouth and his inhuman absoluteness in his quest for the impossible.

The truth which grew organically in a truthful body is a truth that combats the fake truth grown in rigid minds which deny the reality of nature and its manifestations. The sap of life has gone from their blood. They believe that truth is what follows logically from a given premise. The truth is what reveals to you first of all why truth is so rare and so difficult to obtain, and why there exist impostors of truth who disclaim the reality of our existence.

The system of a lunatic is not truthful though it follows logically from its premises. However, there is *some* kernel of truth in everything proclaimed by men.

People avoid the truth because the first bit of truth uttered and lived would draw more truth into action and so on indefinitely, and this would rip most people right off the customary tracks of their lives. But people, basically, know what is true and what is not, even if they so often render help to the lie. They support the lie because the lie has become a crutch without which life would not be possible. Therefore, in common human intercourse, the truth, and not the lie, is suspected as being phony.

From the lie in daily living has developed a technique to know the lie and be reconciled to it, to live with it, as it were. To use the truth against this lie would set the crusader beyond the pale of the human community.

It is not a matter of " proclaiming truth " but of *living truth ahead of one's fellow man.* And this *is* possible, but only if the truth is a *true* truth, and not a made-up, cooked-up, proposed or propagated truth. The truth must be a piece of your Self as is your leg or your brain or your liver. Otherwise, do not try to live a truth which is not akin to your whole being. It will turn into a lie in no time, and into a worse one to boot, than the lie which has grown organically in the makeshifts of social living.

And this is the true difficulty in getting across the truth one lives. You are in danger of being a voice in the desert if you preach the truth. *Don't preach truth.* Show people by example how to find the way to *their own* resources of truthful living. Let people live *their own* truths, *not* your truth. What is organic truth to one is no truth at all to another man or woman. There is no absolute truth just as there are no two faces alike. And yet there are basic functions in nature which are common to all truth. But the individual expression varies from body to body, from soul to soul. It is true that all trees have roots in the soil. But the concrete tree A could not use the roots of the concrete tree B to draw nourishment from the soil since they are not his. To maintain the special in the common, the variation in the rule is the essence of wisdom. The variation, divorced from the common, the differentness, is the way of the freedom peddler in his youth. The way of the common and the dictatorial rule for all is the way of the freedom peddler *when his youth has gone out of him.*

The world is split up between the one and the other. It is called " individualism " and " statism " at present, and will be called many other names before it will vanish from the surface of the earth. The children have not been born yet who will live the laws of Life as they are in the trees of a forest or in the birds or in the corn in the fields.

Freedom peddling robs the truth of its opportunity to prove itself, to sharpen its tools, to structuralize its conduct, to know its enemy, to cope with trouble, to persist in danger, to learn where it can turn into a lie worse than the native lie. Therefore, no rules can be given as to how to use the weapon of truth, as many a reader may have expected from these pages. It is again a sign of the mystification of Christ that rules of conduct common to *all* are expected from *another* prophet. This is to escape the trouble of finding your own special truth within your own special Self as it fits *you,* and not somebody else.

There is only *one* common rule valid in finding the special truth valid for you. That is to learn to listen patiently into yourself, to give yourself a chance to find your own way which is yours and nobody else's way. This leads not into chaos and wild anarchism but ultimately into the realm where the *common truth for all* is rooted. The ways of approach are manifold and none alike. The source from where the sap of truth is streaming is common to all living beings, far beyond the animal man. This must be so because all truth is a function of living Life, and living Life is basically the same in everything that moves by way of pulsation. Therefore, the basic truth in all teachings of mankind are alike and amount to only one common thing: *To find your way to the thing you feel when you love dearly, or when you create, or when you build your home, or when you give birth to your children or when you look at the stars at night.*

Accordingly, common to all sages who knew the truth or were searching for truth, was the expression in their eyes and the meaning of the alive movement in their faces. It is sad but true that the great clown in the circus carries this expression behind his mask. He has touched upon great truths. It is the exact opposite of the howling of a mob throwing stones into windows. It is far from the giggle of a coquettish girl who lures men to find out again and again how dangerous a man could be to her. It is contrary to the looks of an executioner or the expression in the face of a dried-up, cruel, cunning, sneaking, hiding, ruthless, unscrupulous liberator of peoples. *Know the faces of the fake liberators.* Learn to see them wherever they turn up, potential ones and mature ones. Learn to know the clever bandwagon rider who cannot look straight into your eyes. And you will know, by contrast, what the truth looks like.

Truth knows no party lines, nor national boundaries, nor the difference of the sexes or of ages or of language. It is a way of being common to all, and potentially ready to act in all. This is the great hope.

But truth is only *potentially* there; it is not ready to act as yet, like the seed in the field is only potentially there to yield the bread in the fruit. Drought and freezing cold can stop it where it is and prevent it from bearing fruit.

The emotional plague is the freezing cold and the drought that keeps the seed of truth from yielding the fruit. The plague reigns where it is not possible for the truth to live. The eye, therefore, should be centered primarily on the plague and not on the truth, on the prevention of drought and freezing rather than on what the seedling will or might do. The seedling will know its ways toward the Life-giving sun. It is the plague that kills the movement of the stem and it, therefore, requires all our attention. It is not the learning to walk in the infant, but the rock or the precipice in its way that is to be watched. It is a part of the tragedy of man that he did not see the precipice and believed in a perfect, readymade walking of the infant, instead of removing the obstacle in the way of the growing truth.

This is how truth should be used.

TRUTH AND COUNTERTRUTH

Using the truth as a weapon implies not only telling what has been found true but also, and in the first place, knowing why this particular truth had *not* been found or mentioned before. It could have been for lack of technical or scientific knowledge; it also could have been because knowing such truth would have endangered an important institutional or structural formation. Therefore, before proclaiming a truth, one should know the *obstacle* to this truth. Otherwise, the evasion of this truth will be counteracted only by way of freedom peddling, i.e., by proclaiming truth as salvation. And this is exactly what is far worse for the establishment of truthful living than the institutional lie.

Human bondage is always apt to establish an institutional lie. A family is held together by human bondage which in many cases rests to some extent on an institutional lie. Consideration for the children may preclude frankness in sexual matters which could upset the living institution. Telling the truth and establishing truthful living always goes with risking friendship and human bondage. Both truth and human bondage are rooted in living necessities. Therefore, if human bondage obstructs truth, no decision as to which to follow is possible unless one knows exactly the *other truth*, the " *counter-truth* " which maintains the institutional lie. Thus one truth must be weighed against the other truth: *Which is* FOR THE MOMENT *more crucial?* And which is in the long run or with regard to the majority of living humans more important?

If the truth would involve the risk of destroying the institution of this particular family, with no particular benefit derived for the wider aspects of human interrelationships, the countertruth must prevail and the truth must recede or wait until it gains ubiquitous, practical validity. In the latter case, the countertruth must recede. If you can save a thousand children's lives by risking the familial security of two or three children in one family built on an institutional lie, the interest in the thousand children surpasses the interest in the two or three children. But if the risking of the security of two or three children does not help the many children, there is no sense in proclaiming a truth " on principle."

In using truth as a weapon against the plague, the relationships of the truth *on principle* to truth *in particular* must be well considered. It is basically and on principle true that the problem of adolescent genitality and with it the scourge of what is called *"juvenile delinquency"* cannot ever be solved without the full establishment of a full, gratifying and well secured love life of all adolescents. This truth must basically and under all circumstances be adhered to if the long-range solution of the problem of youth as a whole is to be secured. However, in the particular case, it is a matter of considering the *countertruth* which may tell you that in a certain group or in a certain situation the application of the basic truth would be disastrous. The group of adolescents in question may not be socially or structurally ready to live this truth, or their environment may react to such living in a manner more dangerous than the misery which already is entailed in their present situation. In another case, the particular truth will be in accord with the basic truth; then there will be no trouble, for example where the school and the home are in agreement as to the basic solution of the problem of adolescence.

When people, as they are so prone to do, put their social interrelations far ahead of the pursuit of truthful living, which is inseparable from risking friendships, the truth must always be weighed against the countertruth. Do these people now resist the truth because they needs must rely on the countertruth, or is it because they are cowardly, afraid of their neighbors and friends and keep patting them like wild animals to calm their wrath lest it break out? In such cases, the pursuit of truth is clear: One does not yield in matters of truth, valid in wide basic realms, to such malignant calming down of wild animals, if one's job is to get the lifesaving truth across. This would apply to any psychiatrist who is in charge of a mental hygiene center, or to a group of social workers who are to take care of a sector of the city where juvenile misery is rampant on a large scale.

If one yields to backslapping and backpatting, which is to save one from the embarrassment of making enemies in the pursuit of truth, one is a coward, pure and simple, and no good for the job. In this case, the particular worker is interested in his own security only and he does not care what happens to the people under his care. He best be removed from his job if it requires a pioneering spirit and courage as well as skill in coping with the plague.

However, if a social worker is only to provide families with crude facilities of living such as living quarters or jobs, which usually does not entail any obstacle on the part of the plague, he should not risk the pursuit of such job by proclaiming more basic and more risky truth.

Thus the use of truth is an art in itself, an art that must be developed patiently by experience, like any other art, in order to acquire the necessary skill in using important truth as a weapon in the fight against the plague. Otherwise, one will only add the "truth peddler" to the "freedom peddler" and make a nuisance of everything without reaching a single objective of one's labor.

Neither can or should truth be "sneaked" into a group or into a social situation if they are not ready to absorb it. The use of sneaky methods will inevitably render the truth itself sneaky and thus utterly useless. It is a quite different thing to find the countertruth, to eliminate its *raison d'etre* and to replace it carefully with the basic truth. An orgonomist who starts upsetting a whole hospital and endangers his own position by proclaiming truth about orgonomic medicine, is only a nuisance. People in distress sense the truth and will *come to you* if you wait patiently and give them an opportunity to mature up to what they need. Then meeting them will not be difficult.

However, such a rational procedure can easily be replaced by the backslapping type of a nuisance calming-the-beast procedure and even be carried as a shield to maintain one's inner security. This should be fought with all the means of basic truth. Such backslapping and cheek-petting socialite cheats are part of the vast army of the plague which is out to maintain its position and does not care how many children die or how many people starve to death if only their fake friendships are secured. It goes without saying that this has nothing to do with *true* friendship. It is like the friendship of crooks who know exactly that each one of them only waits for the opportune moment to cut the other fellow's throat. The world of diplomacy and sociality and tea-partying and delegating and bargaining is full of such machinations to evade the truth which with one stroke would make all the backslapping unnecessary and would replace fake friendship with true teamship of people putting their shoulders to one and the same wheel. Such people are not afraid to put friendships to the supreme test, which is to risk going over the rim of tolerance.

The new leader will have to be an expert in the distinction between genuine human friendship and the empty sooth-the-wild-animal stuff that poses as friendship. The latter is the twin brother of the sucking leech who seduces the abortive genius, by its mystical admiration, into dictatorial leadership or religious martyrdom.

To know the countertruth which supports and justifies the institutional lie is a part of the job of overcoming social misery, to be carefully done lest the truth, pregnant with future developments, turn into a lie worse than the one it was to put out of this world.

Briefly, truth must be protected from being put into a mirror for empty adoration and for the explicit purpose of covering up another Murder of Christ.

Let us now see whether the publication of such a book as THE MURDER OF CHRIST complies with its own rules to avoid truth-speaking on principle. The countertruths to such a publication five hundred or even one hundred years ago, would have precluded publication of this truth, had it been known. There existed at that time no general awareness of the sexual misery; there existed no knowledge of human character structure; there was not a trace of an inkling of masses of people awakening to Life; there was no knowledge available to cope with medieval scholasticism; there was no trace of or experience in scientific sexology; the Christian church had not its present-day nature which—at least—talks about the problem of human love life; there was no knowledge of contraception, antiseptics, character armoring, infantile genitality, sexual repression; these things had to come about before the Christian church could start changing. The reformation of Christianity had to shake up the world of Catholic asceticism. At present, a new reformation is developing within the church, such as talking about planned parenthood, handling of child sexuality, even of love outside of marriage.

The science of man has come closer to the cosmic view of man in Christianity (see Cosmic Superimposition), and the church had to face the full realities of Life. Renan's book on Christ had to be published, and psychiatry had to take hold of mankind. In the light of all this, we may hope that the Christian church will soon change its viewpoint on the Love of Christ which is bodily love. There is no other way for Christianity but to change with the times.

In other words, with the development of the knowledge of man, the countertruth against the full truth about Christ, maintained by the church of Christ, melts slowly away, and the full truth about the meaning of Christ is mature to see the light of day. The functioning of the cosmic energy in man as Life Energy, and the realization of the meaning of God in terms of the cosmic rooting of men, have bridged the gap between religion and knowledge considerably. We are about to reach the common denominator which for such a long stretch of time has separated man's spiritual from his biological existence. Still, a long stretch is ahead of us to be mastered. But, doubtless the meeting has taken place, whether the respective representatives are aware of it or not. The courts themselves will awaken them to the full truth of the situation. And the honest, the true Godly ones will be with us.

THE LITTLE MAN PARALLEL

In politics everyone blames everyone else, never oneself. It is time to stop blaming the scapegoat. It is high time to see what splits mankind apart. It is the emotional plague, called "sin" in Christendom, which splits mankind apart. It is the armoring which renders man helpless and prostrate. It is again the armor, which is the terror of living, flowing Life, which creates the sergeants of the plague, who become the sergeants in the vast armies of fiendish nations.

TO EVERY GREAT HUMAN THOUGHT WHICH STRIVES TOWARD THE COMMON
DENOMINATOR OF MANKIND, THERE IS A LITTLE MAN'S PARALLEL WHICH BRINGS
TO NAUGHT EVERY SINGLE HOPEFUL THOUGHT OF MAN.

*There is no use in thinking new liberating thoughts as long as Modju,
the Little Man Parallel, continues to spoil the good job.* Here are a few
examples of the Little Man Parallel of great principles:

Creative Thought	*Little Man Parallel*
The God of Moses	Revengeful, punishing Jehovah
Fisher of Men	Holy wars, Crusades, Jesuitism
Christ's Heaven on Earth	Paul's angels in heaven
Liberty	"I-can-do-what-I-please," license, 4-lettering
"Love thy neighbor"	"Fear thy neighbor" and pat him on the back
The Golden Rule	Compromise devoid of principle
Ether as general substratum	One special ether for every natural function
Free enterprise	Robbery, Squeeze, Cheat, get the competitor into jail
Un-American discrimination, oppression and hatred	"Un-Americanism," prosecution of every truth that is disliked
"Human labor creates surplus value" (Marx)	Russian slave labor camps (Stalin)
Human interrelations	Politics, power over men
Knower	Expert, authority
The genital embrace, mating	"*Making*" love, "laying" a woman
The Law	The bureaucrat, the "lawmaker"
Underground revolutionary activity	International diplomatic spying, subversion
Rebel against social injustice	The bank robber
Society	State, Statist, Socialism
Contribution to social security and safety	Tax to soak the rich and individual effort
Organization of labor	Union boss
Free thinking	The free-thinker
Fight against industrial exploitation	"Me, too, a rich man"

Creative Thought	*Little Man Parallel*
Leader, Guide, Adviser	Dictator, Tyrant
Fight against Dictatorship	Slander and persecution of liberty and pioneering thoughts
Free expression of opinion	Shooting one's mouth off
Factual criticism	Personal slander and lie
Free competition of effort	" Squeeze the small fry "
Honest fight	Knife in the back
Civil liberties	*Gullibility;* tolerance of sneaking murderers
Justice	Prosecution, persecution
Thrill of adventure	Gambling, killer of the highway
Sport	The " fix "
Human destructiveness	Death instinct
Searching and finding "GOD"	Litany, Klu-klux-klan, religious convulsions
Diplomatic intercourse among nations	Common horse thievery in international relations
Orgastic potency	Salvation, redemption without effort
Sublimation of secondary drives	Cultural snobbism
Natural morality	" Thou shan't," " Don't touch it "
Self-regulation	" Regulate yourself " *ideal*
Fighter for human freedom	The Freedom Peddler
Scientific psychology	EVERYBODY a " psychotherapist "
Scientific neurology	Brain surgery in emotional ailments
Curative discharge of pent-up bio-energy	Indiscriminate shock treatment, " shock him "
Sovereign — The People	" Hail the Sovereign "
Nation	Race
Social democracy	Dictatorship of the proletariat
National defense	Brass-hat, Junker in uniform
Socialism	State capitalism
Priest, Man of God	The religious jobber
Emotional Plague	A " plague," everything I don't like

Creative Thought	*Little Man Parallel*
Giving	Suck dry the giver
Give and take	Take and never give
Truth	Eavesdropping
Hunting	Kill every deer you encounter
Fishing for food	Fishing to hurt fish
Social administration,	Government above the people, " STATE "
Public servants	Little Men pushing buttons
Convincing people of an accomplishment	Being " recognized "
Reporter, journalist	Character assassination, smearer, slanderer
Social economy	State machinery
The knowing people	The silent people
The critic	" Me too. . . . "
The medical orgonomist	Muscle squeezer, armor pusher
Laughing	Giggling
Research Foundation	Tax-free salary foundation
Forestry	Cut every tree in the forests
Money saving	Usury
Plenty	Waste
Economy of produce	Black market, inflation of prices
Heredity of characteristics	Racial segregation, " hereditary degeneration "
Genius	Crackpot
Healthy child	Child who makes no trouble
Clown in circus	Jokes on the radio to appease bad taste

WHO IS THE ENEMY?

Truth is the most potent weapon in the hand of Life. Whoever uses a weapon must know his enemy. The weapon of truth must be used against the enemy of Life. A gun can be used against the friend as well as against the enemy. The truth as a weapon cannot be used against itself. You can no more attack the truth of living Life by means of truth and kill it, than you can lift yourself up from a hole by your own hair. You cannot cure health and happiness and you cannot destroy the truth of Life by the truth of Life. Just as knowing the ways of happiness and health and life will only enhance happiness and health and Life, and never destroy them, so also knowing more truth about the truth of Life will never, never destroy Life but only further it.

But, *truth is dynamite which can kill Life in the hands of sick life.* Sick life cannot use truth about itself and not kill its sickness. But sick life can use truth about Life to kill *other, happy* Life. And this is another meaning of the plague.

The enemy of Life is, therefore, *truth about happy living in the hands or the mouth or the brain or the guts of sickened life if this truth concerns healthy Life.* Just as rotted meat brought together with fresh meat will make the fresh meat rot, and never will the fresh meat make rotted meat fresh, so also will knowledge of the ways of healthy Life in the hands of rotted life, always poison good Living, and never the other way around. Healthy Life will never make good living out of rotted life, pestilent life. The pestilent, rotted life knows well that this is so and therefore hates good living worse than anything else. You cannot ever make a crooked tree grow straight again. This is bad, indeed, but it is a *fact* to be known well in the process of protecting healthy Life.

It is also true that crooked life can maim, ruin, shoot to pieces or otherwise destroy a million pieces of good Life, but never, never can evil, sick life make a single tree or flower grow faster or make birds out of fish. On the other hand, healthy Life, good living, can make trees grow faster and it can make birds out of fish and men out of apes.

And this is the great tragedy of sick life and the good luck of happy Life; and sick life knows it and, therefore, revels in killing healthy Life and persecuting it wherever it can.

How, now, is good living to prevail and to grow if sick life can kill happiness wherever it comes in contact with it? How should the fresh meat be kept from rotting when it meets rotted meat, and how is a healthy baby to be protected from going rotten if in contact with evil life?

Through many ages, people have asked for an answer to this question and could not find it. They could not find it because the answer was sought in whole groups, in whole institutions, in whole social bodies and not in the principle of rotten life itself. Thus, attention was directed away from the poison in one's own camp when it was sought for in the other camp only. And then it had to happen that the rot in one's own camp infested the whole region while the rot in the other camp was fought with the fury of a holy war.

The enemy is the infectious rot itself, no matter where you find it, and not a special group or state or nation or race or class.

The remedy is not fighting-contact with the plague. This will always cause infection by the plague of the healthy life. Gay and happy children will easily pick up the ways and expressions of sick children. But sick children will never pick up the ways and expressions of healthy children. A single messed-up, pestilent person can upset a whole group of well-functioning men and women. A single infernal spy in the midst of a thousand trusting honest people will make a thousand innocent spies out of the many. But a million trusting people will never make a trusting human being out of a structurally spying scoundrel. Therefore, the answer cannot be contact with and direct killing of the plague. Never has direct killing of the plague been successful; it only infected the arm of justice. The answer is so far, with the given means of knowledge about the ways of the plague: ISOLATION AND QUARANTINING OF THE INFECTIOUS PLAGUE-RIDDEN PERSON OR GROUP. And the full truth about both the plague abroad *and* at home, ruthlessly, relentlessly revealed for all to know, as was done in the USA in the excellent film " When the Earth Stood Still " (1951).

There is an objection to this solution which has remained untouchable; a silent agreement, as it were, between the plague and its victims over a long stretch of time. The silent rule was: *"Never mind the ugly plague. This has always been and always will be so. There is nothing you can do but ignore it. If you fall prey to its murderous ways, too bad. It happened over the ages. The truth always had to suffer, and there must be martyrs of truth. No prophet was recognized in his own homeland, because truth has always been persecuted. The world is as it is, and nothing can really make it better. Do not get excited about it. You will not only burn up your wings if you fly into the fire of human madness and try to rescue Life. Mankind is rotten and will remain rotten. Keep off politics and do your job quietly and without conspicuous behaviour. Be a good citizen, shoemaker, and stick to your lasts. Do not try to improve the world; it cannot be improved. Sin is inborn, malignancy is the very essence of man. Be courteous toward your killer, say 'thank you' to your hangman and show modest reconciliation with the ill fate that kept you in the pen twenty years for no committed crime. Doesn't it say in the holy book, 'Love thy neighbor as thyself' and 'forgive your enemies'? It does. Therefore, keep quiet. Your life is short, and you are an unimportant worm anyway. Therefore, behave with dignity and do not pay attention to the murderer of Christ. Nobody has ever paid attention to him; he always was despised and nobody cared about him. The truth will ultimately win out, no matter how long it takes and how many victims the pursuit of truth will cost. We all know very well that no war has ever changed anything and that everything has always remained as it has been for ages. There is nothing you can do about it. If you wish to do something, try to be nice to your enemy and to convince him of your good will. You may or may not succeed in changing his heart."*

All such talk was created by the plague underground to maintain itself. Nobody at the source of living Life has ever said that one should forgive the enemy, not even Christ, who punished his enemies and the enemies of mankind and cursed the hell out of them. It was the plague which, in order to protect itself against the just wrath of living Life, changed the meaning of Christ's words from "understand your enemy" into "forgive your enemy under all circumstances and by all means. Do not touch your enemy, do not fight for your life, your honor, your reputation against the plague that defiles you. *Turn the other cheek* to receive another blow." It was the pestilent character here as everywhere else who turned the meaning of words upside down to continue his evil doings unopposed. And the pestilent carrier of the plague is being supported by principles of liberalism, wrongly interpreted and based either on unconscious sympathy with or on fear of the plague.

Nobody at the inception of humanitarian liberalism had ever claimed that one should give the right of free movement to the criminal spy, the underhanded, cunning fox who stabs you in the back while he presents you with a bouquet of roses that explodes in your face. It is the Little Man, again, who admires the cunning efficiency of the strong-armed plague, who turned the meaning of a true liberalism into the nonsense of letting murderers and thieves and men who are out to kill you sneak around your house at night, without using your gun.

Who, then, is the enemy of living Life which is the eternal victim of the plague? The enemy is the slyness of the pestilent character in all camps, right and left, in high and in low social strata, in the government office as well as in the shoe factory, in the bacteriological laboratory as well as in the church of St. Maria, in the democratic as well as in the communist party, in every school, family, group, class and nation on this earth.

The enemy is everywhere. No geographical or racial boundaries separate the friend from the enemy. How then can we trust each other? How can "good will among men" and "peace on earth" ever be built on earth if this is so?

The answer is:

Learn to know what Life is and how Life works. *Learn, finally, to fight for Life as heretofore you have only fought for emperors and dukes and fuehrers and ideas and honors and wealth and ephemeral fatherlands and motherlands. Finally, start fighting for Life!* And: *Learn to distinguish the expression of an honest, open face from that of a sneaker and characterological liar.* IF YOU LOVE YOUR CHILDREN, LEARN TO READ THE FACIAL EXPRESSION OF A MODJU.

Do not be patient toward the killer of Life if your patience with the single killer helps to kill thousands of babies and drives millions of people into the gutters to die. What are your high values worth as long as people starve from hunger of the stomach and from hunger for love, as long as you evade the true, crucial issue which is the habitual turning away from the full facts that make Life miserable? What is your good will worth if you dare not expose the poisonous rot which infests your neighborhood with gossip so that no unlicensed loving couple can move freely, and that drives to suicide or insanity many a man and woman and boy and girl at your neighbor's door?

Your values are all right, but *make them work.* Your calm poise in the face of hidden evil is evil itself, nothing but a subterfuge. Your sociality is not worth the smile on your face if it is only to calm the wild animal in your friend or to gain some advantage. Your gaiety and your good will and your good neighborliness are all right and very good things, but watch the underground mole which undermines its very foundations and which is protected by your false liberalism.

You say: "To touch complete freedom of expression and action is very dangerous. Who should be the judge as to what is good and what is bad?" You are right: Who should be the judge? But why not judge the judges, read the expressions on faces and distinguish the face of a scoundrel from the face of an honest soul? How do you otherwise própose ever to stop the Murder of Christ?

The enemy is this talk of yours. The enemy is in the midst of all of us. The enemy is your reluctance to fight for the Life and happiness of babies as you fight for your high ideals. Your ideals are nothing outside living Life.

The enemy is your secret sympathy for the killer of Life; a sympathy based on your fear of deep sorrow and exhuberant joy. The enemy is your own dullness which is to protect you against the full feel of Life.

Therefore, you protect the plague and drivel about the love for the neighbor. Therefore, you will choose the plague rather than living Life, if you can, to escape the thrill of Life, and will give yourself to dullness instead of to fullness of experience. The evil attracts you because you shun the stir connected with the good. You want your little pleasures only, the little 4-lettering, the little paper read at the convention, the little meaning in the big teaching, the little and small and tight and dull and uneventful in everything.

HIDEOUS DISTORTIONS OF ORGONOMIC TRUTH

In the twentieth century, society went through the frightful experience of what a system of thought, distorted by armored man, can do. No leader conscious of his importance and responsibility will ever dare forego the lessons from the mass murder that followed the distortion of sociological teachings in the heads of men in power who were forced to keep society together. And the leaders who will be responsible for the new Life processes which will emerge from the discovery of the Life Energy, will be forced to be more careful a hundred fold. *A teaching of living Life, taken over and distorted by armored man, will spell final disaster to the whole of mankind and its institutions.* There should be no mistake about this.

A brief survey will easily show in what direction such distortions of a teaching based on Life Energy will act:

By far the most likely result of the principle of "orgastic potency" will be a pernicious philosophy of 4-lettering all over the place everywhere. Like an arrow released from the restraining, tightly tensed spring, the search for quick, easy and deleterious genital pleasure will devastate the human community.

The constant, patient struggle for improvement of *health*, based on carefully drawn experiences, will be replaced by the idea of a "perfect," readymade "health" as an absolute ideal with new social stratification in " healthy " and in " neurotic " people.

Physicians and philosophers, to judge from past distortions, will probably establish a new virtue, the perfect ideal of *"freedom of emotion"* which will harass human interrelations. Rage will have no reason nor rational direction. It will rage for rage's sake only, to be *"emotionally free."*

Self-regulation, instead of being the easy, spontaneous flow of events with up's and down's, to follow and to guard, will become a "principle" to be applied to life, to be taught, to be exercised, to be imposed upon people, possibly with prison or death penalties, no matter whether it be called "sabotage of the holy living principle of self-regulation" or "crime against the freedom of Life and Liberty." And those revolted by the sight of the evil doings will most likely blame an innocent, distorted, misinterpreted orgonomy for the actions of living beings bare of any sense of proportion.

The function of *work democratic interrelations among working people* will most likely drown in the verbiage of what work-democracy *should* be like (not of what it actually *is*), and new political ideas will emerge to depict and secure the new hope of mankind: *"work democracy."*

Orgastically impotent physicians in the realm of medical orgonomy will mess up the medical techniques to establish the orgonotic streaming in sick organisms or will forget them altogether and start quibbling about whether the jaw or the shoulder muscles should be attacked first, for centuries to come.

They will form one end of a line at the other end of which they will be opposed by the 4-letterers who will demand *"freedom of love"* and the right to live life according to the *"principles of orgonomy."*

Self-regulation in the upbringing of newborn infants will not work in hands which will not know what a *spontaneous* decision or action is, and the enemies of children and even the friends will rave about the evil consequences of that cockeyed idea of self-regulatory upbringing in infancy.

We can imagine all these developments and many more very easily, and there will be those wisecrackers who will tell everybody that nothing can be done anyhow, that it always has been that way and always will be . . . . . until some new Living Christ will walk upon this earth in the midst of the nightmare and will preach the principles of Life only to be nailed to the cross again by the high priests of the "Science of Living Life."

All this will actually happen unless man will find the exit from the scarred battlefield of the human emotional plague, the entrapment of poor souls.

The prostitute in politics, the glib freedom peddler, the mystical liberator are not to be blamed for the great misery. They are to be blamed for *obstructing the access* to the realization of their own ideals and the removal of the misery they created. They are not to be blamed for peddling "freedom" and "bread" and "democracy" and "peace" and the "will of the people" and all the rest of the register. They are to be blamed for persecuting everybody who clarifies what freedom is and what *obstacles* are in the way of self-government and what *obstructs* peace. They are not to be blamed for promising land to poor, starving peasants. They are to be punished for *obstructing* the access to making the peasant capable of tilling his land *freely* and *efficiently* so that the mass murder of peasants in the process of compulsory collectivization as in 1932 becomes impossible in the future. They are not to be blamed for holding out hopes for heaven on earth, but for betraying and obstructing every single step in the direction of true betterment of human conditions. They are not to be blamed for having ideals but for having *emptied all ideals from any content whatsoever,* for having put human high ideals into the mirror and for killing everyone who *lives* an ideal or tries to bring reality somewhat closer to the ideal; in short, they are to be blamed for being characterological scoundrels. They are not to be blamed for having theories or for feeling themselves the "sole" liberators and the "only" possessors of the holy truth, but for killing millions for not believing in their alleged truths and for torturing those who do not think that they liberate anything. They are not to be blamed for speaking about the liberation of those in low social standing but *for doing exactly the opposite* of what they are talking about, for depriving the lowly ones of all and every opportunity to get on their feet because it does not fit the ghastly corpse of a theory.

The Catholic hierarchy is not to be blamed for preaching Christ's teachings, but for obstructing these very same teachings by the mystification and disembodiment of the living, true, original Christ. They are not to be blamed for being ignorant of the identity of Life and God and sweetness in the genital embrace, but for hating and killing everything that even remotely reminds one of Christ's true living existence, and for keeping from mankind the knowledge of Christ's relations to the love of the body. They are guilty of ossification of a living creed and of murdering Christ in the bodies of countless infants and children and adolescents, thus creating the very Sin they later punish with fire in hell. We accuse them of obstruction to learning and development and improvement and recognition of obvious, simple, clear facts of Life. They are guilty of not joining, with their great power those who have looked a bit deeper into the darkness of human existence and who have thrown some, if ever so dim a light upon what is meant by the word "God." They are to be blamed for having remained sitting since the fourth century A.D.

A kneeling and praying humanity, two and a half billion strong, feels Life in their frozen bodies when they pray, though they call it by different names. They fight holy wars over the kind of name to be given to what they have *in common*. And the high priests have abandoned their sacred duty to lead these kneeling and bowing and praying multitudes toward exactly what they have in common when they feel in their streaming blood what they call "God." And here nothing has changed since Christ cursed the Pharisees at the temple of the Jews. Nothing! The priests have not learned anything at all, and, worse, they obstruct and fight tooth and nail those who are trying to learn. This is what they are guilty of.

An ossified humanity has put ossified priests into its temples, and the ossified priests maintain the ossification in every newborn generation. This is what religion is guilty of, not its original true teachings of Buddha and Christ and Confucius. They all strove toward the same goal. Ossified humanity could not understand or accept these teachings, and they established the right kind of priest to keep the teaching frozen, unreachable, in the mirror. This is the great tragedy: *The obstruction of the penetration of the fog,* not the fog itself; the *threat against the realization of religious beliefs and goals and morals,* not the religious, original moral teachings.

Not the freedom of speech and its advocates are to be blamed but the abuse of the freedom of speech by liars and cheaters and gossipers and maligners and underground moles who destroy the foundations of liberty because they cannot live or stand liberty. To be blamed is not the ignorant psychiatrist but the *gossiping* psychiatrist who maligns the revealer of the misery of frustrated love.

It is true: *If anyone had the guts and power to decree that freedom and self-regulation be established overnight, the greatest disaster in the history of mankind would inevitably swamp our lives like a flood.* If revolution by force, guaranteed in the Constitution of the USA as a right of the people against *evil* government, would and could do the job of true liberation, no sane mind would hesitate to be all out *for* it. It was the essence of the downfall of all freedom movements based on such belief, that freedom can *not* be established by decree or force, because fear of freedom *is in the peoples themselves*. As long as people fear the streaming of living Life in their bodies, they will fear truth and avoid it by all means.

TO TOUCH THE TRUTH IS THE SAME AS TO TOUCH THE GENITALS. Therefrom stems the *" Touch-It-Not "* of anything serious, crucial, life-saving, of anything leading toward true self-reliance. This explains the great taboo " TOUCH-IT-NOT " against genitals as well as against truth. This is the subversive power of the plague. *To turn mass attention away from the conferences of the political windbags toward these crucial facts will be the primary job.* From this job, once done, other developments will follow. Therefore, the current Biological Revolution which has gripped humanity over the past thirty years, is of such tremendous importance. It opens the gates toward the truth by making mankind aware of the great taboo: " DON'T TOUCH IT," and, by making people aware of it, it brings them closer to their genitals as well as to their inner truth. This means the reversal of a situation of some ten thousand years' standing. To be aware of the scope of this penetrating process means to be aware of a huge sweep of history over the following two to three thousand years. No freedom peddler and no political prostitute will accept this. They will talk, gossip, malign, fight, slander and lie it away wherever they meet it. *To the same extent to which the problems of human genitality become accessible to multitudes, will truth be wanted and no longer avoided or killed.* And then things will run their own logical course.

Catholicism, which denies the love in the body, can survive this revolution in our lives only if it returns to Christ's true, original meaning which was so badly and thoroughly transformed into the exact opposite. Should it happen that Christendom will not, swimming in the general stream of life, revert to the original meaning of Christ, more, much more blood, innocent blood will be spilled, and still Life will remain stronger and the church will slowly vanish from the surface of this earth. Otherwise, it will survive as a great institution which, in spite of the terror and darkness it has spread over the ages, had done so much to keep a miserably despondent humanity somehow going. It is those who feel Life in the body's streaming and want the sweetness of true love who know better than the representatives of a distorted Christ that the perversion of Christ's true meaning was, in the face of the sexual misery of mankind, *absolutely necessary.*

St. Paul is not to be blamed for having introduced the most cruel system of sexual starvation mankind has ever known. He *had to* if he was to build up the Christian church. *He had to build strong dams against the pornographic, filthy, sick mind of man in sexual matters, even at the price of killing the true Christ.* But he would in the person of his representatives be guilty of treason against mankind if he were to obstruct the *way back* to the true Christ, by fire and sword, by a knifing-in-the-back of the new leaders who will arise in this struggle, and by conniving in secret conferences to *kill* Life. It won't work any longer; it will only cost innocent blood. And this blood, spilled for no good reason, will be on the consciences of the obstructors of the truth of Christ.

The safeguarding of a healthy, natural, life-saving love life in the newborn generations is the task of the new type of physician and psychiatrist. It is *their* domain; here the truth of Life was born and protected against evil attacks. The church is the domain of the priests. Let each domain have its own rights, equal and honest. Just as no psychiatrist or physician will try to interfere with the *inner* affairs of the church, no church should be permitted to extend its influence and power beyond its own domain. Let us keep to our own domains and not interfere with what is none of our business. This is *mutually* valid.

Life surpasses by its very nature all boundaries, all little frontiers, all custom barriers, all national restrictions, all racial biases; it is truly supreme in the cosmic sense, just as the Christian thinks the Lord supreme in the cosmic sense. But Life only lives its way, it does not *force* anyone anywhere to live its way. It does not interfere with what is none of its business. This is its greatness. Once discovered and understood, it is bound to come to govern all that derives from it. It is in no disagreement with either the true original meaning of God or of Christianity, nor with the true, original meaning of socialism, nor with any other true striving toward human life, liberty and happiness. The yearning and striving for Life, Liberty and Happiness is the common denominator of *all* factions of human political organizations which today are at each other's throats. It is and always has been the emotional plague which split the basically identical human strivings apart and drove them against each other. Therefore, the enemy is not a particular belief but the work of the plague in man.

Red Fascism is the sum total of *organized* techniques to split into pieces and apart the common roots of Life in all people. It has shut every single entrance to the knowledge of living Life. It has banned the laws of the unconscious human mind, the laws of infant and childhood genitality, the knowledge of repression and armoring and secondary drives and natural self-regulation from its schools and its books. Thus it will never reach anything positive in human affairs. And this will, ultimately, be its downfall. The mechanistic mind cannot possibly, in the long run, win out against the cosmic point of view in man.

THE RATIONAL ROOT OF THE "RESURRECTION"

The plague divides and separates men by shutting out what is common to man.

The new leader will clearly see the common root and emotional meaning of the Catholic *and* the Red Fascist belief: the "resurrection of Christ," i.e., the RESURRECTION OF LIFE IN MAN. The resurrection of Life inevitably entails the resurrection of Love, of full, streaming, uniting *genital* Love. *Being eternal Life and Love in the hearts of men, Christ* COULD NOT *have died; he rose again, in the emotional meaning of the word.* The Life-starved, Love-starved people simply would not yield to the final, irrevocable death of Love and Life. It *had to* stay alive by resurrection; it *had to* be as they felt it in their bodies, moving and enlivening the limbs: *immortal,* no matter whether as immortal soul, or immortal spirit, or immortal Christ "within you" or as immortal Christ "in Heaven." Christ, by his very Life meant emotionally to people *the resurrection of true, primal Love of the body.* His mystified existence after his death rested accordingly, on a *rational* basis, i. e., *on the streaming of Love and Life in the limbs of the people who carried on the mystification,* i. e., the divine resurrection of Christ, at about the fourth century A.D.

But this mystification had at the same time, and under the pressure of the compulsion to continue the Murder of Christ *within themselves,* removed the realization of Life and Love into heavens, far away from man's reach. The Son of Man had to die first before he could reach heaven and sweet Love and eternal Life.

Against this mystification, deification, transposition and transfiguration of living Life in the Body, another sector of humanity revolted some fifteen hundred years later. This sector of humanity did not wish to die before having lived a full life; it wanted heaven *on earth right away* and in a *practical* manner: to be given and guaranteed to them by the "freedom movement" which installed the laws of liberation from marital straightjacketing and Murder of Christ in the womb: this was the early Communist movement of 1900-1917, two thousand years A.D., which started with materialistic thinking in the seventeenth century.

The common root of a two thousand years' old Christianity and a three hundred years' old mechanistic rationalism which culminated in an imperialist Russian Red Fascism, taking their true rooting in human emotions, is the liberation of the body streaming, call it Freedom or Christ, it does not matter. Armor plus pornography in man turned Christ into papacy; it turned the body streaming into Sin, and original Communism into Red Fascism. Both mystified their originally rational roots in man's rational dreams and longings. Both Christianity and Communism turned *against* their origin and source of strength at the roots of their continuous existence, *against Life and Love* in the body. *They had to,* both of them, since the road to living Life in the body was shut off in the people who carried and nourished them into power. Both had to land in mystification and the Murdering of Christ, each in its special way. And finally, the variation of the way of suppression of Christ turned them against each other with the threat of future mass slaughter. These are the realities of the meadow as against the show on the stage which speaks of spies against the State, or of Sin versus the Holy Spirit.

Seen from the common roots and emotional meanings of both Christianity and Communism, the solution of their mutual animosity on principle is simple. A new leader could or will tell them:

"*Stop quibbling about spies and motherlands and fatherlands and Sin and holy smokes. You differ only in the ways you choose to murder Christ. It is unimportant whether by mechanization or by mystification and transfiguration. He is dead in both cases. It is immaterial whether you call his domain the Kingdom of Heaven or the Third Phase of Communism. You will fail to reach it because you have murdered, long ago, what alone can lead toward your dreamland. In order to reach your set destination you must reinstate Christ in his original meaning: As love in the body, as freedom of Love from the shackles of a frozen humanity, as freedom of the mind to investigate and live its root in the streaming blood and in the body. You both are rooted in one and the same longing of man. If you mean what you preach, you will return to your origin and help realize the dream of man which is realizable. You will stop punishing little children for touching Christ or adolescents for living Christ in the body as Christ himself has lived. And you will reinstate the first laws you had established toward the freeing of Christ from deadened bodies. You will bring about the Kingdom of God and true brotherhood of peoples. You have the power to do so, both of you.*"

The enemy of Life and Love in both the Christian and the Communist domain, the enemy of the child, will inevitably turn up and fight the new leader. They will keep man's interest spellbound in empty formalities and condemnation of bodily love and in patriotism and war-making and peace propaganda and shooting enemies of the State and many other things the sole aim of which is to talk God away and to keep the Devil reigning. These enemies in both camps, inimical toward each other, will certainly unite to fight their new common foe, the Love of Christ. This Love is their true foe since it will turn their whole organization and existence upside down, unless they return to their original emotional meanings in man.

It is thinkable, theoretically possible, even of crucial importance for the church to return to Christ of 25 A.D. and for Communism to return to the old dreams of an international human brotherhood of 1848. It would save both movements from inevitable decay in a terrifying morass once Life starts marching on the streets of the great cities of the earth. But will they, can they? Will the Murder of Christ be more powerful than reason? They cannot make the big turn because they are rooted in hardened, stiffened, frozen souls who had to carry the last flicker of an old dream along through the ages, the dream of a Living Christ and a Loving God and a peaceful community.

No matter how hard it will be: There cannot be a moment of hesitation as to whether to keep Christian and Communist alike aware of their origins and meanings in people's souls.

The new leader will use many ways to divert the burning attention of Man from the present nuisance to center it on the interest in future generations. And the center is and will remain for a long time, until peace has returned to the plague-ravaged earth, the living "God" in the streaming feelings of Life in the body, and all the knowledge in biology, medicine and education that is necessary to master man's living Life in newborn infants all over the planet.

An immobilized, sitting humanity is waiting for an answer to its search for the ways of living Life. While it drudges along on a bare minimum of subsistence, waiting, dreaming, suffering agonies, submitting to new slaveries after ages of futile revolts, it is harassed by theories and dogmas on human living. To add a new dogma of human living to the maze of philosophies, religions, and political prescriptions, means adding another piece of confusion to the building of the Tower of Babel. The task is not the construction of a new philosophy of life, but diversion of the attention from futile dogmas to the ONE basic question: WHY HAVE ALL DOGMAS OF HOW TO LIVE LIFE SO FAR FAILED?

The answer to this new kind of inquiry will not be an answer to the question of sitting humanity. However, it may open the way for *our chil-*

dren, as yet unborn, to search in the *right* direction. They have over the ages long past, in the process of being born, carried all potentialities within themselves; and they still do. *The task is to divert the interest of a suffering humanity from unfounded prescriptions to* THE NEWBORN INFANT, THE ETERNAL "CHILD OF THE FUTURE." THE TASK IS TO SAFEGUARD ITS INBORN POTENTIALITIES TO FIND THE WAY. Thus the child, yet unborn, becomes the focus of attention. It is the common functioning principle of all humanity, past, present and future. It is, on account of its plasticity and endowment with rich natural potentialities, the only living hope that remains in this holocaust of human inferno. THE CHILD OF THE FUTURE AS THE CENTER OF HUMAN ATTENTION AND EFFORT IS THE LEVER WHICH WILL UNITE HUMANITY AGAIN INTO ONE SINGLE PEACEFUL COMMUNITY OF MEN WOMEN AND THEIR OFFSPRING. In emotional power, as an object of love everywhere, regardless of nation, race, religion or class, it far surpasses any other interest of human striving. It will be the final victor and redeemer, in ways nobody can as yet predict.

This seems to be obvious to everyone. How is it possible, then, that nobody had as yet conceived the idea to center one's effort on this single hope and lever of true freedom? To unite man on this basis and to drain off his misdirected interest from futile, aimless, senseless, bloody convulsions?

The answer to this question was given: *Man lives and acts today according to thoughts which grew from the splitting up of the common stem of mankind into countless variations of thoughts which contradict each other. But the common root and stem of humanity remained the same: to have been born without ideas, theories, special interests, party programs, clothes, knowledge, ideals, ethics, sadism, criminal impulses; to have been born* NAKED, *just as the heavenly power has created it. This is the common root and stem of all humanity. Accordingly, it contains the common interest and power of unification of humanity. It is designed by the very condition of its emergence into the world to be beyond and above as well as at the foundation of everything man thinks, acts, does, strives for and dies for.*

A brief survey may, in the end, show in what manner the kind of thinking influences the use or the neglect of this common root and stem:

The world of Red Fascism, thoroughly mechanistic in its economic system and perfectly mystical in its conduct of human affairs, meets with human sitting on the spot and immobility, badly equipped to do anything about it. It has, in sharp contradistinction to its spiritual founders, remained sitting on "economics" and a mechanistic, industrial view of society. It has thrown out and kept away with fire and sword all knowledge about human emotions beyond those known to the conscious mind. It has condemned the bio-energetic drives as "bourgeois ideology." It rests its philosophy of man on a merely conscious mind which is superimposed on Pavlov's reflexes and automatic responses. It has thrown out the function of love completely. Accordingly, when it meets with human inertia, which is due to the armoring of the biosystem, it believes, quite logically from its own standpoint of thinking, that it is dealing with *conscious spite* or *conscious* "reactionary" "*sabotage*." Again, in full agreement with its way of thinking, and subjectively honestly (apart from the conscious scoundrel of politics whom we find everywhere), the Red Fascist shoots to death the "saboteur." This must be so since, to this kind of thinking, what a man does or does not do is due solely to conscious determination and resolve. To believe otherwise, to accept the existence of a living domain beyond the conscious will, and with it the existence and power of an unconscious psychic domain, of a rigid character structure, of an age-old impediment of bio-energetic functioning, would right away and irretrievably undermine the very foundation of the total system of suppression of the "saboteur of the Power of the State." (Never mind now "proletarian" or otherwise.) It would, with one stroke, reveal MAN as he *is*, and the interest would be diverted from the "Capitalists" who are no more than ultimate results of an economy of armored, helpless, sitting mankind. It would reveal the truly capitalist character of Sovietism. The whole system of arch-reactionary oppression of living Life, of the total mess in the disguise of a "revolutionary" ambition, would inevitably collapse.

So far the influence of thinking in terms of a "conscious mind" alone, upon social action.

Let us now for a moment imagine that the psychoanalysts had acquired social power in some country. They would, from their point of view of the existence of an unconscious mind, acknowledge a vast domain of human existence *beyond* the conscious will. They would, if meeting with the "sitting" of humanity, attribute it to "bad" unconscious wishes of one kind or another. Their remedy would be to "make the spite conscious," to exterminate the evil unconscious. This, of course, would not help, just as it does not help in the treatment of a neurotic, since the spiting itself is the result of the total body armoring, and the "evil unconscious" is the result of the suppression of natural life in the infant; an "I won't" is superimposed upon a silent "I CAN'T." This immobility, expressed as an "I Can't," is naturally inaccessible to mere ideas or persuasion, since it is what orgone biophysics calls "STRUCTURAL," i. e., *frozen emotion*. In other words, it is an expression of the total being of the individual, *unalterable*, just as the shape of a grown tree is unalterable.

Thus, an emperor, basing his attempts to better the human lot on the making conscious of the unconscious and condemnation of the evil unconscious, would fail miserably. The unconscious mind is not the last thing and not the last word. It itself is an artificial result of much deeper processes, the suppression of Life in the newborn infant.

Orgonomy holds the view that human lethargy and sitting on the spot is the outer expression of the immobilization of the bio-energetic system, due to chronic armoring of the organism. The "I can't" appears as an "I won't," no matter whether conscious or unconscious. No conscious drill, no amount of making conscious of the unconscious can ever rock the massive blocking of man's will and action. It is, in the single individual, necessary to break the blocks, to let bio-energy stream freely again and thus to improve man's motility, which in turn will solve many problems arising from inertia in thinking and acting. But a basic immobility will remain. Character structure cannot basically be changed, just as a tree grown crooked cannot be made straight again.

Accordingly, the orgonomist will never aspire to break the blockings of life energy in the mass of humanity. *The attention will center consistently upon the newborn infants everywhere*, upon the infants who are born unarmored, mobile to the fullest. To prevent the immobilization of human functioning, and with it the spiteing, the sitting on the spot for ages, the resistance to any kind of motion or innovation ("sabotage" in Red Fascist terms), becomes the basic task. It is the Emotional Plague of man, born from this very immobilization, which fights living, motile Life in the newborn infants and induces the armoring of the organism. *The worry is*, therefore, the *emotional plague*, and not the mobility of man.

This basic orientation precludes, naturally, any kind of political or ideological or merely psychological approach to human problems. *Nothing can change as long as man is armored*, since every misery stems from man's armoring and immobility which creates the fear of living, *motile* living. The orgonomic approach is neither political nor sociological alone; it is not psychological; it grew out of the criticism and correction of the psychological assumptions of psychoanalysis of an absolute unconscious, of the unconscious being the ultimate giveness in man, etc., and out of the introduction of bio-psychiatry into socio-economic thinking. It is BIOLOGICAL and BIOSOCIAL, resting on the discovery of the Cosmic Energy.

The newborn infant thus, naturally, comes into the center of preventive medicine and education. In this manner the common principle of mankind is obtained; not as an ideal to be striven after, not as a political program to be carried through by mass meetings and proclamations, but as the focus of the deepest root of humanity, as the rock foundation upon which to build: To build as an engineer builds a bridge or an architect a house, and not as the Red Fascist builds up his empire over man and his society, with the help of slander and denunciation and spies and gallows. Modju is the name for the millions of little destroyers of human hope, the killer ants at the foundations of human society; the "poor little fellow" who is so insignificant that no one has as yet mustered enough interest to fix an eye on him and stop his subterranean evil activities.

Orgonomy, which is the factual comprehension of the universal "Cosmic Orgone Energy" ("God," "Ether") touches upon Christian as well as old East Indian thought in the depth of the cosmic existence of man. It is basically not in disagreement with religious thought. It differs from religious thought by its *concreteness* in formulating the concept of God, and by its insistence on the bio-energetic, INCLUDING THE GENITAL, point of view, eschewed in all other systems of thought. But, basically, orgonomy operates in exactly the same realm as Christianity and Hinduism, far deeper than any technological, materialistic or mechanistic conception of Man's roots in Nature. There is no contradiction to Christ's *basic* tenets in Orgonomy, though there is much disagreement with the Christian mythology of Christ.

THE MEANING OF COUNTERTRUTH

To understand the leader, one must first understand the led ones. To beat the foe, one must know his strength and rational roots well. To comprehend the power which the Black or Red Fascist exerts upon multitudes of common people, it is necessary to know the *people*. From this the orgonomic investigation of fascism as "mass psychology" grew in 1930.

In order to use the tool of truth efficiently, one must know the COUNTERTRUTH proficiently. The problem is not why there is truth about things but why truth cannot prevail. If in spite of all the truth and peace-preaching the liars and cheats and gossipers so abundantly prevail, there must be something very powerful that obstructs the truth. It cannot be the lie itself, since lies do not last. There must be some crucial truth of a *different* kind that obstructs the truth proper. We call it the COUNTERTRUTH.

A woman who has taken a lover besides her legal husband lives an important truth. The marriage has worn out, or the husband treats her badly or he is impotent, or he just does not fit her, though he may be important in other respects. Life is rich, too rich to be caught in medieval straightjackets. Yet, this woman does not live the truth without a lie. The lie in this case hides a serious countertruth: If the husband knew, he would kill her or her lover, or both. Nobody would be served. The countertruth is, in regard to telling the truth in this case, more powerful than the truth.

There were at the time of the conferences of the political leaders at Teheran and Yalta, grave reasons NOT to tell the truth about the coming deception of the Americans by the Red Fascists. The countertruth in this case was the compulsion of a companionship with *Red Fascists* regarding defense against the *Black Fascists*.

Royal representatives of people are strictly held NOT to tell any truth, to remain aloof from truth, to avoid embarrassing, truthful questions, to adhere to empty formalities, to " represent " only and not to deviate from — WHAT??? *From custom?* What is custom and why is there this custom? *Good behaviour?* Is strict evasion of the truth good behaviour? *From regard for the public eye?* Why does the public eye shun the truth? *Why is a man who tells a simple truth proclaimed a hero?* Because the multitude consists of cowards? Why is the multitude composed of cowards as regards telling the truth?

There are crucial COUNTERTRUTHS to be guarded against the invasion of the truth. Before searching for the rational in the countertruth, let us survey its domain:

The Jewish people were not permitted to enter the holiest of the holy in the temple. Why? Would one not expect that, in order to elevate a people, one would let them touch the holy every single day? This is not the case. There must be a crucially important reason for keeping the people away from the holy enclosure of the truth.

The cosmic energy which pervades everything and functions in the very senses and emotions of the searchers and thinkers, was never touched in a concrete manner. This is the more astonishing since its functions such as flimmering in the sky, twinkling of stars on clear nights and stoppage of twinkling on nights before rainy weather, the energy field of living bodies, the disappearance of the field in the process of dying, the blueness and the sparkling in "complete darkness," the envelopes of the heavenly bodies, and many other functions such as the vesicles in all tissues that disintegrate, are simple functions easily observed; yet they were not touched for a period of some twenty-five hundred years of human dealings with nature. And when, finally, the cosmic orgone energy was discovered practically and *"touched"* powerfully, there was an uproar, a great hustling and bustling, a loud chit and a chat; but no one, for years, touched an accumulator or looked into a microscope. Why this evasion of the obvious? Why are *geniuses* required to detect the obvious?

The weapon of truth requires that questions are asked regardless of whether they are liked or not, no matter what the results. If your most bitter enemy states falsehoods, you must find the falsehoods. *If he states truth, you must find that he speaks the truth, no matter how painful* the truth of your foe.

The truth of your enemy is the countertruth to your own truth. If the enemy of your truth speaks the truth, then there is something wrong or premature or incomplete in your own truth. Before Hitler's murders could be fully comprehended, the truth he told about Marxists and Jews and Liberals and the Weimar Republic had to be acknowledged. To acknowledge his truth, i. e., your countertruth, was crucial in order to take the next step; to ask, *"How is it possible that a Hitler can come about in the first place? How can seventy million German people, knowing and toiling people, be seduced into such a nightmare by a clear-cut psychopath?"* Without such a question, no answer could be obtained. Hitler clearly presented a countertruth.

The answer to Hitler was found in the character structure of the people at large which made his murders possible. It was *the people* who made Hitler, and not Hitler who subdued the people. Without *Hitlerism or Stalinism in the people* there could be no Hitlers nor Stalins. This was the countertruth in 1932. It became the foundation on which a whole new piece of knowledge grew, the science of orgonomic *"mass psychology,"* the knowledge of the role of the authoritarian family, of the fear of freedom within people, of the structural incapacity for freedom and self-government, of the pornographic and basically sadistic structure of the "middle layer" in people's character; and from here there followed . . . .

THE DISTINCTION OF THE BIO-ENERGETIC CORE AND THE PRIMARY NEEDS. Thus it was the truth, spoken by a biopath in the disguise of a national hero, which led to basic, new answers, to new truths.

The countertruth is in the beginning of a new development, often more important than the truth. The truth will be the firmer and sounder, the better comprehended is the countertruth. And in order to find the countertruth, one must be able to "advocate the devil," to identify with the enemy, to feel like the lout.

Had early sex-economy in the late 1920's succeeded in fully developing a mass movement on a *"sex-POLITICAL."* basis, one of the gravest disasters in the history of mankind would have been set into motion; not because what was told in public at that time was not the truth, but because it was not the FULL truth, which always includes the *countertruth.* And the countertruth in this case was: *The genital suppression in infants and adolescents was necessary; its omission would have been fatal, since these children and adolescents had to adjust to a social structure which* REQUIRED *armoring against emotional freedom. Unarmored children could not have existed in the society of 1930 anywhere on this planet. Therefore, the truth about the evil effects of armoring children and adolescents could not gain the upper hand at that time. This truth, as it stood then, without the knowledge of the countertruth which blocked its way, could not possibly have operated according to its own design and purpose.*

This is truly *"advocacy of the devil."* The countertruth is more cruel at times than any truth could ever be; it is, however, also more fruitful to the final fulfillment of truth:

In the abstract, sex-economic self-regulation is " perfect," much better, cleaner, firmer, sounder, and more decent than moral regulation. Practically, this is borne out in many cases in living Life. The genitally gratified person is not harassed by filthy pornographic thoughts and dreams. He has no impulses to rape or even to seduce against anybody's will. He is far removed from acts of rape and perversion of any kind. *It is the fully genital character who truly fulfills the moral law of Christianity, and of every other true religious ethics.*

THE NEW LEADER

History teaches what major mistakes can be avoided while thrusting forward into the unknown. It cannot teach the coming leader what the future will be like if the future is dreamed of as *different* from present and past social life. It is certain that human society moves onward, steadily, resisting any arrest of motion. Even the great Asiatic societies which had remained the same for long stretches of time, have begun to move onward, and even came into rapid flux when they touched upon Western thought.

The Russian Revolution of 1917 has provided the experience that shows there is no certain goal to be derived from the past. The Marxian view of "historical necessity" only held so far as the necessity of change was concerned. It failed completely so far as the contents and forms of future development were predicted: The actual result of the breaking away from feudal slavery in Russia in the nineteenth century, was increased slavery instead of growth of human self-determination.

With the entry of the great human masses of peoples onto the social scene everywhere — peoples which carry all the miseries and distortions as well as the hopes of the past into an obscure future — mechanical determination of fixed goals and sharply outlined objectives of social development have naturally become impossible. One of the major reasons for the ubiquitous chaos of this twentieth century of transition and transformation of human society, is that masses of peoples in motion have met with heaps of human ideas, most of which are either remainders of the past, devoid of knowledge of human nature, or entirely irrational to begin with.

Molding human destiny according to plans, akin to the building of industrial empires, has become obsolete. In fact, it never was possible, since the great empire enterprises of a Napoleon or a dictatorial mass leader of recent times are no more than brief, insignificant episodes in the tremendous motion which has gripped human society all over the planet.

It is another major reason for the chaos of our times that the crucial issues which are at the bottom of all the commotion are entirely outscreamed by issues of a nuisance nature which govern the scene of politics and politicians. As a physician or a social worker in a small community anywhere, compare what you see with your eyes in the realm of human misery with what you read in the daily newspapers about man's existence, and you will immediately understand the deep chasm between official and private, true life.

It is, furthermore, another characteristic of the times that an entirely new type of social movement is being born, and that people who have not the slightest inkling of what it is all about are the leading statesmen; these leaders of men have shaped their ideas according to past patterns of thought and are sticking rigidly to error.

At first glance, it is astonishing, but quite logical, that none of the basic issues of peoples' movements and upheavals are mentioned anywhere in the screaming, yelling, gesticulating meleé which has taken possession of our lives.

It is common knowledge, and needs no further proof, that the present commotion in human society has no true leaders; in other words, there is nobody so far visible on the horizon who would develop into what a Christ came to mean for the Christian era or a Confucius for Asiatic culture. The present-day leaders are no more than agents of the security of this or that aspect of the status quo, or simply brigands on lawless seas. They are like the looters of goods in a free-for-all robbery during a flood or an earthquake. Unfortunately, these robbers are mistaken for the new leaders by many greatly impressed Babbitts sitting amidst islands of what is left of a happier past.

Let us now outline such a leader who would emerge from today's chaos and be able to observe and handle the main currents in the social upheaval. What task, what fateful decision would such a leader have to face?

It is often said that a leader in our time would have to be very much like a superman, a Nietzschean man far outdistancing his fellow man. Accordingly, such a leader is hard to imagine.

Such an image of leadership for our times derives clearly from man's old, worn-out need for mystification of leadership even before the leader has entered the public scene. It already has promoted and removed the leader in the chaos of our days into a region where no one can reach him, so nobody can even come near being like him.

If we understood the lesson of the Murder of Christ well, such a leader would certainly fail to direct the movements of the masses of people-in-commotion out of the past into a rational future existence. He would *have* to fail since he would do little more than provide another mystical symbol to sexually frustrated, love-starved multitudes bare of the basic securities of life.

If, as we have reason to believe, we have learned our lesson from the Murder of Christ well, a leader of peoples in our times would be nearly the *exact opposite* of what people are so eager to see or to acclaim as their leader. He would, in his everyday life, stand out little from the usual ways of people's lives. He would be a man who would submerge into the stream of life and peoples' movements again and again, learning their bloody lessons of repeated failure; he would make most stupid mistakes and would have to learn to correct silly errors without drowning.

He would have to go through every hell of human inferno within his reach to know human nature *practically* and efficiently inside out and out side in. He would have to have lived with publicans and sinners and harlots and criminals to know the soil from which grows human hope as well as misery. (If he were a leader as people like him to be, he would only add another clown to the mass of little and big noise-makers who do not mean a thing in the long run of human history.)

Such a leader would have to possess or to develop an extraordinary quality, never heard of before, unimaginable to the current view of what leadership of men should be like.

HE WOULD HAVE TO FOREGO ANY TEMPTATION TO BECOME A LEADER AND TO AVOID ANY LURE ON THE PART OF PEOPLE TO SEDUCE HIM INTO LEADER-SHIP. HIS FIRST GREAT TASK WOULD *be to refuse to be a leader.*

Such a leader would immediately sense the danger that threatens to engulf every leader of people, namely *becoming a mere object of admiration and provider of salvation and hope for the people.* Such a leader would make the first step in guiding people by *taking people seriously* and by *letting them save themselves,* with the necessary social safeguards, economic and psychological, backing them up.

Such a leader would certainly have either read the story of the Murder of Christ or he would soon, from his own experience, learn that the people create their live Christs in order to submit to them, or, if the Christs refuse to become Barabbases, to kill them outright only to promote them to heaven for salvation's sake, without themselves moving a finger.

From his own painful and dangerous experience, our leader would know that to become a leader of people with their given structure would mean that one of the following things must happen: ·

He would yield fully to people's ways and remain sitting on the spot with them. The great promises and expectations and programs would soon be mere holiday recitals and routine litanies with no meaning or sense whatsoever in them. People would be silently disappointed, but they would not do much to effect a change since this would be quite in agreement with their lethargic sitting on the spot. This sitting would go on until the more active and reckless type of leader would appear.

This other type of leader would be equally a victim of people's need for salvation and promises of heaven on earth. The *future dictator* is this type. Dictators of this type are carried away by the genuine yearnings of the masses. They are seduced into promising to the people whatever people wish to hear.

Quite unknowingly and honestly (unless we are aware of this honesty of dictators, their power over people cannot really be understood) they will heap people's hopes, impossible of fulfillment, upon their own hopes, impossible of fulfillment, until they will have erected in front of the people a magnificent edifice of a great empire, of a final heaven, of power and glory or of a land where only honey and milk flow in the rivers.

In doing so, these leaders honestly believe that they lead and direct the people, that they are the saviours of society. They are entirely unaware of the fact that they have only fallen prey to the most typical as well as the most pernicious dream of peoples everywhere. They were carried away by a giant stream, and still they believe that *they* are the ones who *make* the stream flow. They are, of course, only tiny dolls play acting as the great emperors of the stream which actually carries *them* along and away. They have no inkling whatsoever of the nature of the stream on which they helplessly float; nor would they know in the least about how to direct the stream into a different kind of bed or of how to build a dam against its flooding potentialities. They are like the clowns in the circus who make certain gestures to make the audience believe that they are the ones who make the show start or stop, who move mountains on the stage by mere gesture. They are like magicians who make people wonder until the tricks are fully exposed and other magicians with different kinds of tricks appear on the scene.

Our leader who is not of this kind would still, for a while at least, feel and behave like such a dictator, driven by his natural inclination to taste from every little bit of human affairs, to know everything by his own personal experience. Our leader, too, would therefore let himself drift on top of the waves of human hero worship. His enjoyment of the hailing would have to be genuine in order really to know how it feels to be hailed and worshipped and looked upon as the saviour of people. He would differ from the true future dictator in that he would sooner or later develop a bad taste in his mouth about all the hailing and the gestures of people expecting salvation. He would certainly feel somehow emptied of the sap of his vivacity and natural productivity. He would feel that he was running out of spirit and ideas, and he would certainly begin to feel the dullness and the emptiness in people's stereotypical, ever returning ways of making their leaders proud of themselves. Only the first few times would he feel that the ardor of the speeches are seriously meant; that determination professed to bring the good into this world is self-sustaining; that, once in power, one would simply go at the misery and sweep it up with a big broom.

Our leader, thus doped into high fake spirits and a continuously high-riding mood of saviourship, would begin to feel stale. And he would make a most distressing discovery:

THEY DO NOT REALLY MEAN IT. It is all a *show of humanity*. It is no more than an empty promise. This he would realize in small matters; matters which usually do not attract much attention.

Our leader, naturally, if he is to fit his function, has to know how to work, how to accomplish a certain job, how to make a living with practical things, how to build a table, or to dress a wound, or to stop a child's choking anxiety, or to repair an entangled situation in a family, or to fly a helicopter, or to grind glass into lenses, or to fell a tree, or to paint a picture, or to disentangle the riddle of a sickness, or to arrange an experiment in order to solve a problem of nature, or how to go about handling an adolescent in the agony of genital frustration, and many more of such things highly uninteresting to a dictator's soul.

Our leader would, briefly, know how to *work* and what work really means; how much effort, detailed, minute effort goes into even a small accomplishment. He would have the feel of it. And this feel would sooner or later make him realize that what people do to him is just empty talk. The moment he would attempt to start them on the road to *doing* practical things they would begin to dislike him, or they would just talk, talk, talk about the high ideal of carpentry or medicine or education or industry or flying. But, really, they would not move a finger, just talk and sit in droves around pleasantly arranged tables with food or drinks upon them, or they would just sit immovably.

He would at first refuse to accept his distinct notion that they are just talking, transforming every little practical task into mere *ideas* of doing this and that. They would sit as the millions of Russian peasants sat for ages when they had not worked their backs sick and stiff for a piece of bread. They would sit as the Chinese coolie has sat for ages when he did not draw his ricksha through the street of some big city, sweating to earn his daily bread. This sitting the talkers call the " *philosophical nature of the oriental man,*" knowing nothing about the Eastern mass disease which is *rigidity of the body through armoring.* And they would dreamingly talk about what they *would* do once they grab power over an eastern or western nation, how they *would* enlighten the people and bring them freedom, and lead them toward Socialism which is inevitably coming, having just reached the end of the first phase as described in the socialist gospel, and being just about to enter the second phase of the development, full-blown Communism.

Sitting amidst this talking crowd, our new leader would remain silent. He would wonder: But how about the mystical mind, the belief in ghosts and the signs of howling hounds and the witches, and how about the misery in the marital chambers, and the beating of the children for nastiness, and how about the nightmares of the ones entering puberty? How about spontaneous work, and taking good care of tools, and safe driving, and running trains and airplanes on time safely, and all the rest of it? How would you go about it all, he may dare to interject. Oh, this is mere bourgeois stuff. A planned economy will do away with it. And who will plan? The Planning Commission, of course. And our leader will see with his inner eyes the burned villages of Ukrainian peasants shot to death or driven to Siberia for "sabotage." These peasants just sat and were unable to move beyond the most essential daily chores necessary to keep life going; and they simply had no inkling of what it was all about, why they had to be led to "freedom" by ignorant, cunning little boys who smelled the smell of power and got drunk from it, and began shooting peasants who were carrying the result of a thousand years' old plague in their stiffened backs and transmitting it to their children with beatings.

From this immobility of the body, from this restriction of life in the limbs and loins emerges all the irresponsibility, because *people have simply been rendered incapable of taking responsibility;* all are helpless, because they were beaten into helplessness or otherwise rendered impotent by a cruel, ignorant way of life of many thousands of years standing.

Our freedom peddlers soon and easily become freedom robbers. There is nothing else they can do since there is nothing they know about this mass disease. And even if they knew what they dare not know, since it would make them run, they would not know what to do about it. The freedom peddler is not to be accused for raving against the misery in front of thousands of listeners. He is to be exposed for NOT MEANING WHAT HE SAYS, or, if he means it, for not knowing at all how to go about things once he has cheated people into the yoke of his power with his promises.

Our leader would be drawn into the very same stream of agony if he were not a *man of* WORK who knows what it means to go about things, to DO, to BUILD, to THINK. He would, once in power, be carried to the top by the need for salvation on the part of the immobilized multitudes of people; he would, merely in order not to be torn to pieces by his own admirers, *have* to keep the mines and railroads going; he would *have* to keep children going to school; he would *have* to provide the nation with bread and corn and potatoes and sometimes even with meat. And because he had only talked and did not prepare anything to fulfill the promises he so lavishly bestowed upon his crowds, he now *must* become the cruel dictator, far worse than the industrialist of the nineteenth century or the emperor whom he had shot dead.

It is always the average character structure of masses of people that determines the nature and activity of leadership. This has been one of the best secured realizations of social orgonomy. It holds for the king as well as for the dictator. Kings and dukes and dictators and priests and freedom peddlers are products of people. It holds also for our new type of leader. The leader of the future who will have learned the lesson of the Murder of Christ well, will also be a result of the character structure of the people in general.

The necessity of realizing the basic importance of the average man's social conduct has been forced upon the world by the dictatorships which grew from people's yelling " Hail, my Fuehrer." It is to be expected that in just the same lawful manner, the great compulsion in the people to Murder their Christs will force the emergence of a new type of leader of men.

Let us survey these characteristics as they needs must emerge from those traits in people's behaviour which periodically culminate in the Murder of some Christ:

The new leader will have to choose between acclaim by the people and adherence to his realization of what people do to themselves by their eternal sitting. He will, accordingly, do little of what makes up the actions of the politician of today. He will not cater to public approval. He will realize that such acclaim, comforting and pleasant as it is, " recognition " as it seems to be, is the first sure step to extinction of what he stands for. He will, therefore, not care for or will even try to avoid as much as possible what is called public recognition. *The claim for " recognition " is, on the part of the pioneer, fear of having to stand alone, and on the part of the people in general, it is cowardice in thinking for themselves. The claim for recognition is basically fear of non-comformity and its resultant social ostracism.*

This does not mean that the new leader will play the role of a neglected wallflower. On the contrary: he will feel greater independence in the pursuit of his tasks. This will require far greater determination and genuine strength than is required from the politician who climbs up some social tree. It will make for far greater solidity in the foundations of the new leader's activity.

It does not mean that this new leader will despise people, or that he will not be desirous of public acclaim. If he is to do his job he will remain human to the last. But, knowing *why* people bestow honors on the victims of their adoration, he will silently evade this trap like a good educator who avoids certain actions if he knows that they will not serve his ultimate purpose of helping adolescents under certain conditions.

The new leader, accordingly, will not " go to the people "; he will not " write for people " and he will not try to " convince people " of the truth or social importance of his knowledge. *He will write about things* he believes to be true, and *not* for people. It is amazing to find how the most elaborate and most realistic human teachings fell prey to the old habit of doing things "for people" or to "going among people" to teach them what appears to be good for them.

If people need the good and the helpful and the clarifying, let them search for it; let them find it *themselves*. Let they themselves develop the skill of discriminating between the saying of a scoundrel or a political windbag or a freedom peddler and the teachings of some serious man. The problem is not that Hitler wanted power, but that he got it. It is a great problem: how millions of grown-up, industrious, efficient, serious men and women could let him get power over their lives.

In such changes of basic views about people, the new leader will grow up to his task. A new rule is growing which sounds strange at first:

If you hear salvation proclaimed in a manner which is of the past, you may suspect that the truth is exactly at the opposite end of the line.

This is quite natural in the face of the basic characteristic of man to avoid the essential and to stick to the unessential. If a whole generation of psychiatrists will have labored hard on the energetic core of man's confused ideas about his existence and found frustrated sex the common denominator of it all, be sure that people in general will try to get away from it and will foster and make famous those psychiatric schools which will delete this crucial piece of knowledge and replace it by some banal, babbitty babble of a hundred years ago, dressed up as a new doll to play around with innocently. It will find its apostle who will thus ride high on the waves of public acclaim. Let them! They won't do much harm as long as there are centers which keep the issues clean and clear. There will certainly come times of distress when the evasive doctrine will fall away like a rotted leaf and when what had been growing in silence for many decades, ready to emerge into the general current of the times, will be searched for with eagerness.

The new leader will feel impatient but he will learn to wait endlessly. He will know or learn by experience that the good things in life cannot possibly soar to heaven like rockets, that they must grow slowly, that no step in crucial developments can be jumped over without endangering the whole, and that lasting things must test their wings in little dangers long before they transform the world the big way, growing by dangers. Waiting patiently is only possible if you have no ambition to lead or to save people. *Let people save themselves.* It will do them a lot of good finally to learn how it feels to drown because of one's own stupidity. Such lessons are never forgotten and very productive of new possibilities.

The old type of leader had to learn how to make friends and to avoid making enemies. In order to make friends, the gist had to be sapped off from most fruitious ideas. Sharp formulations had to be smoothed out in order to offend no one, edgy corners had to be rounded, and the indirect expression had to replace the direct and the open one: the sneaking way, quite in accordance with people's fear of immediate contact, prevailed. Yet, people always like the straightforward man better than the politician. They fear him more, it is true; they avoid him and they seem to cherish the crooked one only. But in the end their admiration, even if from a great distance only, is for straightforwardness.

Here the basic split in their own structure reveals itself: They live, actually, according to the rules of evasion of the essential, but they wish, at the same time, for the direct, full, simple contact with things. People come around in the end; they really do. To realize this initial fear in people of the direct and straight is a major requirement of the new leader.

The new leader will not be afraid to make enemies, if necessary. He will not stop thinking straight because someone might hate him for it. He will sooner or later learn that some of these enemies are far closer friends and knowers of his essence than many a close friend. He will not try to prove his point by offending people, but he will distinguish offense for its own sake from offense by way of telling what is right. The thing that is certain to kill the political plague rampant in this twentieth century is the way the fascists attacked their foes with a deep truth, the force of glowing yearning for Life; however, this force was used in the negative sense only, not in the positive way. They really had nothing to offer and fell prey to people's foible for show of strength and toughness. The new leader will naturally be firm, but he will have no trace of showmanship within him so far as toughness is concerned. He will, of necessity, hit hard but always fairly.

After numerous and dangerous experiences with man's clinging to the strong one, the new leader will slowly develop a sharp sense for people who are apt to cling like a louse to the fur or a leech to the skin. He will sense the friend who will go along a stretch and then remain sitting on the spot like a mule, not budging an inch, thus forcing the doer to slow down his pace or to stop moving altogether. The new leader will also know well the hatred that is bound to develop from people who are left behind, sitting. He will carefully guard against such possibilities by a continuous mentioning of this prominent characteristic of men who are leeches. He will give them prophylactic mental injections, as it were, by telling them *beforehand* what they will most likely be inclined to do against him if he leaves them behind, sitting, doing nothing. They will, in order to suffer less from the loss of the leader, make him appear bad, less important, even picture him as an evil character.

The new leader will face the painful task of loving people and at the same time of not becoming bound to them the usual way; to know their weaknesses and not to despise or to fear them. He will, first of all, face loneliness, living in vast spaces alone with only few friends. And even these friends may turn out to be a bother or nuisance, since all want salvation. Everyone wants something from him, anyhow. He will slowly realize with amazement how infinite are the desires to get *things* on the part of people. It does not matter *what* they want. It is the wanting and the *getting* that matters. And he will be well aware of the price paid to him for the getting: empty admiration. He will accordingly, not fall prey to the temptation, so common in the politician, to soak up this admiration like a sponge.

The new leader will have to do without many things which usually make up for the various hardships of leadership. He will not enjoy much of the ease with which movements usually spread out by way of praising the leader. He will always be aware that what counts is what a leader found or said or proposes and not what he himself would like to enjoy. He will have learned from past history that sacrifice of the essence of one's hard labors is the price paid for formal success. He will, briefly, always be aware of the well hidden tendency in people to see things in the mirror only, to take over great things only to render them impotent, to care far more for the admiring of someone than for what he has to offer, to flock around the unimportant and to force the crucial thing toward impotence.

With this the new leader will cause many to turn against him. He will have robbed these many of an object to hold on to, like a bean stalk would feel robbed of comfort if you took away the supporting stick of wood.

The new leader will have to risk that he remain ignominious in his lifetime. But he will also be certain that it is far better for his cause and for the public good to remain alone than to see his good cause take possession of the world in a *bad* way, in a way contrary to what was intended, even distorted to such an extent by the people that it can only spell disaster. This will apply especially where matters of sexual living are concerned. The armored animal is bound to make a 4-lettering religion out of the tremendous fact of orgastic potency, just as it had made the most elaborate, infernal system of spying and looting *against* freedom out of the good old conspiracy of revolutionary fighters *for* freedom.

The new leader will feel somewhat comforted by the conviction that truth and what is useful to people is bound to come about even if it takes a million years. He will still not do anything FOR people but will simply do things, doing them well. Again, *he will let people save themselves.* He will know that no one else can do it for them. He will simply *live ahead of people* and leave it to them to join him or not. He will be a guide rather than a leader. The guide only tells how to get safely to the peak of the mountain. He does not determine which mountain the tourist wishes to climb. The new leader may very well be leading a whole world without knowing himself that he is leading, or with the world unaware that it is being directed by this one leader. Christ was such a leader. The new leader's way of being, his ideas, his conduct and goals may have penetrated the public mind imperceptibly, unnoticed by anyone. He still may have to take the blame for distortions which are not of his making or for evil doings he never propounded, and he may in the end be put to the cross just as Christ was put to death. The new leader will know that this could very well happen to him. He feels responsible not for people but for what is going on in the world, just as every single citizen of the world feels responsible for world events. This, too, is a new feature in the new leadership: *The feeling of responsibility in every citizen of the world for everything that is going on, even at far-away corners of the globe.* The chatting, back-slapping, gossiping, bad-joking, 4-lettering, empty bag of an irresponsible citizen of a free country is a matter of the past. So much is certain.

The new leader will have more enemies among his closest friends, and fewer but more dangerous enemies among the multitudes. Every schizophrenic mystic, every religious fanatic, every political power drunkard is his potential enemy or would-be killer. He will not adhere to the belief in martyrdom. He will want to *live,* and not to die for his cause. And he will carefully prepare against disaster. He will have a loaded gun in his home and he will, if he can, be careful whom he permits to enter his house. He will live a lonely life and will avoid as much as possible empty, babbling, fake sociality.

He will keep at a distance and yet will not despise or feel enmity toward people. This he will have won in hard battles against himself. When he first encountered people's fake admiration and the fury of their *getting something for nothing,* he felt inclined to join the conservative leader of society who knows that people are that way and who never dreamed of changing it. He will fully understand the mind of the American pioneer of industry in the 1880's. But he will also surpass the " sitting " of the conservative industrialist of 1960.

To understand the motives of people's behaviour and yet not to fall prey to pitying them and saving them, in line with the freedom peddler, will be a major task to be faithfully carried out. How is one to know the plight of a farmer woman with ten children and yet to expect from her that she do *not* gossip and that she tell her mind frankly, just as she feels it in her guts?

The freedom peddler would prolong her misery by his fearsome " understanding" of her malignant gossip about her neighbor, which would mean *confirming* it. The new leader would quarantine a maligning, gossiping woman by social ostracism. Gossip is murder and the exact opposite of the free opinion of a free man or woman.

The freedom peddlers are supported by the brain intelligence machines whose sole function is to keep their genitals dead. These walkitalki brain intelligences are the brain trusts of the plague. They can talk away mountains and rivers right in front of you. They can talk away the scent of every flower, since they are dried-out mouthpieces of a long past truth without emotion or soul. They populate the offices of many a modern, progressive government. They are the Talmudists of the Marxian gospel. They are horrid. Every living feeling is killed by their mere presence. They cannot cry and they cannot sob. They love with their brains and they hate with their genitals. To be human in their presence is impossible. The man or woman of toil to them is a tool of " historical necessity," and nothing else. Therefore, they will not hesitate, while sitting themselves safely in the sanctuary of Manchuria, to drive millions of poor Chinese boys in uniform, called " volunteers," before the muzzels of American cannons in Korea, merely in order to prove the " eternal vigilance and the courage of the bolshevist *avant garde*." They are the offspring of a degenerated mechanical age, making a religion out of their intellectual concoctions. All this the new leader will have to know.

He will also know that these brainy mechanists, while 4-lettering right and left, hate true love of the body like poison and therefore will obstruct with fire and sword any attempt at a reconstruction of the human character structure. They will subsume all human problems under one single aspect only: The dog's stomach excretes saliva when he hears a bell ring which once rang together with the sight of meat. This is all. Isn't it perfect materialism? It is. In perfect agreement with this view of human problems, their brain excretes intelligence when they smell the scent of power. This is all that has been left over of a great teaching of human emancipation.

The new leader will meet with many dangers and pitfalls. Among them the fear in people of the gossipy plague which chokes their simple knowing in their tight and frightened throats. He will have to recognize the first signs of the presence of a hidden plague. He will have learned that a single pestilent person can upset a whole peaceful community, just as a single wrong tune in an orchestra can upset a most beautiful symphony.

He will know that the plague is infectious. Somehow, it manages to bring out the latent plague in most decent people, nobody knows as yet how. You can recognize it happening by the mess which suddenly, as if from nowhere, breaks into a harmoniously cooperating group of people if a single pestilent character is present; once you have learned to scent it, it is immediately recognizable by a definite emotional smell.

Our new leader will encounter another most peculiar thing: People who seemed to be most devoted and reliable in their cooperation with living Life will start crowding around the center which spreads the plague. This seems to be so because the plague offers the *emotion* of heroism without the *effort* of heroic endurance. It seems to protect the human soul from its own emotional depth. The process of rebuilding human character structures needs must require centuries of continuous vigilant, strenuous effort by many educators and physicians of the soul. The pestilent educator will have people flock around him for the simple reason that he will promise a perfect system of education without effort within a month. Just send him children and he will do it. Or, why bother to dig up carefully and skillfully the involved dynamics of the plague in one's own emotional system? Is it not simpler to submit to dianetics which not only cures all ills in the whiffy breeze of a single breath but in addition enables the soul, purified so speedily, to do the same speedy thing to many other sick souls?

Because the plague is the result of the evasion of the depths of things and because people in general are afraid of the depth, they will swiftly choose the plague and abandon the laborious, long range task of decent labor. Not unless this is fully realized, can the plague in the realms of education, medicine, social administration and public hygiene be overcome with efficiency.

The new leadership will, therefore, keep the manifold manifestations of the plague under careful supervision. It will learn how to know in time and how directly to attack the plague-ridden obstructionist of every fruitful human effort. The plague-ridden person is empty and therefore is a coward. He sneaks well in the night, but he melts away in the clean, clear daylight.

Liberals will tell you that the plague has a right to free speech, too. Yes, but in the open fresh air only, not in the dark corner of my backyard, in the middle of the night with a knife in the fist ready to strike me in the back.

The help rendered to the plague by the liberal soul is enormous. The new leader will have to surmount the defense of the plague by the liberal soul. He will rebuke their excuse that " it always has been so " and accordingly can continue this way into all eternity.

The new leader will explain to the liberal that sneaking up on one's fellow man in the dark of night, or sending a bouquet of flowers to his birthday party which explodes in his face has nothing to do with free expression of rational opinion, but is cowardly Murder of Christ. He will have a hard time convincing the liberal soul that liars and murderers and gossipers and defilers of honor are criminals against the security of freedom and happiness of men, women and children. He will have to be successful in convincing the world around him that, finally, one must begin to learn to read honesty and dishonesty in the faces of Asiatic or European or American envoys to distinguish the scoundrel of a spy from the representative of a social administration.

The contempt for practical psychology and the delay in studying the expression of the character have cost the Western world the secrets about their atomic weapon which they so ardently tried to protect. Bombs, of course, will never change the world. Bringing into action the people's innermost living qualities will. But protection against the plague is possible by reading the expression of a scoundrel in the face of a diplomatic envoy; this belongs to the task of bringing people's qualities of living Life into action.

Here the liberal, meek souls become truly dangerous. Weak in their guts, with no prospect ahead of themselves, resting only on a once valid, great doctrine of humanism, they delivered the German society to the Nazis and they may succeed in delivering American society to the habitual spies of the reactionary Russian empire. Such liberals are deeply impressed, though they may not feel or know it, by the skill and show of power on the part of the generals of the organized plague; they succumb to the temptation like virgins weakened in the virtue of abstinence submit to the knight in shining armor. Beware of the soul which always appears meek and softspoken and which never raises its voice in anger or revolt against evil. There are many sneaks among them, ready to betray Christ in our children for thirty shillings. They are only concerned with their own emotions of a fake fairness. While protecting one murderer of Christ, they forget that thousands could be saved from evil. They indirectly empower the plague to fulfill what they themselves are incapable of accomplishing. Their guts are filled with green hatred and the lust of murder. They are the more dangerous in that they use the most peaceful and innocent dreams of people for their evil doings.

Learn to support the man or woman who is straight and outright in the expression of opinion, and who knows well when to love and when to hate, what to protect and what to leave to its own devices; who knows and lives the love of the body and the sorrow of the soul, and who knows what tears in silent nights are. They are the ones hated most by the walki-talki brain intelligence machines and the fakers who drivel words of honey with poison hidden in them to kill the gullible victim.

The new leader will beware of the bandwaggon rider, the empty bag who jumps on your car loaded with rich fruits of your hard toil to fill himself to the brim, only to knife you later on, or to get bigger than you and to suck power over people from *your* strenuous efforts without moving a finger. Beware of him who dares not look into your eyes straight and simple, who always turns his face away from you lest you see and know him. He will be the next president of your organization and he will take everything over and kick you out, no matter how much good you did to build him up. And he will not care for what you have worried about over many years. He only wants to fill his empty ego, endlessly, without effort. The worst of it is this: *He does not know at all that he is betraying you.* Did he not, so runs his argument, have everything coming to him? Is this not so because his mother frustrated him when he was a suckling, and does he not now have the perfect right to suck you dry and empty and then to knife you in the back? Of course he has, and he does not understand at all that you question this right of his. He is one of those who disfigured Christ's fighting love for man into the evil idea that man has to give away everything he possesses so Modju can get all for nothing.

Also, many an evil liberator of peoples comes from such frustrated infancy; but never mind their infancy. Mind the children yet to be born.

The honest leader of men will meet distrust of his doings because these leeches have filled the world with their cunning, murderous sucking of power and knowledge and love and self-esteem and position and honor from those who were abundant in these natural gifts. They never could reproduce and nourish these gifts, and therefore they had to continue to suck other victims dry all through their lives. Honesty will be distrusted because human society has become accustomed to dishonest conduct. If you will give honestly without expecting anything in return, you will be suspected of cheating. If you will give your soul to your pupils to make knowers or doers of them, the world will ask " where is the catch? " And this is so because of the leeches who have sucked the world dry.

The new leader will have to learn to give wisely and with circumspection. Otherwise people will take him for a sucker and make a fool of him with deep contempt for his ways. He will be hailed as the " hen that lays the golden eggs " to be swallowed into empty stomachs. Unless you are prepared to meet still worse than you ever dared to imagine, don't ever try to save lives or to protect children. You will appear as a fool only or, worse, as a criminal in the eyes of many judges. " It is not being done." Love without interest is simply not of this world; but the new leader will have to muster a lot of love. Love has become homeless in a loveless age where politics is ruling the scene. All this the new leader will have to know and to suffer.

An empty space will develop around him when people will feel that he represents Life and is a giver of Life. He will feel hurt, he will go through agony for having suffered hate for deeds of love; and he himself will be tempted to hate for all this ugly performance. Distrust of people and need for revenge will threaten to poison his soul. Many will fall and be lost as leaders in this manner. The people themselves will have done it to their leaders, who will feel like rats in well-set traps, like fools and good-for-nothings. Only very few will survive this hell.

The people will isolate and quarantine the leader in many ways. One way to drive him into solitude is to adore him, to crowd around him, to hang onto his lips and to drink every single word he speaks. Some leaders love it. Others run when they encounter it. They feel like animals in the zoo stared at by crowds who are amazed that animals have not developed shame of their genitals. People are apt to undress the leader when they crowd around him, to get at every one of his secrets: how many women he eats up for dinner, whether he goes swimming and whether he plays bridge, whether he has illegitimate children, or whether his wife has a lover.

The crowd will isolate and kill the leader eventually by centering the spotlight on him, figuratively and literally speaking. They will bind him down and render him impotent by criticizing every single one of his moves without moving a finger in practical action themselves. Hasn't the constitution granted the right of free speech? And aren't they free people of a free land? It does not matter which land; they always feel free, or just liberated or just about to jump into freedom. And what they mean is jumping out of the marriage straight-jacket for just one night or going on vacation or sleeping while others work in the office on a hot summer day in a steaming big city.

All this would be all right if it would not kill every move of a truly free mind. The leader, in order to survive, will have to keep clear of all this staring and criticizing and doing nothing but chatting and 4-lettering. And slowly, in painful realization, he will learn to see the complete emptiness of people which is out-screamed with a lot of noise, a noise which is made to distract them from the gnawing sensation of just nothingness. From this nothingness only malignancy can grow. The leader will know this and feel like one drowning in an ocean of tasks impossible to perform.

The isolation which he suffers at the hands of the people around him will endanger his health and his ability to work. He will lose the right to live a normal life among other people. While people have perfect understanding for the secrets of couples, married and otherwise, they will look askance at a leader's changing a partner or not living up to some set's nuisance standard of conduct. The leader will soon learn that to him is denied what otherwise is taken for granted in the case of the average citizen. He will find it more and more difficult to move freely with mates. He will have to start hiding. And hiding will drive away many a mate who will want to parade among the crowds with the lover, who is a " leader."

Such things will endanger the whole structure of the leader's job. He will be in danger of growing morose or of brooding in a hole, incapable of being productive of thoughts, thus becoming a Caligula or a proletarian mouthful of freedom-peddler-slogans. LEADERS OF MEN WILL HAVE TO LIVE A FULL, SANE, GRATIFYING LOVE LIFE WITH WOMEN WHO UNDERSTAND THE WORKINGS OF LIFE. If the leader is to accomplish his job he will keep clear of the entanglements of a dulling, noisy family life. Here he will be in line with Christ who left his family and requested that his followers do the same. But he will under no circumstances preach the dissolution of the family, as some freedom peddlers are so prone to do. He will have and enjoy children, his own and others. He will know that what is valid for his life is not always valid for everybody else's life. At any rate, the new leader will have to maintain a *pure emotional system,* and he will do everything to escape the filth of the soul which goes with sexual starvation. His senses and his thoughts must stay clear of the ravages of abstinence from gratifying bodily love.

Keeping the core of his living being constantly in high gear, he will be able to penetrate through the gossiping and tea-partying and socializing and backslapping and bad-joking and 4-lettering of the men and women in the street and in the palaces, to the core of their living emotions. He will eventually succeed in finding out why so many people gifted with all kinds of potentialities sooner or later fall into the rut of a dull life. Why there is so little productive thought and action coming from the people; how all the fertility in people is being killed in so many ways and so early in life, even as it just emerges from the womb.

People will not like being driven to feel their very living cores of stirring emotions; not in the movie, but at the sight of a child being beaten up in a park; not in a dancing and shoving and panting and rubbing and sweating crowd, but in the slums and in the impoverished regions of the nations and in the big cities where white proletarians kill black proletarians. Briefly, the task of generations of leaders of men will be to find ways to *stop the evasion of the essential* and the cheap thrill felt at the sight of bleeding faces in a boxing match.

Just as the emotional attention of people in general will have to turn or to be turned toward the *essential,* lest everything perish, so the new leader will also carry the burden of turning the tide toward *concentration on the essential in human life* instead of on the foolish and nonsensical and long forsaken old, rotten stuff of public affairs. The *evasion of the essential* had followed the tracks drawn by the general evasiveness and had established over the ages powerful centers of distraction from the crucial issues of life, equipped with great power to maintain itself against intrusion by Christ in any form. To confirm this, read the headlines of any newspaper today.

The new leader will tell the people that voting is not enough, and that to admonish people to partake in government is not enough either. It will all start in the early infant environments and in the nursery schools and in the kindergartens and in the schools. The courageous, knowing school superintendents will be supported against the ossified school teachers. The ways and means of the plague which keeps living Life away from the schools will be detected and fought as only grand larceny or murder is fought today.

Once the attention will be focused on the great evasion of the essential as the most dangerous enemy of mankind, the means will be found to kill it — the evasion, not the evader — wherever it will be met. The problem is not the problem to be solved. The problem is the determined evasion of any major problem.

Many a true leader will face death and extinction one way or another. The plague will be raving as never before. But, once dragged into the open fresh air and into the brilliant sunlight, the ugly, evil breeding of monstrous mischief and of pernicious thoughts all through the ages, will slowly begin to melt away. To the same extent, Life will begin to move onward.

There is no reason to worry about what forms Life on its march will choose for its existence. Whatever it may choose; once it will be freed from the chronic Murdering of Christ, it will choose what is good for itself, and it will learn by its own experience what to abandon. Life is productive, Life is flexible, Life is decent. Therefore, do not worry about what Life will choose to do. The only worry is how to free it for action against the murder of Christ, against those who have lost the feel of Life in their bodies.

No thunder and no earthquake will accompany the awakening of living Life in our children. It will be a slow process of growth, straight and clean if the plague will be hamstrung, difficult and crooked if the plague will escape *full* extinction.

It is quite certain that in no case will or can Life choose a form of existence which is anti-Life, against children, against truth, against the delight of living happily, against accomplishment or the full flowering of the inborn initiative in every single carrier of the spark of Life. To let Life stream freely, unimpeded by the distortions which render it ugly and murderous, will be the first step toward freedom and peace on earth. This little piece of insight will in itself spark freedom into action. The concern for the welfare of the newborn baby which carries Christ within itself right from heaven onto earth, is quite general and can be surpassed by nothing on earth; it will prove a power of tremendous dimensions, outdistancing everything that evil men have ever tried to invent for the sake of killing Life.

A new type of man will grow up and transmit his new qualities, which will be the qualities of unrestricted Life, to his children and children's children. No one can tell what this Life will be like. No matter what it will be like, it will be *itself*, and not the reflection of a sick mother or a nuisance of a pestilent relative. It will be ITSELF, and it will have the power to develop, and to correct what will impede its development.

Our task is to protect this process from the evil plague, to safeguard its growth, to learn in time what distinguishes a child who grew as Life prescribed, from a child who grew as the interest in this or that Culture or State or Religion or Custom or cockeyed idea of life prescribed. Unless this is accomplished, there will be no hope whatsoever to end the mass slaughter.

In short, the new leader will refuse to ride toward Jerusalem to conquer the enemy. He will turn toward the streaming of Life, which is God, in the little bodies of the unborn sons and daughters of man. On them he will rest his resolve *not to yield to the temptation* of the people to become their leader in perpetuating their ways of life gone stale; not to yield to the very people whose lives must be changed basically in letting infants grow as Life's God has created them.

CULTURE AND CIVILIZATION HAVE NOT BEEN YET. THEY ARE JUST BEGINNING TO ENTER THE SOCIAL SCENE. IT IS THE BEGINNING OF THE END OF THE CHRONIC MURDER OF CHRIST.

BIBLIOGRAPHY

1. AKHILANANDA, SWAMI: *Hindu View of Christ*. Philosophical Library, New York, 1949.
2. AQUINAS, ST. THOMAS: *The Summa Theologica, Vols. I, II, III*. Benziger Bros., Inc., New York, 1947.
3. ARNIM, L. A. und BRENTANO, CLEMENS: *Des Knaben Wunderhorn*. Max Hesses Verlag, Leipzig, 1806.
4. ASCH, SHOLEM: *The Nazarene*. G. P. Putnam's Sons, New York, 1939.
5. AUGUSTINE, SAINT: *The Basic Writings of Saint Augustine, Vols. I, II*. Random House, New York, 1948.
6. BACHOFEN, JOHANN JACOB: *Mutterrecht und Urreligion*. Ulfred Kröner Verlag, Leipzig, 1927.
7. BATELJA, MICHAEL J.: *Value of the Holy Bible*. Published by the author, Portland, Oregon, 1951.
8. BERNARD, THEOS: *Hindu Philosophy*. Philosophical Library, New York, 1947.
9. BERNFELD, SIEGFRIED: *Das Jüdische Volk und Seine Jugend*. R. Löwit Verlag, Vienna and Berlin, 1920.
10. BETHGE, HANS: *Chinesische Fiöte*. Im Inselverlag, Leipzig, 1918.

BIBLES

11. HOLY BIBLE: New Analytical Bible and Dictionary of the Bible. Authorized King James Version. James A. Dickson Publishing House, Chicago, 1950.
12. HOLY BIBLE AND CONCORDANCE: Scofield Reference Edition. Oxford University Press, New York, 1909.
13. DIE BIBEL: Britische und Ausländische Bibelgesellschaft, Berlin, 1910.
14. NEW TESTAMENT: Revised Standard Edition. Thomas Nelson & Sons, New York, 1901.
15. WORLD BIBLE: Edited by Robert O. Ballow. The Viking Press, New York, 1948.
16. BLANSHARD, PAUL: *American Freedom and Catholic Power*. The Beacon Press, Boston, 1949.
17. BONHOEFFER, DIETRICH: *The Cost of Discipleship*. The Macmillan Co., New York, 1949.
18. BURNHAM, JAMES: *The Coming Defeat of Communism*. John Day Co., Inc., New York, 1950.
19. BURNHAM, JAMES: *The Machiavellians*. John Day Co., Inc., New York, 1943.
20. CALDWELL, ERSKINE: *God's Little Acre*. Secker and Warburg, London, 1937.
21. CARSON, RACHEL L.: *The Sea Around Us*. Oxford University Press, New York, 1951.
22. CARUS, PAUL: *The Bride of Christ*. The Open Court Publishing Co., Chicago, 1908.
23. CARUS, PAUL: *God*. The Open Court Publishing Co., La Salle, Ill., 1943.
24. CARUS, PAUL: *The Gospel of Buddha*. The Open Court Publishing Co., Chicago, Ill., 1915.
25. CERVANTES, MIGUEL DE: *Don Quixote*. Modern Library, New York, 1930.
26. CLADEL, JUDITH: *Rodin*. Editions Aimery Somogy, 1948, France. (See Plate 35, "Le Baiser.")
27. CLAUDEL, PAUL: *Mittagswende*. Hellerauer Verlag. Jakob Hegner, Dresden-Hellerau, 1918.

28. GROSSMAN, RICHARD, Editor: *The God That Failed.* Harper & Bros., New York, 1949.
29. DASGUPTA, S. N.: *Hindu Mysticism.* The Open Court Publishing Co., Chicago, 1927.
30. DANTE, ULIGHIERI: *Die Göttliche Komödie.* Volksverlag der Bücherfreunde, Wegweiser-Verlag, Berlin, 1922.
31. DANTE, ULIGHIERI: *The Divine Comedy.* Modern Library, New York, 1932.
32. DA VINCI, LEONARDO: *The Drawings of Leonardo da Vinci.* Reynal & Hitchcock, New York, 1945.
33. DA VINCI, LEONARDO: *The Notebooks of Leonardo da Vinci, Vols. I, II.* Reynal & Hitchcock, New York, 1945.
34. DE COSTER, CHARLES: *Tyl Ulenspiegel, Vols. I, II.* Kurt Wolff Verlag, München, 1926.
35. DE COSTER, CHARLES: *Tyl Ulenspiegel.* Pantheon Books, Inc., New York, 1943.
36. DE PONCINS, GONTRAN: *Kabloona.* Garden City Publishing Co., Garden City, New York, 1943.
37. DOSTOYEVSKY, FYODOR: *The Idiot.* Modern Library, New York, 1935.
38. DRIESCH, HANS: *Philosophie des Organischen.* Verlag von Wilhelm Engelmann, Leipzig, 1921.
39. FARRAR, CANON: *The Life of Christ.* Commonwealth Publishing Co., New York, 1890.
40. FOREL, AUGUST: *Die Sexuelle Frage.* Ernst Reinhardt, Verlagsbuchhandlung, 1904.
41. FOSDICK, HARRY EMERSON: *The Man from Nazareth.* Harper & Bros., New York, 1939.
42. FRANCE, ANATOLE: *The Well of St. Clare.* Dodd, Mead & Co., New York, 1928.
43. FRANCIS, ST.: *The Little Flowers of Saint Francis, etc.* Everyman's Library, E. P. Dutton & Co., New York, 1950.
44. FRAZER, SIR JAMES GEORGE: *The Worship of Nature, V. 1.* The Macmillan Co., New York, 1926.
45. GEDAT, GUSTAV: *Ein Christ erlebt die Probleme der Welt.* Verlag von T. F. Steinkopf, Stuttgart, 1935.
46. GELBER, KARL VON: *Galileo Galilei und Die Römische Curie.* Verlag der F. O. Gotta'schen Buchhandlung, Stuttgart, 1876.
47. GIBRAN, KAHLIL: *Jesus.* Alfred A. Knopf, New York, 1928.
48. GOLLANCZ, VICTOR: *Man and God.* Houghton Mifflin Co., Boston, 1951.
49. GOUZENKO, IGOR: *The Iron Curtain.* E. P. Dutton & Co., Inc., New York, 1948.
50. GRAVES, ROBERT: *King Jesus.* Creative Age Press, New York, 1946.
51. GRIMM, GEORG: *Die Lehre des Buddha.* R. Piper & Co., Verlag, München, 1919.
52. GUNTHER, JOHN: *Behind the Iron Curtain.* Harper & Bros., New York, 1949.
53. HALL, G. STANLEY: *Jesus, The Christ, in the Light of Psychology, Vols. I, II.* Doubleday, Page & Co., New York, 1917.
54. HEIDEN, KONRAD: *Adolf Hitler.* Europa-Verlag, Zurich, 1936.
55. HERSEY, JOHN: *The Wall.* Alfred A. Knopf, New York, 1950.
56. HITLER, ADOLF: *Mein Kampf.* Central Verlag der NGDAP., Frz. Eher Nachf, München, 1938.
57. HOEL, SIGURD: *Sünder am Meer.* Carl Schünemann Verlag, Bremen, 1932.
58. HOENSBROECH, GRAF VON: *Das Papsttum.* Druck und Verlag von Breitkopf und Härtel, Leipzig, (undated).

59. JAMES, WILLIAM: *Varieties of Religious Experience*. Modern Library, New York, 1902.
60. JOHNSTON, JAMES A., Warden: *Alcatraz Island Prison*. Charles Scribner's Sons, New York, 1949.
61. JONES, JAMES: *From Here to Eternity*. Charles Scribner's Sons, New York, 1951.
62. *Journal of Clinical Pastoral Health*. No. 4, Winter 1948. Council for Clinical Training, Inc., New York.
63. KAYE, JAMES R.: *A Systematic Study of the New Analytical Bible*. John A. Dickson Publishing Co., Chicago, 1951.
64. KEMPIS, THOMAS A: *The Imitation of Christ*. Everyman's Library, E. P. Dutton & Co., New York, 1947.
65. KLAUSNER, JOSEPH: *From Jesus to Paul*. George Allen & Unwin Ltd., London, 1946.
66. KOESTLER, ARTHUR: *Scum of the Earth*. The Macmillan Co., New York, 1941.
67. THE KORAN: Everybody's Library, J. M. Dent & Sons, Ltd., London, 1948.
68. KRIMSKY, JOSEPH HAYYIM: *Jesus and the Hidden Bible*. Philosophical Library, New York, 1951.
69. LAGERKVIST, PAR: *Barabbas*. Random House, New York, 1951.
70. LAWRENCE, D. H.: *The Man Who Died*. Alfred A. Knopf, Inc., New York, 1928.
71. LEVI, CARLO: *Christ Stopped at Eboli*. Penguin Books, Inc., New York, 1947.
72. LEWIS, JOSEPH: *In The Name of Humanity!* Eugenics Publishing Co., New York, 1949.
73. LEY, WILLY: *The Days of Creation*. Modern Age Books, New York, 1941.
74. LIEBMAN, JOSHUA LOTH: *Peace of Mind*. Simon & Schuster, New York, 1946.
75. LINDSEY, BEN B. and EVANS, WAINWRIGHT: *Die Revolution der Modernen Jugend*. Deutsche Verlag-Anstalt, Stuttgart, Berlin und Leipzig.
76. LONDON, JACK: *Martin Eden*. The Macmillan Co., New York, 1938.
77. MAILER, NORMAN: *The Naked and the Dead*. Rinehart and Co., Inc., New York, 1948.
78. MALINOWSKI, BRONISLAW: *Das Geschlechtsleben der Wilden*. Grethlein & Co., Leipzig und Zürich, 1929.
79. MEADE, MARGARET and BATESON, GREGORY: *Balinese Character*. The New York Academy of Sciences, Special Publications, Vol. II, 1942.
80. MICHENER, JAMES A.: *Return to Paradise*. Random House, New York, 1951.
81. MORGAN, LEWIS H.: *Die Urgesellschaft*. Verlag von T. H. W. Diek Nachf, 1908.
82. NIETZSCHE, FRIEDRICH: *Also Sprach Zarathustra*. Alfred Kröner Verlag, Leipzig, 1918.
83. NIETZSCHE, FRIEDRICH: *My Sister and I*. Boars Head Books, New York, 1951.
84. NORTHROP, F. S. C.: *The Meeting of East and West*. The MacMillan Co., New York, 1946.
85. OURSLER, FULTON: *The Greatest Story Ever Told*. Doubleday & Co., Garden City, New York, 1949.
86. PAPINI, GIOVANNI: *Life of Christ*. Harcourt, Brace & Co., New York, 1923.
87. PRESCOTT, WILLIAM H.: *Conquest of Mexico*. Blue Ribbon Books, 1943.
88. *Pronunziamento XIV*, AMORC, The Rosicrucian Order.
89. RAKNES, OLA: *Motet med det Heilage*.
90. RODIN, AUGUSTE: Phaidon Publishers, Inc. Distributed by Oxford University Press, New York. See plate 6768 The Eternal Idol.

91. RENAN, ERNEST: *The Life of Jesus.* Modern Library, New York, 1927.
92. ROLLAND, ROMAIN: *Mahatma Gandhi.* Rotapfel-Verlag, Erbenbach-Zürich, 1923.
93. ROUSSEAU, JEAN JACQUES: *Collected Works.* Walter J. Black, Inc., New York, (undated).
94. ROUSSEAU, JEAN JACQUES: *The Social Contract.* E. P. Dutton & Co., Inc., New York, 1941.
95. RUTHERFORD, J. F.: *Was ist Wahrheit?* Internationale Bibelforsher-Vereinigung, Brooklyn, New York, 1932.
96. SCHOEN, MAX: *The Man Jesus Was.* Alfred A. Knopf, New York, 1950.
97. SCHNITZLER, ARTHUR: *Reigen.*
98. SCHWEITZER, ALBERT: *The Psychiatric Study of Jesus.* The Beacon Press, Boston, 1948.
99. SERGE, VICTOR: *The Case of Comrade Tulayew.* Doubleday & Co., Inc., Garden City, New York, 1950.
100. SHEEN, FULTON J.: *Peace of Soul.* McGraw Hill Book Co., New York, 1949.
101. SILONE, IGNAZIO: *Brot und Wein.* Verlag Oprecht, Zürich, 1936.
102. SILONE, IGNAZIO: *Die Schule Der Diktatoren.* Europa Verlag, Zürich and New York, 1938.
103. SILONE, IGNAZIO: *Fontamara.* Verlag Oprecht & Helbling, Zürich, 1933.
104. SINGER, DOROTHEA WALEY: *Bruno: His Life and Thought (with Annotated Translation of His Work " One the Infinite Universe and Worlds ").* Henry Schuman, New York, 1950.
105. SINGER, JACOB: *Taboo in the Hebrew Scriptures.* The Open Court Publishing Co., Chicago, Ill., 1928.
106. SMALLEY, BERYL: *The Study of the Bible in the Middle Ages.* Philosophical Library, New York, 1952.
107. SMITH, PRESERVED: *History of Christian Theophagy.* The Open Court Publishing Co., Chicago, 1922.
108. SMITH, WALTER BEDELL: *My Three Years in Moscow.* J. B. Lippincott Co., Philadelphia and New York, 1950.
109. SPERRY, WILLARD L.: *Jesus Then and Now.* Harper & Bros., New York, 1949.
110. SPINOZA: *Ethics, etc.* Everyman's Library, E. P. Dutton & Co., Inc., New York, 1941.
111. SPITTELER, CARL: *Imago.* Verlegt Bei Eugen Diederichs, Jena, 1910.
112. SPITTELER, CARL: *Olympischer Frühling, Vols. I, II.* Verlegt bei Eugen Diederichs.
113. STEIG, WILLIAM: *Till Death Do Us Part.* Duell, Sloan & Pearce, New York, 1947.
114. STEINBECK, JOHN: *The Pearl.* Viking Press, New York, 1947.
115. STENDHAL (HENRI BEYLE): *Über die Liebe.* Im Propyläen-Verlag, Berlin.
116. STIRNER, MAX: *Der Einzige und Sein Eigentum.* Druck und Verlag von Philipp Reclam, 1892.
117. TROTSKY, LEON: *The Revolution Betrayed.* Faber & Faber, Ltd., London, 1937.
118. VALTIN, JAN: *Out of the Night.* Alliance Book Corp., New York, 1941.
119. VAN PAASSEN, PIERRE: *Why Jesus Died.* Dial Press, New York, 1949.
120. WAGENKNECHT, EDWARD, Editor: *The Story of Jesus in the World's Literature.* Creative Age Press, Inc., New York, 1946.

121. WEDEKIND, FRANK: *Die Büchse der Pandora*. Georg Müller Verlag, München, 1919.
122. WEDEKIND, FRANK: *Franziska*. Verlag von Georg Müller, München, 1912.
123. WEDEKIND, FRANK: *Frühlings Erwachen*. Georg Müller Verlag, München, 1919.
124. WHITMAN, WALT: *Leaves of Grass*. Aventine Press, New York, 1931.
125. WILDGANS, ANTON: *Die Sonette an Ead*. Verlag von L. Staackmann, Leipzig, 1913.
126. WRIGHT, RICHARD: *Black Boy*. The World Publishing Co., Cleveland, Ohio, 1945.

Printed in Great Britain
by Amazon

VINTAGE
LIVING
TEXTS

Susan Hill

THE ESSENTIAL GUIDE
TO CONTEMPORARY
LITERATURE

I'm the King of the Castle
Strange Meeting
The Woman in Black
A Bit of Singing and Dancing

V
VINTAGE

Published by Vintage 2003

2 4 6 8 10 9 7 5 3 1

Copyright © Jonathan Noakes and Margaret Reynolds 2002

The right of Jonathan Noakes and Margaret Reynolds to be identified
as the authors of this work has been asserted by them in accordance with
the Copyright, Designs and Patents Act, 1988.

First published in Great Britain in 2003 by Vintage
Random House, 20 Vauxhall Bridge Road,
London SW1V 2SA

The Random House Group Limited supports The Forest Stewardship
Council (FSC®), the leading international forest certification organisation.
Our books carrying the FSC label are printed on FSC® certified paper.
FSC is the only forest certification scheme endorsed by the leading
environmental organisations, including Greenpeace. Our
paper procurement policy can be found at
www.randomhouse.co.uk/environment

The Random House Group Limited Reg. No. 954009
www.randomhouse.co.uk

A CIP catalogue record for this book is available from the British Library

ISBN 0 099 45218 9

Papers used by Random House are natural, recyclable products made
from wood grown in sustainable forests: the manufacturing processes

Addresses for companies within The Random House Group Limited can be found at:
www.randomhouse.co.uk/offices.htm

Printed and bound in Great Britain by Clays Ltd, St Ives PLC

CONTENTS

VINTAGE LIVING TEXTS: PREFACE

SUSAN HILL

VINTAGE LIVING TEXTS

I'm the King of the Castle

Strange Meeting

The Woman in Black

A Bit of Singing and Dancing

VINTAGE LIVING TEXTS: REFERENCE

Acknowledgements

We owe grateful thanks to all at Random House. Most of all our debt is to Rachel Cugnoni and her team at Vintage – especially to Ali Reynolds – Jason Arthur and Liz Foley, who have given us generous and unfailing support. Thanks also to Caroline Michel, Marcella Edwards, Philippa Brewster and Georgina Capel, Michael Meredith, the Provost and Fellows of Eton College, Angela Leighton, Harriet Marland, to all our colleagues and friends, and to our partners and families. We would also like to thank the teachers and students at schools and colleges around the country who have taken part in our trialling process, and who have responded so readily and warmly to our requests for advice. Susan Hill has been part of this project from the start, and we thank her, with love.

Preface

About this series

Vintage Living Texts: The Essential Guide to Contemporary Literature is a new concept in reading guides. Our aim is to provide readers of all kinds with an intelligent and accessible introduction to key works of contemporary literature. Each guide suggests techniques for reading important contemporary novels, and offers a variety of back-up materials that will give you ways into the text – without ever telling you what to think.

Content

All the books reproduce an extensive interview with the author, conducted exclusively for this series. This is not to say that we believe that the author's word is law. Of course it isn't. Once his or her book has gone out into the world he or she becomes simply yet another – if singularly competent – reader. This series recognises that an author's contribution may be valuable, and intriguing, but it puts the reader in control.

Every title in the series is author-focused and covers at

I

least three of their novels, along with relevant biographical, bibliographical, contextual and comparative material.

How to use this series

In the reading activities that make up the core of each book you will see that you are asked to do two things. One comes from the text; that is, we suggest what you should focus on, whether it's a theme, the language or the narrative method. The other concentrates on your own response. We want you to think about how you are reading and what skills you are bringing to bear in doing that reading. So this part is very much about you, the reader.

The point is that there are many ways of responding to a text. You could concentrate on the methods you might use to compare this text with others. In that case, look for the sections headed 'Compare'. Or you might want to do something more individual, and analyse how you are reacting to a text and what it means to you, in which case, pick out the approaches labelled 'Imagine' or 'Ask Yourself'.

Of course, it may well be that you are reading these texts for an examination. In that case you will have to go for the more traditional methods of literary criticism and look for the responses that tell you to 'Discuss' or 'Analyse'. Whichever level you (or your students) are at, you will find that there is something here for everyone. However, we're not suggesting that you stick solely to the approaches we offer, or that you tackle all of the exercises laid out here. Choose whatever most interests you, or whatever best suits your purposes.

Who are these books for?

Students will find that these guides are like a good teacher. They introduce the life and work of the author, set each novel in its context, explain key ideas and literary critical terms as they arise, suggest comparative exercises in a number of media, and ask focused questions to encourage a well-informed, analytical approach to reading the novels in a way that is rigorous, but still entertaining.

Teachers will find in this series a rich source of ideas for teaching contemporary novels and their contexts, particularly at AS, A and undergraduate levels. The exercises on each text have been tailored to meet the various assessment objectives laid down in the subject criteria for GCE AS and GCE A Level and the International Baccalaureate in English Literature, and are explained in such a way that they can easily be selected and fitted into a lesson plan. Given the diversity of ways in which the awarding bodies have devised their specifications to meet these assessment objectives, a wide range of exercises is offered. We've had fun devising the plans, and we hope they'll be fun for you when you come to teach and learn with them.

And if you are neither a teacher nor a student of contemporary literature, but someone reading for your own pleasure? Well, if you've ever wanted someone to introduce you to a novelist's work in a way that will let you trust your own judgement and read more confidently, then this guide is also for you.

Whoever you are, we hope that you will enjoy using these books and that they will send you back to the novels to find new pleasures.

All page references to *I'm the King of the Castle*, *Strange Meeting* and *A Bit of Singing and Dancing* in this text refer to the Penguin editions. Page references to *The Woman in Black* refer to the Vintage edition.

3

Susan Hill

Introduction

In an early plan for a ghost story, which later became *The Woman in Black* (1983), an 'evil ghost', wanting revenge on the living world, targets a vulnerable child. This child is 'clever – sensitive – anxious – [has] frightened eyes – not like his brothers and sisters – he is the one it has got at'. The boy is both 'got at' and 'got'; both attacked and possessed.

The narrator wakes in the middle of the night, sensing that this child is in acute danger. He finds that the child has destroyed the nursery in a rage; the boy's eyes have changed colour, from grey to green; 'there is a confidence and self-possession about him'. The phrase is arresting, because the child's self-possession is really possession by another. The most sinister aspect of this 'possession' is the child's unnerving mixture of innocence and knowing: polluted by the spirit that occupies him, a spirit that knows skewed adult passions, he is changed by this adult knowledge.

This story of the possessed child (see Contexts, p. 137–40) was not used in *The Woman in Black*. Perhaps the child too closely resembled Miles in Henry James's *The Turn of the Screw*. As an intelligent reader, Susan Hill was aware of the influence of that story. As an individual writer, it was an

5

influence she wanted to escape (see pp. 34–5).

So that particular plot frame was discarded. But Hill could not so easily escape her own special fascination with the idea of the haunted – and haunting – child, and it was a subject to which she returned with *The Mist in the Mirror*, written almost a decade later. Children, especially children who don't quite 'fit in' and are vulnerable, are an intriguing subject for Hill, along with the sense of menace that cannot be fully understood. Cheerful normality that gives way suddenly to a terrifying unknown is a recurrent theme. So are ghosts with deep and unresolved feelings, who cannot rest, and who haunt the living, invading their consciousnesses, desiring to possess them. These are the obsessions of Susan Hill.

Between 1969 and 1974, Hill wrote six novels and two collections of short stories, as well as numerous radio plays. She describes the force of her creative drive during these years as irresistible. 'I couldn't stop,' she says, 'and what I wrote came from deep inside me, it *had* to be written, I couldn't have done anything else. I don't think I "enjoyed" what I was doing, I was writing compulsively.' Where the stories come from during the process, she does not know: 'It is no good enquiring too closely into the origins of it all, and I am slightly superstitious about doing so. I have learned, over the years, simply to trust the workings and productions of my subconscious and of my imagination.'

For Hill, stories have an occult power. Through them, the daylight world of ordinary consciousness opens on to the hidden and sometimes disturbing unknown, tapping into turbulent currents of emotion. In an unused preface to *The Woman in Black* Kipps's stepson Oliver comments on the story that follows – the novel itself. 'I heartily believe and trust that the setting down of the story may at last have exorcised these unhappy ghosts, and the terrors they aroused, from my stepfather's mind,' he says. 'Is it also too much to hope that the powers of evil here described as working through these places, these human circumstances, may have been overcome and obliterated? I pray so daily.'

Lying behind his Christian prayer is a pagan superstition about storytelling, going back through classical tragedy to ancient oral narratives. This is the idea that stories have the power to protect: through them we express our deepest, most haunting fears, and we purge them.

A study of the notes, drafts and manuscripts of Hill's novels reveals that her writing methods follow a distinct pattern. The initial ideas come to her imagination as glimpses: images, atmospheres, smells. There follows a stage of trying to find the right elements of plot and character to allow these glimpses to emerge as a fuller picture; until, suddenly, everything surfaces – the story and characters arrive in her consciousness complete. At this moment Hill writes the first full draft. Subsequent alterations are minor and stylistic. In other words, the novels have their origins in an instinctive imagination, where they seem to take on an almost independent existence. 'Susan Hill' – the writer, if not the person – is haunted by ghosts and characters whose stories she must tell in order to exorcise them.

I'm the King of the Castle (1970) belongs to an early period of Hill's work. She records that 'one of my own strongest and regularly recurring obsessions has been with childhood; my own, indirectly, but more, the state of childhood; what it feels like, how it truly is and how adults misinterpret it. Particularly, I have been interested in children who are in some way at odds with the rest of the world.' Kingshaw and Hooper fit this type, but each in different ways. Unable to assert or defend himself, Kingshaw has always found sanctuary through anonymity; he cannot cope with Hooper's relentless pursuit. Kingshaw's respect for others and his sense of limitations are moral strengths, but to Hooper they seem to be weaknesses. For

Hooper is not just a misfit – he is a psychopath.

And this, too, is a story of a struggle for possession; initially, at least, in the sense of 'ownership'. Hooper's purpose is to strip Kingshaw of his ownership: first of Warings, then of the wood, then of Fielding, and finally of his mother. In the end, the only thing Kingshaw owns is himself, and Hooper's inevitable next step will be to take that, too. The Hoopers' collection of moths is a family totem, symbolic of killing as an act of possession and of connoisseurship. Hooper certainly enjoys the hunt, but he wants Kingshaw dead. He will 'own' Kingshaw and he will 'know' him.

Yet, though Kingshaw's final act may seem to be his surrender, it is also his victory. He is proving his self-possession and self-knowledge in the only way he can.

Hooper's self-possession is not so hampered, indeed it is unnerving. He shows flashes of cunning – almost of genius – that delights in its own cruelty. It is a quality not easily explained; a quality which, for want of another explanation, people call 'evil'.

Strange Meeting (1971) also belongs to this period of writing. It is Hill's only novel based on historic events. She had first thought of writing a novel set during the First World War in 1964, but the prospect was daunting and she delayed it for years. 'What did I know [of the First World War]? I hadn't been there, I only knew what I had read, and imagined.' The problem was not the task of researching and recreating the past – that was the easy part – nor was it that her imagination could not embrace the strangeness of the soldiers' experience. Rather, what worried her 'was the knowledge that I should have to sink myself completely and utterly in imagination, in emotions, into the experience of that awful war'.

When Hill felt that she could put off writing the novel no longer, the experience was harrowing. 'It was, as I had expected and dreaded, a devastating subject to get involved in, a terrible world to enter, imaginatively, an appalling business to be with young soldiers, day and night, in the trenches and in battle, in danger and fear and dirt. I felt exhausted, tense, horrified, depressed and angry the entire time.' And 'when I had finished the book and sent it off, I knew absolutely that I had exorcised my ghosts, all of those poor young men long dead . . . and that I would probably never want to think of any of them again'. The dead, possession, exorcism: it's the same metaphor, the same process, the same obsession.

However, *Strange Meeting* is not only about the First World War. The physical realities that predominate in this novel – the details of trench life and its effects on the human body – are the grounding that enables her to focus her emotional themes. The landscape of the trenches is the background; the foreground is the landscape of the inner life. Hill's work delights in creating external landscapes, but it is the inner landscape which is the primary interest. *Strange Meeting* is about fear and courage: the fear of physical danger and the courage needed to meet that fear. But above all, it is about Hilliard's fear of emotional intimacy, and the courage he shows in risking intimacy with Barton, in their 'strange meeting' of hearts.

Hilliard is another example of the misfit, and his story is also about possession. He is the misfit child whose parents are absent, physically and emotionally, as we learn from the childhood memories that are so prominent in the early part of the novel. And he is also the misfit adult, still stuck in this state of emotional isolation, still at odds with the world he inhabits. As Hill says in the interview (on p. 29), he is Kingshaw again, or what Kingshaw might have become in adulthood. *Strange Meeting* describes his inner journey, from meeting Barton, to realising his own need for him, to wanting to possess him, to letting himself love him, and then facing the loss of what he loves.

When Hilliard learns to love, he learns also that he cannot

possess what he loves. His loss of Barton is cruel, the inevitable price for giving up the safety of detachment: but by giving up the determination not to be involved he has learned to grow, to change and – in the end – to let go. As the novel ends, he is no longer looking back, as he did at the start, but looking 'up, and ahead' (p. 179). By giving up 'ownership', by giving up possession, he is himself released.

The Woman in Black (1983) marks a clear break from these earlier novels. No longer haunted by the ghosts that she felt compelled to exorcise, Hill created a ghost she had full control of, as an exercise in old-fashioned storytelling. *The Woman in Black* is a classic ghost story, modelled on Hill's favourite examples of the genre by Henry James, M. R. James and others (see the interview p. 31 and pp. 34–6).

The classic ghost story is a genre that suits her talents especially well. Character and atmosphere are important, much more so than plot. Hill's method was pragmatic: to create a list of all the typical elements of the genre, and to incorporate them all. The reliably 'normal' narrator, the familiar storytelling-round-the-fire opening, the railway journey, the isolated house, the sea mists, the sudden injection of the strange into the ordinary, the ghostly sounds, the spirit that haunts a particular place and cannot rest, the children who are vulnerable – all of these are stock elements of the ghost story.

The Woman in Black is, in this sense, highly derivative. But it is also recognisably a product of the same imagination as the earlier novels: it is a tale about fear, and about menace from beyond the threshold of the normal world; it is about death in loneliness and about revenge; it is about the isolated individual made vulnerable before something that he does not understand; it is – in the figure of Jennet Humphrye – about the importance of coming to terms with loss and with pain. And finally, it is about the mystery of evil.

If that sounds too grand a claim for a ghost story that is

meant to entertain, you'll see that in the interview (on p. 15) Hill describes herself as 'a Christian writer' – not just as a writer who is Christian. For Susan Hill, even when she is offering us 'A Bit of Singing and Dancing', fiction must also have that 'only thing worth writing about' – an inner life.

Interview with Susan Hill

Ebrington: 24 October 2002

JN: *I'm the King of the Castle* shares with much of your work a focus on childhood – on what it really feels like to be a child, and how adults misinterpret children. What are you saying about childhood?

SH: It is that strange thing – though not by any means unusual – the novel about childhood, but not a children's book. I think I'm saying partly that it's equally valid to have children as principle characters as it is to have principle adult characters. Because they're young, they're not necessarily minor characters, or characters about whom you talk but you don't get inside them. I think I'm saying that childhood is the most formative and important time of our lives, of any adult's life. I take this from Graham Greene who said that the first twelve years of a person's life – of a writer's life particularly – are the most important. Obviously, you have to exclude sexual love from that. But apart from that, and certain adult experiences that can only happen when you're an adult and are not necessarily very important, I think that the essential person is fixed during those first twelve years. So childhood is terribly important. Not just for itself, but for everything that happens later. It sounds

13

rather silly to say that children are to be taken seriously, but children's greatest fear is not being taken seriously. Not having their emotions taken seriously, not having their fears taken seriously, having things that, to them, are huge and important dismissed by adults. Obviously, adults know that some things that loom large for children are actually not as large as they seem, and the sting has to be drawn a little bit. If you fall over and have a minor bump, you don't have to scream your head off as if you'd had your arm cut off – you know, that sort of thing. But to a child, that is an outrage, 'it hurt me'. When adults don't take it seriously, children just shut up, they shut the door. I think that's really what it's about. It's all inside. And whenever those boys [in *I'm the King of the Castle*] try to communicate fully with an adult, they're dismissed in some way or another.

JN: It's very frustrating for the reader to see Kingshaw trying to persuade the adults that he should be listened to and they won't. On the other hand, I also find it frustrating to see the way that Kingshaw doesn't take any advantage of Hooper's moments of cowardice. He seems to let those moments come and go and he makes no capital out of them at all. Did you intend that the reader should find him frustratingly weak?

SH: No, one never plans those things in that particularly rational, logical way. But it's the one thing that comes out when I'm talking to school pupils. They get very annoyed with Kingshaw. They say, 'Oh, why didn't he seize those moments? Why is he being so wet? Why couldn't he see?' I think the answer is, not because he's obtuse, but because he's too nice. He knows that those moments are there. He'd never make an aggressive footballer, because he gives the ball away all the time. Kingshaw knows that Hooper has got this moment of weakness, the chink in the armour, which he could seize, but in that chink he sees himself. I think he's just too kind, he lets him off every time. And I don't see this as a weakness, I see this as a huge strength, a moral strength sadly – but of course it doesn't do him any good.

JN: Kingshaw also has a quality that Hooper completely lacks, which is a sense of moral limitations.

SH: Yes. Hooper is a psychopath, in the proper sense in that I think he has no real feelings or empathy at all. He has no sense of what another person feels. He just can't imagine it. That's what a psychopath essentially is – somebody who cannot feel what other people feel. So you squash an insect and you can't even imagine. It's not that you don't try, or blot it out, you just don't. I think that's the difference between them. Whereas Kingshaw is the archetypal non-psychopath – he feels everything, not only what he feels, but he imagines what other people feel.

JN: Like *The Woman in Black*, this novel is concerned with evil. But whereas in *The Woman in Black* evil is formalised by the ghost-story genre, here it's very raw, and the style also lacks the irony and the humour that most of your work has. Why did you make it such a harsh novel?

SH: Well, again, I didn't sit down and think, 'I'm going to make this a harsh novel.' It just came out that way. There are fifteen years between the two books. But the question of evil is something that interested me, it always has. You have to remember that I'm a Christian writer, and although Christianity doesn't come in in any obvious sense, I always have a moral purpose in a story, and there is always the conflict between good and evil. In *The Woman in Black*, it's very formalised, it's a genre, and in a book like that there is the inevitable feeling of evil, but it's got all sorts of formulaic expressions. In *I'm the King of the Castle*, there is no formula. It is about pitting good against evil. Ted Hughes said something about his poetry which is 'what is my writing about? what am I about?' and he said something like 'it's about the eternal conflict between the living and the dead, or life and death and the area and the pull between them'. If you substitute good and evil, then it's sort of the same thing. I think that's what I'm always about. This is really what *I'm the King of the Castle* is about, the various expressions of good and evil. It's a bad boy versus a good boy, and the bad boy wins – apparently.

JN: Edmund Hooper is partly the product of cold and distant parenting, but is there also an element of motiveless malignity in his make-up?

SH: Yes. This is the old thing of how much is the genes, how much is environment and upbringing and so on. And it's a bit of both. He's like his father, and his father is the same as his father and the whole family have generated this cold distant upbringing, with an inability to express emotion, to sympathise with others, to allow open affection to be shown, all of that. But, after all, that didn't always make cruel psychopaths. Quite a lot of people endured that environment and came out the other side perfectly well. I think Hooper has got this, the pleasure of killing flies – which many small boys have – multiplied by whatever, it's the enjoyment of watching somebody else not so much be hurt in the physical sense, but certainly wriggle on the hook of being afraid. It's the bully's absolute ultimate thing, isn't it? The delight of watching the fear. And this is why you should stand up to a bully and challenge them and they wilt because there's no pleasure in that, not only because they're then afraid, but because it's all gone. I don't like the word 'bullying', all it means is unkindness really. Hooper takes pleasure in unkindness and watching the other person react to it.

JN: The image you are using there of 'the moth collection' is the idea of pinning something down. Is there also the idea in Hooper that, at the end of the novel, he owns Kingshaw? Has he killed him in order to possess him?

SH: I'm not sure about that. I don't know that Hooper would know that consciously. I think the real pleasure is 'now I've got everything else'. He's got Kingshaw's mother, and his own father, the place and the set-up, and he's the 'king of the castle'. I think he's just jolly glad that he's won and that Kingshaw is out of the way really.

JN: Though one can't imagine a very happy family life with the three of them in future!

SH: No, no! And he'd have to find somebody else to replace Kingshaw, because that kind of person always does. Who it's going to be, who knows? Maybe somebody at school, some hapless child, but there's nobody there, and of course he doesn't realise that straight away. That's all for the sequel!

JN: It's very interesting how not only do these children find it difficult to fit in, but the adults do, too. They're like people playing adults in a world they don't fully understand. The misfit is a recurrent figure in your novels.

SH: Yes, I think so, and you're going to ask me why and the answer is I don't know, except that I've seen an awful lot of them. It all comes down to those first twelve years. I grew up in Scarborough just after the war and it was then full of people like that. The war had taken away a lot of men, so you had an awful lot of youngish widows and people who hadn't got much money, unmarried women living with elderly parents because they hadn't managed to marry and then the war had intervened, people who'd come out of the war (and indeed the previous war) in a shocked state. There were an awful lot of people who didn't quite fit, and didn't have the normal relationship to other people, a marriage with children or a normal uncomplicated set-up. I was an only child and I used to observe people, as children do. Children look and think about things while adults are busy doing the shopping, because they're not doing anything else. And I think it always interested me. And misfits from the point of view of some sort of disability – usually a mental disability, because those people are always going to be misfits, this is long before 'social inclusion' as we call it – people who were in some way disabled or odd were outcast really. They were either shut away in homes or they were outcast in society. People were afraid of them and regarded them with suspicion. I found that interesting, and again I found it extremely sad as a child. We had a gentleman who lived in the bottom flat of the block of flats in which I lived – a sort of converted Edwardian house – he lived with his sister and he'd been in the First World War and was obviously suffering from shell shock because occasionally he would wander along the street talking to himself and would throw himself down into the road and put his hands over his ears and shout, clearly suffering from a whole war scenario still going around in his head. People just said, 'Oh, that's Mr Morris, he's shell-shocked,' and I remember thinking that somehow this was terribly sad and ought not to be allowed to go on, somebody ought to look after him or do something about it. I remember saying to my mother, 'Why doesn't somebody make him better?' 'Oh, well, they can't.' I suppose people were rather hard about things because they didn't think they could do anything. I think now, probably, there would at least have been some attempt at helping him. That has just always stayed with me, all of those things, and I think that the subject of the outsider, the odd person, the misfit, is of interest. But beyond that, who knows? You just do find some things of interest, and some things not, to write about.

JN: Eleanor Kingshaw has a habit – that infuriates her son – which is to talk about herself in the third person. I was struck how, in a sense, she is always performing a part, she doesn't seem to fit in with herself very well, or to sit very easily with her real character. Was that part of how she and Joseph Hooper are misfits? The fact that they really just don't sit very easily with themselves or know themselves very well?

SH: Eleanor Kingshaw's desperate to find a place, isn't she? So she's acting a part for a purpose. She sucks up to Hooper and Mr Hooper in order to get the place as the housekeeper and hopefully become the wife and mistress of the household. I think she's playing a part semi-consciously – 'I must appear to be' – as people always do when they go for a job. When you go for an interview you put your best foot forward, you try to be the person that they want. So to that extent this is perfectly all right; she's a woman who needs not just a man, but a home, a base, a household and somewhere to live with her son. But I think it goes further than that – she's trying on roles. This awful way of speaking in the third person – it's what nursery school teachers do to three-year-olds, isn't it? She's patronising to the boys.

JN: Both adults also have that infuriating habit of telling the boys what they really think, or what they really feel, rather than listening to them.

SH: Oooh . . . ! Yes. I know. And that's interesting, isn't it?

The other night I happened to say to Clemency [her daughter] something about 'I don't want you to feel X . . .', and she said, 'Don't you tell me what I should feel and not feel,' and I said I wasn't, I was just meaning I don't want you to be upset about something, that's all. But children or young people quite rightly don't like this. You're not inside their heads, you don't know what they are feeling. We all do that to a certain extent with young children, and to a certain extent we *do* know what they're feeling because you've been there yourself. However, a) it doesn't do to show it, and b) you can't extend that, as these two characters do, into assuming that because these boys are young, they – the adults – have knowledge of absolutely everything inside them. They don't. This is what we learn in the book which is why young people like it, I think. It proves to them that it's perfectly possible for an adult to understand that principle – that we *don't* always know what's going on, and we should never assume that we know.

JN: I've noticed that in your work there's a fascination with the inner life, and especially with the fears that lie deeper than a rational explanation. Why does this interest you particularly?

SH: The simple answer is that I don't know. I think for a lot of writers it's almost what makes you a writer, or I suppose perhaps a dramatist. You have your own inner life, and you know that other people have theirs, and it is of endless fascination and interest, because it's always there and it often bears no relation to what's on the outside, either in everyday things or everyday conversations. There is this deep river flowing on in all of us, with all sorts of depths, and that is what is fascinating. That's why I think the sort of writing which never addresses this, never ever looks into the deep river and doesn't even acknowledge that it's there, is so dull to read. That's why the best children's books – something like [Lewis Carroll's]

Alice in Wonderland – address this, the inner life is there from the beginning. Nothing else is worth writing about really.

JN: And fear is a major creative catalyst for you, isn't it?

SH: Joanna Trollope said something that struck me when I was interviewing her last year. She said, 'I don't think all children by any means have an unhappy childhood, but I think almost all children have an anxious childhood.' And I think she's absolutely right. There's something essentially anxious making about being small and powerless. All children do have an anxious childhood, but some more than others. I think fear in children is grossly underestimated. I think children are always anxious and some children are very, very afraid. Not just of shadows on the wall that aren't really anything – but those do loom very large. It's something that needs to be addressed and understood, but can never really be taken away. It's also something to play with; if you play with it, in a sense you diffuse it. That's why we like watching ghost stories, horror stories and thrillers – because you're slightly diffusing that fear.

JN: I want to ask you a bit about how you present nature in the novel. It seems to be both frightening and liberating for Kingshaw in particular. Why does it contain those two qualities?

SH: Oh, I think because it does. Nature is that. You can walk in beautiful countryside on a sunny day, but you only have to find yourself going through a woodlandy bit where the sun suddenly goes and a slight wind blows up and your response to nature immediately becomes a fearful one, because this is instinct, isn't it? This is animals looking behind them in case there's a predator, and that is what nature does to you. I think this is why places are so important; they have no emotion in themselves, yet the important thing is what they produce in us, and we respond as animals respond – to atmosphere, to places, to slight changes in the weather, to slight sounds – and that really is the thing, you can get so much out of that. It's terribly important. Some people have it more than others, but every-body feels that slight shudder when the sun suddenly goes.

JN: You're very good at menace, aren't you?

SH: Yeah, I like menace. It's another good thing to play with. Because, you know, writers play. We're going on doing what we did as children. We play. We're saying, let's pretend. Let's take these imaginary people and pretend – just like little children do. You play with things, and you play with emotions, and menace is a great thing to play with. Don't take it *too* seriously, I think.

JN: Are you aware of how you create menace, in a technical sense?

SH: No, I'm not, because I'm never aware of how I do things technically. I think if I were, I wouldn't be able to do it. I really do think I just have to do it and hope that it works. You just have to trust your instinct. I think that if I planned, just beyond the next paragraph, I'd be sunk. No: you have to trust to instinct and all those years of practice. You just do it and it either works or it doesn't, and you hope it does.

JN: I've been very interested to look at the manuscripts and notes and drafts of your work. One of the things that has interested me is that, quite often, it's not the storyline that will come to you, but images and atmospheres, a *feeling* in other words, and then you build from those. Is that right?

SH: Always. This is why I can never outline what's going to

happen in advance, because in a way what's going to happen is of least interest. It comes out of those other things which start me off, which are: places, people in places, little tiny things. It might start with somebody going through lovely sunlit countryside and suddenly the shadow comes over and they have to walk into a wood . . . It sounds like a children's story maybe, but it's things like that. Then gradually those crystallise into particular people, in particular places, and out of that the story comes. And it was the same with *The Woman in Black* – very much so – atmosphere and place come first. That's what gets me going. Every writer's different in that sense. Some writers have to start with character and character analysis. My characters are very two-dimensional at first – the depth gets added later. When I first see them they're just walking around, almost like people in a film.

JN: I was also interested by the way in which, when you jot down the very first ideas, you slip in and out of the first person. I'm thinking of the scene in *The Woman in Black* in which the narrator Arthur Kipps goes into the bedroom and is overcome by a feeling of sadness. In your very first jottings, it reads 'I' – 'I am overcome by a feeling of sadness', then it switches back to 'he'.

SH: I wonder whether that's because I was toying with the idea of writing in the first person and not quite having settled on it. This is always a difficult one. Some books absolutely fall into place straight away, as first or third person, but not many. And you've got to get that one right. If you get it wrong it's a false start, and it's really difficult. I do an awful lot of thinking ahead; let's try it in the first person and think in that way. And then it doesn't quite work, so I make some notes in the first person, and 'yes, that's it', or 'oh dear, but if I do that, then I can't do so and so'. It's difficult. I always want to make sure that I've chosen right for each particular book. Some people always write in the first person, so it's easy for them.

Tense matters as well. I hate reading books in the first-person present, and I couldn't write in it except for the odd paragraph which must work for a particular thing. So that one's out for me. But tense matters as well – you've got to get that right. That's a technical thing. The limiting factor is that, of course, once you've done it in first person, then that person isn't inside the heads of the other people. That's your great limitation.

JN: So you have to find other devices like, for example, the letters Barton writes in *Strange Meeting*?

SH: Yes. And that can be phoney. It can work, or it can be a device that doesn't; it's a trick to try and get round the fact that you are in first person.

JN: When you began writing *Strange Meeting* you clearly had to do a different kind of preparation as well, which was the research in the novel. You researched it meticulously, down to the kind of music that Barton listens to on his gramophone, or the fact that mustard gas smells of garlic. What did you use for your research?

SH: I read at first, for about a year, just about everything I could lay my hands on about the First World War. Thank God I'm not writing it now because the literature has quadrupled or sextupled. I read official histories and I read accounts. I didn't read any novels at all except [Erich Remarque's] *All Quiet on the Western Front*. Then I discarded most of them, having just seeped myself in the whole thing. I really only kept one very dry official history which just referred to facts, and I also had a little book, a small red book, which was rules or procedures for officers during battle. That told me all sorts of facts about – you know – guns and so on. Little details like mustard gas smelling of garlic or whatever, you just pick those up from all over the place. I don't know where I first read that. Those are the things you have to include. It's the only book I've ever written which had proper research. I had to get it right. Then when I'd finished the book, I checked as much as I could and sent it off to a military historian, who actually checked facts: whether that particular gun would indeed have been used then and all those sort of things. You've got to get that right and I'm not good at that sort of thing, so the historian checked all that.

JN: The First World War is an awesome subject to take on. What drew you to it?

SH: Well, in a way it was less awesome when I did it because few people had done it – no woman had done it – and there weren't very many First World War novels. Now there are just so many that you wouldn't do it for that reason. Every writer has an obsession and when I was a child we used to spend a lot of time with my maternal grandmother. She lived with her sister, my great-aunt, and in that family there were seven girls, and one had died, and there was one boy. Their surname was Owen – quite coincidentally – and the boy's name was Sidney, George Sidney Owen, but always known as Sidney, and there was a photograph of him on my great-aunt's piano wearing his uniform, with a poppy always there. I was always told from a very young age, 'Yes, that's your great-uncle Sidney.' This was the great sadness of the family: the one boy – the golden boy – was killed on his nineteenth birthday in the Battle of the Somme. Indeed, I found that wonderful website which the War Graves Commission now has – you can trace anybody if you've

25

got their date of death, or their name, and every single soldier who was killed is accorded a Web page, with his name and 'in honour of'. It took me thirty seconds to find George Sidney Owen and there is my great-uncle commemorated and I found out where he'd died. With some, of course, it's simply not known. They just know that they were in the war. But we know exactly where he fell and which battle. That's a great service to humanity, that website. I was just always struck by this story, so it began there.

After the last war there were an awful lot of people left who still celebrated 11 November – it went through a great decline, and it's interesting that it's come back now and it is much more celebrated – and I went to the Remembrance Day service with my mother and my grandmother dressed in solemn black with the poppy which they planted in the churchyard and it was a very ceremonial occasion when we remembered my great-uncle. And that impresses a child of five, six, seven, eight. Then I heard Benjamin's Britten's *War Requiem*, the first performance in Coventry Cathedral, and the whole thing just lit me up because here was this obsession that had always been there, and I just knew then that one day I was going to have to write something about it. But every time I thought about it I thought, 'I can't do it.' Because I imagined the long historical novel, in which I'm not interested. I didn't want to write a thousand pages in which whole battles and whole wars are depicted. It took me nine years to realise that I could do exactly what Britten had done, which is to boil everything down into something very small, and all you want is the story of two or three people set in this context, and a lot of it is exactly the same as writing any other novel really. The minute that I realised that, it was fine. That was the key. I didn't have to write two thousand pages in which I depicted the entire war. It seems obvious now, but it wasn't obvious then. So that's how that came about.

JN: Clearly, this is a novel about war, but it's also a novel about love, isn't it?

SH: Yes. And that's why I say you could take that and put those two people somewhere else.

JN: Yes. And the war does give a particular context in relation to the stresses and strains on the relationship, but in another sense the big stress on the relationship is the fact that Hilliard finds it so difficult to trust and to love. Is it partly about the courage that it takes him to love Barton?

SH: I think he's an example of the English public school boy, isn't he? He's the sort of inhibited anxious person who hasn't ever really known much about love. He has a distant relationship with his parents, a pleasant relationship with his sister, and he's never encountered a real feeling of love for anybody. So he doesn't quite know what to do with it. It's unknown to him. I suppose, observed in other people, it's just slightly alarming, and I think this is very common. Perhaps not as common as it was, but still very common. So he's the person really waiting to be awakened, in the cliché fairy-tale way.

JN: Their friendship is in one way very easily achieved. In what sense is this a 'strange' meeting?

SH: In the sense that I nicked the title from Wilfred Owen really – that's all!

JN: There's a great stress on objects and things in this novel – on the physicality, particularly of trench warfare, and the importance of bodies. How does that grounding help you to focus your ideas?

SH: Well, it came about because what I had to do when I was researching the book was not just read, but talk to people who'd been there. In 1969/70 there were still an awful lot of people about. So I asked various friends if they knew anybody who'd been a soldier in the First World War, and I talked to perhaps twenty people. All these men who were then in their sixties or seventies said virtually the same things. These same images kept coming back and coming back: the mud; the bodies; living in the damp underground; the sensation of living down in a hole. There weren't very many things, but they just kept coming back, so that they all had the same experience. When you read the poems, these things keep coming back. It was a little bit like discovering that I didn't have to write two thousand pages and the whole war, it was discovering that most people who had been in the trenches in the First World War had this very small area, their experience was quite a small one, and they were all rather similar – one trench was much like another wherever it happened to be. Doubtless if I'd spoken to Germans, it would have been the same. It's interesting, because since then Belgium and France have opened up the War Graves sites to visitors and they've mocked up real trenches. There are visitors' centres where you see the original photographs and the original films, you see actual things that they have found. But the main thing is you go and sit in a trench. Now, if I'd been able to do that it would have been even more immediate, I think. I just had to imagine it. But it is the detail, it's the small, rather ordinary, detail. Mud seemed to be it. Just living in mud.

JN: It's very interesting that you chose to set this story of love against a situation in which human beings are forced to live like animals.

SH: Yes, and I think that there are things we will never know.

Hundreds and thousands of stories of individual affection, love, friendship, courage, solidarity, must have been re-enacted day after day in that situation – many of which we will never know about. Some we do.

JN: Why did you choose to tell it from Hilliard's point of view?

SH: Because he's somebody I understood and knew. I'd been inside his head. I'd been there before with Kingshaw and Hooper – maybe not Hooper so much. Hilliard is kind of Kingshaw grown up, in a way. I knew his kind of person, whereas I wanted to observe David Barton and to have the impact of his kind of person influence the other. I couldn't have written it the other way around. It just wouldn't have worked. I never even considered it – at least I don't think I did. I still feel very sympathetic to somebody who finds this inability to communicate emotion, and it's luck, isn't it, whether or not such people are unfrozen or not? Some people have gone through their lives never having had the luck of that encounter.

JN: The luck of the encounter certainly, but then it's cruelly taken away.

SH: It was inevitable, wasn't it? I mean, the chances are that both of them would have died. Certainly one of them was going to, but it was very unlikely that both would have survived. And of course there wouldn't have been a book. There was no way round that ending. It just had to be. I've often wondered, what happened to Hilliard in the next twenty years? I don't think I'd ever write about it, but . . . usually when a book's over the characters are dead for me. But he's still there. I do wonder what happened to him.

JN: So that final image of Hilliard looking up and ahead, he's not just looking ahead because it's too painful to look back, he's looking up to a future because he has one?

SH: I think it's a hopeful image, yes. It is looking ahead. We also know that if Barton had survived he'd just have gone back into this big happy family; in a way it's much more interesting to speculate about what would have happened to Hilliard rather than what happened to Barton. And I think readers like to stop and think. Some books you go on with, don't you?

JN: Are you tempted to write a sequel?

SH: I've often thought about it. I don't think I could, but you never know. Something might happen.

JN: You've talked about how, when you came to write *The Woman in Black*, you were moving on to an entirely different kind of writing. Whereas the earlier novels that we've been looking at were novels that absolutely *had* to be written, that came from somewhere deep inside you, with *The Woman in Black* you chose a particular genre, you researched it, and you decided you were going to tell a tale in an old-fashioned sense. One of the things that this reminds me of is the idea of the writer as entertainer as in *A Bit of Singing and Dancing* where the very title suggests performance. Do you see the writer's role as to entertain and perform?

SH: Yes, and I think I very much divide my work in two. I pick this up from Graham Greene, who's been a great influence on me, all my writing life. He divided his own work into 'fictions' and 'entertainments'. Sometimes the division with him is not always easy to spot, but I very much followed on from that. So: the entertainments are not to be taken so seriously, they don't come from so deep a level; you're playing more, they're not books that *have* to be written in that urgent sense coming from within. And *The Woman in Black* is perfect as an entertainment. It is an entertaining genre – the classic ghost story – and one I've always really enjoyed. I also had a bit of a sense of mission about it, because I felt that it was a genre which was disappearing in a welter of gore. Horror stories are not ghost stories, thrillers are not ghost stories. Or the ghost story is not those things. And I wanted to rescue it really from this new way, from these grey areas where people always lump them together. I get furious when people call *The Woman in Black* a horror story. It isn't. There may be horrible things in it, but essentially it is a ghost story, which is different. Because whereas you can have a ghost story which is not horrible (you can have rather gentle ghost stories, or funny ghost stories, or sad ghost stories), you can't have a horror story that isn't horror.

JN: The ghost story must have the supernatural in it, mustn't it?

SH: Yes. I made a list of what it had to have, and the first thing was a ghost. And I reckoned that a ghost was a presence seen, heard, felt, usually by the living, someone who had been alive and is known to have died. There had to be a defined ghost, so it's not a spook, it's not a monster from the marsh, it's not an alien from outer space, it is a human ghost – though I suppose you could have an animal ghost. And that was absolutely the definition, and everything stemmed from there. Then came the ingredients of the ghost story – which I realised were all the things I loved writing about – atmosphere, and sense of place. But I felt, as always, even with my children's books, there's always got to be a moral point somewhere. I can't just have fun, I'd got to pay for it. There is a moral point to *The Woman in Black*.

JN: Am I right in thinking that the moral point is that there is a fight between good and evil going on in the world?

SH: Yes, there's that. And there's also the pointlessness of revenge and pursuing revenge. As long as this woman in her misery as a ghost continues to try and get revenge for what happened to her child, she will walk the earth unsettled and evil will just go on and on. Also, the other thing of having to let go – she's got to let go to move on to wherever she's going to move on to, and people have to let go. You can't bear a grudge because it will haunt you, it's damaging beyond its natural term. I mean, everybody has to have a sense of wanting revenge, up to a point, for something terrible that's happened, but not endlessly. It's got to be laid to rest.

JN: So although you wrote this partly as a bit of fun within a chosen genre, you're also saying something very serious, aren't you, about evil?

SH: Yes. It is not only a bit of fun. Both the play and the book have to retain this, otherwise it doesn't work. I've always got to have this backbone, somewhere, so that people have got to do more than just put it down and think 'oh well'. It's got to have something to make them think, and a moral point – or moral points.

JN: Why did you decide to set it in period?

SH: I toyed with this. In the end I came down on setting it within a period, but it's a very unspecified period. It's kind of between 1900 and 1929 or something, it's vague. It's not Victorian. Edwardian possibly. Or if it's Victorian, it's just tipping over. I would like to write a contemporary ghost story, but there's too much unspookiness about the modern world. You've got to find it and get rid of all the rest.

JN: You also play on the tension between the familiar, the ordinary, and the strange within. Of course, by setting *The Woman in Black* in period and giving it a very nostalgic feel, you make the familiar and the ordinary feel very safe.

SH: Yes, of course. It's easier to do, in a sense.

JN: Do you feel compassion for Jennet Humfrye?

SH: Oh yes. She is perpetrating evil, yes, but anybody who cannot let go, and cannot let rest, is to be pitied, in themselves, because the person who is most tormented by it all is her. A person in life who is like that, the person who is most tormented and hurt by it is themselves. We're not punished for our sins, we're punished by them. Yes, I do have compassion for Jennet. On the other hand, she's not a good person. Evil goes on. I think, you know, of the old thing of 'can you feel compassion for the absolute monster killer' — can you feel compassion for Hitler as it were — the old moral problem. There comes a point where it must be extremely difficult to feel compassion for a person except to say, well, they're mad, so let them be pitied for that reason alone. You have to leave some of the worst evil just for God to deal with. Yes, I do feel sorry for the fact that she hasn't been able to let go and forgive. Because, after all, what happened was an accident. It may be somebody's fault, but it was still an accident.

JN: And the very fact that she had to give the child up in the first place was because of social pressures which no longer exist, of course.

SH: That's the other thing, yes. You couldn't set *The Woman in Black* book now, in a sense, because it doesn't happen. You could set it forty, fifty years ago. That's about the limit. People did have to give up their babies, or the pressure was on them to do that.

JN: You mention that you're not aware of how you set about doing things technically, but there's clearly a lot of technical skill involved in suggesting evil because evil is mysterious, and inevitably it can't always be stated: it needs somehow to be pointed to, and the reader's imagination presumably must do a lot of the work for you. I notice that you prepare for the moments when Kipps confronts evil very carefully. How aware were you of doing that? Of manipulating the reader?

SH: I think you have to. The gaps are terribly important, because they're what the reader's imagination fills. And you've got to give them the right gap at the right moment. Sometimes it falls naturally, instinctively, it's what you feel – you're the reader as well. I think the one thing about this book that had to be fairly carefully planned – although again it's something that comes instinctively – is not just the build-up from the beginning to the end of the book, but lots of little build-ups. You build up, and then there's a slight release, and then you're building up again. And this is why the play is so clever. This is what Stephen [Mallatratt, the playwright] has picked up so well and this is why audiences are absolutely gripped. They're sort of screwed up and then they're released a bit and they think 'phew, that's all right' and then it gradually comes on again. This is why *The Turn of the Screw* is such a wonderful title. Because you're turning it a little bit, and then stopping.

JN: Was [Henry James's] *The Turn of the Screw* one of your models?

SH: Well, it was, but I tried to keep away from it a bit because it was almost the obvious role model. I think because it's a full-length ghost story, whereas most ghost stories are not full-length, most of them are short stories. This is one of the few. It's very near to me in time, and then there's the Britten opera of course, which makes it even nearer – Britten uses ghosts quite a lot. You can use the ghost for a very serious purpose as well as for fun. I try to do the two really.

JN: Did you have any other particular models?

SH: No, not really. Henry James did write some very good serious ghost stories, 'Owen Wingrave' – there's Owen again – probably he wasn't exactly a model, but he was an influence. I mean, nobody is an actual model. But he was more of an influence than say M. R. James. I find M. R. James frustrating, because he's *so* wonderful on the atmosphere and the places, and then I find his actual plots, or the actual denouement, sometimes odd. Either they're baffling and you don't know what's happened really, or they just don't quite work. I think a real ghost, a human ghost is so much more frightening than a creature of slime or something, which is just silly, children's comic stuff. I never can take seriously the ghost story where some sort of squat hairy black creature creeps into the room, and you think, 'Oh, please!' It's not frightening. Well, it is, but only in the most 'yuck, hate spiders' sense. And I wanted to avoid that. To have really fairly ordinary settings: a solicitor's office; a train; a rather beautiful stretch of water which happens to have tide coming and going; a house which is rather ugly – it's everything that we bring to it. What is a graveyard? It's only where people bury their dead. Those places are quite straightforward, aren't they? They're not, in themselves, frightening. It's what we bring to them.

JN: This is where point of view is so important of course, because it's all told by Arthur Kipps and therefore we get, not just what he saw, but his response to what he saw. His emotional reactions become the reality, don't they?

SH: Yes. I think one very important thing that you have to have in a ghost story is this attitude – 'Well, of course I don't believe in ghosts . . . and nobody will ever make me believe . . .' – and then gradually this person is proved wrong. These things do happen after all. It's the conversion of the unbeliever.

JN: So it's a bit like Horatio in that first scene from [Shakespeare's] *Hamlet*, who says that he wouldn't have believed it had he not seen it with his own eyes. Horatio is a rational man, but he's seen it, it can't be denied.

SH: Yes. Doubting Thomas, oh yes. I don't have to have the sort of person who is completely credulous about everything, about ghosts and crystals, and whatever – they'd fall for anything straight away. You've got to have somebody who has to be convinced and is only convinced when the going really gets tough.

JN: Even then this particular type of character *insists* on trying to get to the bottom of it, on going back again.

SH: Yes. 'There must be a rational explanation' and 'It can't possibly have really happened like that' – that's where he falls down, every time. 'And all these people here who keep telling these stories . . . come on . . . let's prove this false.' That's always interesting to watch – pride coming before a fall.

JN: Why do you suppose the play of *The Woman in Black* has been so popular, and so many people have responded to it with so much enthusiasm?

SH: Oh . . . it's the X factor. I think it uses theatre wonderfully for what theatre is for. It involves the audience from the beginning. It is like a book in the sense that they have to use their imaginations. It involves everything. From the very start you're alert – 'Who is this man walking down and pretending to read things?' It's engaging. I think people like to be involved and engaged. It also engages expectations, because it is supposed to be a frightening ghost story. People go in with anticipation – 'What is going to happen that is going to make me frightened?' And of course most people go in thinking . . . 'Oh yeah . . . frighten me! . . . I've seen Hannibal Lector and worse, and I've seen every horror film. How could a *theatre* do that' – they go in challenging it to frighten them. And it's *very* amusing to watch how they gradually change their attitude. I think it is genuinely frightening. It's unexpected. It plays on a few obvious chords. It's extraordinarily powerful in the way it uses every theatrical device – it's pure theatre – to frighten, to engage, to excite, to mystify, to make you want to know what's going to happen next. It's a real effort, you can't go into that and sit back, you can't *not* be involved in it. It is completely true to the book, but it is also totally itself and totally theatrical. It's just got that magic combination that works. It isn't just being frightened. It's the old-fashioned power of theatre, and it demonstrates it to me more than almost anything – that theatre *works* still and always will. If you get it right, those ingredients, I think that's what makes it so powerful. What happens is that the play trusts that the audience will *immediately* start to imagine. And the imagination, of course, is worse than anything the theatre can do.

VINTAGE
LIVING
TEXTS

I'm the King of the Castle

IN CLOSE-UP

Reading guides for

I'M THE KING OF THE CASTLE

BEFORE YOU BEGIN TO READ . . .
— Read the interview with Susan Hill. You will see there that she identifies a number of themes:

- Childhood
- Menace
- Misfits
- Adults and children
- The idea of evil
- First- and third-person narration

Other themes that may be useful to consider while reading the novel include:

- The creation of atmosphere
- Sense of place
- The presentation of the natural world
- Possession and manipulation

Reading activities: detailed analysis

Focus on: the title

The title comes from a children's game. How is this game played? What connotations of power, status and territory do the images of 'king' and 'castle' suggest? Can you think of other children's games or songs that concern power struggles? What do these games suggest about children's awareness of issues of power and status? Now think of ways in which children's games ritualise the idea of the 'chase' or the 'hunt'. What is the difference between a game of 'It' and genuine victimisation – what determines the difference?

CHAPTER ONE
SECTIONS 1–4 (pp. 7–11)

Focus on: openings

ANALYSE WITH CLOSE READING . . .
— What is a novelist likely to want to achieve with the opening of a novel? When you read these opening sections of *I'm the King of the Castle*, pay attention to how Hill:

- begins to create a mood through setting, incidents and images
- introduces the characters of Edmund and Joseph Hooper, and how they relate to each other
- introduces key themes (central ideas)
- 'hooks' the reader's interest
- sets the 'tone' of the narrative voice

Make brief notes on what Hill conveys in each of these areas, and how she does this. Although you do not yet know what the key themes of the novel will be, look for references to difficult communication between parents and children; to issues of territory and power; to feeling out of place in the world; to images of oppression and claustrophobia.

CHAPTER ONE
SECTIONS 5–6 (pp. 11–15)

Focus on: narrative point of view

ASSESS . . .
— From whose point of view were the first four sections told, and what happens to the narrative point of view in these two sections? Now consider how 'point of view' in a narrative – which character's view of events dominates at any particular moment – is created partly by the style, the tone and the imagery of the narrative. When events are narrated through the mind of one of the characters, the reader needs to stay alert to how that character thinks, feels and responds – and to how these are conveyed implicitly by the narrative.

Focus on: collecting

COMPARE AND CONSIDER . . .
— *The Collector* (1963) by John Fowles portrays the actions of a psychopath who feels compelled to collect, and whose prize catch is a girl he admires. Compare this depiction of a deranged world view with Hooper's world view. Commenting on his novel, Fowles has said that there is 'something wrong with all forms of collecting'. Consider how the Red Room, with its collection of dead moths and animals, contributes to the sense of 'something wrong' in the atmosphere of Warings.

Looking over Chapter One

QUESTIONS FOR DISCUSSION OR ESSAYS
1. 'He knew himself to be an ineffectual man' (p. 11). How is Joseph Hooper's view of himself supported by his portrayal in Chapter One?

2. How does Hill create a sense of emotional distance between the characters in this opening chapter?

3. Consider how relations between different generations are portrayed in this chapter.

CHAPTER TWO
SECTIONS 1–2 (pp. 16–23)

Focus on: anxiety

LIST AND EXPLAIN . . .
— List and explain the various anxieties that the four characters feel on pp. 16–18.

45

Focus on: self-assertion

ANALYSE . . .

— Analyse the different ways in which Hooper and Kingshaw try to assert themselves on pp. 18–23. How does Hooper win and why is Kingshaw vulnerable?

CHAPTER TWO
SECTIONS 3–5 (pp. 23–8)

Focus on: 'should' and 'ought'

UNDERLINE AND EVALUATE . . .

— Underline each instance of the terms *should* or *ought* in Joseph Hooper's thoughts and words on pp. 23–6. What do these instances reveal about the way in which he views the world?

Focus on: adults and children

INTERPRET . . .

— In what ways do the adults misunderstand the children in these sections?

Looking over Chapter Two

QUESTIONS FOR DISCUSSION OR ESSAYS

1. Compare and contrast the characters of Hooper and Kingshaw. Quote the phrases that convey their respective characters, and comment on what these quotations reveal.

2. 'Both Mrs Kingshaw and Mr Hooper . . . are to some extent still at odds with the normal, adult world' (Hill). To what extent have you found this to be true of their characters in Chapters One and Two?

CHAPTER THREE
SECTIONS 1–2 (pp. 29–38)

Focus on: crows

CONSIDER AND COMPARE . . .
— In what ways is the crow made to seem menacing in this section? (If you have seen Hitchcock's 1963 film *The Birds*, compare it with the way the crow is depicted in the first section of this chapter.) What is it about crows that makes them sinister? Read a selection of poems from Ted Hughes's collection *Crow* (1970) and compare the symbolic uses that Hill and Hughes make of this bird. Why does Kingshaw think that the fact that the crow on his bed is not real 'made it so much worse' (p. 37)?

CHAPTER THREE
SECTIONS 3–5 (pp. 38–44)

Focus on: aloneness

COMMENT . . .
— Comment on the extent to which Kingshaw has come to terms with his aloneness by the end of this chapter. Which details on pp. 38–44 are telling in this respect?

Looking over Chapter Three

QUESTIONS FOR DISCUSSION OR ESSAYS
1. 'He could not have imagined the charm it afforded him, having Kingshaw here, thinking of things to do to him' (p. 35). 'Hooper was unpredictable. Clever. Inventive.' (p. 36) Using these quotations as starting points, study how Hooper torments Kingshaw, and attempt to explain why he enjoys doing this so much.

2. Examine the methods that Hill uses to convey Kingshaw's fear in Chapter Three.

CHAPTER FOUR
SECTIONS 1–3 (pp. 45–9)

Focus on: Kingshaw

COMPARE AND IDENTIFY . . .
— Kingshaw is changing. Compare his portrayal on pp. 45–9 with his depiction on pp. 18–23, and identify specific ways in which he is changing.

CHAPTER FOUR
SECTIONS 4–9 (pp. 49–57)

Focus on: redrafting

COMPARE AND COMMENT . . .
— At the top of p. 52, between 'he might relax for a short time' and 'They scarcely spoke', Hill's first manuscript draft included this passage:

> After a while, Hooper finished counting a score, and then said, 'You've still got to go in the copse.'
> 'I don't have to do anything you say.'
> Kingshaw bent down and sent one of the silver balls racing noisily around the wood. He had spoken the truth in that he didn't have to go, into the copse or anywhere. But he would have to go, because now, he always made himself do things, however terrible. He seemed to be aiming for greater and greater

endurance, though he was too wise, now, to fancy it might make him any less afraid. It made him more, like the jumping into the swimming pool. He had got himself into a trap.

And then, he let go of another ball abruptly, before he was ready. Because he had thought of what he must do about the copse.

They went on playing and scarcely spoke again.

Comment on whether the episode gains or loses something by the removal of this passage in later drafts.

Focus on: escape

DISCUSS . . .

— Hooper, realising that Kingshaw is planning to escape, says, 'I shall come with you' (p. 55). In what ways does their relationship resemble that of stalker and prey, in Chapter Four and earlier?

Looking over Chapter Four

QUESTIONS FOR DISCUSSION OR ESSAYS

1. 'We cannot fathom the minds of young children' (p. 47) thinks Joseph Hooper. How is this idea emphasised by the narrative in Chapter Four?

2. Analyse the way that Hill presents the adults in this chapter. Look in particular at how they speak. How are they kept on the periphery of the narrative focus?

CHAPTER FIVE
SECTIONS 1–4 (pp. 58–62)

Focus on: the child in the adult

DISCRIMINATE AND COMMENT . . .
— Analyse the way that Helena Kingshaw is depicted on pp. 58–60. In what ways does she seem childlike? Identify the exact phrases and images that convey this impression. What is the effect of depicting her in this way? Now compare her thoughts with those of her son on pp. 60–2. In what ways are they temperamentally similar, despite the contrast in their world views?

CHAPTER FIVE
SECTIONS 5–7 (pp. 62–9)

Focus on: language

ANALYSE WITH CLOSE READING . . .
— How does Susan Hill create a sense of atmosphere on pp. 62–4? Underline the most effective words, phrases and images, and analyse what effects they have.

TRANSFORM AND COMPARE . . .
— Using images from the original prose, transform this description into a poem. Compare the different effects created by your poem and Hill's prose. How important is form in creating these effects?

Focus on: characterisation

RESPOND PERSONALLY . . .
— We learn more about Kingshaw and about how he relates

to boys of his own age at school. In what ways is he a misfit? What does he think of himself? How do you respond to his character: do you feel sorry for him? Do you find qualities to admire in him, or do you despise him? Write an episode of about three hundred words on his life at school in which you manipulate the reader's responses to Kingshaw, then write a brief commentary on *how* you have set out to control the reader's reactions.

Looking over Chapter Five

QUESTIONS FOR DISCUSSION OR ESSAYS

1. Contrast the exterior setting of this chapter with the earlier interior settings at Warings. What contrasting effects are created by the two settings? How important is 'sense of place' in the novel so far?

2. 'All the characters are misfits, unable to relate to others in normal, healthy ways.' Discuss, with reference to the first five chapters of *I'm the King of the Castle*.

CHAPTER SIX
SECTION 1 (pp. 70–81)

Focus on: imagery

SELECT, COMMENT AND COMPARE . . .
— Select ten or fifteen lines that offer the most vivid description of the natural world in this chapter, and comment on what impressions the images convey of the natural world. Contrast your chosen passage with the description of Hooper's visit to the Red Room on pp. 14–15.

Focus on: the theme of nature

COMPARE AND CONTRAST . . .

— Compare and contrast Kingshaw's attitude to nature with Hooper's. You might start by looking at their contrasting attitudes to the deer on pp. 76–8. In what ways are their different reactions revealing of their contrasting characters?

Looking over Chapter Six

QUESTIONS FOR DISCUSSION OR ESSAYS

1. Warings was Hooper's 'territory, he was master. Here, they were somehow more equal' (p. 75). Consider how the power balance between the two boys shifts in the shared 'territory' of the wood, and account for why this happens.

2. Consider the fact that Kingshaw would much rather face the dangers and discomforts of the natural habitat than the threat posed by Hooper, and discuss why this might be.

CHAPTER SEVEN
SECTIONS 1–2 (pp. 82–91)

Focus on: Hooper

COMMENT . . .

— 'But he had forgotten the sort of person Hooper was' (p. 86). What sort of person is he? Comment on the presentation of Hooper on pp. 82–91.

Focus on: the theme of death

REVIEW AND RESPOND . . .

— There have been numerous references to death in the novel

so far. Think back and make a list of them. To what extent does the novel support Hooper's view that 'Dead things are finished, they don't matter', or Kingshaw's response that 'they do. Well – dead people do, anyway' (p. 87)?

CHAPTER SEVEN
SECTION 3 (pp. 91–102)

Focus on: the presentation of the natural world

COMPARE WITH OTHER WRITERS . . .

— Compare the presentation of the natural world, and the boys' sense of their place within it, with 'Nutting' by William Wordsworth and with 'The Horses' by Ted Hughes. What aspects does Hill's portrayal of mankind's relationship with nature share with either or both of these poems? See the Contexts section (p. 74) for further exercises on this topic.

CHAPTER SEVEN
SECTION 4 (pp. 102–8)

Focus on: motive and character

ANALYSE AND COMPARE . . .

— Why does Kingshaw not leave Hooper in the woods? Analyse his motives carefully, and identify the assumptions about how people should behave that underline them. In what ways do his assumptions and Hooper's contrast?

Looking over Chapter Seven

QUESTIONS FOR DISCUSSION OR ESSAYS

1. 'Humans are only animals' (p. 88). Does the novel support Hooper's claim?

2. 'Hooper's fear was a straightforward response to an outside situation. But his own was quite different, and Hooper had the measure of it, he had done so from his first day at Warings' (pp. 97–8). Comment on Hooper's power over Kingshaw in the light of this comment.

CHAPTER EIGHT
SECTIONS 1–2 (pp. 109–14)

Focus on: manipulation

ASSESS . . .
— Assess the ways in which Hooper manipulates and controls Kingshaw on pp. 109–14.

CHAPTER EIGHT
SECTIONS 3–4 (pp. 114–23)

Focus on: nightmares

TRANSFORM AND CREATE . . .
— What do you imagine Hooper's nightmare was about? Describe it either as a prose account or as a poem. Remember the importance of imagery in dreams, and try to create some of a nightmare's emotional intensity.

Focus on: inner tension

DISCUSS . . .

— 'His own violence astounded him' (p. 122). Although he has an impulse to be violent, he also has (unlike Hooper) a strong sense of inner restraint, of conscience. Discuss what competing impulses are at work in Kingshaw on pp. 114–23.

Looking over Chapter Eight

QUESTIONS FOR DISCUSSION OR ESSAYS

1.   'Kingshaw felt aware of himself, and of his own resources' (p. 123). What has Kingshaw learned about himself in Chapters Six, Seven and Eight?

2.   Whereas Hooper fears the violent aspects of nature, Kingshaw is prone to fear of the *super*natural. During the episode in the wood his mind turns to spells, warts and death (e.g., p. 114). In her first jottings for *I'm the King of the Castle*, Hill wrote of Kingshaw: 'He must believe in spirits and hauntings . . . They talk of death and afterlife. The [other] boy very cool & matter of fact about disbelieving. All atmosphere.' Compare the effects created during this chapter with those created in the film *The Blair Witch Project* (1999). Why, in your opinion, are most human beings so open to fear of the supernatural?

CHAPTER NINE
SECTIONS 1–3 (pp. 124–6)

Focus on: the motif of birds

CONSIDER THE EFFECTS . . .

— What effects are created by the references to birds in this chapter? How do the references to birds and birdsong build upon or alter the way that birds have been used in the novel so far?

Looking over Chapter Nine

QUESTION FOR DISCUSSION OR ESSAYS
1. In what ways does the arrival of the search party seem an unwanted intrusion into Kingshaw's peaceful sense of freedom?

CHAPTER TEN
SECTIONS 1–3 (pp. 127–35)

Focus on: miscommunication

ANALYSE AND ASSESS THE EFFECTS . . .
— Analyse the miscommunication between Kingshaw and his mother. What creates her failure to understand him? In particular, compare the language that each uses, and decide what their choices of words reveals about the ways they think. What hopes and fears underlie Mrs Kingshaw's rather genteel and clichéd way of expressing herself?

Looking over Chapter Ten

QUESTIONS FOR DISCUSSION OR ESSAYS
1. How does Hill convey Kingshaw's sense of entrapment and isolation in this chapter?

2. Write Mrs Kingshaw's diary entry after the events of Chapter Ten. Use it to imagine and express her most secret thoughts, relieved of the need to make the right impression, about Joseph Hooper, Edmund and her son. Try to emulate her way of speaking, and in particular her vocabulary. If the

reader of the novel were given this depth of insight into Helena Kingshaw's heart and mind, how would that insight alter our responses to her? Why has Hill kept her inner life distant from the reader, do you think?

CHAPTER ELEVEN
SECTIONS 1–5 (pp. 136–46)

Focus on: theme of entrapment

LOOK FOR A PATTERN . . .
— Kingshaw's experience at Warings is a process of gradual entrapment. Consider how this theme is brought to a new pitch of intensity throughout Chapter Eleven. In what ways has a pattern emerged in Hooper's methods of bullying? What relevance might his name have in this respect?

Focus on: dream symbols

INTERPRET . . .
— Dreams are often thought to be symbolic. Attempt an interpretation of the symbols in Kingshaw's dream.

Looking over Chapter Eleven

QUESTION FOR DISCUSSION OR ESSAYS
1. Kingshaw often thinks of Hooper as 'cunning' (p. 138). Explain what is cunning about the way Hooper bullies Kingshaw in this chapter.

CHAPTER TWELVE
SECTIONS 1–3 (pp. 147–54)

Focus on: satire

ANALYSE . . .

— In places the portrayal of the adult characters borders on satirical. What aspects of middle-aged behaviour are satirised on pp. 147–8?

Focus on: Kingshaw

EXAMINE, RESPOND AND REWRITE . . .

— Once again Kingshaw has the chance to humiliate Hooper, to make use of Hooper's weakness and cowardice. But instead he responds to Hooper's fear with kindness (which literally means the care one shows towards one's kin, or family). Why does he do this? Do you admire his unselfishness, or are you annoyed by his inability to stand up for himself? Rewrite the conversation from 'Look, you'll have to go down first . . .' (p. 151) so that Kingshaw takes full advantage of Hooper's fear. Which responses from Kingshaw most ask to be changed?

Looking over Chapter Twelve

QUESTIONS FOR DISCUSSION OR ESSAYS

1. Analyse and comment on how Hill creates tension in this chapter.

2. What actually happened when Hooper fell? Remember that the events were told from Kingshaw's point of view. How sure are you that it was an accident? Does the narrative make this clear?

CHAPTER THIRTEEN
SECTIONS 1–4 (pp. 155–66)

Focus on: film techniques

COMPARE DIFFERENT MEDIA . . .
— The forward movement of a narrative can be speeded up, slowed down or even paused altogether, rather like a film. How does Hill use film techniques in her presentation of time and of point of view on pp. 155–6 (up to 'Slowly, Kingshaw began to climb down from the castle')?

Focus on: themes

INFER . . .
— What might be the significance of Kingshaw's memories of Lesage? Think not only about Lesage's reading at the carol service, but all the associated memories, and how these might tie into the novel's main themes. Now consider the relevance of the film that Mrs Boland is watching to the themes of the novel. Consider the ways in which the adult characters seem to experience life at one remove, and contrast this with the boys' raw experience.

Looking over Chapter Thirteen

QUESTION FOR DISCUSSION OR ESSAYS
1. 'Susan Hill's main focus is on emotional states – on the interior landscape of the mind and heart.' Evaluate the validity of this claim with particular reference to Chapter Thirteen.

CHAPTER FOURTEEN
SECTIONS 1–4 (pp. 167–72)

Focus on: unspoken subtext

REWRITE . . .

— Rewrite Kingshaw's conversation with his mother on pp. 167–8, inserting with each of his responses the unspoken subtext of what he is actually thinking. How much is he *not* expressing? Looking back, can you find any instances in the novel of free and open communication between Kingshaw and his mother?

Focus on: the adults

INTERPRET THE JUXTAPOSITION . . .

— Look at the way the narrative juxtaposes Kingshaw's unspoken thoughts with those of his mother and of Joseph Hooper on pp. 170–1. In what ways does this strategy emphasise how ineffectual the adults are?

CHAPTER FOURTEEN
SECTIONS 5–8 (pp. 172–84)

Focus on: addresser and addressee

REFLECT AND TRANSFORM . . .

— What is the point of a prayer? Whom does Kingshaw think he is addressing on p. 173? What do you think would be a Christian way for Kingshaw to deal with Hooper? Transform Kingshaw's prayer into a conversation between him and God.

Focus on: Fielding

INFER . . .
— 'Kingshaw decided to trust him' (p. 177). Do you think that
Kingshaw is right to trust Fielding? What is it about Fielding
that appeals to Kingshaw?

Focus on: redrafting

COMPARE AND COMMENT . . .
— At the top of p. 180, after 'Tomorrow, they are bringing
Edmund home!', Hill's first manuscript draft included this pas-
sage:

> He did not want to tell her anything, not anything at
> all, about Fielding, and the farm, and going back
> there to dinner, but he had to, sitting in the break-
> fast room, she made him go on and on answering
> her questions. When he was allowed to go, he rode
> very slowly back through the village. He thought, it
> is all spoiled, it is spoiled and finished, it is no
> longer just mine.

Comment on whether the episode gains or loses by the removal
of this passage. You might also look at p. 211, where similar
thoughts go through Kingshaw's head.

Looking over Chapter Fourteen

QUESTIONS FOR DISCUSSION OR ESSAYS
1. Compare and contrast Kingshaw and Fielding.

2. Discuss the relevance of the calving episode (pp. 177–8)
to the themes of the novel as a whole.

CHAPTER FIFTEEN
SECTION 1 (pp. 185–94)

Focus on: playing roles

DISCRIMINATE . . .

— 'He squirmed, hating the way she spoke of herself like that, as though she were another person' (p. 189). In what senses is it true that Helena Kingshaw is not herself, but has taken on a borrowed persona? Consider the claim that Mrs Kingshaw is a character who is out of touch with her own feelings.

Focus on: unfairness

REVIEW AND CONSIDER . . .

— 'He almost burst out at her in his fury at the unfairness of it' (p. 190). This has been Kingshaw's repeated complaint. Review previous scenes in which he gave up trying to explain what he was thinking and feeling, but resented his mother's lack of understanding all the same, such as on pp. 129–30, 159 or 167–8. Has Helena Kingshaw actually been unfair on him, do you think, or is Kingshaw guilty of failing to explain himself properly? Consider the idea that the real unfairness is against Helena Kingshaw.

— 'As long as you make the very best of your chances, there, that is all I ask you, as long as you remember how lucky you have been' (p. 191). Now think about the claim that Helena Kingshaw is unfair in continually bringing emotional blackmail to bear on her son. You might want to read on to the end of the chapter before you consider this idea.

CHAPTER FIFTEEN
SECTIONS 2–4 (pp. 194–7)

Focus on: adult complacency

GAUGE THE IRONY . . .

— Joseph Hooper reflects that 'boys are very simple animals' (p. 195). Consider the ironies in this thought within the terms of *I'm the King of the Castle*.

Focus on: identity

COMPARE AND ANALYSE . . .

— Joseph Hooper and Helena Kingshaw have taken on new identities, and are glad. But when Kingshaw 'looked in the tall glass, and saw himself like Hooper, in the black and gold uniform, looked into his own eyes, he knew that there was no more hope for him' (pp. 196–7). Compare Kingshaw's situation with theirs, and analyse why Kingshaw feels such despair at his change of identity.

CHAPTER FIFTEEN
SECTIONS 5–6 (pp. 197–8)

Focus on: physical abuse

INTERPRET AND COMMENT . . .

— Why is the moment when Mr Hooper hits Kingshaw a defining moment in their relationship? Comment on Mrs Kingshaw's reaction.

Looking over Chapter Fifteen

QUESTIONS FOR DISCUSSION OR ESSAYS

1. 'The worst feeling had been the aloneness . . . His terror of Crawford had been absolute' (p. 188). Reflect on how central 'aloneness' is to Kingshaw's world view.

2. Consider how the theme of ownership – of place, of status, of support, of identity – is developed in Chapter Fifteen, and how these ideas relate to the novel as a whole.

3. 'Mr Hooper did not listen' (p. 196). To what extent is this the source of Joseph Hooper's failure to understand his son or Kingshaw?

CHAPTER SIXTEEN
SECTIONS 1–2 (pp. 199–204)

Focus on: insincerity

GAUGE . . .

— 'There had been something in her tone of voice, something in the over-emphasis of words, that made him suspect her' (p. 200). Looking back over the novel, consider the claim that Mrs Kingshaw's lack of sincerity is the primary reason for her failure as a mother.

Focus on: Joseph Hooper

SUMMARISE AND ASSESS . . .

— Summarise Joseph Hooper's view of himself on pp. 202–4. Assess how accurately he knows himself, measured against your impressions of him from the novel so far.

CHAPTER SIXTEEN
SECTIONS 3–8 (pp. 204–18)

Focus on: Kingshaw's isolation

EXAMINE . . .
— Examine how Hooper destroys Kingshaw's friendship with
Fielding. Why does Kingshaw react as he does on pp. 212–17?

Looking over Chapter Sixteen

QUESTIONS FOR DISCUSSION OR ESSAYS
1. Joseph Hooper 'had suffered from the cold gap between
his permitted behaviour, and his desires' (p. 203). Examine the
tension between 'permitted behaviour' and 'desires' in the novel
as a whole.

2. Review the things that Kingshaw fears in this chapter, and
discuss whether he is neurotic.

CHAPTER SEVENTEEN
SECTIONS 1–6 (pp. 219–23)

Focus on: fear

WEIGH UP . . .
— Fielding has earlier remarked to Kingshaw that 'You needn't
be frightened just of what somebody else *says*, need you?'
(p. 181). Is Kingshaw's fearful anticipation of going to school
with Hooper understandable, do you think? Consider the claim
that Kingshaw's real enemy is his fearful imagination.

TRANSFORM . . .
— 'Time, when you are eleven, still moves relatively slowly,

65

and the future for Kingshaw, six or seven years of Hooper at home and at school, is an eternity ahead' (Hill). With this comment in mind, write a suicide note for Kingshaw that explains in detail why he has decided to kill himself. Recreate both his view of the world and his 'voice'.

Focus on: the ending

COMMENT ON . . .
— Hill records that Kingshaw's suicide has been criticised as 'melodramatic and unlikely'. Do you find it so? Consider Kingshaw's character, and consider also the understated style in which it is described.

Looking over Chapter Seventeen

QUESTIONS FOR DISCUSSION OR ESSAYS
1.   Hooper's reaction to Kingshaw's death is 'a spurt of triumph' (p. 223). What are your impressions of Hooper by the end of the novel?

2.   Discuss who among the characters must take some responsibility for Kingshaw's suicide.

Looking over the whole novel

QUESTIONS FOR DISCUSSION OR ESSAYS
1.   Hill has commented that she is obsessed by childhood, by 'what it feels like, how it truly is and how adults misinterpret it'. What does *I'm the King of the Castle* say about how childhood is and how adults misinterpret it?

2.   'I have been interested in children who are in some way at odds with the rest of the world' (Hill). In what ways are

Hooper and Kingshaw at odds with the world?

3. By what means and with what success does *I'm the King of the Castle* evoke the emotion of fear?

4. Consider the significance of shame in *I'm the King of the Castle*.

5. Comment on the presentation of the natural world in *I'm the King of the Castle*.

6. Hill has said that 'settings are always very, very important to me, every bit as much as characters or themes'. Discuss the significance of 'setting' in *I'm the King of the Castle*.

7. What does the character of Fielding contribute to *I'm the King of the Castle*?

8. Kingshaw repeatedly thinks of Hooper that 'There was nothing he wouldn't do.' Consider the theme of conscience in *I'm the King of the Castle*.

9. Discuss the portrayal of the adult characters in *I'm the King of the Castle*. In what ways are their thoughts and words more formalised, less naturalistic than those of the boys?

10. '*I'm the King of the Castle* is about characters who fail to come to terms with aloneness.' Discuss.

11. An early review commented on how Hill's novels 'all focus on the same kind of lonely, dislocated experience. The characters are always somehow unaccommodated, outside ordinary intercourse, there is always the pathos of an excited, complex sensibility that has to stay closed off and inarticulate' (*Times*

Literary Supplement, 25 January 1974). To what extent does this quotation accurately describe the characters in *I'm the King of the Castle*, in your opinion?

12. Consider the themes of entrapment and release in *I'm the King of the Castle*.

13. In what senses can *I'm the King of the Castle* be called a 'tragedy'?

14. Write an episode to fit into *I'm the King of the Castle*. Imitate the novel's style, and make sure that your characters and actions are in accordance with those of the original. Your piece should be about five hundred words.

15. What do you imagine will happen to Hooper, his father and Kingshaw's mother after the end of the novel? Write the plot line of a sequel which gives an account of subsequent events.

Contexts, comparisons and complementary readings

I'M THE KING OF THE CASTLE

These sections suggest contextual and comparative ways of reading these four books by Susan Hill. You can put your reading in a social, historical or literary context. You can make comparisons – again, social, literary or historical – with other texts or art works. Or you can choose complementary works (of whatever kind) – that is, art works, literary works, social reportage or facts which in some way illuminate the text by sidelights or interventions which you can make into a telling framework. Some of the suggested contexts are directly connected to the book, in that they will give you precise literary or social frames in which to situate the novel. In turn, these are either related to the period within which the novel is set, or to the time – now – when you are reading it. Some of these examples are designed to suggest books or other texts that may make useful sources for comparison (or for complementary purposes) when you are reading Hill's work. Again, they may be related to literary or critical themes, or they may be relevant to social and cultural themes current 'then' or 'now'.

Focus on: children and the idea of evil

COMPARE THEMES AND SETTINGS . . .

— Children as vessels or instruments of evil figure in Henry James's novella *The Turn of the Screw* (1898) and in William Golding's *The Lord of the Flies* (1954). Compare Hill's treatment of the theme of evil committed by children in *I'm the King of the Castle* with one or both of these stories. Other novels that you might like to look at include Marianne Wiggins's *John Dollar* (1994) or Annabel Donald's *Be Nice* (2002). These last two are based on the characters of girls, as opposed to the earlier stories which are about boys. You might like to compare the characters in these stories set in different times. Alternatively, you might like to compare the handling of settings in these narratives.

Focus on: children and their experience of adult secrets

RESEARCH AND COMPARE . . .

In the interview at the front of this book, Hill mentions that she has been much influenced by the work of Graham Greene. Read Greene's story *The Fallen Idol* (1935). It was made into a film starring Dirk Bogarde and directed by Carol Reed (1948). In this story, the child, who is the central character, is left alone with the butler and his wife. The butler – the 'idol' of the title – is having an affair and his wife determines to do away with the girlfriend. The child is an ignorant – though not altogether innocent – witness of these events. Compare the way in which the child's view of an adult world that he doesn't fully understand is presented in Greene and in Hill. Another text that you might like to look at is L. P. Hartley's *The Go-Between* (1953) where a child staying in a country house in the early years of the twentieth century is drawn into, and exploited by, the protagonists in a secret love affair.

Focus on: the notion of the 'psychopathic' child

COMPARE EXAMPLES OF A CHARACTER TYPE . . .
—— The so-called 'psychopathic' child was a commonplace figure in 1970s fiction and in films of the time. For example, you might read Stephen King's *Carrie* (1974), which shares with *I'm the King of the Castle* the theme of bullying and the characters' fear of isolation, but in *Carrie* it is the psychopathic character who is the victim of bullying, not the perpetrator. Compare the characters of Hooper and Carrie, and consider the ways in which the authors control the readers' responses to them.

RESEARCH . . .
Look for examples of stories about real children who were diagnosed as 'psychopathic' in an on-line newspaper, such as http://www.the-times.co.uk, http://www.guardian.co.uk or http://www.independent.co.uk. This is an emotive topic that provokes strong reactions in adults. Analyse the news coverage of an instance involving a real so-called 'psychopathic' child and comment on the attitudes, implicit or explicit, that you find in them.

Focus on: parents and children

COMPARE THE PORTRAYAL OF EMOTIONAL RELATION-
SHIPS . . .
Read Hill's novel *A Change for the Better* (1969), which she wrote immediately before *I'm the King of the Castle*. Compare James Fount's relationship with his mother with that between Kingshaw and his mother. What similarities emerge, and what

do these suggest about Hill's concerns in this period? Or read more widely on the theme of parents and children. You might try Ivan Turgenev's *Fathers and Sons* (1862), D. H. Lawrence's *Sons and Lovers* (1913), Esther Freud's *Hideous Kinky* (1992), or Iain Banks's *The Crow Road* (1992). In what ways are the relationships between the parents and their children in these texts portrayed as tense or vexed?

Focus on: childhood in Susan Hill's work

READ AND COMPARE . . .

— 'Children – and especially those who are set apart from their fellows, who are parentless or sickly or "not quite right" – have also become significant figures in Miss Hill's private world of suffering' (*Times Literary Supplement*, 30 March 1973). With reference to *I'm the King of the Castle* and at least one other work by Hill, discuss her depiction of childhood suffering. You might look at *A Bit of Singing and Dancing* (1973) (especially 'Halloran's Child', 'The Badness Within Him' and 'The Custodian'), *A Change for the Better* (1969) or *The Mist in the Mirror* (1992).

Focus on: bullying

FIND OUT AND RESEARCH . . .

— Hill says that she does not like the label 'bullying'. As far as she is concerned 'bullying' is just another manifestation of unkindness. Many people are anxious about the problems of bullying in the classroom and the playground, and many writers have addressed this topic. Foremost among them is the writer Jacqueline Wilson whose stories have been well received and loved by many young readers. Look out any – or all – of Wilson's work. You will find that she takes these questions seriously and attentively. Find an appropriate example among her books and compare it to the concerns of *I'm the King of the Castle*.

Focus on: allusion

DESCRIBE AND ASSESS . . .
— Do you know the children's rhyme which is alluded to in the title of Hill's novel? If yes, how does it go? Why do children play this game? What is the surface point of it? What is the underlying struggle that might be going on among the participants? If you don't know the chant, find out about it, and then ask yourself these questions.

CONSIDER . . .
— This is a diary entry written by an eleven-year-old staying in a castle in Scotland. How might the ideas in it relate to *I'm the King of the Castle*?

When we first arrived I was amazed because it really looked like a castle. To me it has to be one of the most beautiful buildings I have ever seen. I love the interior, not the naf things most would expect. After a day it was home. The wonderful feeling of being king of the castle was always felt. The feeling of shutting the door and knowing no one else could come in. It was my castle. Every night we had a grand meal in the dining room. I could never understand the jokes in the crests on the ceiling but liked sitting looking at them. My cousin Bill adopted the grand fireplace in the dining room as his workshop and sat there for hours whittling sticks. The lovely freedom of being able to go where you wanted on your own was dominant. Everybody was so friendly and trustworthy you could leave them with a bag of gold for a moment knowing they wouldn't run off with it. One day a group of schoolchildren invaded the castle. About 20 kids were charging about the outhouses, ages varying from 5 to 16. My cousin and I were furious. We had to act fast. We could not bear the sight of all these other people tearing round screaming and shouting, kicking and laughing. This was war, my cousin was in the courtyard setting traps and I ran round the battlements keeping watch. In the end my dad came and sorted them out. After they had gone we felt a sense of triumph. But in some ways we wished the battle of the castle hadn't ended. We met a girl called Ruth from the village, she was 9 and came to walk here most days. She was never very well known but always very nice.

Focus on: the natural world

READD AND COMPARE . . .

— Hill's presentation of nature borrows from the pastoral tradition, but with a twentieth-century emphasis the violent and frightening aspects of nature are set alongside the beautiful aspects. Compare Chapters Six and Seven of *I'm the King of the Castle* with Chapter Two of Joseph Conrad's 'Heart of Darkness' (1902) from 'Going up that river . . .'; or with Chapter Eight of William Golding's *Lord of the Flies* from 'The wood was not so dry . . .'; or with the descriptions of living in the Honduran jungle in Paul Theroux's *Mosquito Coast* (1982). What common themes and images can you find? What light do these comparisons throw on what Hill is saying about nature in *I'm the King of the Castle*?

Focus on: drafts and manuscripts

READ AND COMPARE . . .

— Hill's first jottings for *I'm the King of the Castle* are reproduced below. Read them carefully. What do they show about the way the novel first presented itself to her? Hill has remarked that 'the process of sorting out what will eventually be memorable and important enough to find a place, however small, in [a writer's] work, goes on the whole time, deep in the subconscious'. Note how the novel came to her consciousness in fragmentary images and scenes rather than in a plot line. Which of these images and scenes have found their way into the final novel, and which have been dropped or altered?

Short novel – long short story. 1 single incident.
Macabre. Atmospheric. The boy. Start with him. The
butterflies pinned to their cases. He opens one and
they disintegrate to powder. He is waiting for the
other boy to arrive & doesn't want him to. Very
cold. Scraps of conversation. Frightens him. In the
wood – + down by the stream at night. Moonlight.
Trees rustling.

Goes into the church. The other follows him like a
dog. Fascinated & because he has been told to keep
him company. The way they can't reveal the state of
things to the outside world, & the adults can't perceive anything of it either.

The boy is an R.C. The chapel. He must believe in
spirits and hauntings, mustn't he?

They talk of death and afterlife. The boy very cool
& matter of fact about disbelieving. All atmosphere.

— The opening of the first full manuscript of *I'm the King of the Castle* is reproduced below. Compare it with the final version and comment on what the alterations reveal about the process of writing the novel.

Three months ago, his grandfather had died and then they had moved into this house.
'I will not go there until I can be called master,' his father had always said, ~~though~~ though the old man lay ~~ignored~~ on upstairs ~~and~~ after ~~a stroke~~ a second stroke, lingered on for months and gave no trouble.
~~Redmund's father The Boy was~~ The boy was taken up to see him and 'You must not be afraid' his father had said anxiously. 'He is a very old man and now very ill.'
'I am never afraid of what I see.' And that was no more than the truth. ~~It will be a mov~~ It will be very moving, ~~Arthur Redmund~~ ~~Henry Redmund said Redmund~~ Joseph Hooper had ~~thought~~ decided, ~~and he imagined~~ the 3 generations together, ~~around in the~~ eldest son of eldest son of eldest son. ~~For he~~ For in middle age he ~~had acquired~~ was acquiring a dynastic sense. But it had not been moving. The old man had ~~not woken~~ breathed noisily + dribbled a little + not woken.
'Ah well' Henry Redmund had said, and coughed ~~a little~~. 'He is very ill you know. I'm glad that you have seen him.'
The boy looked down. His ~~face~~ skin is ~~like the wing of those moths, he thought, downstairs in the Red Room~~ already dead, he thought, & is old ~~white~~ & dry. ~~Already~~ Already it is dead skin ~~and there was a shimmer where the bone of the nose shone through~~ but the bones of the eye-socket & the nose & jaw

showed through & gleamed. ~~'He'~~ Everything about
him from the hair, down to the line of the sheet,
was ~~greyish white~~ ^{faded and} grey-white.
'He looks like a moth' ~~said Henry Redmund's son.~~
~~(John)~~ ~~Mark Mark~~ ~~Redmund~~ Edmund Hooper said. ~~'perhaps~~
~~he isn't~~
'That is not the way to speak, ~~I will not have you~~
~~being disrespectful.~~ I will not have it said that my
son cannot show proper respect.'
And his father led him ^{out} away. Though I am only
able to show respect, he thought, ~~and~~ to behave
towards him as I should, now that he is ~~already~~
almost gone away.

VINTAGE
LIVING
TEXTS

Strange Meeting

IN CLOSE-UP

Reading guides for

STRANGE MEETING

BEFORE YOU BEGIN TO READ . . .
— Read the interview with Hill. You will see there that she identifies a number of themes:

- Love
- Death
- First- and third-person narration
- Physical detail in fiction
- Scale
- War, and the effects of war

Other themes that may be useful to consider while reading the novel include:

- The creation of atmosphere
- Sense of place
- The presentation of the natural world
- The family

Reading activities: detailed analysis

Focus on: the title

The title alludes to a poem with the same title by Wilfred Owen, whom Hill has called 'the greatest of that rich generation of poets who flowered to such quick maturity in the Great War'. What is the *'Strange Meeting'* of the title? What is the poem saying about 'the pity of war, the pity of war distilled'?

PART ONE
SECTION I (pp. 7–32)

Focus on: characterisation

EXTRAPOLATE . . .

— In these opening pages it is essential that the reader comes to some understanding of the character of Hilliard. Read this section, close the book, and then jot down six words that seem to you to summarise the kind of person that Hilliard appears to be. Then ask yourself how you arrived at these six words. Are they derived from particulars in the text? Or have they come from somewhere else, and, if so, how have they been suggested by what *is* in the text? Are you sympathetic to this character? Why might it be important that you should be? Why do think that Hill chose to present him during a period of leave *away* from the battlefield that will be foregrounded in later parts of the text?

COMPARE . . .

— If you have read Hill's *I'm the King of the Castle* you might compare her characters of Hilliard and Crawford with those in her earlier novel, Hooper and Kingshaw. What does the relation between these two sets of characters tell you about each one? How important is it that Crawford and Hilliard knew each other as boys?

Focus on: openings

NOTE AND COMMENT . . .

— Read the first two sentences of the novel: 'He was afraid to go to sleep. For three weeks, he had been afraid of going to sleep' (p. 7). Note how these sentences work on you as the reader. In what ways might this suggest – if you did not know better – that the subject of this story might be a child? What makes you think that it can't be a child? At what exact point does a change occur, from telling you about something that might be 'ordinary' (not being able to go to sleep) to something that is extraordinary?

Focus on: the women

TRANSFORM . . .

— Look at the passage from pages 22 to 26 where John Hilliard goes to his sister's room and holds a conversation with her. Imagine that you are going to transform this scene either into a scene for a radio play or into a scene for a television drama.

— Write out the dialogue that would take place in either case. Then write out the sound effects you would use – if you are doing the radio play. Also write out directions for the actors as if you were producing their interpretation of your script.

— If you are working with the idea of a television drama, write out the camera angles you would use. Again, write stage directions for the actors explaining how and where you want them to move, and write production notes to help with their interpretation.

— In either case, how are you going to convey the tensions and the unsaid – but thought – elements that come across in the novel? There are also references to shared memories – how are you going to convey those to your audience?

TRANSFORM AGAIN . . .

— Now look at the passages concerning John's mother Constance Hilliard on pages 26–32. Rewrite the episode from the point of view of Constance. Remember to include details to do with her clothes, her anxiety about Fortnum's parcels and her social arrangements. Is she really – in your view – as unfeeling as she seems when the story is told from John Hilliard's point of view? Is there any way of making her more sympathetic?

RESEARCH AND CONSIDER . . .

— Find a copy of Siegfried Sassoon's poem 'The Glory of Women'. It was written during the years of the First World War and – in spite of the title – is not a very flattering portrait of the attitude of women to the men who went away to fight in the trenches. Consider how you might align the sentiments – arguments or complaints – that are in the poem to the pictures of Beth and Constance Hilliard in Hill's *Strange Meeting*.

PART ONE
SECTION 2 (pp. 32–46)

Focus on: settings

ASSESS . . .
— The novel moves through several settings here: the Army and Navy stores in London, the deck of the ship as Hilliard travels towards France, the stopping place on the railway where he is met by Coulter, and the farmhouse where Hilliard is to rejoin his battalion. Pick out two or three words from the descriptions of each of these four settings and assess their importance in creating your own image of the scene.

Focus on: clues

DISCRIMINATE . . .
— Read the passage on pages 40–1 where Hilliard encounters the signs of Barton's habitation of his quarters. Make a list of all the things that we are told that relate to Barton's character. If you have not already read on from this point, think about what picture you have built of the man from the clues offered here. Keep your list of clues and add to it whenever you encounter them again.

Focus on: Colonel Garrett

IMAGINE AND REWRITE . . .
— This is the first episode in which we encounter Colonel Garrett. There will be others. Jot down some notes on what kind of person you think Garrett is – based on your reading so far. Keep these notes so that you can assess their accuracy when you meet Garrett again.

PART ONE
SECTION 3 (pp. 46–74)

Focus on: David Barton

ANALYSE . . .

— Look over these passages and focus your reading on the picture of David Barton that you are offered here. How does he first appear, to Hilliard? to you? What are the distinctive props with which he is associated? What do you make of his physical appearance? How do you assess his devotion to his family? Why do you suppose that Hilliard is attracted to him?

NOTE . . .

— The way in which the relationship between Hilliard and Barton is set up is contrived very delicately and with a great deal unsaid in the text. Try to allow your interpretations of their relationship to be expressed in the same economical and restrained terms. Remember that Hill is writing about a time and a class and a social situation where emotions were held back, or where the expression of such emotions might have been considered to be 'bad form'. Try to let yourself be influenced by this delicacy as you read.

Focus on: plotting and key moments

ASK YOURSELF . . .

— Consider the last passage in this section (pp. 73–4) where Barton and Hilliard find the corpse of the German pilot. Given that Part One ends here, what might be the significance of this discovery? How important is it that it takes places in the orchard where Hilliard and Barton have spent such happy times? Remember that Hilliard and Barton have been sharing a room in the apple loft where the fruit would have been stored after harvest.

87

Looking over Part One

QUESTIONS FOR DISCUSSION OR ESSAYS

1. Consider the imagery of colour employed in the novel so far. How does it work? How are you affected by it?

2. Contrast the characters of David Barton and John Hilliard as you know them at this point in the novel.

3. What is the function of Colonel Garrett's role in Part One of *Strange Meeting*?

4. 'Women fail. Only men understand.' Discuss with reference to Part One of the novel.

5. 'And is there honey still for tea?' (Rupert Brooke, 'Grant-chester'). How far do the frames of either a) nostalgia or b) routine inform the emotional structures of Hill's *Strange Meeting*?

6. Trace the ways in which David Barton is being 'hardened' to the experience of war in this section.

PART TWO
SECTION I (pp. 75–95)

Focus on: narrative methods

DISCRIMINATE AND DISCUSS . . .

— In the course of this section, the narrative – still using the third person and mainly following Hilliard's point of view – is interspersed with two other sources of information. One is the commands and instructions for military personnel, and the other is the extracts from Barton's letters home. How are these three types of narrative juxtaposed? In what ways is this an ironic or critical contrast?

Focus on: *characterisation and point of view*

HOW DO YOU REACT? . . .

— We get a clearer picture of Barton as we read longer and longer extracts from his letters home. What kind of a person do you think he is? Is he sympathetic? Why does Hilliard decide that he 'needs' him?

Focus on: *Harris*

ASSESS . . .

— Look over the story about Harris and his fear, Barton's rescue of him and his death (pp. 83–92). In your opinion, did Barton do the right thing? Why does Barton take this death so hard?

ANALYSE . . .

— The incident with Harris is Barton's second induction into the horrors of war – the first being the sight of the German pilot. There are others to come and Barton's emotions are progressively damaged. Analyse the way in which, increasingly, Barton takes personal responsibility for the events. How far does that affect the measure of his reaction?

PART TWO
SECTION 2 (pp. 95–111)

Focus on: *Hilliard's experience*

LOOK FOR PATTERNS . . .

— 'He was happy' (p. 96). Why is Hilliard happy? Just as

89

Barton has increasingly bad experiences of the horrors of war, Hilliard will experience brief bursts of happiness in his relationship with Barton. Keep a note of these, and when you have reached the end of the novel, assess how these two patterns make a structure for the book.

Focus on: Garrett

TRANSFORM . . .

— Write out the story of the meeting between Garrett and Hilliard but from Garrett's point of view. Look back at the first time we met him (pp. 41–6) for some help in portraying his character. In your opinion, has Garrett really asked Hilliard to come and see him to take his mind off Barton's absence, or is it for another reason? Make clear which it is in your story.

PART TWO
SECTION 3 (pp. 111–30)

Focus on: Barton's experiences

ANALYSE . . .

— The narrative switches to Barton's point of view at pp. 111–16. Why is Barton so affected by what happens to him on this tour of duty? Write down six key words that sum up his misery.

Focus on: interspersed texts

EVALUATE . . .

— In his depression Barton writes out quotations from Thomas Browne (pp. 119–20) and then destroys the book (p. 123). Look over the quotations and evaluate how they might be used to provide a counterpoint to the events and concerns of the novel so far.

Focus on: characterisation

ASSESS . . .
— How has the balance shifted in the relationship between Hilliard and Barton? Why is it important that a mutuality now develops so that neither one is always taking the lead? When Barton says, 'I love you, John' (p. 131), why is this moment so moving? And why does this declaration occur here, at the end of Part Two?

IMAGINE . . .
— Hilliard replies to Barton, 'Yes.' It is in line with his character, as Hill has created it, that he responds so sparingly. Write two hundred words to describe his reaction to Barton's statement. If you have read to the end of the story, imagine that he is telling this to Barton's mother Miriam.

Looking over Part Two

QUESTIONS FOR DISCUSSION OR ESSAYS
1. Compare and contrast the French settings that we have encountered so far: the farmhouse, the billet at Feuvry and the trenches.

2. To what extent does Hilliard's and/or Barton's experience of childhood affect their attitudes as adults?

3. Hill says in the interview (pp. 24–8) that the physical facts of the experience of the trenches was a key to her method. How does the text convey these facts?

4. Discuss the language of *Strange Meeting*. Choose three paragraphs and analyse the kinds of vocabulary employed there.

5. Discuss EITHER the theme of 'self-discovery' OR the theme of 'belonging' as played out in *Strange Meeting*.

PART THREE
SECTION 1 (pp. 131–7)

Focus on: letters

COMPARE AND CONTRAST . . .
— The long extract from Barton's letter (pp. 131–7) retells many of the events that we have already heard about. Look back over the episodes and compare the ways in which the perspective on the events and Barton's experience of them has altered and matured. Try to find specific words or phrases to mark out the changes.

PART THREE
SECTION 2 (pp. 137–59)

Focus on: letters

COMPARE . . .
— Look at Beth's letter on pages 138–9. How does it compare with Barton's letters?

Focus on: Barton's failure

EVALUATE . . .
— Barton is sent with Coulter on a reconnaissance party (pp. 140–51). His own actions imperil the party and result in Coulter's death. We are told about this episode twice over: once from Barton's point of view but in the third person;

and once, again from Barton's point of view, but in the first person as he writes the story in one of his letters. This is the last of Barton's 'hardening' experiences of war. How has he changed?

Focus on: Garrett's decision

ASK YOURSELF . . .
— Do you agree with it?

Focus on: love

CONSIDER THE THEME . . .
— Hill says in the interview (p. 27) that this is a novel about love. Look at the exchange on pages 157–9. This, and the moment at the end of Part Two, is as close as Barton and Hilliard come to a declaration. How can you tell that this is about love?

PART THREE
SECTION 3 (pp. 159–70)

Focus on: the battle

ASSESS THE VOCABULARY . . .
— Look over the description of the battle and its aftermath. What kinds of words does Hill use to describe the events? How exactly can you visualise what is going on? Close the book and write down your six most vivid physical impressions. What difference does it make that Hilliard keeps losing consciousness? What is the effect of this on your attitude as reader?

RELATE . . .
— Hilliard has a delirious dream (pp. 165–6). Regard this dream as the summing-up of the themes of the novel and relate as

93

many elements as you can to things that you have already read about in Hilliard's story or character so far.

PART THREE
SECTION 4 (pp. 170–9)

Focus on: endings

CONSIDER . . .

— The novel comes to a rapid conclusion. How is the sense of loss conveyed? In what ways does this ending take us back to the beginning? What specific elements are returned to, revised and reassessed? Why might it be important that Hilliard recognises the landscape from Barton's descriptions (p. 178). In what sense has he really 'been here before'? How would you assess the implications in the very last sentence of the novel?

IMAGINE . . .

— Imagine that you are Barton's mother. Write an account of your first meeting with Hilliard.

Looking over Part Three

QUESTIONS FOR DISCUSSION OR ESSAYS

1. Discuss the themes of reintegration and reconciliation in Part Three.

2. Contrast the war scenes of Part Three with the scenes at home in England.

3. Compare the characters of Constance Hilliard and Miriam Barton.

Looking over the whole novel

QUESTIONS FOR DISCUSSION OR ESSAYS

1.   'We have to learn things, and also give things up, and those things include the cosiness of ignorance and the safety of uninvolvement and personal detachment.' How accurately does this general comment by Hill describe Hilliard's development in *Strange Meeting*?

2.   How hopeful do you find the end of the novel?

3.   '*Strange Meeting* is essentially not about war, but about love.' Discuss.

4.   Examine the variety of forms of love in *Strange Meeting*.

5.   Discuss the idea of 'family' as it is presented in the novel.

6.   Discuss the themes of innocence and guilt in *Strange Meeting*.

7.   What does *Strange Meeting* say about faith and despair?

8.   Consider the significance of letters in *Strange Meeting*.

9.   Examine the theme of memory in *Strange Meeting*.

10. What is the significance of Captain Franklin's role in *Strange Meeting*?

11. What does the character of EITHER Crawford OR Beth bring to *Strange Meeting*?

12. Consider how Hill presents the physical realities of war in *Strange Meeting*.

13. Examine the theme of courage in *Strange Meeting*.

14. Compare and contrast Hilliard's and Barton's characters in *Strange Meeting*.

15. How is the natural world presented in *Strange Meeting*?

16. 'Despite Hilliard's failings and weaknesses, he is presented as an admirable character by the end of the novel.' Discuss.

17. Discuss the ways in which characters in *Strange Meeting* make sense of their experiences by telling stories about them.

18. 'My subject is War, and the pity of War' (Wilfred Owen). Could this statement be accurately applied to *Strange Meeting*?

19. Hill says in the interview (p. 30) that she is sometimes tempted to write a sequel to *Strange Meeting* in which she describes Hilliard's later experiences. Write EITHER a plot summary for this sequel, OR the opening chapter.

20. Why, in your opinion, and based on your reading of this novel, does the First World War have such a power in the modern imagination?

Contexts, comparisons and complementary readings

STRANGE MEETING

Focus on: the ordinary soldiers' experience of World War I

READ AND COMPARE . . .

— For comparison with Hill's achievement in recreating the experience of warfare, and trench warfare in particular, you might read Sebastian Faulks's *Birdsong* (1993), which includes the experiences of tunnellers; Jennifer Johnstone's *How Many Miles to Babylon* (1974), which also explores a friendship put under strain by war; or Pat Barker's trilogy, *Regeneration* (1991), *The Eye in the Door* (1993) and *The Ghost Road* (1995), which mixes fictional characters with real figures such as Siegfried Sassoon, Wilfred Owen and the psychiatrist William Rivers.

— Erich Remarque's *All Quiet on the Western Front* (1929) was the only novel about the First World War that Hill allowed herself to read while she was researching *Strange Meeting*: it is an account of the experiences of ordinary German soldiers. For fictional portrayals of the First World War written by those who had experienced trench warfare, you might read A. P. Herbert's *The Secret Battle* (1919), a powerful account of a soldier's battle against himself and his fears; or R. C. Sheriff's play *Journey's End* (1928), which similarly deals with the devastating effects of trench warfare on young men's sanity and friendships. For autobiographical accounts of experiences in the First World War, read Robert Graves's *Goodbye to All That* (1929), Siegfried Sassoon's *Memoirs of an Infantry Officer* (1930) or Guy Chapman's *A Passionate Prodigality* (1933).

Focus on: historical context

RESEARCH . . .

— *The First World War* by John Keegan (1998) is a clear, detailed study of the political and cultural origins of the war and of the experience of warfare, which he relates to military strategy. For accounts of the ordinary soldiers' experiences, Malcolm Brown's *Tommy Goes to War* (1978) and *The First World War* (1991) are historical studies based on letters and diaries written at the time as well as on memoirs and interviews. Denis Winter's *Death's Men, Soldiers of the Great War* (1979) is an account of the experience of war based on letters and diaries as well as on historical data. It has particularly powerful descriptions of the experience of 'going over the top'. Another useful historical and factual account is Ian Ousby's *The Road to Verdun: France, Nationalism and the First World War* (2003).

Focus on: the theme of the Great War in modern memory

SEARCH . . .

— If possible, visit the World War I exhibition at the Imperial War Museum in London. Afterwards, write one side on the three aspects of the exhibition that surprised you the most. Describe what they were, and why they surprised you.

— If you are reading the novel around the time of early November, watch the commemorations of Remembrance Sunday. What is said about the Great War on this occasion? The main purpose of this day is to remember the dead of all wars in which British and Commonwealth soldiers have fought, but especially those who died in World War I. What attitude to war do you glean from these commemorations?

— Read the chapter 'Persistence and Memory' in Paul Fussell's *The Great War and Modern Memory* (1975).

AND SEARCH AGAIN . . .
— If you can, watch the video of the BBC's 1964 twenty-six-part series on the Great War. It is available from the BBC as a five-volume video box and includes documentary footage filmed in the trenches. How do these images of the reality of war compare with the fictional portrayal that is in Hill's *Strange Meeting*?

Focus on: the poetry of the First World War

READ, AND IMMERSE YOURSELF . . .
— Hill read a lot of First World War poetry as part of her research for *Strange Meeting*, in part because the poetry that came from the experience of World War I gives insights into the first-hand experience of trench warfare. The exercises that follow introduce the poetry of the First World War, so that the reader of *Strange Meeting* can compare Hill's treatment of experience of war with some of that poetry. For the purposes of these exercises, it would be very helpful to have access to the anthologies *Up the Line to Death*, ed. Brian Gardner (1976) and *The Penguin Book of First World War Poetry*, ed. Jon Silkin (1979).

READ AND COMPARE . . .

— Read Rupert Brooke's 'War Sonnets'. In the sonnet 'Peace', why does the speaker welcome war? Brooke's sonnet sequence was widely read and admired during the war, but his critics say that these poems, written in 1914, are sentimental. One such critic was Charles Hamilton Sorley, who said that Brooke had 'clothed his attitude in fine words, but he has taken the senti-mental attitude'. Compare Brooke's 'The Dead' with Sorley's 'When you see millions of the mouthless dead'. In particular, compare the tone, the imagery and the handling of the sonnet form. Both men died in 1915.

— Although patriotic verse was written and published in British newspapers throughout the war, there was a noticeable shift in attitudes towards the war in much of the poetry written from 1916 onwards. The ignorance of people at home and the incompetence of the senior ranks were particular sources of bitterness (see Sassoon's 'Does it Matter?', 'Base Details' and 'The General' for well-known examples).

— Most poets were public school boys, trained like Brooke or Sorley to write in traditional verse forms. They struggled to find new forms of expression that were adequate to convey the full intensity of their experiences in the trenches. Read Sassoon's 'Counter-Attack', which includes graphic images of corpses. Are these images made to serve the poem's effects, or are they too direct, too photographic, to be contained? The retainer that literature seems to have put on these public school poets was challenged, almost from the start, by Isaac Rosenberg, a working-class Londoner. Read his poem 'Break of Day in the Trenches' and assess how he achieves more subtle effects than Sassoon using tone and imagery.

— Wilfred Owen's poetry – from which Hill took her title, and the only poetry that she took with her when she settled at Aldeburgh in the winter of 1970 to write *Strange Meeting* – is remarkable partly for its technical mastery, but still more so for Owen's extraordinary gift for compassion. Read 'Exposure', 'Anthem for Doomed Youth', 'Futility', and 'Strange Meeting' for examples.

— The poetry of the First World War was probably at least as influential as contemporary photographs in forming our ideas about the ordinary soldiers' experiences of the war. Are there images in these war poems that find echoes in *Strange Meeting*?

Focus on: drafts and manuscripts

READ AND COMPARE . . .

— In order to write *Strange Meeting*, Hill undertook some detailed historical research. As well as reading military histories and biographies, she looked at texts that gave an ordinary soldier's view of war: autobiographies, such as Robert Graves's *Goodbye to All That* and Siegfried Sassoon's *Memoirs of an Infantry Officer*. She also read contemporary diaries, letters and poetry.

— Hill's reading notes illustrate how she set about using the information to recreate the past. For instance, she read the letters of Edward Thomas and of Wilfred Owen, and selected details under headings such as 'in camp', 'the march', 'in the line', 'guns', 'clothing', 'dugouts', 'no man's land', 'working parties' and 'snipers'.

— Under the heading 'ugliness', she noted from Wilfred Owen's letters the following ideas: 'Hideous landscapes, vile noises, foul language, everything unnatural, broken . . . the distortion of the dead, whose unburiable bodies sit outside in the dug-outs all day, all night.' And from his account of the march to the Somme in July 1916, this: 'Swimming & sunbathing in a stream. Flints underfoot. Overhead, observation balloons. A [German] plane, coming down in a field. The pilot dead.' Hill added in parentheses 'Barton took the handkerchief', revealing that even as she was taking notes, her imagination was already turning Owen's account into fictional episodes for the novel. Many of the details in the novel that lend a sense of historical authenticity were gleaned in this way: from the layout of a trench, to the experience of muddle, error and fear; from the kinds of music officers played on their gramophones at headquarters ('The Charlie Chaplin Waltz', Schubert, Mozart or Bach) and the kinds of birds that soldiers saw (reed buntings, wagtails, jays), to the smell of mustard gas (like garlic). 'To reconstruct the battlefields of the war, and life in the camps, and the hospitals, and conversations about it all, back in England, was really very straightforward,' Hill records. The greater difficulty lay in 'the knowledge that I would have to sink myself completely and utterly in imagination, in emotions, into the experience of that awful war'.

— As with all of Hill's novels, *Strange Meeting* began in the form of fragmented images and ideas, clustering around characters and episodes. For instance, 'H.' (the main character's name was Hemmings and Hillary before Hill settled on Hilliard) brings books with him to the front: 'Keats's letters. Favourite S'speare. Trollope. Thought he would want adventure stories but there's enough here.' Further notes say: 'The men play football – he envies them their easy comradeship.' 'Washing in green water of a shell hole. Drinking from water in a chlorinated tank.' 'In the ordinary course of trench life day & night seem distorted. They smell.' 'Black beetles in the trenches. Lice and rats; all taking on a monstrous aspect.' Even single images are recorded at this stage: 'a lizard runs across a wall in the sun'. The first detail that seems to have come to her about Barton was that 'Barton has a v. fine nose – narrow bridge – no spare flesh'.

— Next, Hill began to group ideas under headings. Under 'Barton' she wrote this:

Is the youngest of 5 or 6 children.

Tells of a holiday he spent alone in a French cottage – eating cheese & milk & fruit – reading. Mirages the heat cast – only saw the man from a farm nearby, the postman & the man on the bicycle selling bread.

Walked. That was 1913. He was 18 or 17. Happy. Long letters from his sisters and brothers. He has a family sense – terrific feeling. Jokes – all the parcels, etc.

A loose, easy family. Father a doctor? Hillary envies him – they talk about the visit H. will pay them after the war.

H. 'I don't think I'd want you to visit my house.'

— Look at the mixture of factual information with memories and snippets of conversation. What does this mixture tell you about how Hill creates her characters? Her own explanation for how she created Barton and Hilliard's story is that 'all the details of their personalities and backgrounds . . . and the day-to-day details of what happened to them, all those came to me as I went along, each day, rising up into my mind ready-formed'.
— Under 'Emotions' Hill noted the following:

1. Barton's horror that he begins not to feel anything except for himself – the dead bodies too numerous. He cares more for a dead horse which he sweats alone to bury.
2. His feelings of terror. How ashamed he is of telling H.
3. The change to loathing & bitterness – need to destroy himself.

4.   The sense of telepathy between them. The *shock* of their mutual attraction.

5.   Loathing the Captain.

6.   No patriotism, no hatred of the enemy, but s[ome]times a sudden exhilaration, making a charge for its own sake.

7.   Hemmings's desperate concern to save Barton from himself.

8.   B. tells him of how he did gym & athletics & stretching exercises to make himself grow, he was so afraid of being small.

9.   They have a terrible, violent argument after Barton has tried to get himself shot – they come to blows, or one strikes a blow.

— Narrative episodes began to form, such as 'Leaving rest camp' and 'The meeting with Barton'. Under the heading 'What he dreams of', Hill writes:

1.   Seeing a straggle of men returning from a battle – their faces – and the contrast between them & the young, fresh men going out.

2.   Walking through an area now deserted & finding decaying horses. Somehow worse.

3.   Guns in his ears until his head will burst.

4.   A German with a bayonet. Soft voices behind a curtain in the dugout.

5.   In the hospital – the man dying left to him. Wouldn't talk to him because he was so afraid & now he feels endlessly guilty.

6.   Burying a horse on his own.

— The next stage is a rough narrative plan. For the opening:

1. Hilliard is on his last night of leave at home,
goes to walk by the sea. After he has woken up
from an appalling nightmare – the sounds, smells,
sights of the trenches. Quiet, still sea. Moon. It is
late summer. Warm. He is 22. Thinks of his family's
lack of understanding – his sister & he have been
close & now he finds he can't talk to her. He goes
back up to her room, planning to talk. She has
woken as he went out. But when it comes to it,
there is nothing he can say. He looks at her & sees
how their relationship has changed. Tries to
remember things of their childhood with her. She is
thinking of other things – her world & his will
never be the same.

2. After the scene + Beth. Up till he leaves the station his mother has appeared formal, distant, a little
disapproving. When he goes she suddenly becomes
human – loves him – wants to come to London
with him & is desperate when he goes – he realises
in a flash that it is simply a 'code' with her not to
seem to love him – he & Beth have always been
wrong. Then? As Beth suddenly moves away from
him, so he moves closer to his mother – for the
length of time they are on the platform at the village station. He watches her go & feels suddenly
moved. Remembers that as a young girl she was a
great beauty; wonders whether she has had a happy
life with his father after all – realises that he has
never really thought or been curious about her
before.

Compare these draft notes with pp. 7–32 of *Strange Meeting*.
How has Hill woven these ideas into her final narrative? Are
there any that she has changed her mind about?

VINTAGE
LIVING
TEXTS

The Woman in Black

IN CLOSE-UP

Reading guides for

THE WOMAN IN BLACK

BEFORE YOU BEGIN TO READ . . .
— Read the interview with Hill. You will see there that she identifies a number of themes:

- Menace
- Misfits
- The idea of evil
- First- and third-person narration

Other themes that may be useful to consider while reading the novel include:

- The creation of atmosphere
- Sense of place
- The presentation of the natural world
- Possession and manipulation

Reading activities: detailed analysis

Focus on: the title

The title alludes to a Victorian novel by Wilkie Collins called *The Woman in White* (1860), the first and most influential of the Victorian 'sensation' novels. It pursues questions of identity and insanity in English country houses. Compare it with *The Woman in Black* for its creation of atmosphere.

ONE: CHRISTMAS EVE
(pp. 9–24)

Focus on: openings

NOTE AND COMMENT . . .
— Look at the Contexts section (pp. 133–41) for a consideration of the genre of the ghost story, and for Hill's first notes on this opening section of *The Woman in Black*. Why might an author begin a ghost story with a scene that is so normal, so familiar, so safe? Read the first chapter, making notes as you read in answer to the following questions:

● What atmosphere is evoked at Monk's Piece on Christmas

Eve on pp. 14–17, and how is it created?

- What impressions do you form of the narrator, from what he says about himself, from his description of his family life and from the tone of his 'voice'?

- What details on pp. 9–20 hint that the safe and peaceful surface of the narrator's life hides memories and experiences that are far from safe or peaceful?

- How does the narrative hold in tension images of innocence with images of experience?

Focus on: memory

EXAMINE THE METAPHORS . . .

— What do we mean when we say that a memory 'haunts' us? And in what senses can we say that memories 'live on'? In what way can writing down a story of some terrible events help to 'exorcise' the memory of them?

RESEARCH THE ALLUSION . . .

— The narrator quotes 'some lines of poetry, lines I had once known but long forgotten' (p. 23) – another reference to how memories can lie dormant and revive. The quotation comes from *Hamlet*, act 1, scene 1, ll. 163–9. Read the whole of this scene, which is set in the bitter cold of night in Elsinore. Note the tension between the normal and the extraordinary. Horatio, a balanced and rational man, has to see the ghost to believe it, but see it he does: 'Before my God, I might not this believe / Without the sensible and true avouch / Of mine own eyes' (ll. 59–61). We later learn that the ghost cannot rest because he was murdered, and he is tormented by a desire for revenge on his murderer. As you read on, you will see how this allusion to *Hamlet* links to the themes of *The Woman in Black*.

Focus on: the power of storytelling

COMPARE . . .

— The idea of storytelling having an almost magical power is ancient. Sometimes storytelling is seen as a kind of conjuring, 'as imagination bodies forth / The forms of things unknown . . . / Turns them into shapes, and gives to airy nothing / A local habitation and a name' (*A Midsummer Night's Dream*); at others it is seen as the repository of arcane wisdom or knowledge. The figure who is haunted by some terrible knowledge, who has to tell his story in order to relieve the agony of knowing too much, is an archetype in literature. Compare the narrator's need to tell his story of terrible knowledge in this opening chapter with Coleridge's 'The Rime of the Ancient Mariner' (1798), in which the mariner intrudes into the normality of a wedding in order to tell a story about a strange world, both beautiful and terrifying, which lies just beyond our own. The final ten stanzas express his agonising situation.

Looking over Chapter One

QUESTIONS FOR DISCUSSION OR ESSAYS

1. 'I had never been an imaginative or fanciful man and certainly not one given to visions' (p. 13). Why might Hill choose such a straightforward character as the narrator of a ghost story?

2. In keeping with many ghost stories, Hill uses several techniques in Chapter One to create the illusion that what we are about to hear is true. Identify those techniques and comment on how effective you find them.

3. Examine the tension between the familiar and the strange in Chapter One.

TWO: A LONDON PARTICULAR
(pp. 25–33)

Focus on: literary influence

COMPARE . . .

— Before writing *The Woman in Black*, Hill read extensively and used works that she admired as models. Dickens is her greatest literary hero, so it is not surprising to find that passages in the novella recall passages from his work. Compare, for instance, the opening four paragraphs on pp. 25–6 with the opening two paragraphs of Chapter One, 'In Chancery', of Dickens's *Bleak House* (1852–3). What similarities can you find in imagery and sentence structures? How does Hill's playful imagery of fog also recall the third and fourth stanzas of T. S. Eliot's poem 'The Love Song of J. Alfred Prufrock' (1917)?

Focus on: connotations

IDENTIFY AND DISCUSS . . .

— The narrator's description of London in the fog on pp. 26–7 suggests connotations of hell. Reread the paragraphs from 'But what is perhaps remarkable' to 'they became red-eyed and demonic.' Identify the images that suggest witchcraft, hell or the underworld, and discuss why Hill has used them. Consider in particular the significance of distorted perceptions and of the unfamiliar in the normal.

Looking over Chapter Two

QUESTIONS FOR DISCUSSION OR ESSAYS

1. Hill has included a number of hints in this and the previous chapter about when the story is set: the pony and trap (pp. 10–11), London peasoupers (p. 25), 'railway stations and journeys on steam locomotives' (p. 26). Later, he rides in a car (p. 40). How

do these details contribute to the atmosphere of the story? Roughly when is the story set, do you think? See Hill's comments on this in the interview (pp. 32–4). Why might Hill have chosen to set a ghost story at that time, rather than in the present?

2. Discuss Hill's use of metaphors and symbols in Chapter Two.

3. Which details on pp. 28–33 suggest that Mr Bentley is hiding something about Mrs Drablow?

THREE: THE JOURNEY NORTH
(pp. 34–9)

Focus on: archetypes

CONSIDER AND RESEARCH . . .

— Arthur Kipps (we now know his full name) meets a stranger on the train. Because this is fiction, we can guess that the meeting is to be a significant one, although we must wait to find out why. The word 'stranger' derives from a French word meaning 'foreigner'. Who is the real stranger in the parts of England that they are now in (by implication, somewhere on the east coast)? In what ways is it emphasised that Kipps is in unfamiliar territory, in every sense? Note that we are repeatedly reminded of his youthfulness. He recalls an archetype in literature: the young innocent who travels away from home, unaware of the dangers that he will be exposed to. Interpreted on this level, Sam Daily recalls the archetype of the guide or the guardian spirit in strange territory, and the journey represents an excursion into the unknown that will put Kipps to an extreme test. Does this way of interpreting the text seem helpful to you, or pretentious? Recall that Hill set about writing *The*

Woman in Black by emulating models of ghost stories. 'Archetypal criticism' maintains that readers recognise archetypes in literature whether or not they are consciously aware of their existence, and that characters, images or narrative designs that fit these archetypes evoke a profound response from the reader. To learn more about literary archetypes, refer to Northrop Frye's *The Anatomy of Criticism* (1957), or to Frye's 'The Archetypes of Literature' in *Fables of Identity* (1963).

Focus on: names

LIST AND INFER . . .
— 'I've come to the land of curious place-names, certainly' (p. 38). Hill gives each character and place a name that is suggestive of its nature. List all the names in the novel so far, and give a brief description of the characteristics that the name suggests.

Focus on: mystery

LOOK FOR CLUES . . .
— As with Mr Bentley, so with Samuel Daily: what he says about Mrs Drablow hints that he knows more than he is saying. Identify the statements that convey this impression, and make an intelligent guess about what he might be hiding.

Looking over Chapter Three

QUESTIONS FOR DISCUSSION OR ESSAYS
1. Comment on Hill's employment of delayed revelation and the power of suggestion in the first three chapters of *The Woman in Black*.

2. In what ways is Arthur Kipps presented as reassuringly normal in this chapter?

FOUR: THE FUNERAL OF MRS DRABLOW
(pp. 40–57)

Focus on: the known and the unknown

NOTICE AND INTERPRET . . .

— Everything about Arthur Kipps's first night at Crythin Gifford (pp. 40–1) feels reassuring and comfortable, until he has a conversation with the landlord that unsettles him. Kipps has an uncomfortable sense that something 'had been left *un*said' (p. 43). How does he explain this sense away, and what does his reaction reveal about him? How does the narrative on pages 42–4 contribute to our sense that he is an innocent stepping into an unknown that he is unprepared for?

Focus on: mood

EXAMINE . . .

— Examine how the mood of the narrative changes between Kipps leaving the hotel (p. 46) and attending the funeral (pp. 48–50). How is a sense of encroaching sadness and isolation created?

Focus on: the woman in black

ANALYSE AND COMPARE . . .

— Read carefully the description of the woman in black on pages 48–50. Identify all the words that suggest sickness or death. How do you react to her? How does Kipps react? Notice the developing irony that the reader is beginning to understand more than Kipps does, an impression that is strengthened by Mr Jerome's reaction when Kipps asks about her on pages 51–3, and by the farmer's reaction over lunch on pages 56–7.

Focus on: children

INTERPRET THE JUXTAPOSITION . . .
— What effects are created by the juxtaposition of the description of the woman in black and the image of the children on page 51? You might think back to the narrator's unwillingness to tell his story in front of the grown-up children in the first chapter, and the contrast of innocence and evil that was created then.

Looking over Chapter Four

QUESTIONS FOR DISCUSSION OR ESSAYS
1. 'Kipps is likeable but complacent.' Discuss, with particular reference to Chapter Four.

2. Analyse the narrative strategies that Hill has used so far to create a sense of a strange and threatening reality that cannot be spoken of and that lies just beyond the threshold of normality.

FIVE: ACROSS THE CAUSEWAY
(pp. 58–71)

Focus on: landscape

ANALYSE WITH CLOSE READING . . .
— How does the description of the changing landscape on pages 58–60 suggest the sensation of crossing boundaries from one world to another, from one reality to another?

COMPARE MEDIA . . .
— The description of the landscape is 'picturesque' – similar to a picture. But is it? Look at some landscape pictures, and

contrast the different ways in which words and paint represent landscape. In what ways does language require a greater imaginative collaboration from the reader than representational painting?

Focus on: the 'senses'

ANALYSE THE CONNOTATIONS . . .
— Look at the description of the journey on pages 59–62 (from 'Today, all was bright and clear' . . . to 'deep in my imagination, too.'), and note the emphasis on Kipps's five physical senses. He wants to 'wander about freely and slowly, take it all in through every one of my senses' (p. 61). Does this, by implication, also include his 'sixth sense'? What do we mean by this phrase? Is it linked to a 'sense of place'? Look for hints – here and elsewhere – that Kipps has a sixth sense, but that he distrusts it.

Focus on: atmosphere

ANALYSE THE NARRATIVE STRATEGY . . .
— How does Hill build tension in the paragraphs on pages 62–5 (from 'But I did not go inside . . .'), leading up to the second appearance of the woman in black? Consider the way in which she uses images to create atmosphere. How does the narrative play on our ironic sense that Kipps is an innocent who is in more danger than he realises?

Focus on: representations of evil

ANALYSE THE DESCRIPTIVE TECHNIQUE . . .
— When a writer represents 'evil', she or he has to get around the difficulty that the experience of evil is by its nature mysterious. Kipps's comment that 'the words seem hopelessly inadequate to express what I saw' (p. 65) acknowledges the problem

of expressing a sensation that seems to lie beyond words. However, evil can be suggested, using a combination of images, symbols, situation, atmosphere and – principally – a focus on the effects on a character who experiences it. Analyse how Hill suggests the evil nature of the woman in black on pages 65–6 (from 'In the greyness of the fading light' to 'out of sight'). How significant is it that Kipps's normality, health and alertness have been stressed during the preceding pages? Consider other representations of evil in literature and on film. See the Contexts section for examples (pp. 133–5). What techniques are usually employed in each medium to evoke a sense of evil? How are they similar, and how do they differ?

Focus on: the danger of knowledge

CONSIDER THE IMPLICATIONS . . .

— 'I was consumed with the desire to find out exactly who it was that I had seen, and how, I could not rest until I had settled the business' (p. 67). This statement implies that what Kipps wants is not possible, and that to attempt it will take him out of his depth. How is this implied?

Focus on: the extraordinary and the everyday

COMPARE AND CONSIDER . . .

— Kipps expected the house to be 'like the house of poor Miss Havisham' (p. 69), the reclusive and embittered old woman in Dickens's *Great Expectations* (1861) who, after being abandoned at the altar on her wedding day, had shut herself up in her large house and kept everything as it had been on that day, including her wedding feast. Read the relevant passages from Chapters Eight and Eleven of *Great Expectations* (pp. 56–60 and 83–5, Penguin Classics) and compare them with the description of Eel Marsh House. Dickens describes the house in minute detail, but conveys an overall impression of the bizarre and extraordinary; Eel Marsh House, by contrast, suggests the ordinary and everyday. Consider why a setting that seems normal is more effective in a ghost story than a setting that is bizarre.

Looking over Chapter Five

QUESTIONS FOR DISCUSSION OR ESSAYS

1. 'How one old woman had endured day after day, night after night, of isolation in this house, let alone for so many years, I could not conceive' (p. 70). Imagine that you are Mrs Drablow. Write a diary entry from a few months before Kipps's visit in which you describe what it is like to live alone in Eel Marsh House.

2. Discuss how Hill creates atmosphere and a sense of place in Chapter Five.

3. Do you believe in ghosts? Have you ever had an experience of the supernatural? Write either a discursive essay in which you argue for or against the existence of ghosts, or a descriptive essay in which you describe an experience of the supernatural.

4. Consider how Hill interweaves naturalistic and fantastic elements in this chapter.

SIX: THE SOUND OF A PONY AND TRAP
(pp. 72–83)

Focus on: distorted perceptions

ANALYSE THE EFFECTS . . .
— How does the narrative create a sense of distorted perceptions on pages 73–5?

Focus on: nostalgia for normality

DISCUSS . . .
— Shaken by his experiences, Kipps becomes angry at his foolishness in ignoring 'all the hints and veiled warnings' he had received about Eel Marsh House, 'and to long – no, to pray – for some kind of speedy deliverance and to be back in the safety and comforting busyness and clamour of London, among friends – indeed among any people at all – and with Stella' (pp. 76–7). However, as the opening chapter suggested, even if Kipps can get back to London, he will never regain the normality he craves: he now knows too much. What knowledge must he now carry with him for ever that will rob him of his peace of mind? Discuss the validity of the claim that *The Woman in Black* can be interpreted as a story of lost innocence, of 'paradise lost'.

Looking over Chapter Six

QUESTIONS FOR DISCUSSION OR ESSAYS
1. Give an account of the ways in which Kipps has changed during the course of Chapter Six.

2. Kipps notices in Keckwick and in the landlord 'the same extreme reserve, a barrier put up against all inquiry which I had the sense not to try and break down' (p. 83). Give an interpretation of why these two men are so uncommunicative with Kipps about Eel Marsh House. You could express your answer either as a commentary or, if you prefer, as if you were one of these two characters, talking to yourself.

3. Write a short story on the theme of secrecy.

SEVEN: MR JEROME IS AFRAID
(pp. 84–93)

Focus on: facing the unknown

EXAMINE THE IRONY . . .
— 'I must face it out, Mr Jerome. Such things one must face'
(p. 90). The night before Kipps was desperate to leave Eel
Marsh House, so why does he now say this to Mr Jerome?
What has happened to his perspective? And what effect do
these words have on you, the reader? How is Hill playing on
the irony that the reader can see the foolishness behind Kipps's
bravado?

EXAMINE THE LANGUAGE . . .
— There are several references in this chapter to souls, to
prayer, to death, to spirit, to spells and to being in thrall. Find
these. How does this language suggest that Kipps is up against
a dimension of experience for which 'the evidence of [his]
own senses and nothing more' (p. 91) will be inadequate?

Looking over Chapter Seven

QUESTIONS FOR DISCUSSION OR ESSAYS
1. What does Mr Jerome contribute to the story in Chapter
Seven?

2. Discuss what Kipps means by 'I was living in another
dimension' (p. 92).

EIGHT: SPIDER
(pp. 94–101)

Focus on: intuition and will

DISCRIMINATE AND REFLECT . . .
— Kipps suppresses his intuitions by an effort of will several times in this chapter. What is his intuition telling him? Why is he so keen to ignore it? How does he view his own return to Eel Marsh House? How do you react to his claim that 'If I go there and see her again, I am prepared' (p. 99)?

Focus on: worldliness and otherworldliness

ASSESS . . .
— Samuel Daily is very much a man of the world, who represents a view of life that is firmly rooted in 'normality' (as his name suggests). Which aspects of his characterisation in Chapter Eight emphasise this? What seems to be his attitude towards Eel Marsh House? How does this affect our view of Kipps's experiences and of whether he should return there?

Looking over Chapter Eight

QUESTIONS FOR DISCUSSION OR ESSAYS
1. 'Fools rush in where angels fear to tread.' Is Kipps a fool to go back, as Daily says, in your opinion? Or is it better that he faces out his fears? Explain your answer.

2. Write an account of Kipps and Daily's conversation in Chapter Eight from the latter's point of view.

NINE: IN THE NURSERY
(pp. 102–22)

Focus on: normality

IDENTIFY . . .

— In what ways does Kipps strive to emphasise a sense of normality in his account at the start of this chapter (pp. 102–6)?

Focus on: light and shadow

COMPARE . . .

— Compare the description of the day on pages 103–5 (from 'The sun was high in the sky' to 'as the sun declined') with Kipps's first experience of the site of the graveyard on pages 63–6 (from 'Then, thinking thus fancifully' to 'wretched patch of ground'), paying particular attention to images of light and shadow.

Focus on: mounting tension

ANALYSE . . .

— Having established a sense of normality up to page 106, from pages 107–11 the narrative introduces a number of incidents and details that create increasing tension. Identify them and analyse why they have this effect. Refer to Hill's comments on this in the interview (p. 34). How important is context for their effect?

Focus on: Stella

IMAGINE AND CREATE . . .

— Stella remains on the edge of the story, a part of the normal world that Kipps has temporarily left behind. Using your understanding of Kipps's character, and imagining what Stella likes about him, write the letter from her that Kipps reads and carries in his pocket on page 112.

Focus on: inverted innocence

EXAMINE THE JUXTAPOSITIONS . . .
— From page 113 onwards, the narrative places images of love, innocence and childhood security against images of hatred, misery and danger. Discuss the effects created by this juxtaposition. And what effects are created by the confusion of Kipps's memories of his own nursery with the nursery in Eel Marsh House?

Focus on: the secret story

LOOK FOR CLUES . . .
— This chapter begins to reveal – in glimpses – the story of Jennet and her child. Which clues on pages 116 and 120–1 link her story with the house? Can you guess how these details will throw light on the woman in black?

Looking over Chapter Nine

QUESTIONS FOR DISCUSSION OR ESSAYS
1. What part does Spider play in Chapter Nine?

2. Describe how you felt as you were reading Chapter Nine. Did you enjoy reading this account? If so, account for the pleasure that can be derived from vicarious fear.

3. Using any elements you choose from Chapter Nine, write your own narrative to provoke fear in your reader.

TEN: WHISTLE AND I'LL COME TO YOU
(pp. 123–32)

Focus on: the title

READ AND COMPARE . . .

— The title of Chapter Ten recalls M. R. James's ghost story 'Oh, Whistle, and I'll Come to You, My Lad' (1904), which Hill reread as part of her preparation for writing *The Woman in Black*. Read M. R. James's story and consider whether (and how) it might have influenced Hill's novella.

Focus on: weather

COMPARE GENRES . . .

— Read Ted Hughes's poem 'Wind' (1957) and compare his use of imagery with Hill's in the first two paragraphs of Chapter Ten. Does imagery work in similar ways in poetry and in prose?

Focus on: outward and inward experience

EXAMINE . . .

— Earlier, Kipps was determined to trust only what his physical senses told him. Note how in Chapter Ten his usual senses are disoriented: the events take place in darkness, and the sounds he hears are confused with the wind. Only on one level does he sense things with unmistakable clarity and force: the emotional. Examine how the narrative emphasises inner experience of 'feelings' over the 'outward, visible and audible' experience from pages 124–8.

Focus on: clues

INFER . . .

— 'But the feelings that must accompany the death of someone as close to my heart and bound up with my own being as it was possible to be, I knew then' (p. 128); 'But she was alive and so was I and . . . cradling Spider like a child in my arms, I began to stumble back across the marshes towards the house' (p. 131). What clues do these sentences give for the reasons why the woman in black haunts Eel Marsh House and how she wants to exact her revenge?

Looking over Chapter Ten

QUESTIONS FOR DISCUSSION OR ESSAYS

1. Consider the relationships between the outward landscape and the inner landscape of the emotions in Chapter Ten.

2. Discuss the use of images of light and dark in Chapters Nine and Ten.

ELEVEN: A PACKET OF LETTERS
(pp. 133–53)

Focus on: hubris

COMPARE . . .

— Kipps stubbornly persists in believing that 'If I could uncover the truth, perhaps I might in some way put an end to it all forever (p. 135).' In Greek tragedy, the hero who suffers from the failing of 'hubris' stubbornly persists on a dangerous path despite the warnings of the gods. 'Hubris' amounts to insolence, or pride – the hero's excessive belief in his own abilities, which leads him to transgress divine laws. It leads finally to his nemesis, the punishment that the angry gods dole out in retribution. In the case of Oedipus, his mistake was to persist in uncovering an awful truth. Is Kipps guilty of hubris, do you think?

Focus on: faith

DISCUSS . . .

— 'Now, I realized that there were forces for good and those for evil doing battle together and that a man might range himself on one side or the other' (p. 151). This statement reflects the traditional message of the Christian church that Kipps was 'brought up within'. To what extent do his experiences at Eel Marsh House actually support this Christian message? Does the novella as a whole support the idea of Jennet as evil, or as a victim of circumstance and her own insanity, and therefore deserving of sympathy – or both? Is there any common ground between religious faith and belief in the supernatural, in your opinion?

— Do you believe that the world is a battleground for forces of good and evil?

Looking over Chapter Eleven

QUESTIONS FOR DISCUSSION OR ESSAYS

1. Consider the ways in which letters are used in the novel to give an illusion of truth, of a concrete reality that is not mediated by the narrator.

2. How important is it to the effectiveness of Chapter Eleven that it is told by Kipps from his subjective point of view, and not by an omniscient narrator?

TWELVE: THE WOMAN IN BLACK
(pp. 154–60)

Focus on: anticipation or shock?

ASSESS . . .
— 'I could not have been less prepared for what was to come' (p. 157). Is the reader also unprepared for this final scene? To what extent does it depend for its effectiveness on our anticipation of tragedy, or on the shock of our being unprepared for it?

Focus on: forgiveness

REFLECT . . .
— Kipps concludes of the woman in black that 'Her bitterness was understandable, the wickedness that led her to take away other women's children because she had lost her own, understandable too but not forgivable' (p. 155). This seems at odds with his profession in the previous chapter of Christianity, which maintains that all sins may be forgiven. Do you believe that she is 'not forgivable'?

Looking over Chapter Twelve

QUESTION FOR DISCUSSION OR ESSAYS
1. The story ends where it began, with the narrator an old man living at Monk's Piece with his stepfamily. How does the final scene force a re-evaluation of the opening chapter?

Looking over the whole novel

QUESTIONS FOR DISCUSSION OR ESSAYS
1. Hill has written: 'I've become expert at disguising my lack of ability to plot, preferring to concentrate on atmosphere, character and above all a sense of place.' To what extent do

you find this self-assessment to be an accurate comment on the strengths and weaknesses of *The Woman in Black*?

2.   Give a description of the character of Arthur Kipps, and discuss whether he makes a suitable narrator for his own ghost story.

3.   Hill has made the point that *The Woman in Black* has a serious underlying purpose: 'This is a story about evil: about how suffering and grief may warp a human personality.' How appropriate is the ghost-story genre for tackling such a serious theme?

4.   What techniques does Hill use to give a pretend concrete reality to events – an illusion that these events are true – in *The Woman in Black*?

5.   Discuss the ways in which the sea and the weather are used to create atmosphere in *The Woman in Black*.

6.   Examine the significance of food and drink in *The Woman in Black*.

7.   Through a detailed analysis of three or four passages, discuss images of light and darkness in *The Woman in Black*.

8.   Consider the importance of 'period' in *The Woman in Black*.

9.   Examine the means by which Hill encourages readers to feel some sympathy for the ghost even while they are repulsed by her.

10.   Hill's preparatory notes for *The Woman in Black* include the statement that 'a tension between the known and the unknown,

security & exposure, the familiar and the strange, scepticism and credulity, must always be maintained'. Discuss the means by which the novella maintains these tensions.

11. Discuss the contribution made to the story by two of the following: Samuel Daily, Keckwick, Mr Jerome, Spider.

12. Write an additional episode that could be inserted into *The Woman in Black* and would fit stylistically.

Contexts, comparisons and complementary readings

THE WOMAN IN BLACK

Focus on: the genre of the ghost story

RESEARCH AND COMPARE . . .

— *The Woman in Black* is written in the style of a classic ghost story. Hill records how she had always admired ghost stories, and especially 'the greatest one of all', Henry James's *The Turn of the Screw*. 'As I settled down to reread it, I thought how much I had always admired it and how brilliantly James creates the atmosphere of the house called Bly in which it is set: out of the blue I thought "I wonder if I could write a ghost novel myself?"' Hill researched the genre by reading as many ghost stories as she could and making a list of all the elements that a ghost story should contain. Her reading convinced her that, in ghost stories, plot – which she believes to be a weakness in her writing – was less important than atmosphere and sense of place – two of her greatest strengths as a writer. She noted down the following elements:

- A reason for the ghosts to be haunting the place.

- A narrator who didn't believe in ghosts. Not a sceptic, exactly – but certainly not credulous.
- Mixture of the familiar, ordinary & everyday – but distorted or made to seem strange a little, by fear or weather or fever or odd circ[umstance]s – and the unusual – the *toy*-room, for e.g.
- A tension between the known and the unknown, security & exposure, the familiar and the strange, scepticism and credulity, must always be maintained.

— Research the ghost-story genre yourself by reading Henry James's *The Turn of the Screw* (1878), M. R. James's 'Oh, Whistle, and I'll Come to You, My Lad (1904), 'They' (*Traffics and Discoveries*, 1904) by Rudyard Kipling, 'The Triumph of Night' (*Xingu and Other Stories*, 1916) by Edith Wharton, or 'The Old Nurse's Story' (1906) by Elizabeth Gaskell. Otherwise, you might like to look for more modern ghost stories, such as *A Touch of Chill* (1980) by Joan Aiken, *The Wedding Ghost* (1985) by Leon Garfield or *Uninvited Ghosts* (1991) by Penelope Lively. Note the distinction between a horror story – in which there is a natural explanation for everything that happens, however horrific – and a ghost story, which must figure the supernatural. (Hill makes this point in the interview. on p. 31) As you read, compare the elements of the genre with details in *The Woman in Black*. In particular, compare the uses of the narrators, of landscape and weather, of houses, of children, of animals. Finally, you could read Hill's second classic ghost story, *The Mist in the Mirror* (1992).

Focus on: the idea of the audience

RESEARCH AND COMPARE . . .
— Read the opening section of *The Woman in Black* and then

read the opening section of Henry James's *The Turn of the Screw*. Make a list of things that are the same in the presentation of the scene that frames the telling of the ghost story proper. Some of the things that you might list could include: Christmas, the fire, a manuscript, a memory from youth. But make your own list and consider the implications of all these elements in both stories.

— Then read the opening section of Wilkie Collins's novel *The Woman in White*. This is not (as it turns out) a ghost story. But how many of the same constituents are present in the episode when Hartright tells his friends about the mysterious encounter on the Hampstead Road?

— Ask yourself how the presentation of the scene of the telling and the fact of an internal audience for the tale affects and governs your own reactions as a reader.

Focus on: adaptations

COMPARE DIFFERENT MEDIA . . .

— Do the same traditions and conventions exist for showing the supernatural on film as in writing? A story works mainly by appealing to the imagination, which makes writing an ideal medium for ghost stories. How well suited is the explicit medium of film to representing the supernatural? To answer this question, you might watch the television version of *The Woman in Black* (dir. Herbert Wise, 1989) or the film adaptation of *The Turn of the Screw* called *The Innocents*, directed by Jack Clayton (1961) and starring Deborah Kerr. Or else you might like to investigate Benjamin Britten's opera, also based on the novel, and premiered in Venice in 1954, conducted by the composer, and with Peter Pears as Quint and David Hemmings as Miles. Write a review, of either film or of the opera, commenting in particular on how successfully it has captured the mood of the novel to which it relates.

— In 1987, Stephen Mallatratt adapted *The Woman in Black* for the stage. The playwright recalls that representing Hill's story on stage presented a considerable challenge: 'In the book there are things that are very difficult to show on stage. There's the sea with the causeway running through it, the pony and trap, gaunt Eel Marsh House, the vast open landscape, the little dog Spider, and of course – the woman in black herself.' His solution was to take passages of description from the novel that work so vividly on the reader's imagination and to use them on stage, to make her words 'speak to the audience just as they'd spoken to me. If that could happen there'd be little need for things like scenery, or ponies or dogs; all those things would be there – and real – in the mind of every person in the theatre.' The essential idea in Mallatratt's adaptation is that Arthur Kipps is preparing himself to read out his story to his family and friends. Lacking confidence, he has engaged the help of an actor, who persuades Kipps to start shaping his story into a play, until the two men are performing the story as a play within the play. But their performance evokes the past in a way that neither man could have predicted – or wanted. If you can see the play, write a review; or compare the texts of the two versions, commenting on how successfully Mallatratt has adapted the story for the stage.

Focus on: sense of place

READ AND COMPARE . . .

— Hill's 'greatest literary hero' is Charles Dickens. She shares with Dickens an ability to create a powerful sense of place. Read the opening chapters (especially the start of Chapters One and Three) of *Great Expectations* for examples of Dickens's description of the Essex marshes, and compare these descriptions with the chapter entitled 'The Sound of a Pony and Trap' in *The Woman in Black*. Compare Eel Marsh House with the description of Satis House when Pip first visits it in Chapter Eight of *Great Expectations*. You might also compare it with the description of Manderley in Daphne du Maurier's *Rebecca* (1938), to which Hill wrote a sequel, *Mrs de Winter* (1993).

Focus on: drafts and manuscripts

READ AND COMPARE . . .

— Hill talks in the interview (pp. 22–4) about how she develops ideas from first thoughts to finished novel. As with *I'm the King of the Castle*, *The Woman in Black* appears to have come to Hill first as fragmentary images and scenes rather than as a plot line. The notes reproduced below were her first ideas for a 'Ghost Story', which she jotted on a small notepad. Read them carefully. Notice that the narrative slips in and out of the first person, which suggests that at this early stage Hill had not yet decided whether to use a character narrator or a third-person narrator.

Short story novella. Something very pared down and atmospheric. Sense of pure evil: a place in which, once I stepped within it, it hit, a sadness, came over me. People were embittered, repressed, made suicidal & made vindictive. It affects children and makes them quarrelsome. Animals – dogs bite, horses kick etc. Open in a beautiful place – English Country House – in September sunshine? Golden colours – blackberries in the lanes – blackberries in October having the devil's mark on them – What influences everyone? One part of the house has an evil smell –

the hotel/musty home – haunted by 2 children &
their animals – the place keeps changing.

Railway journey. Fog. Winter. Intense cold, snow,
frost, ice – a snow-land – wind & rain – weather.
Long train, getting emptier – rattling to the last few
places.

Fens marshes. House at the end of the salt flats.
Wind roaring. Beach. Silver water. River looks silver
& clear – all calm, in the morning after the storm.
The house – appeared at the end of all this – perhaps across a causeway?

Next, Hill tried out ideas for the plot and characters. She seems
to have played with two main plots. The first idea was that of
a character who visits the house of a relative who has just died,
in an isolated and creepy place:

Perhaps the first time he has ever been to the house,
it's known to have been haunted – the relative who
owned it . . . recently died – the place was just as it
had been for 60 years – she'd been a Miss Havisham
– he'd gone up in fog, wind & storm: the place
creaked and groaned & was damp – no electricity –
the attic in the house – the funeral & then to sort
out the possessions – boxes – the creepy attic full of
stuff. When is this set? 1920. Turn of the century?
Unspecified past.

The second idea is of a character visiting a relative's or friend's
house for Christmas:

He is middle-aged – 50? – once married as a young
man, widowed – never felt like trying again. A

scholar? He had visited the house years earlier and found it depressing. This time, however, all appears very different.

He makes a journey tired, but cheerful & a case full of Xmas presents – he being an uncle figure – for there will be some children – Xmas in a country house, only relatives/friends – cousins? The journey North and East. And across the causeway – to the house . . .

A cheerful air and friendly family welcome cheer his heart – a widower all these years. But he can't forbear to tell them of how he had been to the house before – and to entertain them around the fire, he tells the story – the gloomy place as it was & the haunted toy-room & the rocking horse etc. but it is all different now – still – one bit he hadn't told them – he'd spun a good ghost story and given them a shiver – but not told them about the *evil* – the child – which haunted, pursued and possessed him – how he was taken by sudden seizures, dread & the terror of a sense of evil & a vision of hell – a smell of it – in London somewhere – how he saw the evil child's face & now he is back there – this night & he wakes & goes to the room again & of course, there is the evil child – & he is planning a revenge and to take one of the children here – [the narrator] is wakened in dread that something is wrong with one of the children – & finds him in a fever & looking near death? White, choking, pale – sweaty – . . . the child on the point of death – he prays – drives the spirit out . . . the child's toys are strewn around – broken here and there – as if he had a fit – one of his sleep walks – when he

139

destroys things. He is the very child – clever – sensitive – anxious – frightened eyes – not like his
brothers and sisters – he is the one it has got at . . .
the child's eyes have changed colour, from grey to
green & there is a confidence and self-possession
about him – a superiority – the spirit has gone into
him.

Some years later – he went abroad – met a wife at
last – happy – travelled – 20 years younger – she
had a family & four children so he was happy & not
alone – they married, it was sad because the boys
went away to school and the place was too far to
keep up & one of them had been expelled? A worry
– that boy – carrying around his burden/evil – possessed by a devil . . .

— The idea of the child possessed by an adult then disap-
pears from the notes – perhaps because Hill was anxious not
to be influenced too much by *The Turn of the Screw*. However,
if you read Hill's later ghost story *The Mist in the Mirror*, you
will see that some of the ideas she rejected for *The Woman in
Black* were used for the later one. Finally, she seems to have
hit upon a way of combining the ideas of a happy family at
Christmas, of a man making a lonely visit to a haunted house,
and of evil wreaking vengeance on a family. At this point, she
started to draft the different stages of the novel. These are her
notes on the opening:

Xmas eve. Their house. A small country house in
the Cotswolds, 1 mile from an upland village hard by
the church. Stone. A sharp frost, clear but dry – no
snow – foxes barking etc.

It was a family gathering. My wife's grandchildren,

her daughter Stella's children, upstairs asleep. The
three sons – aged 22, 20 & 17.

The meal was out – the lull before creeping about
and stockings. They settled round the fire and began
to tell the ghost stories – which quickly became
horror stories. I felt uneasy – why? In the end – he
goes outside & walks around the garden – cold,
kitchen garden, etc. He looks over at the church –
quiet – peaceful graves – no eeriness – why?

Then he remembers – in the paper he has seen perhaps a letter from that home address – & it all
comes back to him.

He is in no mood to tell the story casually around
the fire – but he cheers up for his dear wife's sake –
and promises himself that he will write down his
story & put it in the safe/bank deposit – or a locked
drawer – to be read after his death.

— Hill wrote *The Woman in Black* in six weeks. 'It flowed very
quickly and easily,' she recalls. By the time she started writing
the first full draft, which she has always done by hand, the
working out had all been done. Her subsequent alterations are
usually only minor. However, Hill wrote a preface for *The
Woman in Black* which was never used. It purports to be an
explanation by one of his stepsons, Oliver (who figures as a
young man in the novel on pp. 14–20), of how Kipps left the
story to be read only after his death, and about the family dis-
agreements about whether it should be published at all. It is
reproduced here (still in draft form) by kind permission of the
author.

Preface
By the Reverend Oliver Ainley.

Some word of explanation may perhaps be in order, upon publication of the story that follows. It is a true story. I can vouch for the absolute integrity of the 'author', whom I knew, from the time I was eight years old, until the day of his death some three years ago, as well as I have known any man. Arthur Kipps was my stepfather, and in every respect he took the place of a natural father, to my sister, to my two younger brothers, and myself, when he married our mother, after she had been some five years a widow. He devoted himself conscientiously to his role from that day but there was nothing merely dutiful about his behaviour towards us. He loved us as warmly as if we had indeed been his own flesh and blood, and he loved us equally.

He was an upright and honest man, with a predilection for 'a quiet life,' with a regular, ordered routine that one might have thought bordered on the obsessive. He calls himself, in the course of his narrative, 'a dull dog', and when we were younger, we were inclined to agree with him, though certainly we thought none the worse of him on account of his distaste for surprise, excitement and all domestic disturbance. After reading the story contained in the following pages – the story not one word of which any of us ever heard from his own lips during his lifetime – I understood profoundly and with instantaneous sympathy, the reason for his prefer-ence for that predictable, uneventful existence. What man who witnessed what he had witnessed, felt what he had felt and suffered as he had suffered in consequence, would not make the enjoyment of a life of peace and tranquillity, of both body and soul, his most fervent, oft repeated prayer?

The story was written in ink in his plain, lawyer's hand, on foolscap pages contained loose within a cardboard folder, the whole being sealed in a large brown envelope which was found, together with the rest of his personal and business papers, in the locked drawer of his desk. The envelope, marked 'To be opened only after my death', was addressed to each member of his family by name. A letter, which is here printed, was clipped to the cover [this letter seems not to have been written by Hill].

I, being the eldest, read both the letter and manuscript first, and I then passed them on to my brothers. As our sister was at the time expecting her fourth child, we withheld it from her until some months had elapsed and she had been safely delivered of another boy, when she expressed a strong desire to 'know the worst'. Less than halfway through, her courage failed her, and she was vehement in her refusal ever to read another word, or to hear the story spoken about in her presence. She alone in the family was opposed to its publication, and the violence of her opposition has, unhappily, been the occasion of much distress and anxiety among us. Her brothers would, I believe, have allowed her desires to hold sway, had our mother not over-ruled us all with unwavering resolution.

We had at first also discouraged her from reading the manuscript, and for almost a year, she showed no interest in doing so, so absorbed was she in coping with her own bereavement. Her private grief was acute, her public mourning restrained, but although she was a woman of courage and common sense, I, more than anyone, was concerned that she should not suffer not only any further shock, nor any horror and revulsion, at the contents of the narrative but, perhaps most important of all, any sense of betrayal, on discovering that her devoted husband of almost fifty years, had kept the knowledge of such a ghastly experience completely hidden from her.

She had known, naturally, that she was his second wife, the first Mrs Kipps having lingered, a pathetic invalid, for some ten months before dying 'as the result of an accident'. But of the details preceding and surrounding those events in my step-father's earlier life, she was told nothing, and, being a woman of tact and sensitivity, she did not presume to enquire further.

Who will be surprised that her reaction to the story, when she eventually came to read it, was one of dismay and agitation, followed hard by renewed grief on behalf of her dead husband, that he should have so suffered, borne the burden of his suffering quite alone – and carried it to his grave?

For some time, she would not speak of the matter, but retreated into herself, and into a fresh trough of grief and despond where none of us could reach her – I least of all. Never has there been a more bitter trial of my own faith and my steadfastness in the priesthood. For, on reading my stepfather's manuscript, I realised that I had never once been, as he had, touched by real evil, evil made manifest, evil acting through and upon the innocent

with all its malignant force. He had seen, heard, felt,
been possessed and almost overcome by, an evil
about which I had only read and heard at several
removes, and against which I habitually prayed in
formulae which seemed hopelessly abstract and
theoretical.

I admired my stepfather for having adhered to his
customary principle and decided that, if a job was
worth doing, it was worth doing properly. He did
not scribble down the story anyhow, but has gone to
some trouble over the shaping and the writing of it.
Perhaps mastering some of the skills of professional
authorship had alleviated some of the pain and
horror it must have caused him to revive his
memories. Nevertheless, had it been left to me, I
confess that I would either have burned the entire
manuscript, or at the very least, locked it away in
some bank vault, for another fifty years, and tried
thereafter to expunge it from my mind. My brothers,
and certainly my sister Stella, would have done
likewise.

It was our mother, who insisted that the story
should be published. She did not explain her reasons,
except to repeat, 'It is the truth, and truth should be
told'. Possibly, she believed that Arthur Kipps had
meant the story to serve as a warning, or as evidence
for the continuing presence of evil, battling for
supremacy in both this world and the next. At any
rate, she would brook no opposition, and after much
careful consideration, it was agreed that the manuscript be sent to a very old-established, and highly
reputable firm, whose handling of it would be tactful
and restrained. The last thing we would agree to
would be any exploitation of the ghoulish inclination

of one section of the reading public, nor any preying upon the fears of the weak and ignorant.

The manuscript was read and accepted, and all our conditions agreed to, with but little delay, and the publishers themselves invited me to contribute this preface to the volume that bears their imprint, and my stepfather's name. I am proud to do so, as a last tribute to a man for whom my respect and affection have, if it were possible, been even more increased, and into whose character and virtue I now have a deeper, more tender and intimate insight and understanding.

I heartily believe and trust that the setting down of the story may at last have exorcised these unhappy ghosts, and the terrors they aroused, from my stepfather's mind. Is it also too much to hope that the powers of evil here described as working through these places, these human circumstances, may have been overcome and obliterated? I pray so daily.

My stepfather died, in the peace and serenity of old age, and in joy and freedom of spirit. Two years later, our dear mother, his widow, followed him, and that not reluctantly. In morte non divisi.

Pluckwell Rectory
Old Ilpen
Suffolk.

Looking over the unused preface

QUESTIONS FOR DISCUSSION OR ESSAYS

1. Look at the description of Oliver Ainley as a nineteen-year-old on pp.14–20 of the novel. How closely does the

voice that speaks in this preface connect with his portrayal in the novel? Kipps advised Oliver to become a lawyer. What might be the significance of the fact that he was ordained into the Church instead?

2. In what specific ways does this 'framing' device emphasise the idea of Kipps as a reliable narrator of his own story?

3. How does this preface help to give a pretend reality to Kipps's script, an illusion that it is a real story told by a real man, and published by his family?

4. 'The violence of her opposition has, unhappily, been the occasion of much distress and anxiety among us.' Consider the notion that the influence of the woman in black may 'live on' in the manuscript.

5. Account for Isobel's (Oliver's sister's) reaction to the story. Should her wishes have been observed, do you think?

6. In what ways is it evident that this preface is still only a draft?

7. What does this preface contribute to the theme of good and evil in the novel?

8. 'It is the truth, and truth should be told.' Discuss this claim, or write a story with this title.

9. 'The last thing we would agree to would be any exploitation of the ghoulish inclination of one section of the reading public.' Is Hill poking fun at her own readers and their reasons for reading *The Woman in Black*?

10. What would the inclusion of this preface have added to *The Woman in Black*? Do you think Hill right to drop it from the final text?

VINTAGE
LIVING
TEXTS

A Bit of Singing and Dancing

IN CLOSE-UP

Reading guides for

BEFORE YOU BEGIN TO READ . . .
— Read the interview with Hill. You will see there that she identifies a number of themes:

- Performance and entertainment
- Serious fiction and 'play'
- Menace
- People who are 'misfits'
- First- and third-person narration

Other themes that may be useful to consider while reading the collection include:

- The creation of atmosphere
- Sense of place
- The presentation of the natural world
- Possession and manipulation

Reading activities: detailed analysis

Focus on: the title

ASK YOURSELF . . .

— This phrase is given prominence three times: the overall title for the collection of short stories; in the title of the story that occurs in the middle of the book at pages 97–118; and on page 97 when Esme's mother uses it to describe her fondness for 'spectaculars' on the television. Think about each of these occurrences and define how each one functions in its specific context. How does the implied meaning of the phrase alter depending on the context?

LOOK BACK . . .

— If you look at the interview with Hill (on pp. 30–1), you will see that she is willing to accept a description for some of her writing as 'entertainment'. At the same time, she argues that writing has to have some 'moral point'. As you read consider the ways in which this collection of short stories might balance 'entertainment' as against a 'moral point'. What 'moral points', overall, might be offered to you in this collection?

Focus on: the collection overall

LOOK OVER AND ASSESS . . .

— Although these stories were written individually and at different times, and not designed necessarily as a complete work, it is possible to trace key themes, concepts, concerns and methods through many or all of the stories. Key ideas to look for might include: the idea of the 'misfit'; the treatment of setting – especially resorts (for instance) that are portrayed out of season; the creation of menace or threat; the treatment of the natural world; skewed or difficult relations between people; children and their attitude to the adult world. As you read the collection as a whole, make a list of places where each one of these themes occurs.

— Make your own list of recurring images, themes and settings. What does your list suggest about Hill's preoccupations and interests as a writer?

DECIDE ON ENDINGS . . .

— Read the endings for each one of the short stories in this collection. How often do they come to a definite conclusion? How often do they include a death? How many times is it implied that one or more of the character's lives is changed for ever by the events narrated in the story? How often – or not – is some moral point arrived at?

— As a result of this exercise, what conclusions can you draw about the tone of Hill's stories?

HALLORAN'S CHILD
(pp. 1–18)

Focus on: the child as icon

RESEARCH AND COMPARE . . .

— The first story in this collection is about a child, and a child who dies. Look back at the interview with Hill (on pp. 13–14) to see what she has to say about her ideas on children and childhood. Read her novel *I'm the King of the Castle* which is also about a child who dies. When you have read over the other stories in this collection, note how many times children appear there, and how many of them are similarly doomed. What ideals or images does any one of these children represent? How might you contrast and compare them?

Focus on: the 'misfit'

DESCRIBE THE VOCABULARY . . .

— Both Nate and Bertha Twomey are outsiders in their village and 'misfits' in relation to the community they live in. Write down all the words that explain their alienated social position and assess the effect of this choice of vocabulary in portraying their 'difference'.

Focus on: superstition and fear

WHY? . . .

— Why might Halloran fear and despise Nate Twomey? Make a list of his superstitions and fears about Nate. If possible, look up some of these folk beliefs in a dictionary of superstitions.

Focus on: violence

ASSESS . . .

— This story begins with the rabbit that Nate is eating (p. 1) and goes on to discuss traps and the story of the wounded deer and Nelson's callous reaction to it. How do these images of violence relate to what happens to Nate at the end of the story?

Focus on: forgiveness

ASK YOURSELF . . .
— Does Nate forgive Halloran? If so, why? What significance is there in Nate returning, at the end of the story, to 'the carpenter's shop'?

MR PROUDHAM AND MR SLEIGHT
(pp. 19–36)

Focus on: setting and atmosphere

MAKE A LIST . . .
— In the first paragraph of the story we are told about the 'sleet and a north-easterly wind' and about this being 'the bleakest time of year'. Work through the story jotting down every example of descriptions of the weather and the time of year. How does the list you arrive at convey the setting and atmosphere for the story?

Focus on: first-person narration

ANALYSE . . .
— This story is told in the first person. If you look at the interview with Hill (pp. 23–4), you will see that she discusses the importance of this technical choice in composing fiction. What difference does it make that this is a first-person narration? What extra things might be relayed to you by that choice? (You might also like to look at the discussion in the interview

on p. 35–6 about the narrative point of view in *The Woman in Black*.)

DID YOU NOTICE? . . .
— Who is the narrator? What do you learn about this person from the story? What kind of person are they? What gender? How did you find that out? At what point exactly? What work do they do? How have they been affected by the events that take place in the story?

Focus on: menace

INTERPRET . . .
— How is a sense of menace built up in this story? Which episodes are particularly disturbing or frightening and why?

IN THE CONSERVATORY
(pp. 37–53)

Focus on: museums and collections

COUNT UP . . .
— How many museums and collections of objects are mentioned in this story? Remember to include Boris's lead soldiers. What is suggested by the idea of 'collecting' and 'categorising' here? How does the image of the 'museum' or the 'collection' relate to – and throw light on – the character or the nature of the narrator's affair?

Focus on: atmosphere

WORK OUT . . .
— Consider the description of Fewings: its rooms, the contents of its rooms, its furniture and character. What is the

atmosphere in the house? How is the atmosphere created by these descriptions?

Focus on: point of view

COMPARE . . .

— Although this is a story told in the third person throughout, there are two narrative points of view in this story – the one is the point of view of the woman who is having the affair, and the other is the point of view of the Musrys. Compare these two perspectives. In what ways do they connect to, contradict, or illuminate each other?

WHY? . . .

— Look over the names of the characters in this story. Whose names do you know and whose do you not know? How does that knowledge – or lack of it – affect your attitude to the different points of view with which you are presented?

Focus on: animals

COMPARE AND ASSESS . . .

— Animals of different kinds have featured in all three of the stories in this collection so far. Jot down what kinds of animals appear in each story and assess what symbolic significances they may have in each separate case.

Focus on: vocabulary and sentence construction

ANALYSE . . .

— Read over the first paragraph of this story. For each sentence, try to work out the exact grammatical construction. So, for instance, in the first sentence their 'love affair' is the subject, 'was' is the verb, 'very public' is the adjective, 'From the beginning' is a phrase describing time. Look up grammatical references if you need to, or discuss the constituent parts of the sentences with someone else. When you have worked out and thought about how these sentences are put together, consider how the tone of the story is set in this opening paragraph by means of a specific linguistic style.

HOW SOON CAN I LEAVE?
(pp. 54–67)

Focus on: characterisation

DISCRIMINATE . . .

— There are only four characters in this story. Work out which words and phrases characterise each one. How convincing are the characters of Miss Roscommon and Miss Bartlett? How do the pictures of Miss Roscommon and Miss Bartlett compare with that of Angela and her husband? How many times is Angela called 'the niece Angela' and what effect does that have on your attitude to her character?

THE CUSTODIAN
(pp. 68–96)

Focus on: the natural world and the 'pathetic fallacy'

EXAMINE . . .

— Read the story carefully and assess each of the descriptions of birds, the water, the trees, animals and flowers mentioned. Then look up the term 'pathetic fallacy' in the glossary. In what ways are the images of the natural world used to mirror or comment on the feelings and reactions of the old man who looks after the boy?

A BIT OF SINGING AND DANCING
(pp. 97–118)

Focus on: singing and dancing

COUNT UP . . .

— Every time you come to 'singing and dancing' in the text of this story, note it down. How many different concepts of 'singing and dancing' are suggested, and what is the cumulative effect of these built-up references?

Focus on: mother's sayings

NOTE AND WEIGH UP . . .

— There are several times in this story when Esmé remembers, or imagines, typical things that her mother might say. Look for each time such a quotation appears. Then – as with the exercise above – weigh up the cumulative effect of these allusions. Are there more towards the end of the story? Or fewer? Why does the story end with one such reference? And does the way the allusion is used in that final passage mark it out as different from the other allusions? If so, in what way?

Focus on: parents and children

COMPARE AND CONSIDER . . .

— Several of the stories so far in this collection have featured parents and children – or surrogate parents and children. Look over the collection and note down each such relation. Then consider which relationships are similar and which are different. Go back to the opening of the interview with Hill to see what she says about children and childhood. How do her remarks square with the pictures of parents and children that she presents in this collection of stories?

THE PEACOCK
(pp. 119–38)

Focus on: crisis

DECIDE . . .
— How many scenes of crisis take place in this story? Obviously there is the minor incident where Daisy gets shut in the summerhouse, set against the major event of her husband's heart attack. But there are also other incidents that have occurred in the past and are occurring in the present – Daisy's spurt of hatred directed towards her father, for instance. Make a list, and work out how each relates to and illuminates the others. And what about the peacock itself? How does Daisy's memory of its eyes (p. 138) focus the other crises in the story?

Focus on: timescale

MAKE A CHRONOLOGY . . .
— Think about the differences between story, text and narration. The story is what happens to the characters; the text is the piece of work under your hand that sets it out; the narration is the way it is told. This story takes place partly in the present when Daisy and Humphrey Buckingham meet Vernon and Elspeth Thackeray, but we are told about events in the past. Make a chronology of events as they happened consecutively in time. Then make a separate plan of the events in the order in which they are narrated.

MISSY
(pp. 139–54)

Focus on: dialogue

LOOK AT THE PATTERNS AND COMPARE . . .

— There are several exchanges set out in this story where a nurse is speaking to one or other of the old people in ways which are childish or banal. These may look like simple exchanges, but often they have rhythms and patterns within. Pick out one or two such examples and consider the repetitions, rhymes and shapes that they make. Then look at a play by Harold Pinter, *The Birthday Party* (1958) would be a good place to start, or *The Caretaker* (1960). Read, for example, the exchange about the corn flakes at the opening of *The Birthday Party* or any of the discussions about going to Sidcup in *The Caretaker*. Again, Pinter's dialogues appear artless, but are actually highly contrived. How does Pinter's method compare with Hill's?

THE BADNESS WITHIN HIM
(pp. 155–63)

Focus on: the child who thinks he's bad

COMPARE . . .

— Read Henry James's short novel *The Turn of the Screw* (1898). There are passages in that story where Miles also seems to be 'bad', or to consider himself 'bad'. But we never really find out what this 'badness' might consist of or why the child thinks of himself in this way. If you look at the episode where the governess receives a letter declaring that Miles has been expelled from his school, you will see that no explanation is given as to a reason for this. The implication is that some adult anxiety, knowledge or preconception has been forced on the child. How might the picture of Miles in this plight help you to assess Col's perceptions of his own wickedness?

Focus on: death and moments of transition

RESEARCH AND COMPARE . . .
— Several of the stories in *A Bit of Singing and Dancing* focus on children and the moment of transition from childhood innocence to adult knowledge. Similarly, several of them focus on death, and that death may mark the moment of transition. Read James Joyce's *Dubliners* (1914). The first story in that collection is called 'The Sisters' and concerns a boy and his experience of another person's death. The last story in the collection is called 'The Dead' and tells of a death of a young man many years ago in the past, but that memory pinpoints a moment of epiphany and understanding for the main character in the story. Consider how the episodes and incidents may be linked together in either or both Joyce's and Hill's collections.

RED AND GREEN BEADS
(pp. 164–70)

Focus on: setting and atmosphere

ANALYSE . . .
— Although several stories mention characters who live or work abroad, this is the first story in the collection to be set somewhere other than in England. Pick out the specific references in the story that make this setting clear. What is distinctively French in the atmosphere and references in this piece?

163

Focus on: epiphany and 'the question'

ASK YOURSELF . . .

— What do you suppose is the answer to the Curé's question, given to him by Marcel's action? In what ways is this a revelation, or a moment of epiphany and understanding?

OSSIE
(pp. 171–88)

Focus on: Venice

RESEARCH AND ANALYSE . . .

— Like the previous story, 'Ossie' is partly set away from England, in this case Milan and Venice. Venice, as a setting, is not necessarily important to the story, but it is appropriate, given that it is known as the city of mazes, of disguises, distrust and masquerade. Find some information about the 'real' Venice. One famous example from the nineteenth century is John Ruskin's influential *The Stones of Venice* (1851–3). A well-known text from the twentieth century might be Jan Morris's *Venice* (1960). Other useful books are *Venetian Views, Venetian Blinds: English Fantasies of Venice*, ed. Manfred Pfister and Barbara Schaff (1999) and Tony Tanner's *Venice* (1992).

— Novels and plays often use the image of the city of Venice to disorient and to dismay the foreigner and the tourist. Important 'Venetian' fictions might include Ben Jonson's play *Volpone* (1605–6), Shakespeare's *Othello* (1604), Henry James's *The Aspern Papers* (1888), Vernon Lee's 'A Wicked Voice' (1890), Daphne du Maurier's short story 'Don't Look Now' (1971), Ian McEwan's *The Comfort of Strangers* (1981), and Jeanette Winterson's *The Passion* (1987). Many of these books include themes that are also to be found in Hill's 'Ossie'. Among these you could list: disguise, performance, cross-dressing, surface and depth, the erotic and the transgressive.

FIND OUT ABOUT . . .
— Terence tells us that he is writing a book on the Venetian painter called Francesco Guardi (p. 180). Then a bit later Ossie says to him, 'Venice suits me . . . because it's not a place where you can ever be yourself, don't you see? You have to put on some kind of disguise – look at how it always used to be, in those pictures of yours – masked balls, elaborate costumes, double identity, deception' (p. 181). Find out about Guardi and his paintings, and consider how these themes are worked out in the pictures and in Hill's short story.

RESEARCH AND COMPARE . . .
— The character of Ossie may be compared in some ways to the real-life writer Oscar Wilde. Find out what you can about him and see if you can make such a comparison. You might also like to read Wilde's novel *The Picture of Dorian Gray* (1891). Can you make connections between Hill's short story and this novel?

THE ELEPHANT MAN
(pp. 189–205)

Focus on: characterisation

LIST AND INTERPRET . . .
— There are three main characters in this story: Nanny Fawcett, William, The Friend. Take a moment to think about each of these characters, then write down four key words for each – whatever comes into your head and without looking at the story again. Once you have written down your four words,

reread the story, paying particular attention to the individual characters and ask yourself where you have got your key word impressions from. Are they directly related to the information offered in the story? Or have they come to you indirectly from elements in the story? What does this tell you about the processes of creating character in fiction?

Focus on: symbols

INTERPRET . . .

— This story begins and ends with the Round Pond and its draining. Consider the places where the Pond is discussed and interpret its significance (full or drained). What does it symbolise and how is that shown? Make a list.

FRIENDS OF MISS REECE
(pp. 206–22)

Focus on: the title

ASSESS . . .

— Is the title of this story ironic?

Focus on: children and adults

CONNECT . . .

— There are (at least) two other stories in this collection that deal with the death of an adult from the perspective of a child: they are 'The Badness Within Him' and 'Red and Green Beads' – though, of course, strictly speaking Marcel is not a child but a retarded adult of twenty. Make a list of the similarities between the three stories. Then make another list of the differences between the three stories. How does this comparison help you to analyse and make connections?

Focus on: language as ritual

EXPLAIN . . .

— The boy in this story keeps asking in which room he was born. Count up the number of times this is repeated. Explain a) why he asks the question, b) why the answer has to be always the same, and c) what effect this repetition has on the reader.

THEN LOOK BACK . . .

— Look back at the language and vocabulary exercise for 'Missy' where you were asked to evaluate the apparently banal, but actually artful and meaningful arrangements of ordinary dialogues and exchanges. How might the conclusions you drew there relate to what is going on here?

COCKLES AND MUSSELS
(pp. 223–39)

Focus on: class and setting

INVESTIGATE . . .

— The title to this story alludes to a well-known popular song. If you know the song, think over the lyrics and consider how the song may be relevant to the story. If you don't already know the song, find out about it and work out the relevance.

CONTRAST . . .

— There are two distinct worlds set one against the other in this story: the genteel world of the Delacourt Guest House, and the rougher world of the Lower Bay. Similarly, there is the fantasy status set up by Mrs Hennessey, as against the reality of the life of Mrs Rourke. How are each of these set up?

MAKE A DIAGRAM . . .

— Draw yourself a Venn diagram to represent the distinctions and the overlap between the two worlds in 'Cockles and Mussels'. Miss Parson, for instance, belongs to both worlds. Crustaceans — cockles, mussels, shrimps, crabs and other shellfish — belong to only one. How does setting out these distinctions help you to negotiate a path through the story?

SOMERVILLE
(pp. 240–78)

Focus on: chronological time as opposed to narrative time

DRAW UP A CHRONOLOGICAL PLAN . . .

— This story covers a long span of chronological time, even though the narrative of the main 'events' of the story relates to a very short space of time — maybe a month, or two or three — over the period of Martha's late pregnancy and the birth and early days of her child. Make a chronological time plot of the events. The earliest episodes that we learn about may be to do with Barton and the narrator and their friendship at Oxford. Include as much information as you possibly can, and bring it right up to date with Somerville watching out for the hedgehog again. How does this help you to trace the overlap between past and present that structures Somerville's thoughts as they are represented in the story? Ask yourself why Somerville hides the body of the baby.

RESEARCH AND COMPARE . . .

— Read the book of Exodus in the Old Testament of the Bible and think about the story of the rescue of the baby Moses by the Egyptian princess. Then look at the latter part of George Eliot's *Adam Bede* (1859) where Hetty abandons her baby. In the one story, a baby is abandoned and rescued. In the other a baby is left and lost. How might you relate either or both of these stories to Hill's 'Somerville'?

Focus on: point of view

TRANSFORM . . .

— In no more than two pages, retell the story of the events in 'Somerville' but write them from the point of view of Martha. How does this help you to assess the characterisation of Martha herself, and of Somerville?

Looking over the whole collection

QUESTIONS FOR DISCUSSION OR ESSAYS

1. 'Hill's themes are death, the misfit, childhood and crisis. But always it is the moment of transition that makes her focus.' Discuss the 'moment of crisis' in Hill's short stories.

2. Why are so many of Hill's short stories set in English resorts and out of season?

3. 'Menace and the macabre are never far away if you are reading a story by Hill.' Do you agree?

4. Hill's writing has been described as 'truly organic'. What might you understand by this and how do you think it could relate to her writing style?

5. Consider the kinds of death that appear in Hill's short stories.

6. 'The surface is all that matters.' Discuss in relation to *A Bit of Singing and Dancing*.

7. How much 'performance' goes into Hill's collection of short stories?

8. Make a case for this collection as a unified work.

9. Where is the 'moral point' in *A Bit of Singing and Dancing?* (You may choose to confine your answer to one or two stories.)

10. 'Susan Hill's ability to recreate conversation is masterly.' Discuss, giving examples.

11. Describe and assess the presentation of the natural world in the stories in *A Bit of Singing and Dancing.*

12. 'These are stories about what is not said.' Do you agree?

Contexts, comparisons and complementary readings

A BIT OF SINGING AND DANCING

Focus on: short stories, oral history and folk narrative

EXPLORE CONNECTIONS . . .

— Hill has written a number of short stories and short-story collections. You might like to compare her collections of short stories to those of writers like Edith Wharton, Guy de Maupassant, Graham Greene or Somerset Maugham. Other, more recent, collections that you could look at might include Margaret Atwood's stories in *Bluebeard's Egg* (1987), Helen Simpson's collection of short stories *Hey Yeah Right Get a Life* (2001), Angela Carter's *The Bloody Chamber and Other Stories* (1979) or Emma Donoghue's collection *Kissing the Witch* (1999).

— Take any one of these other collections of short stories and consider how the concept of the collection is used by Hill and by one of these other writers. In what ways are each of the stories in their collections separate, and in what ways do they connect to each other?

Focus on: animal helpers

CONSIDER . . .

— In fairy stories it often happens that the hero or heroine is assisted in their quest by an animal helper who explains something to them, or gives them some crucial clue that allows them to kill the wicked witch/find the gold/rebuild the castle/solve the riddle, or whatever. How are animals used in Hill's stories? Are there any ways in which you could describe her – overall – handling of the 'animal helper' as a theme in these stories?

Focus on: a bit of singing and dancing

LOOK OVER AND ASSESS . . .

— How often do concepts connected with performance figure in these stories overall? Go over the whole collection carefully and assess the importance of the words 'performance', 'presentation', 'entertainment', 'subterfuge'. Which is which? And which idea is most significant in relation to the collection as a whole?

Focus on: shared themes

MARK OUT AND ANALYSE . . .

— At the beginning of the reading guides we asked you to note down the themes that are important in this collection. Here is another list: violence, relationships between men, parents and children, religion, fate, death, childhood, old age, risk-taking, madness or 'difference'. Go through the collection and work out which stories are about which subject. How often are they about more than one subject? How often do the subjects and the stories overlap? Then identify one theme that interests you particularly and write three paragraphs on a) why the theme intrigues you, b) how Hill deals with it, and c) how your own perceptions might be changed, challenged or vindicated by Hill's story.

Reference

Critical Overview

Hill is an intelligent and accessible writer, and one who is skilled in delineating atmosphere, setting and place. For these reasons, she is widely read and popular with her audiences. In recent years, a number of her works have been set by the awarding bodies who are authorised by the government body in charge of public examinations. Either as set texts, or as suggested reading, Hill's novels have been used for GCSE, AS, A level and International Bacculaureate examinations. In particular, *I'm the King of the Castle*, *Strange Meeting* and *The Woman in Black* have been treated in this way. Her collection of short stories, *A Bit of Singing and Dancing*, and her novella *The Albatross*, have also featured in such examinations.

As a result of the popularity of Hill's work both with readers and with examination officers, a number of guides and essays have been published, including several 'forewords' and 'afterwords' to the novels, written by Hill herself. As ever, when studying a contemporary writer (or indeed, any writer) it is your own reading of the text that must come first. Nevertheless, after you've read Hill's work, and jotted down and planned out some of your ideas, it can sometimes help to look at other sources. There is often the pleasure of recognition – 'I thought that too' – but you might also find some new elements in such guides and essays and these can help you to focus your own thinking.

For *I'm the King of the Castle*, Longman produced an edition which offered some brief introductory notes by Frank Downes, explaining how Hill came to write the book in the summer of 1969 when she rented a cottage in a 'remote corner of Dorset'. It outlines the country-house setting of the story and the social environment inhabited by the characters. It offers a few 'main themes' borrowed from Hill's own account in the afterword to the Penguin edition. (If this afterword is included in your edition of the novel, you would do well to read it as it does set out some interesting lines of enquiry.) Hill says that it is a novel about 'cruelty and power'. Downes helpfully adds a few pointers to our new consciousness of the causes of vicious behaviour in children.

In *I'm the King of the Castle* very little analysis is offered as to *why* Hooper acts in the way he does. Instead, we have to make assumptions and investigations of our own. Both Hooper and Kingshaw have lost a parent, neither in the (still) quite 'stiff-upper-lip' world of the 1960s has been offered any help in coming to terms with this loss. Their trauma is unresolved. Add to that a distinct lack of love or sympathetic attention in the family and both boys – but Hooper in particular – become isolated, unable to relate to the sensitivities of others. These are children, but, as Downes points out, in the late twentieth and early twenty-first century we have had to relinquish a Victorian ideal of childhood as an 'innocent' period, in order to face more brutal truths. Language and style are crucial in examining the techniques of Hill's method, and each chapter in this schools edition is introduced with questions to ask yourself and projects to focus your reading. The book also contains brief but useful suggestions for further reading and a 'programme of study'.

For *The Albatross* (1970), Hill also wrote an 'Author's Afterword'. In this, she explains how much she was influenced by the music of Benjamin Britten who lived and worked in the seaside town of Aldeburgh. If you look at the interview with Hill (on p. 35), you will see that she also mentions the influence of Britten there, especially in relation to her novel *The Woman in Black*. So here, again, it is a question of atmosphere, setting and place that initiates a story in Hill's imagination. After that, she says that this is a story about 'the misfit, the odd, the simple, the strange one in the midst of the rest of ordinary humanity, and about the power of love and pure goodness, shining through all manner of human exteriors'. Hill also says that it is about 'possessiveness and cruelty and oppression, about fear and pride'. You will be able to see how all these themes are repeated and reworked throughout all her novels and short stories.

In 1989, Longman produced an edition of the *The Albatross* with some of Hill's short stories. It offers a brief biography, a few 'notes to help with your reading' and some 'coursework assignments' for each of the stories. But the most helpful element of the guide is an introduction by Hill, where she again refers to the combined influence of Britten's opera *Peter Grimes* and to the Aldeburgh setting. She also says, 'I'm occasionally asked which is my favourite among my own books, or which I am most proud of. I always refer to *The Albatross*, because I think the magic of the setting brought out the best in me as a descriptive writer, because the music of Britten runs through its pages, for those who can hear it, and because of Duncan – simple, suffering, blundering Duncan, groping towards light and life, strength, freedom – thwarted, doomed. Yet, I like to think, perhaps eventually redeemed, to experience resurrection.' It is a typical list and one worth attending to when you are reading Hill's work: setting, description, music, struggle, redemption.

In 1989 Hill also wrote an afterword for the Penguin edition of *Strange Meeting*. She mentions the Britten connection again and explains the relation between her own novel and

Wilfred Owen's poem of the same title. But, even more importantly, she says two very crucial and intriguing things: firstly,
that before she wrote the novel she was obsessed, more particularly, 'haunted' by the subject of the First World War, and
that after it was done, she cared no more; and secondly, how
pointless it is to speculate about fictional characters. Readers
ask her two things about the story: 'Were Barton and Hilliard
gay?' and 'What would have happened after the war if they
both had lived?' Hill is impatient with both these questions
and with the assumption that she will always be interested in
the subject of the war – a writer's inspiration comes from
curious sources and cannot always be pinned down. All that
matters is the results. Similarly, it is crass to approach a relation delineated with such delicacy in such a crude manner.
Barton and Hilliard love each other – we don't need to know
more – but it is the responsibility of the reader to analyse how
that love comes across to us, without worrying 'what would
have happened'. This is – as Hill insists – a fiction, which is
how it must be read and enjoyed: as a powerful construct made
of words, images, sounds, sentences that convey whole worlds
from the page into the reader's mind.

Longman published an edition of *Strange Meeting* with brief
notes and suggestions for reading.

There are other 'Forewords' and 'Afterwords' written by
Hill that you might look at in relation to her work. That for
the Penguin edition of *In the Springtime of the Year* (1973) is
helpful for her intelligent explanation of how a writer's works
are – and, more importantly, how they are not – autobiographical.

For *A Bit of Singing and Dancing*, there is a Longman edition which offers a short introduction and some inventive exercises in a briefly outlined study programme. For *The Woman in
Black*, there is a Longman edition with an introduction by Hill
which, once again, emphasises the importance of setting and

atmosphere, and 'Some points for discussion and suggestions for writing' which ask sensible questions in relation to the text, chapter by chapter. This edition also includes a short account of his processes in adapting the novel for the stage by Stephen Mallatratt, and an excerpt from the play. If you would like to obtain a copy of the text of the play you can write to Stephen Mallatratt at Mpress, Stonehurst, Hurst Road, Hebden Bridge, West Yorkshire, HX7 8HU.

In her introduction to *The Woman in Black* and in the interview included in this text (pp. 30–8) you will see that Hill speaks also about the significance of the literary challenge involved in deciding to write a 'classic' ghost story. It is a particular genre, with particular constituents, and sticking to a formula of this kind can often lead to certain perceptions and opening up of ideas. This is the paradox: stick to a formal shape and new freedoms can be found in that process. Hill went on to write another classic ghost story, *The Mist in the Mirror*. Longman produced a study guide for this novel, with a short introduction, advice on preparing reading logs, questions to focus your reading of each chapter and a suggested study programme.

Hill's expertise with genre writing, and the ghost story in particular, led to her compiling a collection of ghost stories for Longman, which includes works by A. S. Byatt and H. G. Wells. She offers there an introduction which persuasively defines the form and its essential ingredients. Hill has also made three collections of short stories for Penguin, *The Penguin Book of Modern Women's Short Stories* (1991), *The Penguin Book of Contemporary Women's Short Stories* (1995) and *The Second Penguin Book of Women's Short Stories* (1997). Each of these books has an introduction which can also usefully be raided for perceptions and explanations that you might find helpful in thinking about the work of Hill.

If you consult the bibliography, you will see that Hill is a prolific writer. As well as novels and short stories she has written a great number of children's books, plays and books of autobiography which often consist – as much as anything – of discerning nature notes and observations of the quirks and peculiarities of the people she sees around her, all of which are facets that go into the special character of her fiction. In addition to the writing, Hill runs a publishing venture called Long Barn Books, and edits and publishes a magazine for readers and book lovers called *Books and Company*. She also runs her own excellent official website which you can find at www.susan-hill.com. But beware – if you go to this website looking for information, make sure that you have done your own reading work first. Once a book has been written and published and gone out into the world, it's your book too, and as reader you must take possession of it by paying attention, by thinking and by enjoying the book. As Hill herself says: 'If you are studying any of my books (or anyone else's books, for that matter) for an examination, or in order to write an extended essay, it is your opinion that counts, not mine. What you think about the book and what you think it is about, as well as what it means to you – those are the things the examiners want to know. And if you have been reading carefully, attentively and thoughtfully, then your opinions and thoughts are as valid as those of any published commentator or literary critic.'

Glossary of literary terms

Archetype Basic mythic formulas of plot or character.

Chronology Timescale.

Cliché A phrase, idea or term that is so familiar that it has no 'cutting edge' any more.

Epiphany In modern fiction, a sudden revelation from an ordinary scene or event.

First person I, as opposed to he, she or they.

Formula Something that conforms to an expected pattern.

Genre A mode of characterisation. In biology, for instance, 'families' of plants are classified as belonging together in one way or another. In literature, 'genre' works in the same way as a mode of classifying and ordering literary 'types' of form.

Ghost story According to Susan Hill, this kind of story – to be strictly so-called – has to have a human ghost involved, i.e. a person who was alive, but who is now known to be dead, who haunts the living.

Horror story Any story which 'horrifies' the reader.

Image A 'picture' which can be conveyed by the text to the reader.

Melodramatic Originally, a drama performed to music (Greek *melos*), but in everyday usage, an over-the-top kind of drama. The most conventional forms of melodrama today are television soap operas.

Narrative The means by which the story is told.

Pathetic fallacy When a narrative supposes that the weather or any other inanimate or unrelated object is in sympathy with the feelings of the characters. Rain does not 'shed tears', but a character – or any person – may imagine that they do if they are in a position that makes them sad and vulnerable.

Plot The facts of the story in the order they are told.

Story The facts of the events.

Thriller Anything designed to have a 'thrilling' effect on the reader.

Third person He, she or they, as opposed to I.

Biographical outline

1942 Born in Scarborough, North Yorkshire.

1945–58 Attends Scarborough Convent School.

1958 Moves to Coventry and attends a girls' grammar school, Barr's Hill.

1960–3 Reads English at King's College London.

1961 *The Enclosure*, first novel, published by Hutchinson.

1963 *Do Me a Favour*, second novel, published. Moves back to Coventry and writes for the local newspaper for five years.

1968 *Gentlemen and Ladies* published. Moves to Leamington Spa and spends some time working and writing in Aldeburgh in Suffolk.

1969 *A Change for the Better* published.

1970 *I'm the King of the Castle* published. Wins the Somerset Maugham Award.

1970 *The Albatross* published.

1971 *Strange Meeting* published.

1972 *The Bird of Night* published. Wins the Whitbread Award.

1973 *A Bit of Singing and Dancing* and *In the Springtime of the Year* published.

1982 *The Magic Apple Tree* published.

1983 *The Woman in Black* published. Adapted for the stage by

Stephen Mallatratt in 1988 and still running.

1984 *Through the Kitchen Window* published.

1986 *Through the Garden Gate* published.

1991 *Air and Angels* published.

1990 Moves to Ebrington in Gloucestershire.

1992 *The Mist in the Mirror* published.

1993 *Mrs de Winter* published.

1997 *The Service of Clouds* and *Listening to the Orchestra* published.

2003 *The Boy who Taught the Beekeeper to Read* published.

Select bibliography

NOVELS

The Enclosure (Hutchinson, London, 1961)
Do Me a Favour (Hutchinson, 1963)
Gentleman and Ladies (Hamish Hamilton, London, 1968)
A Change for the Better (Hamish Hamilton, 1969)
I'm the King of the Castle (Hamish Hamilton, 1970)
Strange Meeting (Hamish Hamilton, 1971)
The Bird of Night (Hamish Hamilton, 1972)
In the Springtime of the Year (Hamish Hamilton, 1973)
The Woman in Black (Hamish Hamilton, 1983; Vintage, London, 1999)
Air and Angels (Sinclair Stevenson, London, 1991)
The Mist in the Mirror (Hamish Hamilton, 1992; Vintage, 1999)
Mrs de Winter (Sinclair Stevenson, 1993; Vintage, 1999)
The Service of Clouds (Chatto & Windus, London, 1997; Vintage, 1999)
The Boy who Taught the Beekeeper to Read (Chatto & Windus, 2003)

SHORT-STORY COLLECTIONS

The Albatross and Other Stories (Hamish Hamilton, 1970)
A Bit of Singing and Dancing (Hamish Hamilton, 1973)
Listening to the Orchestra (Long Barn Books, Ebrington, 1997)

REFERENCE

NON-FICTION

The Magic Apple Tree (Hamish Hamilton, 1982; Long Barn Books, 1998)

Through the Kitchen Window, illustrated by Angela Barrett (Hamish Hamilton, 1984)

Through the Garden Gate, illustrated by Angela Barrett (Hamish Hamilton, 1986)

The Lighting of the Lamps (Hamish Hamilton, 1987)

Shakespeare Country, photographs by Talbot and Whiteman (Michael Joseph, London, 1987)

The Spirit of the Cotswolds, photographs by Nick Meers (Michael Joseph, 1988)

Family (Michael Joseph, 1989)

Reflections from a Garden, illustrated by Ian Stephens with Rory Stuart (Pavilion Books, London, 1995)

PLAYS

The Cold Country and Other Plays for Radio (BBC Publications, 1975)

The Ramshackle Company (Longman, London, 1981)

WORKS FOR CHILDREN

One Night at a Time (Hamish Hamilton, 1984)

Mother's Magic (Hamish Hamilton, 1985)

Can it be True?, illustrated by Angela Barrett (Hamish Hamilton 1987)

Susie's Shoes, illustrated by Priscilla Lamont (Hamish Hamilton, 1989; Puffin, London, 1990)

Stories from Codling Village, illustrated by Caroline Crosland (Walker Books, 1990)

I've Forgotten (Edward Walker Books and Sainsbury's, London, 1990)

I Won't Go there Again (Walker Books, 1990)

Pirate Poll, illustrated by Priscilla Lamont (Hamish Hamilton, 1991)

The Glass Angels (Walker Books, 1991)
Beware, Beware, illustrated by Angela Barrett (Walker Books,)
King of King's, illustrated by John Lawrence (Walker Books, 1994)
The Christmas Collection: An Anthology, illustrated by John Lawrence (Walker Books, 1995)

The editors

Jonathan Noakes has taught English in secondary schools in Britain and Australia for fifteen years. For six years he ran A-level English studies at Eton College where he is a housemaster.

Margaret Reynolds is Reader in English at Queen Mary, University of London, and the presenter of BBC Radio 4's *Adventures in Poetry*. Her publications include *The Sappho Companion* and (with Angela Leighton) *Victorian Women Poets*. Her most recent book is *The Sappho History*.